HANDS TO
FLYING STATIONS

HANDS TO FLYING STATIONS

A RECOLLECTIVE HISTORY
OF CANADIAN NAVAL
AVIATION

Volume 1

Stuart E. Soward

ISBN 0-9697229-0-7

Canadian Cataloguing in Publication Data

Soward, Stuart E., 1924–
  Hands to flying stations

    Includes bibliographical references.
    ISBN 0-9697229-0-7 (v. 1)

    1. Canada. Royal Canadian Navy—Aviation—
History. I. Title.

VG95.C3869 1993   359.9′ 4′ 097109   C93-091608-5

Neptune Developments (1984)
657 Beacon Street
Victoria, BC V8V 1K1

Printed in Canada

CONTENTS

Introduction vi

Foreword viii

Acknowledgements xiv

Dedication xvi

Prologue 1

Chapters

  1 Restarting 35

  2 Airborne 81

  3 Forming Up 129

  4 Climbing Away 187

  5 On Course 235

Prangs 1945-1954 299

Synopsis 301

Abbreviations 307

Bibliography 311

Appendices

  A Senior Officers for Naval Aviation 313

  B Directors of Naval Air Division
     and Directors of Naval Aviation 315

  C Commanding Officers of Aircraft Carriers
     and Air Station 317

  D Commanding Officers of Air Groups 319

  E Commanding Officers of Air Squadrons 321

  F Specifications of Aircraft Carriers 325

  G Details of RCN Aircraft 1945-54 327

Index 331

INTRODUCTION

The commencement of this volume of Hands to Flying Stations began in January 1988, as a result of the formation of the CANAVAIR Group. Since inception, the editorial guidance, constructive criticism and overall assistance provided to me by the other members of the Group, namely, W.H. Atkinson, R.E. Bartlett, C.G.H. Daniel, K.L. Gibbs, G.J. Laurie, J.W. Logan, J.W. Mason, M.H.E. Page, A.H.G. Storrs and G.D. Westwood has been greatly appreciated.

In addition to the listed sources, historical documents from the Public Archives, and various articles, over 125 individuals have provided anecdotes, personal recollections, photographic material and other assistance, all of which was necessary to develop the manuscript. As the reader can readily appreciate, some of the incidents provided in this history not only took place as long as 47 years ago, but also have never been documented. Therefore, in such a situation where our individual recollections have dimmed and tended to differ somewhat, I have used a consensus approach, which perhaps has more accurately portrayed the events as they occurred.

In instances where I was personally involved in the various activities and incidents described herein, I have taken the liberty of reverting to the first person. Hopefully, this minimizes any ensuing confusion to the reader.

Finally, since this book deals primarily with aviation policy and the operational activities of Canadian Naval Aviation, it necessarily concentrates on the flying history of RCN squadrons and groups, both ashore and afloat and on those who shaped our development. The detailed record of the Air Technical personnel who served in the Branch, with their considerable achievements which played such a significant role in the successful development of Canadian Naval Aviation, is best left to those who are qualified to tell their story. Fortunately, such a separate, full history is now being compiled, under the title of "Seafire to Sea King - The Air Technical History of RCN Aviation".

S.E. Soward.
November, 1992.

FOREWORD

The sailors who served on Atlantic convoys during World War II, will remember with vivid clarity those occasions when, with U Boats hovering for attack, they watched the departure of the long range shore-based aircraft whose presence and attacks had so greatly limited the U Boats surface movements. Their concern at the loss of this critical air support was sharpened by the knowledge that the aircrew had stretched their time with the convoy to the limit of endurance and faced a long return flight to a base where the weather may have deteriorated seriously.

However, it was obvious that this kind of limited air cover was operationally inadequate. The long hours of flying needed to reach the operational area and return, so limited its effectiveness, that the necessary air cover could never be given satisfactorily by shore-based air. Shipborne aircraft, immediately available when submarines threatened, were as essential for convoy operations as they had been for other Naval fleet operations.

So, with Canadian Naval forces taking a greater role in Atlantic shipping protection and with their future commitment to the Pacific war, approval was given for a Naval Aviation component and the acquisition of two carriers and aircraft.

This, then is the story of the formation of Canadian Naval Aviation and its development to maturity. It was not achieved without opposition as it exposed the sharply differing philosophies of the Navy and Air Force regarding the place and use of aircraft. To the Navy, aircraft like surface ships and submarines, were an essential vehicle for the conduct of war at sea. They should therefore be an integral part of the Navy and be operated by Naval people. The Air Force felt with equal conviction that aircraft had special qualities that wherever and however used in combat, they should be controlled and operated by a Service with a specialized aviation identity, the Air Force.

Stu Soward, the author of that well researched and thoroughly readable story of the Navy's only VC in World War II, Lieutenant Hampton Gray, now turns his attention to the story of the development of Canada's Naval Aviation.

This is not a definitive history. Though historically accurate, it is largely subjective and anecdotal. Much is autobiographical as the author, an experienced carrier flyer, served as squadron pilot and Commanding Officer and as a Landing Signals Officer much of the time covered in this tale and participated in many of the events described. It is an insiders tale of what it was like. Particular personal views are evident. But through it all, the qualities, attitudes and panache of that assorted gathering of airmen who brought Naval aviation into operation and to maturity is clearly presented. The author makes no effort to play down the early problems and consequent disturbing accident rate. Some due to the teething problems inevitable in a new organization, particularly in the context of time. Some because of the nature of carrier flying. Some because of logistic and support difficulties. Some because of the inevitable bugs in new design high performance aircraft. Some because of the background of the early aircrew themselves.

They came from many sources. Some with very considerable war-time carrier combat experience. Others from RCAF training, no longer needed in that service at the end of the war. They brought with them the attitudes and approach to flying of combat flyers - aggressiveness, exuberant individuality. A readiness to push their flying skills to the limit. The assimilation of this new element into the Navy was not achieved without some rough spots. The immediate post-war period was a difficult one for the Navy anyway. There was no clear cut role on which to focus, and its composition was based on a small general purpose fleet. There was also something of an identity problem. The considerable number of wartime officers and men transferred to the Regular Force to bring it to peacetime strength, did not have the background or much indoctrination into Naval tribal values. There was some reluctance to return to the pre-war style of a Royal Navy sibling. There was difficulty in settling down, a lack of cohesion throughout the Fleet and a general restiveness that produced a few minor mutinies. The story of this is well known. It was openly investigated and causes and remedies suggested in the famous Mainguy Report. Though deeply troubling, it turned out to be a beneficially cathartic experience that helped set the Navy on the road to the assured identity and the high professional quality that it achieved.

While all this was shared by the new air element in varying degrees, there were matters of more direct concern. Many wondered whether the fish-heads, as non air people were known - really understood and appreciated aviation. No doubt there were die-hards as in any community. But most certainly, the Navy generally, clearly recognized that aviation was a major new dimension to sea warfare. It was comparable to, but even more striking than the arrival of the submarine in its time, and it was essential that it should be an integral part of the Navy. But it did entail considerable exchange and initially there was a bit of difficulty in adjusting surface ship procedures to meet the imperatives of aircraft operation.

There was also some ambivalence in the relationship of surface and air people. Some of the former felt a degree of resentment at the new preeminence of aviation. There was also a fair amount of envy. Carrier flying had a mystique and a quality of challenge, danger and glamour not found in the surface part of the fleet. On the other hand, there were aviators who understandably saw themselves as an elite and were sometimes inclined to rub it in.

A source of some weakness then in the fledgling air component was that there were so few senior Canadian officers with a strong aviation background. The RCN was therefore obliged to rely on officers on loan from the RN and on officers of a junior and less experienced level. There was thus, some natural hesitation in the exercise of the more forceful leadership that would have curbed some of the more untidy features of those early days.

On the question of elitism, while Naval policy was totally committed to aviation, it was not seen as a distinct "Arm". There should be no service with a disparate identity within a service. Sea warfare embraced combat above, on and below the surface and required a common outlook. Carrier flying was part of the sea battle and needed flyers who were also sailors, and not flyers just operating from a floating airstrip. To this end, flyers were from time to time given surface ship appointments, which they filled with marked success. Not all, however, considered that the benefits justified the drawbacks, as it was seen a harmful interruption to a flyer's professional development.

It was a pity that surface officers did not receive some sort of similar structured familiarization with aviation, other than some acquired incidentally through non-aviation service at an air station or in a carrier. There was a handful of exceptions, whose flyer friends gave them some illegal airborne experience. But for the most part, not even the surface branch high-fliers, who might be expected to have senior sea command in war, received the kind of air familiarization that would give a commander the gut feeling that he should have for the capabilities and limitations of all his combat resources.

These early teething troubles faded quickly when Soviet aggressiveness led to the recognition of the Cold War and the formation of NATO and of its allied military structure. The threat made it necessary to achieve a level of readiness for war, different from what would normally be expected in peace-time. The Navy thus had the stimulus of being able to focus its efforts on its real purpose - effective combat at sea.

Even so, Naval Aviation remained handicapped to a degree by never having a carrier really suited to its capability. The RN light fleet carrier type, though a satisfactory WW2 craft for its job, was too slow and its sea-keeping performance not good enough to get the best out of the new higher performance aircraft.

There were opportunities to get a better carrier. The USN offered one at a bargain basement price. The RN also suggested negotiating the loan of one on favourable terms. However, the timing was such that the offers could not be considered because of the advanced state of modification of the already purchased *Bonaventure*.

Nor was the originally approved two carrier component ever achieved after the two late war escort carriers. The authorized strength of the Navy was not sufficient to man a second carrier as well as the two cruisers that were part of the immediate post-war general purpose fleet. Then when the two cruisers were paid off, the need for a replacement programme for the ageing destroyers and frigates, unsuitable for the NATO specialized role of the Navy, absorbed all available funds.

But the heyday of Naval Aviation and of the Navy generally, really came with the arrival of the carrier *Bonaventure*. Though still far from ideal as a carrier, she was nevertheless fitted with latest devices and features that allowed the operation of jet fighters and modern A/S aircraft purchased from the USN. There had also progressed to senior seagoing positions, aviators and surface fleet officers with considerable carrier experience. Such people had a high degree of professional assurance and were demanding. The quality of flying was high and backed by a highly dedicated and efficient maintenance staff.

The circumstances were such that the A/S carrier group reached a very high degree of operational efficiency. This was clearly demonstrated in NATO combined exercises and showed that Canadian A/S forces need concede nothing to the best that the USN and RN could produce.

This was also a time when destroyer escorts, converted or built to carry and operate an A/S helicopter, were coming into service. Thus, most of the ocean going part of the fleet had an aviation component allowing the whole Navy to feel, with the exception of shore based air, complete and in control of the resources needed for the conduct of war at sea.

These were heady days for the Navy. A period of immense satisfaction that all too soon, virtually came to an end with the *Bonaventure's* mid-life refit. The costs of this ran considerably over estimates. This was partly due to the nature of ship refits. Costs cannot be accurately judged until closed spaces and machinery can be opened up. It was also partly due to the deterioration of a hastily built wartime hull and a certain level of optimism. The size of the cost over-run caused considerable concern and adverse publicity resulting in a hasty and ill-considered decision to pay off and dispose of the ship.

There remained a ship-borne component of Naval aviation in the helicopters. However, with the poorly conceived and destructive policy of unification of the armed services and the loss of individual service identity, all Naval Aviation became part of Air Command of the Canadian Armed Forces. Later, when some of the more ridiculous features of unification became evident and a measure of Service identity was restored, the naval hierarchy of the time was unable to reclaim its former aviation as an element of "Navy". It remained part of Air Command, of what was virtually a restored Air Force, with its people wearers of Air Force uniform, and part of an Air Force career: a situation that the Royal Navy had experienced during the inter-war years and had been found so unsatisfactory.

The author's account has caught the flavour of those years so very well. It will be read by those who lived through them with immense satisfaction that they were part of it. Others will have wondered what Naval Aviation was like and what manner of people those were. Well - here it is - a lively and most valuable complement to other more academic and objective records.

A.H.G. Storrs, DSC and Bar,
Rear Admiral, RCN, (Rtd).

ACKNOWLEDGEMENTS

The author and the Editorial Board wish to thank the following individuals who contributed photos, comments, suggestions and research material, all of which was essential to the successful production of this Volume 1 of Hands To Flying Stations, A Recollective History of Canadian Naval Aviation.

Louis Audette, QC., T.S. Allan, John Anderson, J.M. Arnold, W.H. Atkinson, G.W. Babbitt, R.V. Bays, C.H.S. Barter, E.M. Barter, R.E. Bartlett, Archie Benton, H.W. Beutel, H.J. Bird, I.T. Bouch, Bob Bovill, F.W. Bradley, S.L. Britton, T.C. Brock, J.J. Brooks, E.G. Brooman, H.D. Buchanan, Roy Budesheim, H.G. Burchell, B.A. Cartwright, Roger Campbell, P.G. Chance, Stan Conner, R.W. Cocks, E.W. Colwell, G.M. Cummings, V.J. Cunningham, C.G. Daniel, R.A. Darlington, E.M. Davis, J.K. Dawson, R.O. de Nevers, J.N. Donaldson, John Doherty, Richard Duiven, G.C. Edwards, R.H. Falls, J.M. Favreau, W.H. Fearon, F.R. Fink, R.E. Fisher, D.L. Foley, Wynn Foster, J.B. Fotheringham, A.E. Fox, Beatrice Geary, K.L. Gibbs, L.J. Gibbs, T.E. Gray, F.A. Harley, J.J. Harvie, J.B. Hayter, R. Heath, S.W. Hopkins, R.L. Hughes, Ed Janusas, J.D.F. Kealy, E.G. Kjellstrom, V.M. Langman, L.G. Laramee, G.J. Laurie, R.J. Legeer, Don Lilley, J.W. Logan, Paul Lord, J.D. Lowe, Phyllis Lowe, F.W. Lynch,

J.J. MacBrien, Roy McCormack, R.E. Maclean, D.M. Macleod, W.W. Maxwell, G.E. McArthur, Gordon McLauchlan, J.W. Mason, B.W. Mead, K.M. Meikle, R.G. Monteith, Jack Moss, D.A. Muncaster, W.D. Munro, V.J. Murphy, E.A. Myers, Len Norris, J.C. O'Brien, C.J. O'Connell, K. O'Connor, B.A. Oxholm, D.D. Peacocke, M.H. Page, J.W. Paton, R.E. Quirt, J.M. Riley, C.V. Rolfe, Douglas Ross, G.A. Rotherham, S.M. Rowell, J.V. Searle, Denny Shaw, E.W. Smith, J. Sosnkowski, J.A. Stokes, A.H.G. Storrs, W.J. Stuart, H.L. Swiggum, D.H. Tate, W.J. Tuck, J.A. Turner, M.E. Wasteneys, Patrick Watson, R.J. Watson, R.P. Welland, H.R. Welsh, B.K. West, George Westwood, J.P. Whitby, P.G. Wiwcharuck, S.C. Wood.

Special thanks and appreciation are extended to Carl Mills, Leo Pettipas, Steve Schaefer and Allan Snowie whose co-operation and generosity in making freely available their own extensive files of material and photographs, greatly reduced the additional research otherwise required for this history. Particular thanks are also extended to Ken O'Connor and J.B. Fotheringham for their exceptional assistance in compiling this manuscript in a revamped computer format, Michael Whitby, DND History, who spent valuable time on my behalf diligently researching the Public Archives and his own files, and renowned artist Len Gibbs for designing the book cover.

Finally, CANAVAIR Group wishes to acknowledge the cooperation and support given by the Ministry of Health and Welfare - New Horizons Program through the Federal Grant provided to initiate this project, and the Arts Awards Services of the Canada Council for the Grant provided to the author.

DEDICATION

Following the formation of the Canadian naval air squadrons as World War Two ended, and the official establishment of the Canadian Naval Air Branch in December 1945, fifty eight officers and men were killed during the period from September 1945 to December 1954. This Volume I of Hands to Flying Stations is respectfully dedicated to their memory.

Lt. Frank W. McCarry, RCNVR	8 September, 1945.
Lt George F. Clarke, RCNVR	18 September, 1945.
S/Lt. L. Wade, RCNVR	2 October, 1945.
S/Lt. Lloyd A Nash, RCNVR	2 October, 1945.
Lt. Robert A. Jacobs, RCN(R)	8 February, 1946.
S/Lt. James C. Philly, RCN(R)	8 February, 1946.
S/Lt. Douglas J.V Shortt, RCN(R)	11 March, 1946.
Lt. George A. Greenwood, RCN	17 October, 1947.
Lt. Clifford R. Gavel, RCN(R)	31 January, 1947.
LCdr. O.W. Tattersall, RCN	31 January, 1947.
Lt. Robert M. Gailbraith, RCN(R)	17 July, 1947.
Lt. John M. Lamon, RCN	17 July, 1947.
Lt. Alexander L. Warren, RCN	16 October, 1947.
PO. James W. MacDonald, RCN	4 November, 1947.
Lt. Gerald Quarton, RCN	17 January, 1948.

Lt. George A. Carter, RCN	24 August 1948.
Lt. Joseph T. Murphy, RCN	13 October, 1948.
Lt. John S. Berge, RCN	14 October, 1948.
Lt. John M. Stewart, RCN	6 December, 1948.
Lt. Thomas A. Coultry, RCN	1 February, 1949.
Lt. Clarence J. Pulfer, RCN	28 March, 1949.
LCdr. Robert A. Monks, RCN	28 March, 1949.
AB.O/M. Joseph R.J. Cambray, RCN	28 March, 1949.
Lt. Glenn W. Hutton, RCN	28 March, 1949.
Lt. Douglas Stevens, RCN	31 May, 1949.
LCdr. Clifford G. Watson, RCN	23 August, 1949.
Lt. Alfred C. Elton, RCN	23 August, 1949.
Lt. Leslie F. Peever, RCN	18 February, 1950.
AB.P/W. Walter D. Mitchell, RCN	30 June, 1950.
Lt. Mervin C. Hare. RCN	30 June, 1950.
Lt. William M. Phillips, RCN	13 September, 1950.
Lt. John B. Hartle, RCN	28 February, 1951.
S/Lt. John J. Morehouse, RCN	27 March, 1951.
Lt. John E. Anderson, RCN	17 April, 1952.
Lt. William J. Hutchison, RCN	17 April, 1952.
Lt. John K. Mason, RCN	17 April, 1952.
Lt. John S. Murphy, RCN	17 April, 1952.
S/Lt. Phillip J. Plotkins, RCN	17 April, 1952.
AB.O/M. William J. Hunter, RCN	17 April. 1952.
AB.O/M. Douglas S. Moffatt, RCN	17 April, 1952.
Lt. William J. Spencer, RCN	24 April, 1952.
Mid. Winthrop F. Wood, RCN	28 April, 1952.
Lt. Michael Milovich. RCN	13 June, 1952.
AS/Lt. James F. Washbrook, RCN	3 March, 1953.
LS.O/M. William E. Dutfield, RCN	3 March, 1953.
LS.O/M. Ernest V. Marshall, RCN	3 March, 1953.
Lt. Fredrick G. Rice, RCN	9 April, 1953.
Lt. Robert C. O'Neil, RCN	9 April, 1953.
Lt. George W. Noble, RCN	4 October, 1953.
P1.E/A. George W. Wraith, RCN	4 October, 1953.
Lt. Leslie H. Terry, RCN	26 January, 1954.
AS/Lt. John A. MacLeod, RCN(R)	6 May, 1954.
S/Lt. James D. Holden, RCN	6 May, 1954.

S/Lt. Robert H. Jones, RCN	6 May, 1954.
P1.RA. John A. White, RCN	6 May, 1954.
AS/Lt. Edmond W. Alexander, RCN	4 October, 1954.
AS/Lt. Ian Robertson, RCN	11 October, 1954.
S/Lt. Charles L. Wright, RCN	4 December, 1954.

"If I take the wings of the morning,
    and dwell in the uttermost parts of the sea;
Even there shall thy hand lead me,
    and thy right hand shall hold me."

Psalm 139.

PROLOGUE

In the spring of 1917, the tremendous loss of allied shipping to the German U Boats had reached such a devastating level that a major increase in anti-submarine measures was considered essential. As a result, the question of forming a Canadian Naval Air Arm was under active discussion by the Interdepartmental Committee of the Militia and Naval Departments. A decision was quickly reached that an air service was necessary to provide an adequate defence for the heavy shipping traffic off the Atlantic seaboard. To achieve this, it was agreed that two seaplane stations should be established in Nova Scotia, one at Halifax and the other at Sydney.

Expert advice was now needed to implement this naval air program and a request for assistance was made to the Admiralty. Wing Commander J.W. Seddon, Royal Naval Air Service, (RNAS), an experienced aviator who had commanded the first seaplane base in England, was selected and he promptly outlined a proposed organization for two air stations, equipped with 34 seaplanes and supported by 300 personnel. Initial cost was estimated to be in the order of 1.5 million dollars.

This plan was rejected by the Privy Council as being too expensive, and also on the grounds that the money could be better spent increasing the capability of surface anti-submarine patrols. An additional factor was the serious shortage of skilled construction workers who were already fully committed on other projects. Seddon then came up with a modified proposal, which was also rejected on the grounds that it was primarily a training scheme, only providing protection to the shipping approaches to Sydney. This ended the first attempt to establish a Canadian Naval Air Service.

By January 1918, the toll of allied shipping destroyed had risen drastically, and the introduction of new, more powerful and lethal U boats by the Germans had greatly increased their submarine offensive capability. In March of 1918, the Admiralty again appealed for help from Canada to meet the increased threat and proposed that Canada set up airship construction factories, balloon works, the establishment of a seaplane manufacturing industry and the opening up of air stations for air patrols. The Canadian Government believed that this proposal was far beyond the capability of the resources available and it was consequently put on hold. As a redeeming alternative, approaches were made by Canada to the United States for assistance, and for the long term, plans were requested from the Admiralty for suitable airship and seaplane designs, while a study got underway to establish the Canadian capability to manufacture the aircraft and equipment in Canada.

On 1 April 1918, the Royal Air Force came into existence. This was the result of the Smuts Committee's final study and whose report of August 1917, recommended that the Royal Naval Air Service and the Royal Flying Corps be amalgamated. This decision was the result of an extensive study by Smuts and his committee to establish the command and control of these two military flying organizations.

It is worth noting that during the far reaching study by the Smuts committee, the Admiralty, although adamant that the RNAS should remain part of the Navy, was not altogether speaking with a unified voice. Captain G.A. (Hank) Rotherham, DSO, OBE, RN, (Rtd.) makes this point clear in his book, "It's Really Quite Safe", when he discloses that Lord Trenchard, head of the RAF, insisted that the Commander-in-Chief of the Home Fleet, Admiral Beatty, be consulted in the matter. The Admiralty did not take time to brief the Admiral since they naturally pre-assumed that a Navy controlled air arm was an obvious requirement. To their dismay, Beatty is reported to have said that, he thought aeroplanes were a nuisance and that he didn't care who controlled the air. What prior inkling Lord Trenchard may possibly have had about Beatty's views is not known, but the

Admiral's offhand comment certainly did not help the Admiralty's case. It is understood that Beatty subsequently recognized his blunder, and later while in his capacity as First Sea Lord, worked hard to overcome the impression created by his careless remark.

The Smuts Committee's report proposing a unification of the RNAS and the RFC was essentially a response to three basic questions:

1. Should there be an Air Ministry?
2. Should there be a single unified air service?
3. How should the relationship between the new air service and the Army and Navy be regulated?

By one brief stroke of the pen the RNAS was taken from naval control. True, the conflicting material demands and overlapping roles of the RNAS and RFC were eliminated, but the long term implications of this historic and controversial decision would now commence to plague both the Royal Navy and the newly formed Royal Air Force for the next two decades. The immediate effect was the transfer of some 2,000 RNAS aircraft and 55,000 personnel to the newly designated Royal Air Force, which resulted in a tremendous loss to the Royal Navy of naval aviation expertise, with the attendant restrictions in the operational capability of the fleet.

In late April, however, an important conference for Canada took place in Washington between representatives of the RN, USN, and RCN. At this conference an agreement was reached and a decision was finally made to establish naval air stations at Halifax and Sydney, with another two stations planned to be built subsequently at Cape Race and Sable Island. These new establishments would be equipped with dirigibles, seaplanes and kite balloons. The United States would provide the equipment and aircrew until such time as the Canadian naval personnel assigned for training in the US, were ready to assume command and control of the stations.

On 3 May 1918, the Privy Council approved the measures adopted in Washington and requested that an officer be provided from the Admiralty to organize a Canadian Naval Air Arm. The British response was hardly enthusiastic observing the Admiralty had just lost their own Naval Aviation, and it was only after detailed explanations to the Secretary of State for Air that approval was given to provide this organizational leadership. Privy Council having given approval to establish two air stations at an estimated cost of $2,189,600, the Department of Public Works was directed to conduct surveys and obtain the necessary land for the two air stations, which were selected to be as originally conceived at Halifax and Sydney. A recruitment plan was approved and a complement of 500 officers and men was authorized for aviation duties to be added additional to the strength of the RCN. Officers would belong to the executive branch with the addition of an "(A)" after their title. The uniform of the branch would continue to be that of the regular service with the addition of an eagle emblem attached to the cuff. Regular rates of pay would prevail, but with the addition of a special air allowance. Each base would be equipped with 3 dirigibles, four kite balloons and 6 seaplanes.

As was fairly typical, the effort by Public Works was a protracted affair and progress was slow in the acquisition of property and drawing up of plans. Under the leadership of Lieutenant Colonel J.T. Cull, DSO, RAF, the British aviation expert, negotiations were re-opened with the USN to commence the provision of aerial patrols and in spite of vague financial arrangements, the USN agreed to provide all the necessary flying equipment at their own expense, if Canada would provide the ground sites, stores and installations. The Americans were prepared to live in tents initially, but since a maritime winter was now approaching, Cull was given added support to push Public Works to get moving and ensure living quarters and mess halls were available in time.

The USN personnel arrived in August 1918 and brought with them 4 Curtiss HS2 flying boats, all under the command of Lt. Richard E. Byrd (who later achieved distinction in the post-war years as both an aviator and arctic explorer). Byrd was also given the additional title of Officer-in-Charge US Naval Air Force in Canada.

While construction proceeded, anti-submarine patrols were commenced from both Halifax and North Sydney, and Cull began to tackle the problems of organizing a Canadian Naval Air Arm. The situation from an organizational point of view however was ludicrous, with Cull and his small staff of ex-naval aviators, now members of the RAF under the General Officer Commanding the RAF in Canada at Toronto for discipline, while at the same time under the authority of the

Proposed RCNAS officers
cap badge 1918. CN 3932

Proposed RCNAS Officers
uniform 1918. CN 3933

RCNAS cadet group, Ottawa 1918. Front row second from left is S.V. Hopkins. Credit S.E. Hopkins.

Group of Canadian military personnel en route UK 1918. RCNAS Cadet second on left. Credit S.E. Hopkins.

Director of the Naval Service, Ottawa for administration. The British Admiralty was vitally concerned with the development of the new naval aviation branch in Canada to effectively increase the anti-submarine capability off the East Coast, but had no direct involvement in the decision making process. The newly created RAF on the other hand, being far more concerned with other matters, was giving the entire Canadian naval aviation project a low level of priority. The USN was greatly involved and constantly dealing both administratively and operationally, with the recently formed British RAF and the RCN, with all correspondence amongst the three, travelling a rather tortuous route. It is no wonder that Cull and his associates often felt that they were engaged in a losing battle by not having any single autonomous and effective voice speaking for them. That so much was actually achieved is remarkable and a major tribute to Cull's abilities and dedication.

It was soon readily apparent that dire warnings issued by the Admiralty concerning the serious threat created by the new German U Boat campaigns were fully justified by the admitted loss of over 110,000 tons of shipping off the East Coast between May and October of 1918, all accomplished by a force of only five submarines. However, the invaluable aerial patrols by the USN flying boats from Halifax and Sydney, if nothing else had a positive effect on stimulating further interest in, and greater justification for, the formation of Canadian Naval Aviation.

On 5 September 1918, by an Order-in-Council, the outline of the new force was established and was to be known as the Royal Canadian Naval Air Service (RCNAS). This title had been selected not without difficulty since Cull prophetically visualized that land-based aircraft would indeed be required in the future, and as such, the air service should be known as the Canadian Air Force. This name change was avoided only by the fact that news was received that such a service was now being formed overseas. Rates of pay for the RCNAS were those of the Canadian Expeditionary Force, with officer cadets receiving the standard private's pay of $1.10 per diem on enlistment and increasing to $2.00 during their ground training. A flying increment would be paid at the rate of $1.00 per day when under a flying status. A special flat rate of $1.50 per day would be paid to a non commissioned rank for the newly created position of airship coxswain to be recruited from RCN ratings. Uniforms for the officers were to be of dark blue serge with a brown leather Sam Browne belt. Ranks would be as used by the old RNAS up to Wing Commander level. Pilot wings would be of the RAF pattern, with a green maple leaf and the monogram RCNAS in the centre. The cap was to be the standard style worn, with a distinctive badge which would consist of a bronze maple leaf, a silver fouled anchor with silver wings and topped with a crown.

Dress for the ratings would be as "men not dressed as seamen" in the RCN and the basic rank would be that of "aircraftsmen". Initially 80 cadets would be trained in the United States on seaplanes and another 12 would proceed to the U.K. for airship training.

Recruiting for the new RCNAS through press advertising actually commenced on 8 August 1918, and was enthusiastically accepted with an immediate response from over 600 applicants, before the new service had even been officially approved. A selection committee was formed and twenty five cadets were inducted by the middle of September with another 39 selected a week later in Ottawa. Drafts of the new candidates were quickly formed up for departure to the training schools in the USA while the first group of airship trainees left for England in October. This small group consisted of 12 Flight Cadets, among whom was Stanley V. Hopkins from Burlington, Ontario, an ex-private of the Canadian Expeditionary Force. He, along with Flight Cadet W.V. Bedell, during passage, contracted the broncho-pneumonia type of flu which had broken out and was raging in epidemic proportions throughout Western Europe and England. Bedell succumbed to his malady and Hopkins was so ill on arrival at Liverpool that he was put in the same ambulance as the already expired Bedell, the medical authorities having already considered that Hopkins would not survive. Hopkins remembers being bedded down on the hospital balcony since all the inside beds were occupied. In an effort to keep the balcony patients warm, they were given medicinal brandy every morning and night, mainly due to the desperate shortage of proper medication. Hopkins had some difficulty partaking of the spirits since his upbringing in a strict temperance Methodist family frowned on such consumption. Fortunately, he recovered from the deadly flu and although now considerably behind his classmates, commenced preliminary airship training at Grove House, Roehampton, near London.

By November 1918, the RCNAS was well established, morale was high and there was great optimism that the new naval aviation branch would be a full fledged fighting force ready for action by the spring of 1919. Colonel Cull was now in full charge, with the title of Director of the Royal Canadian Naval Air Service, and had his headquarters staff established at 30 Rideau Street, Ottawa. As the end of the long bloody war finally appeared to be imminent however, all further recruiting for the branch ceased and no new construction was authorized at the two bases being built. With the signing of the Armistice on 11 November 1918, the overall demobilization process commenced, convoys were discontinued out of Sydney and the United States Naval air operations ceased. The flying operations continued briefly at the Halifax base, then operations there were terminated and Baker Point was reduced to a low level of care and maintenance until such time as the RCNAS was in a position to take over the station.

Three days after the Armistice was signed, Colonel Cull was ordered by the Honourable C.C. Ballantyne to prepare a memorandum outlining the advantages of continuing the naval air service on its current basis. All factors were carefully considered, but on 5 December 1918, an Order in Council was issued to officially disband the RCNAS. A particularly significant factor in this decision was the imminent return to Canada of a considerable number of experienced former naval aircrew now being discharged from the RAF, providing a large pool of well trained pilots, readily available to form any subsequent air branch that might be required.

Training for the RCNAS Cadet Officers in the UK actually continued for about three weeks after the official disbanding of the new Air Branch. Flight Cadet Stanley Hopkins was still undergoing kite balloon training at Roehampton which provided instruction in both free and kite balloons. Hopkins logged three balloon flights in December, the last one being conducted on 21 December 1918. These flights were quite extensive, covering a distance of about 30 miles, mostly over London at an average airspeed of 30 mph, extending over an hours flight time and occasionally reaching heights of 5000 feet. All was not work however, because Hopkins did subsequently relate that while on leave in London the "Ladies of the Night" (also known in WW2 as "Piccadilly Commandos") were in great strength in Trafalgar Square. He also clearly recalled Petticoat Lane, "Where your watch could be stolen at the top of the street and sold back to you at the bottom." Hopkins and another Flight Cadet, N.G. Jackson returned to Canada on 30 January 1919, aboard RMS *Corsican*. Hopkins was discharged from the RCNAS effective 14 February 1919, following the disbandment of the branch.

Colonel Cull and his British contingent returned to England, but since the Naval Service was still interested in the possibility of establishing a naval aviation service, Major MacLaurin DSC, RAF, an ex RNAS Canadian pilot formerly on Cull's staff, assumed the post of Acting Director of the Royal Canadian Naval Air Service. He continued in that position for the next year, although technically he was in charge of an organization that no longer existed. Construction however was still continuing at the two air stations, and in February 1919, the two bases were accepted from the Department of Public Works by the Naval Service. The facilities at the bases were extensive with barracks accommodation for 100 men, a messing and recreation hall able to handle 300 personnel, together with a large stores building. Although the sites were inactive, they were kept under custody and basic maintenance, and indeed in May of 1919, Baker Point was briefly in the news when the former Commanding Officer of the base, now Lieutenant Commander Byrd, USN, made an unexpected landing for repairs to his NC3 flying boat whilst attempting the first leg of his trans-Atlantic flight.

Meanwhile, in the United Kingdom, the situation facing the Royal Navy, as the Admiralty shifted to a peacetime role, was precarious for the remnants of the naval aviation branch. After the armistice, RNAS aircrew were given the option of returning to the Royal Navy as surface executive officers, or transferring to the new RAF. The most enthusiastic, experienced and best fliers opted for the RAF to continue in an aviation career, as a consequence the Navy was left with little naval aviation expertise.

The Halifax and Sydney stations gradually shifted to a minimum care and maintenance status under civilian watchmen and by November 1919, all the remaining aviation equipment was in a state of

First Carrier Deck landing – HMS Furious 1918. Note holding
straps on bottom wing. CN 3932

#203 RAF squadron following amalgamation of RNAS and RFC in 1918.
Lt. Collishaw in naval uniform is Commanding Officer. CN 3987

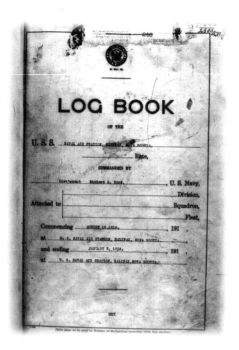

Title page of log book, US Naval Air Station, Baker Point, Dartmouth N.S. commanded by Lt. Richard Byrd USN. 1918-1919 (Courtesy United States Navy)

Group of RCNAS cadets, Ottawa 1918. CN 6533 (Courtesy Mr. J.M. Weir)

Group of RCNAS officers under training in UK 1918-1919.
Credit S.E. Hopkins.

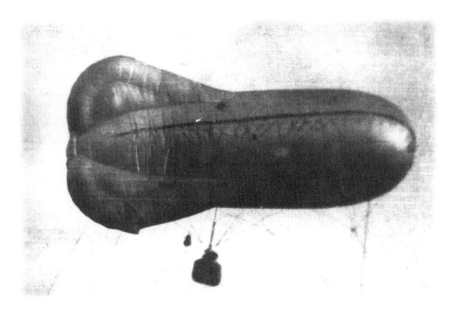

RCNAS officers undergoing balloon training in UK 1919.
Credit S.E. Hopkins

Launching HS2 flying boat on ramp at Baker Point, N.S. 1919.
CN 6508 (Courtesy National Aviation Museum)

USN HS2 flying boats at hangar – Baker Point,
Dartmouth, N.S. CN 6807

HOW TO FLY A JENNY - WW1 BIPLANE TRAINER
By Don Morrison, pilot in World War 1

INSPECTION - It is best not to inspect the aeroplane, if you do, you will never get into it. CLIMBING INTO COCKPIT - Do not climb into cockpit in the usual manner. If you put your weight on the lower wing panel it will fall off, and besides your foot will go through the wing, probably spraining your ankle. The best way to get into the cockpit is to climb over the tail surfaces and crawl up the turtle deck. Be sure to brush the squirrel and gopher nests out of the seat. Be sure not to cut your hand on the remnants of the windshield. INSTRUMENTS - After having lowered yourself carefully into the seat, and having groped in vain for a safety belt, take a good look at the instruments, both of them. The one on the right is a tachometer. It doesn't work! The other is an altimeter and it functioned perfectly up until 1918 when the hand came off. Look at them now, for after the engine starts you can't see them. STARTING THE MOTOR - The switch is on the right. It isn't connected but it does give a sense of security to the mechanic who is pulling the prop, to hear the switch click when you say "switch off". If for some reason the motor doesn't start don't get out to pick up the unconscious and bleeding mechanic as he really did deserve it. WARMING UP - Don't warm up the motor. It will only run a few minutes anyway and the longer you run it on the ground, the less flying time you will have in the air. After the throttle is open, do not expose any portion of your body beyond the edge of the cowling. It is no fun to have your face slapped by a flying rocker arm or be peppered by small bits of piston rings, valves etc. that are continually coming out of what was once the exhaust stacks. THE TAKE OFF - The take off is in direct defiance of all the laws of gravity. If you have a passenger, do not attempt it. THE FLIGHT - After you have dodged through the trees, windmills and chimneys until you are over the lake, you will see a large hole in the left side of the fuselage. This hole is to allow the stick to be moved far enough to the left to get sufficient bank to allow a left turn. Never try a right turn! LANDING - The landing is made in accordance with the law of gravity. If the landing gear doesn't collapse on the first bounce, don't worry, it will on the second. After you have extricated yourself from the wreckage and helped the spectators put out the fire, light a cigarette and with a nonchalant shrug, walk, DON'T RUN, away.

Parachute jump from balloon during RCNAS cadet training in UK 1919.
Credit S.E. Hopkins.

Aerial view of Baker Point air station at Dartmouth in 1923. CN 6800

Aerial view of RCAF Station at Dartmouth in 1923. CN 3963

CMaoL/KE

DEPUTY MINISTER'S OFFICE,

OTTAWA.

26th March 1919

TO:
    Flight Cadet S.V.Hopkins,
        Box 45,
        Burlington, Ont.

            In view of the cessation of hostilities it has been decided to discontinue the present organization of the Royal Canadian Naval Air Service. In consequence, it becomes necessary to effect the discharge of all cadets at present under training.

            The Minister of the Naval Service, therefore, wishes me to notify you that your services will be dispensed with, the date of discharge being February 14th, 1919.

            The Department of the Naval Service will refund the second half of the Uniform Allowance ($75.00), provide transportation to your home address, and grant Post Discharge Pay -- $70.00.

[signature]

            Major R.A.F.,Acting Director
        Royal Canadian Naval Air Service,
           For: Deputy Minister.

Letter of Discharge for RCNAS Flight Cadet Hopkins. 1919.
Credit S.E. Hopkins.

preservation, with only MacLaurin making periodic visits to each site. An extension to MacLaurin's tour was requested, but the RAF refused on the grounds that he was purely engaged in the development of general non-military aviation. He was demobilized from the RAF in December 1919, but remained in Canada as a member of the newly formed Air Board. MacLaurin continued to be most active in aviation, subsequently becoming the air station superintendent at Vancouver. Regrettably he was killed in a flying accident in 1922.

Interest in the RCNAS was briefly revived in December 1919, when Admiral of the Fleet, Viscount Jellicoe of Scapa, GCB, OM, GCVO, was visiting Canada on his Commonwealth tour and in his capacity as an advisor, made some recommendations for the peacetime structure of the Royal Canadian Navy. Although Japan had been on the side of Britain and the allies in World War One, Jellicoe, in a remarkably accurate forecast, considered that Japan would be the most likely enemy in any future war. Accordingly, he made some sweeping recommendations for the future composition and disposition of the RCN. He considered that two squadrons of aircraft, one of flying boats, and the other equipped with torpedo-carrying aircraft, should be established on the west coast of Canada. He also put forward an outline of four proposed fleet building programs, two of which included aircraft carriers. Interestingly enough, he did not consider the two bases at Halifax and Sydney to be part of the permanent base proposal, presumably in view of the anticipated Japanese threat. Unfortunately as far as a re-activated RCNAS was concerned, there was no action taken on his proposals.

The Royal Canadian Naval Air Service by now had virtually been eliminated as an entity. The air stations passed from naval control to that of the Air Board, and other than a brief flurry of activity in August 1921, when the air base at Baker Point under the Air Board Director of Flying, Wing Commander Leckie, RAF (an ex-RNAS officer) was the scene of a flying exercise with ships of the RCN, the base remained dormant. The air station then faded into obscurity until 1934, when it was reactivated by the RCAF from a care and maintenance reserve status to a base for a flying boat squadron.

It is worth while to note that although the RCNAS failed to get launched successfully due to the war's ending, there was considerable foresight and independent thinking demonstrated on the part of the Canadian Government, particularly observing that its former principal adviser, the Royal Navy, upon which the Canadian Naval Service had been founded, was by now virtually stripped of its own naval air branch.

At the end of 1918, everything had been put in place for a successful role for the new RCNAS in the postwar RCN, but the lack of a clear cut peacetime policy and adequate funding primarily clouded its future. Indeed, in a letter written on the same day as the Order-in-Council was published on 5 December 1918, the Minister of the Naval Service Ballantyne clearly stated to his Deputy Minister Desbarats "I wish it understood that the RCNAS is not abolished and the action that is now being taken is only until such time as the Government decides on the details and policy of a permanent Air Service."

It was mainly with the evolution of arctic exploration, the opening up of mail routes, fire patrols, aerial surveying etc. that the original scope of the Air Board increased, and by exclusively controlling and administering the government civil aviation requirements it gradually developed the civil flying organization in Canada into the very "permanent Air Service" previously referred to by Ballantyne. Since military flying was also the responsibility of the Air Board, this role was provided by the establishment of a small non-permanent auxiliary component in 1920, which then became the nucleus of both the Federal Government's civil and military aviation arms. The aircraft initially flown by this formation were war surplus RNAS and USN flying boats, enthusiastically manned by keen volunteers available from the large pool of ex RNAS officers who had returned to Canada following demobilization.

It was not until a few years later, it was recognized that a more permanent military type of organization was required. This resulted in the formation of the Royal Canadian Air Force on 1 April 1924, although for the first few years it continued to be engaged in civil aviation activities. It subsequently expanded and evolved into a firm military posture almost identical to the Royal Air Force, assuming as the RAF had done (with the demise of the RNAS), one new additional responsibility; the shore-based surveillance of coastal waters. In effect, it was the RCAF that became the replacement service for the RCNAS. It was no doubt the desperate straits in which the post war RCN found itself through major budget cuts, reducing the peacetime Navy to the point of extinction, that prohibited any attempt to consider the re-activation of the RCNAS. With the evolvement of the RCAF from a civil air beginning to a military formation, and being the only flying organization in existence, a convenient back door entry was provided for the new service to assume this responsibility for maritime air operations. This is in spite of the fact that it had already been well established that a firm requirement existed during the war for the RCN to provide air patrols which in fact were the prime justification for the establishment of the RCNAS.

In summary, the RCN never did relinquish its primary role or diminish its overall interest in and responsibilities for naval air operations. Rather, they were assumed by the slowly developing application of the wartime flying boats operated by the Canadian Government in a variety of roles and applications, including coastal patrols. It is doubtful if the Canadian Government, or for that matter, anybody in the Defence establishment at that time, ever considered the potentially serious problems that might result from the new air service drifting into the command and control structure of the RCN forces operating in their maritime environment. An environment which always had been, and would continue to be, the prime responsibility of naval forces throughout the world.

About the same time as the Admiralty was attempting to re-establish a flying branch under RAF control, while still capable of meeting the Royal Navy requirements, and the Royal Canadian Navy was at a bare level of existence, the United States Navy was on a steady flying course. Through an Act of Congress in 1921, the Bureau of Aeronautics was created which was "Charged with matters pertaining to naval aeronautics as prescribed by the Secretary of the Navy." Consequently, the United States Navy was most effectively provided with the responsibility to design naval aircraft and equipment to meet its requirements, completely free from interference from the other services. Not only were USN aviators well equipped with modern aircraft, but they were also highly motivated and instilled with the firm conviction that naval aviation was the key to achieving maritime dominance. The only other Navy in the world which believed and was able to follow this same doctrine, was that of Japan, and the Japanese Naval Aviation Branch was developing far faster and achieving a much higher level of combat effectiveness than was generally appreciated by the western world.

The Royal Navy, by 1921, in attempting to establish a reasonable degree of aviation effectiveness, found it necessary to ask currently serving naval officers to volunteer to serve in the RAF, then upon becoming qualified aircrew, return to serve with the Royal Navy. This plan failed miserably since the officers involved, justifiably considered their careers could only suffer if required to transfer from Admiralty control to the RAF. During the next few years it became increasingly obvious that the RAF manned squadrons serving in the Royal Navy were generally unsuitable to perform their naval functions. The provision of manpower and depth of maritime expertise required were proving to be inadequate to satisfactorily carry out what were essentially full time specialized naval aviation sea duties. In an attempt to resolve this matter, the Balfour sub-committee of 1923 made certain recommendations that led to the Trenchard-Keyes agreement of 1924, wherein several modifications were undertaken to address the problems. Under the new arrangements, RAF embarked units would henceforth be collectively classified under the title of the Fleet Air Arm of the RAF. As a concession, the RAF accepted the fact that 70% of the pilot billets would be Royal Navy officers, as would be the observers and telegraphists. The other RAF units operating from shore in the maritime role, ie. seaplanes and flying boats, would remain under RAF control. This small step toward the RN obtaining a degree of control of their Fleet Air Arm operations was only marginally successful and proceeded no further in spite of subsequent Admiralty presentations before Parliamentary Committees in 1925 1928 and again in 1934.

Also in 1934, a rather progressive and interesting concept of a small carrier was introduced to the Royal Navy. This was the plan to develop a 3000 ton high speed aircraft carrier which was designed to launch its complement of seven seaplanes from catapults and recover them with winches towing a landing canvas aft of the ship. This aroused interest in Canadian naval circles, and Commodore P.W.

Nelles, RCN, Chief of the Naval Staff asked for blueprints to be provided to the RCN. Although nothing came of the idea, no doubt mainly due to the severe limitations of the skimpy RCN budget, it did indicate that the RCN was fully aware of the importance of airpower in the naval role.

Returning to the Royal Navy, it is worth describing some of the personnel conditions that existed in the mid-1930's to demonstrate the utter impracticability of operating effectively under the existing two service tangle. In summary: Naval officer pilots held two commissions, and had two ranks, one in the RN, the other in the RAF. RAF pilots held only the RAF rank and commission. Naval observers held only the Royal Navy rank.

Naval observers were appointed to ships, pilots to squadrons. Naval pilot appointments were proposed by Admiralty but required Air Ministry concurrence.

RAF pilots were appointed by the Air Ministry without Admiralty concurrence.

RAF pilots served only an average of two years with the Fleet Air Arm.

In short, the RAF controlled the quality, numbers and length of time that pilots seconded to the Navy would serve.

By 1936, it was obvious that the quality of aircrew personnel provided by the RAF could not keep pace with the specialized demands required by naval aviation. Additionally, the short period of time the RAF pilots served with the Navy was completely out of proportion to the length of time it took to be trained to an adequate standard. This was further aggravated by the greatly increased requirements by the Admiralty for aircrew to meet the expanding aircraft carrier program. Balfour in his report of 1923 had described the problems clearly, when he summarized the situation as follows: "The general system is that the Air Ministry raises, trains and maintains the Fleet Air Arm at sea. At sea, the FAA comes under the discipline and operational control of the Admiralty, which designs, builds and maintains the carriers."

"Naval air policy is concerted by both the Air Staff and Admiralty War Staff."

"The Air Ministry are solely responsible for the supply of all material connected with aircraft."

By his foregoing summary of the situation, it was apparent that the modifications Balfour had previously proposed had merely resulted in compromises dealing with some aspects of the inter-service personnel difficulties, without delving into the heart of the problem. The situation in the UK had now become intolerable. Public interest was stimulated by parliamentary debate and press reports, so finally a Cabinet Committee chaired by Sir Thomas Inskip was formed and in 1937 he made the following remarks when presenting his recommendations:

"I desire to emphasize the vital importance of the Fleet Air Arm to the Navy. No system could be satisfactory which subordinated the first line efficiency of the Fleet Air Arm to the maintenance of that system."

"The Fleet Air Arm, as the phrase suggests, not only co-operates with the fleet: it is an integral part of the fleet."

"I find it impossible to resist the inference that when so much that concerns the air units depends upon the naval element in the ship and in the fleet, the Admiralty should be responsible for selecting and training the personnel, and generally for the organization of the Fleet Air Arm. Again the work of the FAA with its inevitable naval environment and having regard to the high degree of specialization in equipment, is in my opinion more likely to be efficient if the Admiralty are now made responsible. This, if accepted, will mean that a pilot in the Fleet Air Arm will no longer be an Air Force Officer."

The report was accepted, the recommendations implemented, and administrative control of the FAA passed to the Admiralty, but it was not until 1 May 1939, that the long and tedious negotiations between the Admiralty and the Air Ministry were finally concluded. This surely must be a condemnation of the strangely possessive and stubborn view held on the part of the RAF and the Air Ministry negotiators. It is difficult to understand why they would wish to perpetuate a situation which made no military sense, and aggravate the problem further by not making a clean, quick transfer of the Fleet Air Arm back to the Royal Navy. It was obvious over the years that the RAF never understood the priority, concept, or role of the FAA, which to be effective, had to be a true naval air service. That the FAA should never have been separated from naval command and control has since become an established historical fact.

There were only a few short months before war would break out. The ill-prepared Admiralty would now have to throw their newly acquired Naval Air Branch into battle, badly equipped with obsolete aircraft, manned and led by far too few skilled and experienced fliers, and under the control of senior surface officers, many whom understandably had but little experience or basic knowledge of the wartime employment and application of carrier-based naval air power.

Both the administrative and technical aspects of maintaining a naval air branch, had been well pointed out to the RCN by the events that had been taking place in both the USN and RN. The devastating experience of the RN was surely a most sobering example, and the need for a navy to maintain control of its own naval air forces could not have been more dramatically established. On a personal level, individual officers serving in the RCN were provided with a first hand opportunity to witness the aviation problems being faced by the RN since the RCN was still relying on the Royal Navy for junior Canadian officer training in the British capital ships. Quite separately, and on an individual basis, there were additionally several adventuresome young Canadians who applied for a service flying career in the Royal Navy prior to WW2 through direct application to the Admiralty. R.E. (Dick) Bartlett, O.W. (Tats) Tattersal and F.H. (Frank) Harley were three such candidates.

T. E. (Tom) Gray was another such Canadian. He had joined the RAF, flew in the FAA, then transferred to the Royal Navy shortly before the outbreak of war. Tom, (a cousin of Hampton Gray) describes a laughable episode that occurred in 1939 while serving in 802 squadron at Alexandria, Egypt, before the war. The squadron had just re-equipped with the new Sea Gladiator fighters (a Gladiator with a tail hook) and Tom was flying formation on his leader over the desert. The lead aircraft suddenly appeared to brake with remarkable deceleration, and simultaneously Tom saw something from the aircraft whirl away and disappear into the distance, which just happened to be his leader's aircraft propellor. The subsequent story (accompanying the forced landing) was that the propellor had neatly sliced apart an unsuspecting camel below as it sped (the prop) on its errant way.

When war commenced in September, four of the squadron's Sea Gladiators were crated up and loaded aboard the aircraft carrier *Glorious* for shipment to Malta. Three of these little fighters later gained renown as "Faith", "Hope", and "Charity" in the air defence of Malta.

Another young Canadian who entered the Royal Navy in 1930 as a Cadet at the RN College in Devon, was R.S. (Roy) Baker-Falkner, a Victoria B.C. youth. He became an FAA pilot during the pre-war years and had a distinguished flying career being awarded the DSO and DSC for his actions on FAA operations. He was on the *Tirpitz* raids of April 1944 as the Commanding Officer of a Barracuda squadron, subsequently taking part in further attacks on the battleship while flying from HMS *Formidable*. He was declared "Missing in Action" on 19 July while carrying out an offensive ASW patrol and was never seen again. In 1986, what was believed to be the wreckage of Baker-Falkner's Barracuda was found on a remote glacier in Norway.

Dick Bartlett recalls clearly the somewhat unsettling reception his group of Air Midshipmen and Sub Lieutenants received in 1938 as they reported for training aboard the aircraft carrier HMS *Hermes*. They were told unequivocally, by the carrier Captain, following some minor misdemeanour, "That he considered the group nothing but a rabble and as long as they remained in the Air Branch, they would continue to be a rabble." Fortunately the air specialist officers aboard who were a devoted and skilled group of fliers, downplayed the episode, but did warn the young trainees, "That on occasions you will encounter this type of attitude toward airmen by senior officers."

Frank Harley, also thinking back to those early days as a Midshipman, in November 1938, recalls the various members of their group of 54 aspiring pilots. He was rather taken aback at the friction that immediately developed between the snobbish Public School boys and the remainder of the course members who came from varied backgrounds. The three Canadians and a lone Australian were quickly dubbed the "Bolshi colonials" and were invariably involved in any ensuing ruckus.

Harley also clearly recalls as a spectator, the first deck trials of the new Skua fighter dive bomber aboard HMS *Courageous* in January 1939. It was hardly an impressive show. The first one aboard blew a

RN Air Midshipmen Aboard HMS Courageous, Firth of Forth
1938. Canadians O.W. Tattersall on left and R.E. Bartlett on right.
Credit R.E. Bartlett.

Sub Lieutenant Hampton Gray, RCNVR. following wings graduation at Kingston Ontario September 1941. Gray was posthumously awarded the coveted Victoria Cross while leading a carrier attack on Japanese naval ships on August 9 1945. On August 9 1989 a joint Canadian Japanese ceremony was held to dedicate a memorial to him at Onagawa Bay, Japan, at the site of the action. This is the only memorial in Japan which has ever been dedicated to a foreign hero. Credit Phyilis Gautschi.

tire and nearly went over the side, the second nearly stood on its nose, while the third caught the last wire, careened into the island, lost its propellor and reduction gear, then cartwheeled across the deck and plopped over the side. This display terminated the first trials.

Another somewhat amusing incident, also recounted by Tom Gray, concerns the problem of punctured fuel tanks being experienced by the Skuas in combat. Tom, (who was shot down three times flying Skuas), recalls the quaint resolution the Admiralty instituted to eliminate the leaks in the fuselage main fuel tanks which were located between the pilot and the air gunner, and were frequently penetrated by enemy machine gun fire, (often with unfortunate consequences to the crew). The proposed solution was to issue the pilot a canvas bag of 24 different sized corks. These were to be used by the aircrew to select (and reach out in the slipstream if necessary) and hopefully plug the right-sized cork into a matching bullet hole. The cork issue was dutifully signed for by the pilot, taken on his personal inventory and was to be fully accounted for at all times. This particular solution, although the subject of some ribald aircrew humour, was also a sad reflection of some Admiralty thinking.

It should be recorded that Skua operations although generally limited in their effectiveness, did on occasion achieve positive results during the short period the aircraft were in operational service. One such example was the highly successful raid in April 1940, on the German cruiser *Königsberg* at Bergen, Norway. This raid was carried out with 16 Skuas, each armed with a 500 lb. semi-armour-piercing bomb (SAP). The aircraft, flying to the extreme limit of their endurance, sank the cruiser in a surprise dawn raid, with the loss of only one aircraft. This was the first time in history that a naval dive bomber had sunk a major warship, and the significance of this event was not lost on the United States Navy and the Imperial Japanese Navy. It is ironic to note that the event was practically ignored by the Admiralty, and, as written by Major Partridge in his book "Operation Skua", one well known authority on naval affairs reported that the episode was greeted "with roars of indifference."

Dick Bartlett, as his service career continued, later in retrospect, believed, "that, there seemed to be quite a few older and senior Royal Navy officers who, having lived for years in a regulated and unchang-

ing world between wars, found it difficult to accept the thoughts of
such flimsy things as aircraft being any use to them, or alternatively,
any threat to their invincible battleships. Yet enough information about
aviation seemed to have filtered through to them to provide a sense of
unease and insecurity. Hence, those who were perceived to be the
instrument of change to the old structure were often regarded as a
rabble."

Perhaps a no more telling example of such thinking occurred
through the destruction by Japanese naval aircraft of the two RN
capital ships, *Repulse* and the *Prince of Wales*. These ships were
under the command of Admiral Tom Phillips, a staunch advocate of
battleship power, who according to at least two members of his
previous staff at Admiralty, (Commanders Edwards and Rotherham),
had always considered aircraft of negligible value in naval warfare.
More damning indictments are recounted in the book The Longest
Battle by well known author Richard Hough, in which he describes an
incident following the Norwegian campaign where Admiral Sir John
Tovey was being briefed by Phillips. Tovey remarked that "The need
for fighter cover was a lesson he had just learned in the Mediterranean." Apparently according to one witness, Phillips in a temper
virtually accused Tovey of being a coward. In the same book, Admiral
Sir John Cunningham, C-in-C Mediterranean, one of the RN's best
fighting Admirals wrote concerning Phillip's appointment to command
the *Prince of Wales* and *Repulse*, saying, "I thought from the moment
the appointment was announced, the fate of the two ships was sealed."
Ironically, Admiral Phillips son, Lt. Gerry Phillips, later became an
FAA pilot, undergoing advanced service flying training at No. 31
SFTS Kingston, Ont., in April 1944.

Rotherham, in his book also recounts another typical episode
which again indicates the low level of understanding of carrier air
power by some senior officers of the Royal Navy. This particular
incident that took place in 1941, involved the new fleet carrier *Ark
Royal*, when "Admiral Sir Charles Morton Forbes, (his sailors had
dubbed him 'Wrong Way Charlie' because he always seemed to turn
the wrong way when he left harbour) was in command of the Home
Fleet. He had little use for aircraft, and when he led the fleet on a
foray into the Heligoland Bight, (just as in First World War days) he

took the carrier *Ark Royal* with him primarily because it had such an excellent anti-aircraft battery. The first day that they came under heavy air attack the carrier was not allowed to fly off fighters. Despite the Fleet's heavy anti-aircraft fire the attacks continued with no enemy losses. On the second day he allowed *Ark Royal* to launch her fighters and bombing of the fleet came to a halt. Old sea dogs took a long time to learn new tricks, and unfortunately he was by no means the last of the type."

Perhaps the most tragic and bizarre example of the misuse of an aircraft carrier occurred to HMS *Glorious*, sunk later with her two destroyers in June 1940. Over 1500 lives were lost, including the pilots of an RAF squadron of Hurricanes, who had skilfully landed their fighters aboard with no previous carrier experience and without the benefit of an arrestor hook. Also lost was the carrier's Commanding Officer, Capt. Guy D'Oyly-Hughes, a well connected and twice decorated DSO winner of WW1. He was at such odds with and publicly reviled his Air Commander, J.B. Heath, an experienced capable airman, to the extent that he arbitrarily dismissed him from the ship. D'Oyly-Hughes, then taking *Glorious*, left the main convoy then enroute from Norwegian waters to steam independently to England in order to expedite Heath's court martial. The carrier and her two escorts were caught by the German battle cruisers *Scharnhorst* and *Gneisenau*, with no aircraft in the air and no lookouts posted. The justification for the ships precipitous departure was concealed by the Admiralty for nearly 37 years with the official reason given as "a shortage of fuel." Winston Churchill didn't buy that story, stating, "This explanation is not convincing." There were also suggestions of a cover up from the highest level. Remarks were made by those who should know, (including his wife) that on occasions the Captain's behaviour was "somewhat mad." Further, Commander (F) Guy Willoughby, Heath's predecessor, considered D'Oyly-Hughes "mad as a hatter."

It is by no means the intention of these examples to suggest that all senior Royal Navy officers were ignorant and non-supportive of the use of naval aircraft and aircraft carriers. Indeed there were many officers who saw the future domination of sea power through the application of naval aviation. Admirals Fraser, Kennedy-Purvis,

Lyster, Forbes, Henderson and Chatfield to name but a few were all enlightened capable leaders in the late 1930's, and each in his own capacity worked with determination to rebuild the Fleet Air Arm.

There were of course always the humorous interservice and FAA incidents that took place during the early part of the war. Frank Harley recounts a delightful story that took place when serving in 825 squadron during working up exercises out of Scapa Flow aboard *Furious*. Target towing was being done by a Fairey Battle, and some of the ship's AA batteries actually fired bursts ahead of the towed target, much to the concern of the pilot. Being greatly incensed, he radioed to the carrier, "I am towing this bloody target, not pushing it."

A short time later, the squadron was awaiting a lecture by an RAF Wing Commander on something to do with Coastal Command. The 'Wingco' who was flying a Miles Magister was informed that the carrier would be turned into wind, and the landing could be made when the "affirmative signal" was given by the ship. The pilot arrived, circled the carrier which was into wind and came straight into land without awaiting the affirmative signal. He landed alright, rolled up the deck and promptly disappeared from sight down into the forward lift well - the lift still being down! When extricated from the wreckage, he said, "Sorry, I had the directions but didn't bother to read them." As Harley recalls, and much to the chagrin of the few RAF members attending, the ships company that evening put on a hilarious skit, pantomiming the incident and using the wrecked fuselage of the Magister as a prop.

One of the most damaging and critical aspects of the state of the Fleet Air Arm was the appalling aircraft situation. Ian Cameron in his book, Wings of the Morning, quotes an official report, which in a damning indictment stated, "That between the first day of the Second World War and the last, the Fleet Air Arm received not one single British aircraft which wasn't either inherently unsuited to carrier work or which wasn't obsolete before it came into service."

The final sorrowful result was that by June 1940, the cream of the small professional FAA core of superbly trained and highly motivated aircrew had been virtually decimated by the abortive Norway campaign. Over a hundred aircraft and one hundred and fifty aircrew (approximately one third of the Air Arm) had been lost.

As the war increased in scope and intensity, the urgent need for a rapid expansion of the Fleet Air Arm was widely recognized and although no plans yet existed for the formation of a Canadian Naval Air Branch, many Canadians joined the FAA through the RNVR as direct entry, or as RCNVR officer candidates. One such group in 1940, was the 150 "Canadian Raleighites" contingent, of which 23 became FAA aircrew, among them was young Hampton Gray, RCNVR, who subsequently became the only Canadian naval Victoria Cross winner of WW2.

By 1942, the British and Canadian Governments were increasingly aware that adequate naval air forces were essential for the successful prosecution of the war at sea. The British Admiralty facing a critical shortage of manpower, whilst striving to meet the requirement for its rapidly expanding FAA, made a proposal to the Canadian Naval Chief of Staff, Vice Admiral Nelles in late December of that year. This proposal basically consisted of a request for additional Canadians to be trained by the Royal Navy as aircrew while retaining their status as RCNVR personnel, who on successful completion of their courses would be commissioned in the RCNVR.

The RCN had been keenly aware of the need for naval air forces to take part in closing the critical mid-Atlantic air coverage gap, and the timing of the Admiralty's proposal fitted well into the planning being carried out by Acting Captain H.G. DeWolf, RCN, Director of Plans. Similarily, Acting Captain H.N. Lay, RCN, Director of Operations on receipt of the Admiralty communication had given the matter urgent consideration, and prepared a memorandum in January 1943, emphasizing the importance of naval aviation toward a balanced fleet. He followed up this with a series of recommendations, which are described in detail by J.D.F. Kealy in his book, A History of Canadian Naval Aviation, as follows:

" (a)   The Royal Navy's offer should be accepted;
   (b)   Two senior officers should be exchanged with officers of similar rank in the Royal Navy to gain experience in carrier air operations;
   (c)   Officers and ratings should be sent to the United Kingdom for service in escort carriers; and
   (d)   Arrangements should be made to either build, convert or

buy four escort aircraft carriers for use with the four mid-ocean escort groups, C1, C2, C3, and C4, which were providing convoy protection in the North Atlantic at that time, operating from St. John's Newfoundland and Londonderry, Northern Ireland, as terminal ports."

On 2 March 1943, after considering all the factors, the recommendations were approved and the Admiralty was accordingly informed that the RCN was now prepared to loan personnel for aircrew training with the FAA. In April, the Directors of Plans and Operations, in a joint memorandum, outlined the details of the necessary practical steps required to formulate the development of a naval aviation policy.

It is noteworthy that in this joint memorandum, one of the sub headings mentioned helicopters, which were then being recognized as having potential value for convoy protection. The Admiralty had already made progress in this field of operations and had placed orders for 250 operational type helicopters, with pilot training being conducted in the United States by the end of 1943. Ten Canadians were to be included in this course. In addition to helicopters, the subject of airships was also included, as these machines were receiving consideration at Canadian Naval Service Headquarters in the role of air patrols and convoy escort. Since the USN had been operating airships (blimps) successfully on the eastern seaboard, arrangements were made accordingly for two Canadian RCNVR Lieutenants to take an airship pilot's course at the main training base at Lakehurst, New Jersey.

As Kealy notes in his book, "In the final paragraphs of the report, the two Directors recommended that:

(a)   The training of personnel with the Royal Navy for the possible formation of a Canadian Naval Air service be expedited;

(b)   That a naval air division be formed at Headquarters; and

(c)   That a senior officer should be sent to the United Kingdom and, if possible, to the United States as well, to study all aspects of Naval Air operations, including the gaining of experience at sea in a carrier."

Following approval by Naval Board of the foregoing recommendations, Captain Lay was selected for the study task and left for his fact finding tour at the end of April 1943. His tour was extensive and included visits to major USN naval air stations, subsequently providing an analysis of the desirability of training the Canadian naval aircrew in the United States. Lay then conducted an extensive tour of Royal Navy air stations together with an opportunity to observe carrier operations. This was followed by detailed discussions with the Admiralty. Plans also proceeded with Canadian Government acceptance of the Admiralty's proposal, and arrangements were made to commence training of 55 aircrew officers and additional numbers of telegraphist air gunners and air maintenance personnel. At the same time as this training was approved, other proposals were made to incorporate the experienced Canadians already serving in the RNVR (A) with the FAA, and other Canadians serving in the RCNVR, with the intention of encouraging the RNVR members to transfer to the Canadian Navy, for duty in the developing Canadian Naval Air Branch.

By the end of August 1943, Captain Lay released his findings in a comprehensive report. His basic recommendation was to establish a Naval Air Service which, with some modifications, "Would be modelled on the Royal Navy Fleet Air Arm". Following along with the British concept, he also stated that the new service should only be concerned with carrier operations, leaving the existing role of the surveillance of coastal operations to RCAF shore-based aircraft. Lay also stated that the new service should begin by manning two escort carriers, backed with the required maintenance organization and facilities.

It would appear that the decision to follow the Royal Navy's organization of the Fleet Air Arm had been pretty well a foregone conclusion, since the RCN as a much younger service, had always been modelled upon the Royal Navy, and virtually all senior Canadian naval officers had in part been trained by the RN, and were familiar with their system. As such they would no doubt support that decision. On the other hand, not all of the senior officers, including Lay, were completely comfortable under the guidance of the British Senior Service.

As Lay recounted in his biography, Memoirs of a Mariner, "My report was a difficult one to write. I was quite convinced that because of its ASW role in the North Atlantic, the RCN should establish an RCN Air Service but there were great difficulties. To begin with we had practically no officers or men who had any experience in Naval Aviation. It was clear from what I had seen of the organization of the Air Branches of the US Navy and the Royal Navy, that the USN was infinitely superior. On the other hand, the RCN from its beginning, had been trained and operated almost as a part of the RN and even during World War II we had worked with the RN much more than we had with the USN. We discussed the growing importance of air in all Naval Operations and particularly in anti-submarine escort, where escort carriers had just started to play their role. We also mentioned the role of the RCN in the war in the Pacific against the Japanese where Air Operations would perhaps be even more important than they were in the Atlantic. We noted the probable opposition of the RCAF to the RCN for a Naval Air service and pointed out that the answer to this was the experience of the Admiralty when Naval aviation had been under the control of the RAF from 1918-1938 and the resulting unfortunate state of the Fleet Air Arm when war broke out. We pointed out that it was the unanimous opinion of many officers in both the USN and RN whom we spoke to, that control of a Canadian Naval Air service must be completely under naval hands."

Observing the considerable number of Canadians serving in the FAA, and the commonality of training and equipment provided, the choice to go along with the RN was also the most practical and expedient one, since there had been virtually no close liaison, cross-training or experience gained by senior RCN officers with United States Naval Aviation experts. This does not mean that the USN would not have been eager to provide their expertise, and Lay touches on this point when in his memoirs he describes his visit to the USN Pensacola air training complex, remarking, "All the USN officers I spoke to were extremely interested to think that the RCN was considering establishing a Naval Air Service and they were all enthusiastic for such an action."

Following the Quebec Conference, which also took place in August, a meeting of the Cabinet War Committee was convened on 8 September 1943, at which time the Chief of the Naval Staff made an impassioned plea for the proposed aircraft carriers. This request was delayed, pending a more thorough study of the requirement. A joint RCN/RCAF Committee however, was quickly formed and the following month issued its report supporting the RCN proposal that the operation of carriers should be undertaken. As part of the report, it was recommended that the establishment of supporting shore bases should be delayed for the time being since Royal Navy facilities would be available to the carrier borne aircraft and the RCAF would be able to provide the required support when in Canada. Observing the urgency of getting the carrier commitment underway, these support arrangements did make sense for the initial formation of the new service.

On 30 October 1943, it was apparent that the manpower shortage in the RN was adversely affecting the escort carrier building program, accordingly the Royal Navy made an appeal to the Chief of the Canadian Naval Staff for additional manpower assistance. As a result of discussions between the two services, the Admiralty proposed that the RCN take over the manning of two new American-built escort carriers being completed for RN service. This proposal was subject to a series of ongoing meetings by a joint RCAF/RCN technical committee which seemed to drag on endlessly. Admiral Lay was involved in one such meeting in November 1943, as a technical witness and again in his memoirs he described the situation as follows: "When I arrived the discussions had been going on for some time and I remember that Air Commodore Guthrie (an RCAF member of Committee) stated to the conference that it seemed a rather stupid time for the RCN to become involved in a class of ship like the escort carrier when it had been proved that carriers were completely obsolete. This was such a stupid remark that, although I was only an observer, I asked if I could reply and AVM (Air Vice Marshal) Anderson said, "Certainly. Go ahead." I said if A/C Guthrie is correct, we in the RCN should immediately tell the Admiralty and USN what a mistake they are making because these two services are now building about 100 aircraft carriers of various types. This of course brought the house down, and I don't think A/C Guthrie ever forgave me. The committee finally recommended that the RCN should be allowed to acquire and operate two Escort Carriers."

Guthrie's asinine comment, coming after such spectacular aircraft carrier victories at the battles of Taranto, Pearl Harbour, Coral Sea and Midway, perhaps portrays some of the negative and shallow thinking that existed in the higher echelons of the RCAF. Their opposition to the RCN plans for the formation of a Naval Aviation Branch in this instance could only be viewed as nothing but pure emotional nonsense, based on an unfounded jealous fear that their undisputed control of aviation in Canada was under siege.

The Minister of National Defence for Naval Services prevailed on the Cabinet for authority to proceed with the Committee's recommendation and on 12 January 1944, it was finally agreed that the RCN would undertake to man two designated escort carriers, HMS *Puncher* and *Nabob*, while the RN would contribute the aircraft and air personnel. By the implementation of this proposal the required ships and personnel were now being established, and for the first time since 1918 when the RCNAS was formally disbanded, the nucleus of a Canadian Naval Aviation Branch was actively being resurrected.

Captain Lay was given command of HMS *Nabob* and the carrier began working up in January 1944, while command of the other assigned carrier, HMS *Puncher*, was assumed by Captain R.E.S. Bidwell the following April. Although both ships experienced the usual working up problems, with combined RN and RCN crews, different pay scales and victualling standards which created friction, the opportunity for Canadian personnel to man and operate ships other than the small vessels that hitherto had been the main composition of the RCN, was of inestimable value, playing a key part in the successful evolution of a naval aviation branch for the RCN.

The decision to actually implement the October 1943, Joint RCN/RCAF Committee's recommendation that "Carriers be acquired and operated by the Navy," was in the meantime under active study by the Naval Staff with the war in the Pacific being the prime requirement. As a result it was "proposed in principle," that the RCN acquire two Light Fleet Carriers from the Royal Navy. This proposal was pursued further at a Cabinet War Committee in January 1944. However, it was subsequently established that no ships of this class would be available for another year. The timely decision for Canadians to man the *Nabob* and *Puncher* for the Royal Navy proved indeed

S/Lt. Hampton Gray at RNAS Yeovilton December 1941 while undergoing advanced flying training. Credit John Stewart via C. Rolfe.

Captain Bidwell and officers of HMS Puncher 1944. Via B.K. West

HMS Puncher at flying stations. Note Wildcat fighter coming
aboard at far right. Via B.K. West.

HMS Nabob ferrying Mustang fighters to UK in 1944. 0-204-11

Barracuda landing aboard HMS Nabob 1944. HN 2517

Avenger aircraft deck park, HMS Nabob 1944. HN 1488

HMS Nabob badly damaged after being torpedoed
22 August 1944. 0-203-5

Launching of Warrior May 1944 at Harland and Wolff Ltd. shipbuilders, Belfast. Credit E.M. Davis.

to be a practical interim alternative.

The history of both *Nabob* and *Puncher* is well documented elsewhere and it is not considered necessary to detail their service careers in this account of Canadian Naval Aviation. It is of interest to know that it was proposed that *Nabob* become one of HMC ships, following standardizing pay scales for the RN members of the ships company at Canadian rates in March 1944, but no action was taken on this suggestion. This subsequently became an academic point, and no doubt a blessing in disguise, after the torpedoing of the ship in August 1944, followed by her subsequent cannibalizing, since repairs to the major damage could not be effected at that time. *Puncher* meanwhile continued in commission, primarily in an aircraft ferrying role until near the end of the year when after delays with engine trouble, the ship finally began operating with her own squadrons. *Puncher* continued flying on several strikes with the Home Fleet until May 1945, then shifted to serve in a carrier training role until converted to a troop carrier, ending up in January 1946, at Norfolk where she was transferred back to the USN.

Since the proposal to operate carriers had been implemented, and plans did exist to subsequently acquire two Light Fleet Carriers, it now became necessary to establish an aviation authority at Naval Headquarters. On the recommendation of the Naval Staff, the Naval Board on 31 March 1944, approved the formation of an air section under a Director of Naval Air Division. This final and important step established an Aviation Directorate as an integral part of Naval Staff. The new director appointed was Lieutenant Commander (P) J.S. Stead, RCN, who had been filling the appointment of Staff Officer (Air) since September 1943.

On 17 July 1944, an aide memoire was sent to the Canadian Naval Mission Overseas, (CNMO) London, from Naval Service Headquarters (NSHQ) proposing that the two escort carriers being operated by the RCN subsequently be exchanged for two Light Fleet Carriers for intended operations in the Pacific War. The Admiralty was informed and negotiations began with various proposals for the designation of the ships. With the torpedoing of *Nabob*, it was necessary to accelerate the replacement ships and an offer of the Light Fleet Carriers *Ocean* and *Warrior* which would be completed in April and

May 1945 was expected shortly from the Admiralty. The Canadian Cabinet War Committee had by now revised the RCN contribution for the Pacific theatre to a total personnel of 13,000 officers and men involving a fleet of ships including two Light Fleet Carriers. In November of 1944, the discussions became more complicated due to the Admiralty's assumption that the RCN would also be assisting in the manning requirements for escorts and repair ships. Further, the Admiralty had assumed that Canadian participation would include Indian Ocean operations, whereas the view in Ottawa was that the Canadian operations should be directed toward Japanese forces in the Pacific, rather than salvaging the remnants of the British Empire which was Churchill's objective. After considerable protracted negotiations, it was finally agreed by the British Cabinet that *Warrior* and *Magnificent* would be transferred to the RCN and a message was received accordingly on 24 May 1945, from CNMO London.

On 27 June 1945, Naval Board Meeting No. 166 took place which finally established in detail the RCN commitment to provide a Naval Aviation component for action in the Pacific. On the recommendation of Naval Staff, Naval Board agreed that the force would consist of:

Two Light Fleet Carriers
Two Naval Air Stations - One on each coast.
Two First Line Fighter Squadrons - 36 aircraft
Two Reserve Fighter Squadrons - 36 aircraft
Two First Line Bomber Squadrons - 24 aircraft
Two Reserve Bomber Squadrons - 24 aircraft
Two Fleet requirement Units - 12 aircraft
Three Communication Flights - 9 aircraft
Total strength 431 officers and 1675 men.

At the next Naval Board Meeting, it was approved to recommend to Cabinet the initial procurement of:

Two Light Fleet Carriers and four Squadrons.

Once this policy decision concerning the two Light Fleet carriers had been resolved, the "go ahead" was given for the formation of the two fighter squadrons and the two TBR (torpedo-bomber-reconnaissance) squadrons together with air staff for two carriers. Personnel for the squadrons would consist of mixed RN and RCN personnel. Canadians serving in the FAA were an obvious first choice as previously stated, and an additional source was the large number of ex-RCAF pilots who had transferred to the RNVR in response to an Admiralty call for volunteers to serve in the Far East with the FAA. Some of these pilots had already converted to Barracudas, Seafires and Corsairs and were readily available for service in the new "Canadian-ized" units now forming. Air maintenance personnel had previously commenced training following an agreement between the Admiralty and the RCN, and the number of air maintenance trainees in the United Kingdom by January 1945, had reached a total of 482. Senior tradesmen had also begun air conversion training from engine, electrical and ordnance artificers. This was a complicated and extensive program, involving a variety of personnel with divergent backgrounds for training to a common standard, and by May 1945, there were Canadian naval personnel spread through twelve separate training schools in the UK.

On 15 June 1945, 803 squadron, the first Canadian-designated unit, equipped with 25 Seafire Mk. III fighters, formed up at the Royal Naval Air Station (RNAS) Arbroath, Scotland, under the command of LCdr. (A) L.D. Wilkinson, DSC, RNVR. The squadron was desig-nated to join 19 Carrier Air group (CAG) aboard an *Implacable* class carrier, but with the advent of VJ Day, this plan was cancelled, the squadron meantime re-equipping with 12 Seafire Mk. XV aircraft. 803 squadron had a long and illustrious career having first been formed back in 1933, equipped with Ospreys. During the war, flying Skuas, they sank the cruiser *Könisberg* at Bergen in 1940, later taking part in the ill-fated attack on the *Scharnhorst*, where most of the attacking Skuas were shot down, among them being S/Lt. Dick Bartlett. The squadron later reformed and served extensively in both the European and Indian Ocean theatres, aboard various British Fleet carriers including *Ark Royal*, when the squadron took part in operations at Dakar and Oran against the Vichy French. The squadron subsequently flew from Egypt to Ceylon to assist in the defence of Colombo in 1942. Later the squadron served in East Africa, aboard *Illustrious*, one of its former members being Lieutenant Hampton Gray, VC, DSC, RCNVR. The squadron was disbanded in August 1943.

On 1 August 1945, 825 squadron, the first Canadian-designated TBR unit equipped with 12 Barracuda Mk. II aircraft under the command of LCdr. (A) Stovin-Bradford, DSC, RN, formed up at RNAS Rattray, Scotland. The squadron was also earmarked for 19 CAG in the Pacific but, as with 803 squadron this was changed and the squadron re-equipped in November 1945 with 12 Firefly FR Mk. I aircraft. 825 squadron had an extensive and distinguished history, having been established in 1934 as two RAF flights aboard the carrier *Eagle*. The squadron, later flying Swordfish, operated from *Victorious* and took part in the chase of the *Bismark*, crippling the battleship with a torpedo hit. After surviving the sinking of the *Ark Royal*, the squadron under command of Lt. Cdr. (A) E. Esmonde, DSO, RN, took on the suicidal task of attempting to stop the German heavy ships' daylight escape up the channel in 1942. All squadron aircraft were destroyed. Esmonde was awarded the VC posthumously, with the few surviving squadron members also being recognized by decorations. The squadron, after re-equipping, served extensively aboard the escort carrier *Vindex*, flying sorties against the enemy in the Arctic convoys and in the Atlantic, until disbanding in April 1945.

The third Canadian-designated unit to be formed on 15 August 1945 was 826 TBR squadron equipped with 12 Barracuda Mk. II aircraft, at RNAS East Haven, Scotland, under the command of LCdr. E.S. Carver, DSC, RN, moving later in October to RNAS Fearn. This squadron, first established in 1940, was initially equipped with the then new Albacore aircraft. They flew with RAF Coastal Command, later joining *Formidable*, seeing action at the battle of Matapan. 826 later became the first Albacore squadron to fly in operations in the Western Desert. The squadron subsequently re-equipped with Barracudas, flying operational sorties aboard the carriers *Indefatigable* and *Formidable*, finally disbanding in October 1944.

The fourth unit to be activated for the RCN was 883 squadron consisting of 16 Seafire Mk III aircraft, which formed up on 18 September 1945, at Arbroath under the command of LCdr.(A) T. J. A. King-Joyce, RN. The squadron was originally earmarked for the British Pacific Fleet as part of the new 10th CAG. However, the squadron was no longer required in this capacity with the ending of the Pacific war, so moved to HMS *Pintail*, Nutts Corner in November re-equipping with 18 Mk. XV Seafires. This fighter unit had first been activated in October 1940 at RNAS Yeovilton, and equipped with Sea

Hurricanes. In 1941 the squadron joined the escort carrier HMS *Avenger*, flying patrols over the North Russian convoys against the Luftwaffe, and later providing fighter cover for the North African landings. The squadron ceased to exist in November 1942, following the loss of *Avenger* by a torpedo attack.

The number of Canadian aircrew and squadron maintenance personnel continued to grow steadily in spite of a large number of war-time reservists now being demobilized, and as the year drew to a close, the RCN had filled all the pilot billets in 803 squadron (from over 300 volunteers), virtually all of 825 squadron and 60% of the maintenance personnel. The shortage of observers, however made it necessary for some RNVR personnel to remain with the TBR squadron until the first course of Canadians had completed their training. Since 825 squadron had by now replaced their Barracudas with Firefly I aircraft, the first two Canadian-designated units, 803 and 825 Squadrons began working up for flying duty aboard the soon to become commissioned Light Fleet Carrier, HMCS *Warrior*.

The activation of the other two squadrons, 883 and 826, was proceeding much more slowly as they were just re-equipping with Seafire XV and Firefly I aircraft, respectively, and were now embarked on an extended work up period while faced with a major shortage of maintenance personnel.

Although beyond the scope of this recollective history of RCN Aviation, it is important to emphasize that there were a considerable number of Canadian aircrew who served during the war with the Fleet Air Arm, either in the RN, RNVR, or as RCNVR, prior to the establishment of RCN Aviation. To a large extent, their activities were unknown to the Canadian public. As a consequence, both the gallantry and individual exploits of these Canadians, was to a considerable degree unnoticed in Canada and often unrecorded. Suffice to say that their record of accomplishment is impressive enough to be the subject of a separate book. It is difficult to provide precise figures of the numbers involved, due to the fact that the British Admiralty did not necessarily disclose the nationality of the personnel serving in the Royal Navy. The Fleet Air Arm Canadian Register, diligently compiled over the years by B.K. West however, is probably the best source available for these figures. In summary, the statistics make interesting reading as follows:

Total Canadian aircrew serving with the FAA during WW2 in the RN, RNVR, and RCNVR, (excluding the ex RCAF aircrew that transferred to the RNVR as the war ended), totalled upwards of 260 personnel.

Killed in action 14.

Killed in flying accidents 28.

Decorations and honours awarded to Canadian naval aircrew during WW2 were as follows:

Victoria Cross	1
Distinguished Service Order	1
Distinguished Service Medal	1
Order of The British Empire	1
Legion of Merit (US)	1
Distinguished Service Cross	21
Mention in Despatches	20
Total	46

In late 1945, an interesting proposal was made by the USN, and recounted by LCdr. Dennis Foley, as follows:

"In the latter part of 1945, as BNLO(Air), (British Naval Liaison Officer) at Norfolk, Virginia, I was the RN member (LCdr.(A) RNVR) on the USN Team handling the return of Lend Lease RN aircraft. As BNLO, I had two Sikorsky R4 helicopters assigned to me. In October 1945, these were to be handed back to the USN as returned Lend Lease. As the USN had no helicopters or helicopter pilots, they suggested that as I had received my transfer to the RCNVR, and was to report to NSHQ the first week in January 1946, that I take the two helicopters and their spares with me to the RCN. Being a new boy to the RCN, I thought I had better wait until I reported in, and ask if they would accept the two R4's. When I reported in, I advised Cdr. Arbick that the two R4's were there, just waiting to be flown to Canada with spares. I was told, "Helicopters f---, what we want is jets." Had we taken the two R4's, I think we would have got into helicopters much earlier they would have been much better than the old Swordfish we had at Dartmouth, and would have been good for a few years service." (The RN used their R4's until July 1950).

These R4's were obviously some of the remaining helicopters

ordered by the Admiralty in 1943, and were actually used by the RN in the anti-submarine role in 1944. It is interesting to note on the other hand, that up to the end of 1945 the USN itself was not operating any helicopters. It was odd that the matter of a free gift of two helicopters was not more actively pursued by Arbick and his air staff.

A final step in the Admiralty and NSHQ negotiations was completed on 13 December 1945, when the Admiralty proposed the revised terms for the loan to the RCN of the two Light Fleet Carriers. They further proposed that the four air squadrons, when and if they were taken over by the RCN, be effectively transferred with the acquisition by the Canadian Government of all aircraft, equipment and stores.

While these proposals were being studied by Canadian authorities, a most important decision was reached by Canadian Cabinet on 19 December 1945 that "Approved in principle the formation of the Naval Air Component as recommended; on the understanding that it would be confined within the authorized total manpower of the Navy." This momentous decision was exhilarating for all those Canadians serving in the squadrons earmarked for the two carriers and was accompanied with a general feeling of relief. Up to this point the activation of squadrons and the ambitious plans for a naval aviation component had all been based on the RCN requirements for the war in the Pacific. Ever since VJ Day in August 1945, virtually everybody involved was very uncertain if the Air Branch was still a sure thing, or whether it was just the momentum of war plans continuing, with the squadrons actively forming up, until the machinery finally ground to a full stop. In one clear respect, the major decision had been made to "Start up," as compared to the decision 27 years earlier in 1918 to "Shut down." The determination and foresight of the Naval Board to expand the RCN, then the third largest allied navy, to a peacetime force which included carrier aviation was highly commendable, and resulted for the first time in a modern balanced maritime force for Canada.

A significant point in the general euphoria, which was perhaps overlooked by many, was the clearly spelled out restriction that the newly created Air Branch would be necessarily confined to 11% of the proposed 10,000 personnel peacetime strength of the RCN. This meant in fact that the branch would have to man two fighter squadrons, two TBR squadrons, two aircraft carriers and a supporting air station with a total personnel complement of only 1100 officers and men. The ability of the Air Branch to meet all these major personnel commitments was indeed highly questionable, and it would appear the naval planners involved were being excessively optimistic. A final, somewhat "Scrooge type" change was also made about this time with the Federal Government's decision to reduce the wartime $60 per month flying pay or risk allowance for aircrew of the Canadian services to $30. No doubt inspired by some historically minded minion in Treasury, this niggardly step reduced the allowance to the identical scale which had been originally established some 30 years ago in 1918, for the original RCNAS. No doubt, the law of supply and demand took precedence in this case, since in 1945 the RCAF was wallowing in surplus aircrew and could pick and choose their personnel. This low rate of aircrew pay would continue for some years until the availability of aircrew vs. service requirements, came into a reasonable balance.

Chapter One

RESTARTING

Events were moving rapidly in 1945 with the war in Europe ending in the Spring, followed by the shift of additional resources to mount the coming allied offensive in the Pacific against the main Japanese Islands.

By the time hostilities ended in Europe, there were several hundred Canadian naval pilots serving in the United Kingdom, attending various air training courses or being otherwise indoctrinated into the Royal Navy. The largest percentage of these were ex-RCAF pilots who had recently joined the RNVR. Most of these fliers had transferred early in 1945, the majority of whom were recent graduates of the RCAF, the remainder consisting mainly of staff pilots and instructors who had been serving in training stations in Canada. In addition, there were a small number of RCN and RCNVR pilots who were undergoing post-wings operational training at various Royal Navy air stations. All these pilots, the largest group being the 550 from ex-RCAF ranks alone, were available for service in the proposed Canadian Naval Air Branch, now being formed and destined for service in the war against Japan. The ex-RCAF fliers were a highly motivated, adventuresome group, whose main interest was to continue their service career in a flying capacity. The Royal Navy's offer for these men to participate in the war against Japan was eagerly accepted, and many of them, with above average flying experience and ability, saw this new opportunity as a means of fulfilling their individual ambitions. To fly operationally in naval carrier aviation, was therefore looked upon as a new and exciting challenge. In the Pacific theatre, there were also a number of veteran Canadian fliers serving operationally in FAA squadrons, many who were available as valuable additions to the new air branch.

One of the first contingent of ex-RCAF pilots to proceed overseas was a group of some 33 instructors and staff pilots, who on arriving in the UK in March 1945, went directly to HMS *Macaw*, a small induction and holding unit at Bootle, Cumberland. One of them, Sub Lieutenant, (S/Lt.) J.W. "Deke" Logan recalls the somewhat limited success the RN staff at *Macaw* experienced in attempting to mould the individualistic "colonials" to the Royal Navy's concept of RNVR junior S/Lts. Since the war was still on, this exposure at *Macaw* for the group was short-lived and they were bundled off to an Advanced Flying Unit (AFU) at Tealing, near Dundee, Scotland, to fly Harvard trainers. Since most of the pilots in this group had as much, if not more flying experience on the aircraft than the instructors themselves, this training only lasted about a week before they were all shunted back to *Macaw*. The RN recognizing that these pilots were obviously already well trained and capable at the AFU level of flying, had the entire group by-pass any further flying training and in mid June they arrived at Arbroath, Scotland. There, they became the first "Canadian-ized" squadron to be formed for Pacific operations, commencing as previously mentioned, to work up operationally as 803 fighter squadron, equipped with Seafire III's. The squadron, commanded by LCdr.(A) L.D. Wilkinson DSC, RNVR had scheduled the complete equivalent of the Operational Training syllabus for the new Canadian pilots. Wilkinson was ably assisted by an experienced nucleus of four instructors, three of them RNVR and the fourth Lt. (P) A.J. (Bob) Tanner RCNVR. The newly arrived pilots totaled 32 in number and the following members comprised this group: Bill Rikely, Doug Breithaupt, Bob Falls, Jack Hartle, Gord Hoffus, Ian McCuaig, Lloyd Nash, Don Gray, Jack Sloan, Hank Leidl, Deke Logan, Doug Russell, Len Wade, Bob Tate, Jim Anderson, Al Roberts, Harry Rounds, Andy Forbes, Neil MacDermid, Bill Hutchison, Pat Whitby, Mel Douglas, Roger Fink, Roger Cyr, Doc Prescott, Gerry Quarton, Russ Jantzen, Cam MacKenzie, Bob Jeffries, Hal Fearon, Bill Munro and Bob Beach. Regrettably, the first Canadian fatality to occur in this

803 Squadron pilots and Sea fire XV at Nutts Corner, 1945.
Credit W. H. Fearon.

883 Squadron pilots and Seafire XV, Nutts corner, 1946.
Credit H.L Swiggum

825 Squadron Barracuda at Fearn, 1945. Credit S. Britton

803 Squadron at Nutts Corner, 1946. Credit John Anderson

803 Seafire XV on line at Nutts corner, 1945-46.
Credit John Anderson

825 Squadron Barracuda at Rattray, 1945. Credit S. Britton.

Canadian naval squadron took place off Arbroath, when Andy Forbes was killed on 30 July 1945 while on a low-level formation flight, crashing into the sea. Deke Logan who was flying in this formation astern of Forbes, noticed that he was flying stepped down from the lead aircraft rather than the customary position above the leader which is assumed on low level flights. Logan was just about to warn Forbes when he saw him inexplicably edge his Seafire still lower and suddenly hit the water.

One of the early members of the Canadian maintenance team was Able Seaman John "Hoss" Anderson (AM/L) who had been recruited early in December 1944 by Lt. A/E Jack Ratcliffe, subsequently proceeding to the UK for training in air trades. Hoss recalls a particular Royal Navy Commodore who no matter where the training establishment was located, invariably spied the Canada flashes on the uniform of the Canadian trainees, during an inspection and always asked, "How are you enjoying things in the Royal Navy?" He then would absently pass on with the remark, "Splendid", without ever waiting for the answer. Following one such occasion, each Canadian in the group agreed to respond immediately with the identical reply should the Commodore again ask his inevitable question. It happened on the following inspection, and the one Canadian who was asked "How are you enjoying things in the Royal Navy!", shot back immediately, "It's the shits, Sir!" The Commodore walked by genially remarking, "Splendid, Splendid!", to the appreciative snickers of the conspirators. As Anderson was to remember, this disrespect did incur the displeasure of the Captain of the training school, resulting in a general stoppage of leave. Anderson joined 803 squadron in December 1945. He recalls the shortage of maintenance personnel in the early stages, and also the rather casual and relaxed atmosphere in the squadron, this was most evident when on a visit to the squadron of some senior Canadian Navy "brass" to do an inspection, it was artfully avoided by some of the "hands" who immediately disappeared into the tall grass adjacent to the assembly area.

The squadron after a few months stay at Arbroath, re-equipped with Mk XV Seafires in August 1945, then moved to Nutts Corner at Belfast, arriving in September. As Deke Logan comments, "Nutts Corner seemed a very appropriate name for the home of a large number of fighter pilots". Shortly after, the station was augmented by a couple of New Zealand Hellcat squadrons and the formation of 883, the second "Canadianized" fighter squadron.

The operational work ups of 803 continued through the fall of 1945, including the commencement of training in aerodrome dummy deck landings (ADDLS). About the same time, the RCN(R) interview boards had been convened and a number of the squadron members were selected for transfer to the RCN Interim Force for service aboard *Warrior*, while about half of the original 32 pilots, now that the war with Japan was over, elected to be demobilized and departed for Canada. The squadron pilots, now familiar with the new and more powerful Seafire XV's, were continuing with advanced operational flying training, and by the end of November 1945, all were considered to have completed the equivalent of the rigorous "Fighter School Syllabus". Unfortunately, this was not achieved without further cost, since Len Wade was killed on 2 October, when he struck a mountain peak while formation flying near Nutts Corner. The third squadron fatality took place on 5 November, when Lloyd Nash disappeared flying on a formation climb-out from Nutts Corner, crashing south of Belfast as the 16 plane squadron transited en route to Lee-on-Solent for an air show.

As Hal Fearon recalls, the switch from the Seafire III's to the XV's was not a major step for those already experienced on the earlier Seafires, but extra caution and skill was required in both takeoff and in formation flying. The increased power of the Griffon-powered XV's created a major torque effect on takeoff and a swing to the right could not be controlled if excessive power was applied before rudder control was achieved as the speed built up. In formation flying, similar care had to be exercised due to the sudden yaw that occurred when making abrupt throttle adjustments, which in the previous Seafire III's had only a negligable effect. The pilots in 803, being like most fighter pilots, a thrill-seeking lot, also believed in finding out just what their new Seafires were capable of doing. Roger Cyr decided to find out "how fast she would go" in a dive. This he certainly did find out! He wound up in a high speed descent from great heights and hit the sound barrier, achieving a speed in excess of Mach 1. This led to fairly serious complications, the fuselage was twisted, the main planes wrinkled and bent, and violent buffeting was experienced as the aircraft approached the speed of sound. Roger did manage to keep control and get the aircraft back on the ground, but had major difficulty getting the undercarriage down due to the twisted fuselage and main plane damage. The new Seafire which only had a few hours on it was written off, and Cyr was hardly greeted with enthusiasm by his Commanding Officer, for this rather foolhardy experiment.

As Deke Logan was to comment many years later, the fatal accidents experienced by the squadron were fairly commonplace in the FAA, since the wartime attitude, general practices and operational procedures were still very much in effect in the Royal Navy, and the shift to a more controlled and disciplined peacetime operating standard was yet to be established. This applied particularly to instrument flying conditions and the attendant hazards involved in following the lead aircraft in poor visibility and cloud.

Observing the RCAF background of many of the remaining Canadian RNVR pilots, none of whom had ever received any naval training, it was inevitable that the individual on arrival in the UK, would require the basic indoctrination as offered by HMS *Macaw* prior to being fed into the Royal Navy air training organization. Other than the initial group who proceeded directly to 803 squadron, the majority did experience a more comprehensive introduction to the Royal Navy at this small, remote holding establishment at Bootle, which could best be described as in "the booneys". At *Macaw*, the only other perceived habitation in the vicinity was the small village itself, consisting of little more than a few cottages, a pub and a railway station. To arrive there involved passing through Carlisle, where it seems all trains were routed, then often wait endlessly for a train to Bootle.

By common agreement, the best feature of *Macaw*, was the large number of females stationed there, as members of the WRNS (Womens Royal Naval Service). These pert, good humoured and agile group of young girls served in a variety of tasks on the station, among which was the officers' morning "wakeup" with a cup of tea. None of the Canadians had been exposed to this type of morning service in the RCAF and the early morning routine raised more than considerable interest. As a consequence the girls were invariably fleet-footed, or if not, quickly became so.

Since there existed such a lack of knowledge about the Royal Navy among the Canadians at *Macaw*, there was a considerable variety of uniform attire on display, with colour varying from black on through navy blue, and in one instance a somewhat naïve new officer who had apparently purchased his kit from a small town tailor, arrived resplendant in a grey-blue naval uniform. One other poorly advised, or perhaps somewhat innovative young officer, actually showed up complete with what was subsequently identified as Royal Egyptian Railway brass buttons on his naval jacket. The wearers of such gross uniform deviations were accorded no sympathy and treated with raucous humour by their new contemporaries, coupled with varying degrees of horror by the Royal Navy staff. In hindsight, it was probably Gieves Ltd., Naval Outfitters, who did more at that time than anybody, to advise the unwary and provide the proper dress for new officers.

There was little to do at *Macaw*, while the training intake system was temporarily plugged with the large influx of junior air branch officers, so other than a few lectures, sporadic parade drills and training in night vision aptitude, there was not much of interest to keep oneself occupied until the next phase of training was scheduled. The night vision course was often a bit of a skylark, since in spite of the competence of the WRNS (always known as Wrens) instructors, the basic training course was directed toward classes of somewhat bored and restless young pilots lurking about in the pitch black classroom while being subject to the voice instructions on night vision techniques by the senior Wren. Her small staff of girls strategically located about the room would, on command, momentarily activate mini lights randomly suspended from the ceiling to simulate a target location. The object of the exercise was for the class members to visually identify the various objects as the lights were being flashed. Often the routine was interrupted by sound of a smack, giggle and slap, (not necessarily in that order). The girls were very adroit, however, and fortunately being well accustomed to this type of encounter, they accepted it all in good humour.

The Royal Navy had in operation during this time, a marvellous scheme called a "Leave course". It consisted of short term travel periods of up to two weeks granted to the individual service member to spend at various educational facilities and points of cultural interest in the UK, where accommodation and meals were provided at the expense of the British Government. Virtually everyone took advantage of this type of recreational relaxation and trips were taken to various historical places, one of the most popular being Stratford-on-Avon. Others attended the University of Aberdeen, which also included side trips to St. Andrews, Fyfe and Dundee, with plenty of time allowed for stopovers at various places en route. All were so anxious to get away from the dull *Macaw* routine, that the base primarily became a temporary stop for laundry, mail pickup and replenishment of funds.

Normal leave which was granted quite readily, was expensive, particularly in London. In some cases desperate circumstances required desperate measures. S/Lts. Irvin Bowman and John Laurie found themselves in rather embarrassing circumstances while in London on leave - namely without money. They heard from what turned out to be an unreliable source, that one of the major movie studios was hiring extras for an ongoing film. They duly presented themselves in naval uniform, but were informed that if there was any hiring to be done, it was at the film site, and as a chauffeur- driven Rolls Royce just happened to be going there, the two "Subbies" were invited along. Adjusting smoothly to luxury, they proceeded to the out of town location in regal style, with high hopes. Their dreams of stardom however, were quickly shattered when it was determined there were no openings for any extras. The film studio was located well out of London, and now they were truly stranded.

All was not lost however, because the two were given a ride by a sympathetic passing driver, who on learning of their plight, offered a somewhat different level of employment, which was the labour intensive repair of tennis courts damaged during the war. This menial labour comprised filling the bomb cratered courts, at which they toiled alongside the English working class for about two weeks until their finances had improved. As expected, their surreptitious daily coming and going from the well established London Officers Club, where they were living, was more than complicated somewhat as they scurried back and forth in grubby labourers garb.

One particular benefit of the RN which was quickly put to use, was the useful feature provided by the pay accounting organization, namely, the issue of individual pay books. Carried by each service member it was almost as valuable as a cheque book, since every RN establishment and ship, no matter how large or small, would issue a cash advance to the individual upon presentation of the pay book. Since the transient group of roving Canadian trainees were always on the move, the length of time for the individual "casual" (as the advances were called) to be processed through the RN pay system was fortunately lengthly, taking several months to finalize.

It was in the fall of 1945 following VJ Day in mid August, that the pace quickened at *Macaw* for the large Canadian contingent with the final arrival at the station of the three RCNVR officers who had been given the responsibility to interview and select pilot candidates for the manning of the four "Canadianized" squadrons. The selection board members were Acting Commander G.C. "Ted" Edwards and Lieutenant Commanders Jim Hunter and Tom Darling, all veteran Canadian pilots of the Fleet Air Arm. *Macaw* was only one of the many locations where pilot selections were being made, others already having been given to the several Canadian pilots who had already joined squadrons or other training units located throughout the UK. S/Lt. Ron Heath was at Zeals outside Yeovilton, where he had managed to amass some 70 hours on Corsairs, and remembers one of his contemporaries S/Lt. "Moe" Yule being there at the same time and who was also awaiting his board selection. It appears that Moe was doomed from the outset since the night before his interview, he had occasion to share the Officers urinal at the same time as Jim Hunter. Following their individual proceedings, Moe while exiting the washroom, was asked by Hunter, "Do you not normally wash your hands?" Moe's self destructive response was, "I do not piss on my hands when urinating!"

With the ending of the war, and many Canadian RNVR pilots now taking their release, the manning of the four "Canadianized" squadrons was undergoing considerable changes. Plans were now proceeding rapidly to implement the two year special Interim Force commissions for those wishing to join the RCN, and the wavy braid of the RCNVR and the RNVR was now being replaced by the straight stripe of the RCN which was also to be worn by the newly accepted aircrew

825 Squadron Barracuda, aircrew and maintenance team at
Rattray, 1945. Credit F.W. Lynch

RNVR Officers course at Greenwich Naval College 1945. About half the course are Canadian ex-RCAF aircrew. Credit H.L. Swiggum.

members. For some of those selected, the shiny gold single stripe of a new Sub-Lieutenant was a sign of complete inexperience and as a result, a few enterprising, but misguided souls decided that a more tarnished appearance was in order. This was achieved to a certain degree by soaking the braid in salt water or applying black shoe polish, following this, the braid assumed a rather odd looking, somewhat greenish black shade which was decidedly off-colour. Invariably, the individuals concerned were ordered to replace with the required new gold braid, ending up looking even newer than their less imaginative contemporaries.

As the pipeline pressure diminished, the next step in the introduction to the Senior Service was the three week long "knife and fork" course at the beautiful and renowned Naval College at Greenwich. Although the quarters were spartan and crowded, the large buildings and spacious grounds were amazingly well maintained after five years of war, and the magnificence of the Painted Hall, where all meals were served, was particularly impressive. With strict rationing in effect, meat and fresh fruit were still in short supply, which was particularly noticeable to the recent arrivals from Canada. The meals by comparison were therefore dull and lacking in both quality and quantity. Initially, it was somewhat awe inspiring to dine in the splendour of the evening at the great hall, surrounded with a king's ransom in silver flatware, busts and statuettes from long departed ships, complete with ornate chandeliers and intricate candelabra. This feeling of awe was dispelled somewhat once dinner progressed, as each naval steward, serving in all his finery, made a grand flourish on removing the silver dish covers, to disclose the savoury, which more often than not, consisted of a dried up prune cinched in by a tiny strip of bacon, skewered with a toothpick, all resting morosely on a dried piece of cold toast.

There must have been about seventy on each course at the College of which probably one half were Canadian aircrew. With the war now over, the classes were quite relaxed, basic subjects consisting of naval etiquette, administration (letter writing), seamanship (trips down the Thames in the College launches) and knot learning.

One particularly memorable and hilarious instruction period included a lesson in unarmed combat by Commander Street, a remarkably well preserved Royal Navy officer, who had been a boxing champion in the pre-war service, and by this time must have been sixty years old. His first instruction was to personally demonstrate how to break a neck hold when unexpectedly attacked from behind. He mistakenly issued a general challenge for a volunteer to grab him in this manner around the neck, which would then be followed by a routine display showing how easy it was to break such a hold. On that particular occasion it didn't quite work out that way, because one burly individual (believed to be Ken Nicolson) readily accepted with a somewhat roguish grin and promptly put a strangle hold on the old fellow so effectively that the poor Commander was virtually suspended, his toes barely touching the ground, the neck lock inexorably throttling him, while he ineffectually clawed at the ham sized arm around his throat. As the seconds passed, the old man was getting redder in the face, his eyes had begun to bulge, and there was no way he had any hope of breaking that vice-like hold. When the pressure was finally and mercifully eased somewhat, the Commander managed to gasp out that the neck hold was a bit too tight and the class would now take a short break (while he slowly recovered his wind and composure).

As the young ex-RCAF officers were being familiarized with the customs and procedures of the Royal Navy during the summer of 1945, a number of the ex RCAF sergeant pilots awaiting their commissioning boards, were putting in their time at the Royal Navy gunnery school at Whale Island. This was the famous "Spit and polish" school revered by gunners for its tough discipline and time honoured traditions as they pertained to the gunnery world. The Canadian fliers, given the rank of Petty Officer while awaiting their disposal, were under the dubious supervision of Chief Petty Officer Jack "Rummycan" Runciman, the senior member of the contingent. One member of the troop, Bill "Jumper" Babbitt recalls one particular day the group which included himself, Les Peever, Charlie Bourque and Roger Harris, was ordered to proceed to the Clothing Store and off they went, following some vague instructions as to how to get there. After marching dispiritedly about the large base, they were hopelessly lost, so Runciman upon spying a large building decorated with a flag, brass cannon, and surrounded by impeccably kept lawns, told the gang to fall out and he would "locate their position." They all promptly lit up cigarettes and were lying around listlessly on the grass bemoaning their fate being in this strange service, wearing strange clothing while surrounded with strange people with no sense of haste or humour. Their brief moment of self pity was rudely interrupted by the first Royal Navy Gunners Mate to spy them, who with a beet red face screamed at the reclining junior Petty Officers for lying about on the grassy verge and desecrating the hallowed sanctity of the Quarterdeck. There is truly nothing more impressive than an angry Gunners Mate! Apparently the depth of the ignorance of the Canadian group, coupled with their naive bewilderment, left them more to be pitied than chastised for their heinous breach of Royal Navy tradition, so other than quickly "Getting felled in" and departing at the gallop under the stunned lead of Runciman, nothing more came of the incident.

Another rather irreverent incident occurred at Greenwich College that summer, when the Admiralty hosted some of the senior members of the new British Cabinet, which included Clement Atlee and Ernest Bevin, who on this particular occasion, following an official reception, were somehow invited to the subterranean lair (Gun Room) where all the Sub. Lieutenants and Midshipmen held sway with their own bar amid rather ancient battle-scarred leather lounge furniture. It was fairly late in the evening and the Gun Room activities were well on the way to the nightly mayhem, when the VIP group arrived, escorted by a protective screen of Royal Navy Admirals, to meet some of the junior officers attending the College. (Let's face it, at a Royal Navy establishment, there is nothing more junior than a Canadian Acting, Temporary Sub Lieutenant (A) RNVR). In any event, the guests were presented with drinks , and in no time the irreverence surfaced. S/Lt. Ken Gibbs recalls his slightly inebriated drinking partner, S/Lt. "Tommy" Thomas, approaching a seated Admiral and politely inquiring as to what he was drinking. The Admiral looked appreciatively at his nearly full glass and replied "It's gin Sub." Tommy took the Admiral's drink and said "That's what I'm drinking too Sir", and promptly drained the glass. The Admiral was speechless for a few goggle-eyed seconds, then mercifully broke into a loud guffaw, and boomed, "Bloody good!, another drink for the Subbie". Nobody ever recalled how this little caper went over with newly-elected Prime

Minster Clement Atlee and his Cabinet colleagues.

Following the Greenwich course, some members of the group went aboard training carriers for a few weeks as observers. One such ship was the Escort Carrier, HMS *Ravager*, based at Rosyth, where naval pilots having completed their operational training, were given deck landing practice. I remember joining *Ravager* in November 1945, with a small group of other S/Lts, which included Jimmy Pulfer, Doug Short and Peter Kohl. As was customary in the Royal Navy, we were put under the control of a "snotty's nurse", whose responsibility was the overall supervision of our general training and deportment. The introduction to *Ravager*, was a real eye opener! For starters, our assigned Lieutenant by the name of Easum, who looked about fifty years old, opened his welcoming talk by discussing in outrageously frank details, his opinion of the personal qualities and habits of the individual ship's officers from the Captain on down. After mostly disparaging remarks about the various officers, it was readily perceived by us that the ship was run by a "bunch of weirdos". When he was finished with his recital, it became obvious that Easum considered the only two members of the wardroom who were at all normal, were himself and his running mate whom he referred to as "Testicle Tom". Looking back on it all, the wardroom certainly did have some oddballs, not the least of whom was Easum and his buddy "Testicle". There was, however, one definitely strange character that fascinated us all. He was the shipwright, who went ashore every night after tanking up with gin, carrying a silver headed cane (probably complete with concealed sword) and wearing a top hat together with a long black boat cloak. What he did and where he went, was never established by us, but he gave the best parody of Count Dracula anybody could ever have imagined. One night aboard *Ravager* that was remembered by Ken Gibbs, was an invitation to him from his old buddy Jimmy Pulfer, to go out to the anchored ship for a party. Ken recalls the wind was blowing up a storm, and as the drifter came alongside, Jimmy (being somewhat unsteady on his feet from a pub crawl) leaped for the ship's accommodation ladder, missed it completely and ended up being ignominiously fished out of the drink by a crew member armed with a long boat hook.

Training aboard was very limited, with a few lectures on

miscellaneous naval subjects. These lectures, invariably of short duration, were intended only as a fill-in until we could view the main event-deck landings. One of the first landings we had the opportunity to witness, created a lasting impression. A Corsair piloted by Lt. George Olson RCNVR, came whistling aboard, bounced once, swiftly sailed up the deck over all the wires, and finally ground to a halt after being well wrapped up by the first and second barrier cables. It was quite an exciting event, and none of us at the time, even for a moment, considered that it would ever happen to us sooner or later. In the Royal Navy FAA, we were told, that as a general rule, naval pilots were divided into two groups, "Those that have had a barrier, and those that are going to have a barrier". As time went on, this particular philosophy appeared to be prophetically accurate.

One aspect of our exposure aboard *Ravager* was to provide us with the privilege of experiencing a deck landing from the observer's lower compartment in a Barracuda. This we found out, was a rather dubious honour, of questionable training value. My own participation in this event was minimal. When my turn came, I ran out to the the ungainly waiting aircraft, crouched with its engine sputtering, looking not unlike a turkey buzzard with spread wings. I clambered through the rear door into a dark little space in the back of the aircraft and started doing up my harness straps. I found out where to plug in the radio lead just in time to hear the pilot make a garbled transmission. I was still frantically trying to fasten the straps as we started lumbering into the takeoff, and it wasn't until after we were airborne that I finally got them secured. By this time, I noticed a small window on the side of the aircraft, and managed to peer out just in time to see that we were already landing back aboard. So much for observed deck landings! I believe it was about two days later that the same pilot pranged the Barracuda on landing, when it went lurching over the port side and flopped in the sea. Fortunately, he did get out!

S/Lt. George "Knobby" Westwood also did some sea time in an Escort Carrier, in this instance aboard HMS *Premier*. The current role of this ship was to collect the various FAA aircraft that the Royal Navy had received from the USA in the form of Lend-Lease. The agreement governing such equipment required that it must be brought back to a state similar to that in which it was received, before being returned to the United States, which by war's end was knee deep in surplus fighter aircraft. Rather than take the aircraft back, the agreement permitted in lieu, that the aircraft in question could be "disposed of" permanently. As Knobby recounts, his first carrier time primarily consisted of watching perfectly serviceable and sometimes new Corsair aircraft being hoisted aboard *Premier* then taken to sea and unceremoniously dumped over the side. Ron Heath experienced a similar experience, insofar as he was involved in flying Corsairs from the South of England up to Sydenham (Belfast) to see them hoisted aboard a carrier for dumping at sea. Also, Lt. Dick Bartlett, taking a fighter flying refresher at RNAS St. Merryn in November 1945, following his release as a POW, recalls the unusual sight of the FAA airframe mechanics obediently installing the clocks in the cockpit of new Corsairs. After test running the engines, they then watched with stolid indifference as the aircraft were hauled aboard ship for dumping at sea.

At the end of 1945, a number of the seventy five ex-RCAF pilots who had been accepted and transferred to the RCN(R), commenced training at the various flying establishments. The Advanced Flying Unit at the RAF Station at Tern Hill Shropshire, was the first stop for most of the pilots. This was one of the older RAF training establishments and being of pre-war vintage, had a beautifully built and maintained Officers Mess. Apparently the station had a somewhat interesting claim to fame, since there was a plaque mounted in the Mess donated by Charles Lindberg, following his famous flight across the Atlantic. The plaque is specifically inscribed "In memory of the famous November fog", which apparently plagued the Lone Eagle when he was flying about England in the late twenties.

The flying course at Tern Hill consisted primarily of a one month course of 25 hours on Harvards. This, for many pilots was the first opportunity to fly the single-engined advanced service trainer, they having flown only twin-engined training aircraft while undergoing their flying training in Canada. The RAF type that instructed me on the Harvard was a genial Yorkshireman, who, as we flew about the local area, pointed out the various little villages that dotted the Shropshire countryside. Being unused to such a broad accent, I couldn't understand a single word he said, so my map was of little use in verifying our position.

As the year drew to a close for the Canadians in the UK, it was the pilots of 803 squadron that were probably in the best location to organize and participate in the most lavish Christmas festivities. Coincidently, it just so happened that most of the officers had recently received a lump sum payment of their Canadian rates of back pay, and so they promptly planned a gala Christmas weekend in Dublin where food rationing was non-existent. This was no doubt a party to end all parties, and Hal Fearon still remembers the groaning tables loaded with ham and turkeys, with a bottle of Scotch placed prominently at each place setting, the occasion complete with a score of Irish colleens. Later, and much poorer, the Canadians could not help but feel a touch of guilt, comparing the scarcity of food in the UK, to the gourmet choices that were made available to them in the Irish Free State, which had been virtually unaffected by the ravages and deprivations of the war.

Following the course at Tern Hill, pilots went to the Royal Naval Air Station (RNAS) Instrument Flying School at Hinstock, Shropshire and the nearby Rolls Royce Engine Handling Course at Peplow. The basic course of 10 hours flying on Harvards and Airspeed Oxfords lasted only two weeks, which was fortunate in one sense, since the standard of living was a big letdown from the luxury of the RAF facilities. Accommodation was in Nissen Huts, unheated washrooms were in a similar building elsewhere and the conditions were spartan to say the least. Heating consisted solely of a small coal fired stove in the centre of the building, and the amount of coal was not only severely rationed, but the stockpile of fuel was under continuous surveillance by an armed sentry. The accumulative results of this austerity rapidly became evident, when upon inspecting the chest of drawers assigned to each officer in the hut, it was found that the drawers were no longer in existence. What was left consisted of only the front of each drawer, carefully positioned in place to appear normal. The previous occupants, having no doubt used up their coal ration, proceeded to utilize the wood from the available chests. It was a cold and wet winter that year and the huts never did warm up, so we all slept with our greatcoats as supplementary cover. I can recall that Doug Peacocke, Brian Cartwright and myself were in one such frigid space at Hinstock in January 1946, when who should arrive on the scene but S/Lt. Harry Swiggum, "Swig" a member of 883 squadron, who had flown a Seafire XV into the station. Apparently he had been given a weekend leave to fly to Birmingham to visit his girlfriend, but the weather had turned sour at Nutts Corner and he couldn't get back to his unit. Swig's scheduled return seemed pretty flexible so he was with us for awhile with nobody (least of all Swig) being concerned about when he would actually get back to his squadron. I remember one prize comment Swig made when describing what he airily referred to as his experience in Ferry Command. It seems he was assigned to ferry a Seafire from one place to another, and while taxying out and following another Seafire, became understandably somewhat distracted by a couple of friendly girls waving to him from an adjacent road. As Swig related, "I wasn't on Ferry duty very long after I ferried my Seafire up the ass of the aircraft taxying ahead of me".

825 Barracuda squadron had moved from Rattray, following completion of fighter evasion tactics, to RNAS Fearn at the end of August 1945. Jim Watson recalls one incident just prior to leaving Rattray, when after completing the usual Barracuda corkscrewing evading maneuvre, he decided to continue on by trying a roll in the beast. After losing a few thousand feet, and failing to accomplish a semblance of a roll, there was a long pause on the intercom, and finally his observer Tony Sweeting said, "If you try that again Jim, I'm bailing out!"

It was at Fearn as the squadron commenced dive bombing and anti-submarine diving practice, that S/Lt. Sid Britton, RCNVR joined the squadron as AEO, (Air Engineering Officer) replacing the departing RNVR engineer. Sid recalls that the senior squadron NCO's were RAF Flight Sergeants and Sergeants, and the Canadian personnel were primarily Able and Ordinary Seamen. The two senior Canadians were Petty Officers Stephens and Mason who led the group of 60 Canadians as the contingent arrived on the station. The first comment heard by Sid came from the squadron Commanding Officer, LCdr. Stovin-Bradford RN, who told him to take charge of those "Scruffy Colonials", a remark that was most certainly not appreciated. Sid also remembers being in a degree of shock after the individual interviews, to find out that nobody in the group had any actual experience working on squadron aircraft. He also warmly remembers how dead keen the new group was, and their tremendous individual efforts to become proficient at their new trades.

As the end of 1945 neared and the official formation of the Canadian Naval Air Branch took place, there were additional changes in the four "Canadianized" squadrons. 825 Squadron had been transferred to RNAS Burscough, re-equipping in November with Firefly FR Mk I aircraft, which replaced the much maligned Barracudas. Squadron pilots at that time were predominately RNVR, the Senior Pilot being "Dai" Davis and the Senior Observer, Tony Sweeting. The pilots were all greatly relieved by the replacement of the "Barra" with the Firefly, since in the view of many, the Barracuda was not really designed to fly! It is interesting to note on the other hand, that many of the observers that flew in Barras, enjoyed the practicality and comfort of the observers work station, which enabled them to carry out their various functions with relative ease and efficiency.

Canadian aircrew had now commenced to join the squadron ranks in increasing numbers and one of the first ex-RCAF fliers to join 825 was S/Lt. Charlie Bourque, while Davis, Sweeting, Watson and S/Lt. Lynch comprised the RNVR nucleus who remained with the Squadron. Two Canadian observers, S/Lts. Dick Quirt and Dave Gill also joined in late fall to augment the remaining RNVR observers. LCdr. Stovin-Bradford turned over command of the squadron in December 1945, to LCdr. O.W. Tattersall, DSC, RN, now a veteran flier who as previously mentioned had joined the FAA from Canada in 1938. Other Canadians also began arriving to replace the RNVR pilots, who in most cases were now being demobilized. Among the group that arrived at the end of 1945 and in early 1946, were Lts. "Darkie" Lowe, Tom Wall, Dick Bartlett and S/Lts. Cliff "Crash" Gavel, Art Liley, Don Hockin, Howie Clark, Doug Peacocke, Brian Cartwright and myself. We were given to understood that Stovin-Bradford had been offered the opportunity to remain in squadron command on loan to the RCN, but he was very concerned that his chances for promotion in the Royal Navy would be jeopardized if he took the appointment. He feared that being responsible for working up a large number of pilots in the squadron with a non-naval (RCAF) background, with no operational flying experience, would result in a noticeable increase in the accident rate, which would adversely affect his reputation, his career suffering accordingly. At this particular time, the new, revised training program underway in the Royal Navy, scheduled squadrons to reform and re-equip, then work up as a unit to a full operational first line status. Therefore both 825 and 803 Squadrons were working up from scratch so to speak, since most of the new pilots had not been given the benefit of an Operational Training course on the type of aircraft they were now flying when in the squadrons. Therefore, squadron accidents which were normally incurred during training at an Operational Training Unit (OTU) could certainly be expected, as the pilots began to fly operational aircraft in a first-line role. This observation appeared to be realistic, observing the attrition rate that had already been experienced by 803 squadron.

Lt. Freddy Bradley recalls this period clearly after serving previously in the summer of 1945 as an RCNVR senior member of 825 squadron under Stovin-Bradford. He tells of a subsequent interview in London with Air Personnel, who in the throes of organizing the Canadian squadrons' aircrew, were actively seeking an RCNVR officer to take over command of 825 Squadron. Bradley tells of being offered the position, but when told that most of the pilots would be Canadian ex-RCAF trained RNVR pilots who were now being enrolled in the RCN(R) Interim Force, he strongly objected and stated that it would be a disaster working with pilots with that type of non-naval background. Bradley said he would only accept if he could retain a personally selected group of British RNVR pilots as a squadron nucleus. Due to the current policy in effect this was not an acceptable arrangement, so the meeting ended. Later on the same day, Bradley encountered "Tats" Tattersall walking down Piccadilly and suggested to him that there was probably a squadron in the RCN available, if he wanted to take it under the proposed arrangements. Fortunately, Tattersal accepted!

Meanwhile 803 Squadron, operating out of Nutts Corner, was now under the command of LCdr. A.J. "Bob" Tanner, RCNVR, who had replaced LCdr. Wilkinson, who along with his RNVR instructors, was demobilized in November 1945. About this time, 803 was augmented by other Canadian pilots, including Lts. Bob "Dawgface" Monks and Ross McNab, RCNVR, and S/Lts. Paul Stock and Neville "Monk"

Formation of 825 Squadron Barracudas, Rattray 1945.
Credit PA146651

803 Squadron personnel preparing Seafire XV for start up
at Arbroath. Credit PA145551

825 Squadron Fireflies stowed in hangar of Warrior, 1946.
Credit PA141223

825 Squadron Firefly on catapult launch, Warrior 1946.
Credit PA141274

Group of Canadian Air Engineers in UK 1945-46. Front left
Dave Litle, rear left Jack Ratcliffe, rear right Bill Maxwell.
Credit Bill Maxwell

Deck park of 803 and 825 squadrons aboard Warrior
en route to Halifax, March 1946. Credit DND G220

Preparing to launch Fireflies and Seafires of 825 and
803 Squadrons from Warrior off Halifax, 31 March 1946.
Credit DND G238

Warrior approaching Nova Scotia, 31 March 1946. Note Swordfish aircraft at top right. Credit E.M. Davis

825 Squadron aboard Warrior at Gaspe, 1946. Credit S.E. Soward

Geary, both RCNVR. Lt. (E) (AE) Les Turner, RCNVR also joined for engineering duties. Three other Lts. RCN(R), Vic Wilgress, Derek Smith and Barry Hayter arrived at about the same time. Barry Hayter, who had served in the Pacific aboard *Victorious* was designated senior pilot in the squadron, with two other ex-RCAF pilots, S/Lts. Al "Smoky" Bice and George Marlow completing the group.

Under the command of LCdr. "Spike" King-Joyce, RN, 883 fighter squadron was now virtually "Canadianized" and although suffering from a shortage of maintenance men, was continuing with operational work ups. Among the Canadian pilots who remained in the squadron and had completed their selection process were S/Lts. Tommy Boyle, Bob Laidler, Eddy Myers, Ken Nicolson, Jack Runciman, Harry Swiggum, "Wally" Walton, and "Duke" Wardrop. Additionally, S/Lts. Ron Heath, Bert Mead and Knobby Westwood were appointed to the squadron, but their arrival was delayed, pending a leave period and clarification of the future status of the unit, now seriously affected by the major maintenance personnel shortages.

It was during the cold, rainy and boggy Irish weather so common in the winter, that the fertile minds of 803 pilots came up with a graphic visual presentation to emphasize and portray the prevailing climate. Monk Geary appeared in the door of the mess late one night in muddy gum boots after a trip to the local pub. He was promptly set upon and hoisted on the shoulders of some of his larger squadron mates, propelled up the nearest wall, then carried upside down across the low ceiling and back down the other wall of the ante room. The result was a well defined, messy trail of muddy boot prints arriving at one entrance and exiting at the other, via the walls and ceiling. Pre-dictably, the RN air station staff were not overly amused the following morning.

One problem being encountered by 803 squadron at Nutts Corner was the complete lack of aircraft towing equipment. This resulted in the pilots being frequently called out to taxi aircraft from one location to the other to meet servicing needs. Bob Monks finally decided this was becoming too much of a nuisance and proposed that the ground crew do the required taxying. This was rejected because under Royal Navy regulations only aircrew were allowed this dubious privilege. Hoss Anderson was finally allowed the distinction of being the only non-flying member of the squadron to taxi aircraft, but only after he had sent home to Canada to produce his pilot flying log book, which established his qualification as an ex-RCAF Sgt. pilot. Following this, the wearing of wings was nonchalantly granted by Bob Monks, but as Anderson subsequently was to find out, it became increasingly awkward trying to explain to one and all how he could justify wearing a pair of naval pilot's wings on the sleeve of his Able Seaman's uniform jumper. The prevailing miserable weather during the winter of 1945 at Nutts Corner also resulted in more than one ingenious scheme by the Canadian maintenance personnel to augment the miniscule coal ration provided for the stove in each hut. One particularly successful heating unit was developed by scrounging discarded kitchen cooking oil, thinning it out with a small amount of aviation fuel and gravity feeding the mixture into the stove via a metal pipe attached on the other end to a suitable container. This worked beautifully, but was subject to the odd flash back, (perhaps too much gas) which unfortunately on one occasion did attract the attention of the Fire Marshal and his staff. The occupants of the hut were not punished for this innovative heating solution, because there was nothing in the Air Station Standing Orders which prohibited such an arrangement. This however, was quickly brought under control by an amendment to the orders, and the nightly attendance in the hut by S/Lt. Bill Rikely in the role of heating supervisor.

Meanwhile in Canada, following an RCAF proposal that they would consider "sympathetically" the whole question of the management of shore facilities for naval aviation, negotiations commenced in October 1945, at a high level between the Chief of the Naval Staff, Vice Admiral G.C. Jones and the newly appointed Chief of the Air Staff, Air Marshal R. Leckie. It was subsequently agreed that a joint committee should be established to examine the common requirements of the RCAF and the newly formed RCN Air Branch. This committee commenced its studies, presumably based on the original recommendation by the RCN/RCAF Committee of October 1943, which had proposed that the RCAF provide shore facilities for the RCN carrier squadrons when operating from land-bases. This proposal naturally had been based on a wartime expediency situation, but now that this had ended it is difficult to understand why such a restrictive proposal would still have any validity in the post-war establishment of the three services. Unfortunately, the final outcome of these negotiations would severely affect the development of the fledging Naval Air Branch.

825 squadron continued with their operational training program throughout the poor weather of the winter months and into the new year. As Jim Watson recalls, the weather at Burscough was marginal for flying days on end, and coupled with the industrial smoke and haze from the Midlands, there was a severe restriction to the work up program, resulting in most of the flying being confined to formation, slow flying sequences and the on-going airfield deck landing practice (ADDLS) in preparation for flying aboard the soon to be commissioned Canadian Light Fleet Carrier, HMCS *Warrior*. LCdr. Jim Hunter and Lt. Ted Davis were the two DLCO's (Deck Landing Control Officers), better known as "Batsmen", assigned to conduct the ADDL phase of the workups. Ted Davis was an unflappable, good natured officer and an excellent DLCO, who quickly established a good rapport with the pilots of both squadrons. Since Jim Hunter was appointed to *Warrior* as Flight Deck Officer, he concentrated his time initially on training the flight deck personnel, and familiarizing himself with the flight deck equipment aboard *Warrior*, leaving the ADDL workups largely to Ted Davis.

The first major accident to take place during these workups by 825 occurred in February 1946, when Darkie Lowe and Tom Wall took off in a ceiling of about 200-300 feet to conduct ADDLS. This turned into a disaster almost immediately when the aircraft lost sight of each other in the prevailing low ceiling and visibility. Darkie recalls having to climb through the cloud, then trying without success to gain radio contact in order to obtain a homing back to the airfield. Since the only airfield open was on the Isle of Man, and he had no maps (being launched for ADDLS only) he elected to fly out to sea and then let down through the clag until he regained visual contact, which he managed to do, breaking out of the clouds about a couple of hundred feet. He then headed back to where he estimated the airfield should be, narrowly avoiding the shore cliffs that loomed up in the murk while en route. Minutes later, those of us on the airfield, heard, then saw, a Firefly flying in a big orbit around the field at an altitude of about a 100 feet, being lost to view intermittantly in the fog and haze. A high smoke stack on the perimeter of the field was an additional hazard for Darkie and he narrowly avoided hitting this as he circled and finally made a successful pass at the duty runway. After taxying back to the hangar, Darkie remembers the CO (Tats), saying,"I guess you must have been pretty nervous up there Darkie". Darkie of course denied this with an emphatic "Hell no!" Tats then said, "Well why did you taxi all the way in to the hangar with your flaps down?"

In the meantime, as this "hairy effort" was being concluded, Tom Wall, also forced into the cloud, lost control of his aircraft, and ended up in a spin. Fortunately he was able to bale out, but not without considerable difficulty, actually landing close by his spinning Firefly which crashed in Bootle, Lancashire some ten miles south of Burscough. The aircraft exploded on St. John's Road, damaging houses and injuring three children. It was indeed miraculous that nobody was killed and the houses a few yards away were only slightly damaged. Tom was understandably shaken by this unexpected and near fatal episode, but after a medical check, promptly came back to regular flying duties, apparently unharmed by his ordeal.

There were other, but fortunately minor accidents, which took place on the airfield, during these ADDL sessions. Two in particular did have their amusing side. Brian Cartwright deciding he would practice an ADDL on his own, was doing nicely until he got both low and slow coming in on the approach and stalled a few feet above the end of the runway. In the meantime, I was airborne on my first Firefly solo and after a few rolls and stalls followed by a further general familiarization with the aircraft's flying characteristics, returned to Burscough only to find to my dismay the duty runway somewhat cluttered up with Brian's broken aircraft. In attempting to effect a cross wind landing on the other runway and not being all that conversant with the Firefly's cross wind performance, I ended up skipping my aircraft somewhat crab-like down the runway, until the undercarriage finally collapsed under the lateral stress. We now had two runways blocked with pranged Fireflys, so since flying was pretty well finished for the day, the rest of the squadron aircrew went off to the local pub and the two of us spent the remainder of the afternoon being checked out in sick bay (ego damage only) and filling out our accident reports.

Meanwhile, HMCS *Warrior* had commissioned on 24 January 1946, under the command of Capt. F.L. Houghton, RCN. The Executive Officer was Cdr. K.L. Dyer, and the Air department was headed by Acting Cdr. Peter Mortimer RN who was on loan to the RCN. At the same time both 803 and 825 squdrons had formally been transferred to the ownership of the RCN, complete with all aircraft and stores. In order to be closer geographically to the working up area off Spithead, the two squadrons re-located at Lee-on-Solent, at the end of February 1946 and began their final workups prior to joining the carrier. By this time the status of both 826 and 883 squadrons was precarious and their continued existence increasingly doubtful due to the critical shortage of maintenance personnel. Although additional pilots were still being appointed, both units regretfully had to be disbanded on 28 February, although remaining officially on paper as RCN squadrons for future activation. LCdr. C.G. "Clunk" Watson, RCN(R) probably had the shortest tour on record as a Commanding Officer having taken over 826 squadron only eight days previously.

In Canada, arrangements were being made for the newly created Air Branch to locate at the RCAF Station, Dartmouth, N.S. This site had first been proposed in May 1945 by Cdr. (A) J.H. Arbick, OBE, RCNVR, Director Naval Air Division (DNAD), when the RCN began negotiations with the RCAF for transfer of wartime air bases, which would be required for aircraft of the two carriers, *Warrior* and *Magnificent*. Although not the best location from the weather point of view and quality of facilities, the Dartmouth air station was considered the most practical since it was across the harbour from the main RCN naval base complex at Halifax. So, after an absence of 25 years, arrangements were made for Canadian Naval Aviation to return to its original birthplace, the site of the first RCN Air Station at Baker Point, now forming part of the marine section of the RCAF Station.

In November 1945, the first naval personnel, comprising a number of stores ratings, had been drafted to the air station to commence mustering the air stores inventory for the 25 surplus Walrus and Swordfish aircraft turned over to the RCN from the Royal Navy facility, HMS *Seaborn* which was now in the process of being shut down at Eastern Passage (Baker Point). Cdr. Gibbs of the RCN Air Division, Ottawa, took over the small detachment of 3 officers, 6 men and 6 civilians who comprised the RCN group and with the welcome assistance of the last remaining detachment of 44 RN air mechanics who were awaiting passage back to England, they commenced to renovate buildings, inspect the condition of the surplus aircraft and prepare one of the Swordfish for flying duties. Fortunately, additional naval personnel were made available and by March 1946, a semblance of order had been achieved, with the RCN Air Section installed as a small but separate service lodger at the RCAF owned and operated air station. This arrangement was the result of the six months of negotiations between the RCN and RCAF, covering the sharing of responsibility for shore-based naval aviation. The outcome was a sellout! In spite of the well known agonizing consequences of joint RAF and RN control of the FAA following WW1, which had persisted until 1938, the RCN negotiating committee blithely walked into the trap of dual service control of its newly formed Naval Air Branch. That this arrangement was ever allowed to be repeated is incredible! The RCAF was granted the funding, management and control of all naval air shore-based facilities and supporting air services, including such significant sections as air stores and major aircraft repairs and overhaul. One would have thought that Air Marshal Leckie, who had been a S/Lt. in the RNAS in WW1, and later served with great distinction in the RAF and RCAF, would have been more understanding and supportive of the newly-formed Naval Air Branch. This was not the case, and with his RAF background between the wars, it was soon apparent that he understood the ramifications of the situation all too well. Remarks attributed to him while serving in the RCAF as Chief of the Air Staff, suggest that he was prepared to do everything in his power to prevent the development of Canadian Naval Aviation.

The facilities at RCAF Station Dartmouth were in general badly run down, and the limited accommodation made available was in poor shape. The dual control aspect of the air station operation rapidly became unworkable, with the RCAF exercising full control and management of all the various sections serving the needs of Naval Aviation. It was soon apparent to personnel at the working level of both services, that the RCAF commitment was but a hollow promise and the existing arrangements would have to be changed to meet the ever increasing demands and requirements of the the RCN Air Branch, as it expanded to meet its approved role.

Lt. A/E Gerry Daniel, RCN, recalls a rather amusing incident in the spring of 1946, when he made a courtesy call to the RCN Air Section, which consisted of little but a hangar, a few Swordfish, the Engineering Officer, LCdr. Dennis Foley, RCNVR, together with the Officer-in-Charge with his secretary. Gerry was invited to have lunch by Cdr. A.E. Johnson who was now in charge, and was dumbfounded to discover, when after readily accepting, that "lunch" consisted of something the secretary was busily concocting on a hot plate in the Mens Head. As Gerry recounts, he was singularly unimpressed with his first introduction to the newly formed RCN Air Section.

At the beginning of March, *Warrior* completed acceptance trials, embarked the additional 13 Seafire Mk15 and 9 Firefly I reserve aircraft at Glasgow, finished flying trials and then was officially accepted by the RCN. On 17 March, 803 and 825 carried out deck landing qualifications for the eligible pilots. For many of us this was the day that we first heard the bugle call alert, followed by the loudspeaker pipe, "Hands to Flying Stations". This would be a call which many of us would respond to during the next twenty five years on commencement of each day of carrier flying. Flying completed late that afternoon, then *Warrior* came alongside at Portsmouth to embark additional stores and the personnel of the disbanded 826 and 883 squadrons.

On 23 March 1946, with 803 and 825 squadron aircraft embarked, *Warrior* sailed for Halifax to fulfill with great expectations, an essential, established post-war role in Canadian Naval Aviation. A few days later, on 26 March, Naval Board officially approved the acquisition of the four squadrons for the RCN at a cost of $10M.

Since the carrier was newly commissioned, there was little to find fault with aboard the ship. It was quickly apparent however, during the short trip back to Canada while being exposed to the chilly March weather, that the lack of winterization and tropicalization was going to result in uncomfortable living conditions in many of the mens living quarters, in both cold and hot climates. The British Light Fleet Class vessels were built with expedience for wartime use in the Pacific and as a consequence they suffered from a lack of space and offered only limited amenities for peace-time service.

In the meantime, in the UK, there were still many Canadian aircrew serving at Operational Training Units and flying first line naval aircraft for service in the RCN. Unfortunately these various flying courses took their toll of pilots and in February and March there were three fatal accidents. Among those killed were Lt. Bob Jacobs, RCN(R), S/Lt. James Philley, RCN(R) and S/Lt. Doug Shortt, RCN(R) who was killed when his Firefly stalled during takeoff on his first flight. On another occasion there occurred one of those humorous and somewhat bizarre flying escapades which on rare occasions does actually take place. This involved S/Lt. Bert Fiddes RCN(R) who, whilst on an OTU somehow managed to overshoot the firing range during a practice gunnery run, and continued on to spray 20mm. cannon fire into the local cemetery, narrowly missing two grieving residents kneeling at the family plot. He was naturally charged for this "grave" error with a court martial, from which he was miraculously acquitted because he had also committed the cardinal sin of forgetting to sign the necessary pilots authorization form required to carry out the flight. As a result of the lack of an acceptance signature by Fiddes, there was no evidence presented to the court that he had even made the flight, and on this technical discrepancy he was exonerated. Bert's luck also held up on a second misdemeanor when he exuberantly "beat up" the Royal residence at Balmoral Castle. The only witness to this low level violation was His Majesty, King George VI, and since there was no way he was about to be subpoenaed for the investigation, the charge had to be reluctantly dismissed.

On 27 March 1946, the Canadian Cabinet approved the retention on loan of two Light Fleet carriers, two *Crescent* Class destroyers and the purchase of four naval air squadrons with reserve aircraft, stores and equipment, from the Royal Navy. With this approval, the composition of the post-war RCN Air Branch was now established and all was in place for a promising future. On 31 March, *Warrior* arrived at Halifax with great fanfare, welcomed by local and federal dignitaries, while the aircraft of the two squadrons flew ashore to the RCN Air Section at RCAF Station, Dartmouth, where they were scheduled to continue on with operational work ups for the next three months. Due to the inability of the RCAF to meet its commitments to provide the station maintenance for the RCN squadrons, an air maintenance pool had to be formed from RCN personnel, while at the same time, #743 Fleet Requirement Unit (FRU) was established at the section equipped with Swordfish and Walrus aircraft, which were shortly after augmented with Harvard trainers and Avro Anson light transports. 743 squadron was primarily formed to carry out flying training sorties in support of the fleet and provide pilot proficiency flying.

Things were very much disorganized as the two returning squadrons prepared to take their approved leave period. This rapidly developed into an acrimonious situation when it was learned that all the train billets had been assigned to the ships company of *Warrior*, many who were taking extended leave. It was only by considerable complaining and a lot of work on the part of Lts. Hank Leidl and Deke Logan that alternate train billets were finally produced. As Hoss Anderson was to recall, each person proceeding on leave was advanced the princely sum of $30.00 which was the maximum allowed. This did little to placate those who were proceeding on extended leave of 60 days or more. As Hoss was to recount many years later, this unsatifactory situation drove him as close to mutiny as he ever would be!

In March 1946, the air station was the locale of a variety of different activities, but it was soon apparent that the level of support facilities and services was minimal, and the station was one of the most run down and poorly equipped airfields one could imagine for peacetime use. It was a large, sprawling base accommodating the airfield on the north side where the hangars, control tower and runways were located. Crossing the access road was a railway running through the lower part of the station, along which rambled the small train to Musquodoboit. Further to the south was the main highway running east from the town of Dartmouth to Eastern Passage. On the extreme south along the shore was the marine section containing some of the old WW1 hangars and buildings which had comprised the original Baker Point Air Station. Immediately to the west was the large Imperial Oil refinery filled with hundreds of thousands of gallons of aviation fuel and various oil products. It was to become an area of no little concern when repeatedly flying over it at an altitude of 150 feet during ADDLS. On the airfield proper, there were a great variety of WW2 aircraft, some of which were tucked into the revetments built into the slopes on the sides of the runways. In them were parked Lancaster bombers from the RCAF 6th. Group from the UK, which had been flown back to Canada by their crews. Surplus Canso flying boats, Hudson bombers, together with the 22 Swordfish and 3 Walrus amphibians left to the RCN from the RN, all scattered about the field, awaiting disposal. The two decrepit hangars allocated to 803 and 825 squadrons were in sad shape, in spite of the considerable efforts made by the advance naval party. The hangar working conditions for the squadron maintenance crews were sub standard, with leaking roofs, poor heating units and decrepit sliding doors that allowed the seasonal weather to drive wind and rain through the buildings at will. The living accommodation for the officers was badly in need of refurbishing, with little or no furniture and leaky plumbing fixtures throughout. Suffice to say that the quarters for the other ranks was even worse! There was little flying being carried out by the RCAF at Darmouth, which comprised a small Search and Rescue Unit and a couple of Dakotas that maintained a Communication Flight. Commercial air access to the Halifax/Dartmouth area was provided by Trans-Canada Airlines and Maritime Central Airways, which were also based at the airfield. To the east, on the other side of the airfield was a small private flying operation owned by Pulsifer Bros. that ventured sporadic flights in an Anson and two or three other elderly aircraft. All in all, it was a chaotic and somewhat depressing situation, aggravated by the fact that the RCN, being an unwanted beggar tenant, meant that the degree of support from the RCAF was almost non-existent. In fairness to the few RCAF personnel at the base, most were sympathetic to the general situation and poor working conditions of the naval personnel, but with indifferent support from their own Air Headquarters, there was little corrective action that could be accomplished at the local level.

On 8 May 1946, there was a Naval Board Meeting of some significance, insofar as the Board had agreed that for the next four years the air squadrons would be equipped with British aircraft - or until "such time as the question of Hemispheric Defence vs. Empire Defence is more clearly defined". Aircraft would be: - 803 and 883 squadrons - Seafire XV's pending replacement by Sea Furies. 825 and 826 squadrons - Firefly I's pending replacement by Firefly IV aircraft.

It is noted that Captain Bidwell was the Director of Naval Aviation at that time, and there was no question that most of the senior RCN officers were very pro British. It was not surprising therefore, that the policy to continue to buy British naval aircraft would prevail. The mention of Hemispheric Defence vs. Empire Defence is interesting and perhaps requires further examination. Observing that there was as yet no Canadian White Paper on Defence defining defence policy, and NATO had not been formed, Naval Board were necessarily on their own with regard to the overall role and function of the RCN. Since the pre-war policy for Canadian defence was orientated toward the Commonwealth, and the wartime policy provided for Canada to have its own command structure to the maximum practical degree, it was inevitable that the immediate post-war period would undergo a period of uncertainty until a specific naval policy was established by the Canadian Government. During this period of uncertainty, Naval Board was therefore continuing with the re-shaping of the fleet, determined that the RCN would no longer be a small ship Navy.

A major aviation personnel problem developed following the granting of leave to the personnel of 825 and 803 squadrons, which was no doubt aggravated to a degree by the indifferent manner in which the men had been treated by the service when making their leave arrangements. Many of the maintenance personnel elected to opt for discharge once having experienced a long awaited Canadian leave period. Such a critical shortage ensued, that for a time 803 was down to a nucleus of only three qualified Leading Seamen and below, consisting of LS. A/E Callard, AB. A/F Ellison and AB. A/L Anderson. In order to keep the aircraft serviced, pilots were assigned to carry out refuelling and participate in the aircraft daily inspections. In doing so, they were generally under the supervision of Callard who reportedly took great and perverse delight in assigning his newly recruited temporary assistants the additional dirty jobs, such as cleaning the oil covered aircraft engine panels. The white uniform shirts of the pilots quickly became grubby and oil stained, since there was no available alternative work clothing to which they were entitled to be issued.

For 803 and 825 squadrons, following the leave period and personnel changes, the months of May and June were actively spent preparing for embarkation aboard the carrier and getting all the pilots ADDL qualified for deck landing refresher, Acting LCdr. Clunk Watson in the meantime having assumed command of 803 squadron in May from Bob Tanner. ADDLS were not an easy task to schedule, since every time an aircraft, other than the ones conducting the ADDLS, wished to land or takeoff, the squadron deck landing practice was interrupted and the ADDL aircraft required to clear the area. 825 squadron continued working up the newer pilots with the emphasis on formation flying, carrier procedures, and basic navigation and sea exercises carried out by the newly formed crews.

Meanwhile, at another Naval Board Meeting of 12 June 1946, Naval Board considered a recommendation by Naval Staff to acquire 50 F6F Hellcats from the USN at a cost of $3500 each. This recommendation was made as a result of the delay in the production of the British Hawker Sea Fury, the replacement for the Seafires. In its deliberations, Naval Board noted that: "This would be a reversal of present policy (Buy British). The Hellcat was no longer a first line aircraft. It would involve three different types of aircraft. The RN was thought to be ahead of the USN in future design and development." In conclusion, the Director of Naval Aviation (DNA), now Capt. Bidwell, was directed to undertake further investigation.

It was interesting, but also incorrect, for the Naval Board to have assumed that the British were more advanced in the design and development of future naval aviation equipment and aircraft. Although the Admiralty was actively pursuing the angled deck concept, steam catapult and mirror landing aid for aircraft carriers, the USN continued to advance rapidly and maintain superiority in carrier aircraft design and development. There was also no doubt that the Canadian DNA staff members were still of the view that Hellcats would be a viable and inexpensive alternative to the Sea Fury, for use as an interim replacement and for subsequent operational training once the Sea Fury was ready for squadron service.

The matter was still very much alive in any event, because on 31 July 1946, at a Naval Board Meeting, DNA was directed to go to the USN to obtain details with a view to a purchase of Hellcats. At the same time the Admiralty were also to be informed that the RCN was considering the purchase of aircraft from the USN. One of the most ardent and persuasive proponents of the Hellcat purchase at NSHQ, was Lt. H.J. "Dicky" Bird, on the Naval Aviation Staff. He had flown Hellcats during the war, knew of its excellent carrier performance and with his remarkable talent to deal winningly with a large number of USN friends and associates, mounted a very effective campaign to convince Naval Staff to buy the aircraft.

On 20 September 1946, Naval Staff noted that the Admiralty had advised that the RCN would receive priority allocation of Sea Furies and 803 squadron would re-arm in March 1947. 883 would also re-arm in time for the commissioning of *Magnificent* in September, 1947. This abrupt change of delivery dates was no doubt prompted by the disclosure to the Admiralty that the RCN was also looking at a USN fighter replacement. In spite of this acceleration of Sea Fury delivery dates, Naval Staff still recommended that Hellcats be procured for Reserve pilot training and for use in the support and utility role by 743 squadron, the Fleet Requirement Unit.

On 2 October 1946, at another Naval Board Meeting, the subject was aired once again, but the Board felt that in the view of the recently promised earlier delivery of Sea Furies, there was no longer a requirement for Hellcats. There was an odd proviso to this, which added "Unless Cabinet changed its decision on procurement of Sea Furies and Fireflies."

In the meantime there was on-going training of Canadian pilots in the UK during the fall of 1946, one such group was undergoing flying at the RAF Elementary Flying Training School (EFTS) at Panshangar, the satellite field to Hatfield. Included in this group were Lts. Ken Learmouth, Ken Hunt and Al Carter who had remustered from the Observer Branch. The remainder of the Canadian class were comprised of Lts. George Hopkins, Jack Beeman, Alec Cupples, George Greenwood, Roy de Nevers, Joe McBrien and John Murphy. Sadly, their ranks were depleted on 17 October 1946 by a mid-air collision resulting in the death of Greenwood. Apparently George was practicing instruments under the hood, with his RAF instructor, in a Tiger Moth when they collided with an Airspeed Oxford twin engined trainer, piloted by an RAF Wing Commander, as both aircraft simultaneously came out of cloud. George made an unsuccessful attempt to bale out, but there were no survivors from two shattered aircraft which each crashed out of control. Roy de Nevers who was flying a Tiger Moth at the time, witnessed the entire shocking tragedy.

In Ottawa, the subject of Hellcats was again raised a few months later, when both the RCAF and the Royal Navy reported that they would be unable to provide the operational training of pilots for the RCN. This statement concerning the RCAF response is interesting, since they had never provided this training for the RCN, their only involvement with RCN pilots having been restricted to flying training to wings standard and instructor and instrument courses.

At the Air Section at Dartmouth, the flying clothing provided was mostly old RN issue, the summer flying suit consisting of a canvas type of overalls which was so heavy and ill-fitting that it was never worn. Other personal flying clothing items such as gloves and helmets were either in short supply or not available, so many of the aircrew flew in shirt sleeves, discarding naval jackets if the weather was warm enough. A large part of the time, 825 squadron flew over the sea, and although the implications of this were not generally considered at the time, the lack of any type of immersion suit was indicative of the general shortage of aircrew clothing in the immediate post-war years. At one briefing, early in our workup stage, we were all cautioned to be sure and remove our black ties before flying, so that in the event of coming down in the drink, we would escape being strangled by the shrinking neckwear in the salt water. Initially, the complete irrelevance of this instruction did not sink in, and it was only sometime later we realized that in the year-round chilly water off Nova Scotia, one would expire from hypothermia long before a shrinking tie became a threat to survival.

Carrier qualifications and refresher carrier landings were carried out by both 803 and 825 squadrons in early July, but shortly after, the Admiralty advised the RCN that the Mk XV Seafires were experiencing a major defect in the supercharger clutch of the Rolls Royce Griffon engines and it was necessary to prohibit the aircraft for carrier operations until the problem could be rectified. 825 squadron continued on with flying operations in the Gulf of St. Lawrence, after shifting from the waters off Halifax where heavy fog had persisted. Deck landing training was the main objective, and other than the odd instance when an aircraft mislanded and wheeled into the port sponson

825 Squadron maintenance personnel during cruise to Caribbean. 1946-47. Credit S. Britton

FLYING STATIONS

They wept and they wailed, as the carrier sailed,
From Canada's Eastern shore,
For they loved the men, who were in her then,
And wanted them back once more.
So Canada's pride went out with the tide,
To be tried in the open seas,
To prove her crews, who were flying fools,
Doing their DLT's.

The Captain smiled, like a happy child,
And he clapped his hands with glee,
Old "Wings" looked pleased, as he sniffed the breeze,
And playfully slapped his knee,
For this was the day, they started to play,
With this new toy of theirs,
And little did know, what dreadful woe,
Would whiten their graying hairs.

Now the time was ripe, so they made a pipe,
"Hands To Flying Stations,"
And assembled all told, eight pilots bold,
For briefing, in Operations.
The Flight Deck Crew, yellow-green-red-blue,
Fell in with enormous commotion,
The wires were spliced, the barriers triced,
While Jumbo drove into the ocean.

With a mighty roar, all but the four,
that fell, into the sea,
Became airborne, that fateful morn,
And the Micmac picked up three.
Little "F" proposed, with no one opposed,
That a shot, be done off the CAT,
When the shot detonated, the aircraft rotated,
And ended up in the stack.

Approaching from aft, a speedy aircraft,
Just bounced, off the quarterdeck.
the next, a Seafire, caught #9 wire,
But the pilot, broke his neck.
The third who tried, went over the side,
And the fourth, went into the barrier.
As they carried him away, to the ship's Sick Bay,
He cried to "Wings" of the carrier.

"You may well glare, from way up there,
And shake your fist at me,
You may look on the dent, that the barrier bent,
And the place, where my prop should be.
You may look at the crack, in the Firefly's back,
Just above, where the round down hit it."
And again he cried, just before he died,
"I don't know how, I did it!"

"Who now will fly?" Our "Bats" did cry,
As everyone scurried to hide.
After losing his denture, a Looker did venture,
To crawl in the rear, for a ride.
C.O.'s said, "Not me!. Please try Senior "P",
But everyone seemed, a bit nervous,
'Till a Subbie stepped in, well loaded with gin,
And volunteered, his service.

He posed there with pride, as the photographer tried,
To snap him from every direction.
On his chest, "Wings" secured, a ribbon so lurid,
That he wore Poleroids, for protection.
Away in the sky, our bold hero did fly,
While the carrier, developed a list.
As everyone tried, to reach the port side,
And watch him fade into the mist.

Now the maintenance men, are heard from again,
And were all exclaiming with glee,
"Its come to an end, It's now make and mend,
Our aircraft, are all in the sea."
The bridge was so congested, the XO suggested,
That "Wings" was no longer, apropos,
With the Captains assistance and little resistance,
they launched him directly, for Sambro.

And now there's a gushing, of salt water flushing,
But lo, the wrong valve is on.
To make more steam, they have used gasoline,
And she blew, like an atom bomb.
Now the story is told, by a Fisherman old,
And his tale, will long endure,
That as sinking she hurtled, the loud hailer gurgled,
"Flying Stations-Secure"

Air Maintenance Class, HMCS Stadacona, 1946. Credit W. Maxwell

Swordfish aircraft at RCN Air Section, Dartmouth, NS.,1946
Credit DND DNS 5785

Walrus aircraft–type flown from RCN air Section 1946.
Credit DND 0-1344-21

Avro Anson trainer at RCN Air Section 1946.
Credit DND DNS 5785

Officers of 743 Fleet Requirement Unit with Swordfish at RCN
Air Section 1946. Credit J.N. Donaldson

RCN Swordfish aircraft parked at Saskatoon, September 1946.
Credit Alex Kilpatrick Via George Westwood

Canadian Observer course at St. Vincent, UK 1945-46.
Credit J.M. Favreau

HMCS Warrior aground in St. Lawrence, 1946. Credit W. Maxwell

825 Squadron Firefly carrying out ADDL at RCN
Air Section 1946. Credit DND DNS 1020

803 Squadron Seafire carrying out ADDL at RCN
Air Section 1946. Lt. E.M. Davis is DLCO.
Credit DND HS 3478

803 Squadron Seafire deck landing aboard Warrior 1946.
Credit DND 0-909-3

825 Squadron Fireflies being taxied forward for catapult
launch, Warrior, 1946. DND G646

or the occasional landing gear collapsed, flying went fairly well, although plagued again with poor weather, reducing the flying rate. After leaving the Gulf, the carrier returned to Halifax on 10 August.

One particular amusing lark took place on this cruise at Gaspé, when *Warrior* and the plane guard HMCS *Micmac* had anchored overnight after completion of flying. Dai Davis, the happy go lucky Senior Pilot of 825, had a run ashore with LCdr. "Spike" Hennessy, (also known as the "Sea Wolf" in some quarters) the CO of *Micmac*. The ships were preparing to get underway the next morning, when *Micmac* was forced to signal to *Warrior* that her captain was not yet aboard. After sailing had been delayed, two figures could be seen frantically waving from a rocky ledge on the shore. It was Davis and Hennessey! They were finally picked up by a boat dispatched from *Micmac*, which had ventured in close to shore to retrieve her errant skipper. All this unexpected activity had naturally attracted the attention of the majority of the ships' company, and as the boat neared *Warrior*, Dai could be seen in the stern sitting at attention with his arms crossed across his chest, occasionally giving the royal wave to the multitude in honour of the occasion.

It was also during this short cruise that 825 squadron lost their first Firefly, when Howie Clark stalled on takeoff, crashing into the sea ahead of the ship. Howie suffered a broken ankle, but both he and his observer S/Lt. Hand, RNVR were recovered by *Micmac* otherwise unscathed.

In August, *Warrior* proceeded on a "Show the flag cruise" to Montreal while the squadrons remained flying at the air station. It was while en route to Montreal from Quebec that the unexpected happened, when the carrier did not answer the helm and ran aground on a mud bank at Pointe St. Antoine with the rudder jammed to port. The steering motors and all controls were checked, but no defect was discovered, and officially the cause of the failure remained a mystery. Unofficially, it was suspected that some inquisitive novice had mistakenly closed the wrong valve in the after steering compartment of the ship, thus depriving the power to the rudder. It is generally believed that the error was almost immediately detected, and the valve quickly opened by a (knowledgeable) person or persons unknown. Consequently there was no longer any evidence remaining to account for the momentary steering failure.

There were some humorous moments while the ship was aground, with several suggestions to reduce the weight in the bows. S/Lt. Ralph Fisher who was undergoing junior officers' sea training was engaged in busily recording the events on the compass platform, when some senior dimwit came up with a real howler. As Ralph recounts the situation: "Desperate times however, demand desperate measures. It was hastily decided to lighten the bow, and again apply full power astern in a final attempt to unbeach the ship. This was to be done by bringing up at the rush all available aircraft, bombs and stores from forward, ranging them aft on the flight deck. To this would be added the weight of the many hundreds of officers and men who could be spared from essential duties. Then at solemnly timed orders by the conducting officer, the great symphonic mass of humanity would jump up and down in perfectly synchronized unison on the flight deck. The force of their flatfooted impact, it was reasoned, would reinforce the dead weight of stores, wiggle and further lighten the bow and enable reverse thrust of the engines to overcome bottom drag, thus hauling *Warrior* out of her indignity and into the deep channel again. Engineer officers and lesser mortals, with merely a smattering of high school physics, rolled about in near fatal mirth from safe observation posts, choking with laughter at the totally ludicrous spectacle of hundreds of grown men leaping up and down by numbers in a proposition as futile as a swarm of trained fleas doing formation jumps on the rump of a partially beached hippo." Eventually the proponents of this novel idea gave up and *Warrior* was later refloated with the persistent but conventional aid of tugs.

After a short leave period, flying continued ashore for 825 squadron during September, concentrating on formation flying, night flying and crewing up with the new Canadian observers who had just joined the squadron after completing their training in the UK. This particular group was the only all-Canadian Observer Course, consisting of a ten month syllabus commencing at HMS *St. Vincent* and terminating at Rattray, flying Barracudas until wings graduation in July 1946. Among the new observers that joined 825 squadron were Lts. Marc Favreau, "Junior" Swainson, Denny Feagan, Jack Lewry, Bill "Daisy" Farrell, Maurice "Moe" Arpin, Frank "Fever" Lefaivre,

Firefly of 825 Squadron heading for the port catwalk, Warrior, July 1946. Credit PA141237 G. Geddes

Deck landing trials Warrior, 1946. Credit DND G. Geddes

Aircraft Handlers moving damaged Seafire, Warrior, 1946. Credit E.M. Davis

825 Squadron Firefly being given "Cut" signal, Warrior 1946. credit E.M. Davis

825 Firefly on catapult launch, Warrior 1946. Credit DND G1053

along with Peter Grady who assumed the position of Senior "O", and SLts. Jack Steel and Bill Ewasiuk. This now completed the "Canadianization" of 825 with Lt. Dick Bartlett taking over the Senior Pilot position from Dai Davis, who along with Jim Watson, Tony Sweeting the Senior Observer and the remaining few RNVR observers returned to the UK. Two additional pilots, Lts. Don Knox and "Pop" Fotheringham also joined the squadron in August, bringing the pilot numbers up to full complement.

Just to support the general contention that 90% of naval pilots at some time have engaged in unauthorized low flying (the other 10% being liars), Pop Fotheringham, after some 44 years, volunteers a little flying escapade of his own, which is fairly typical of those first few months at the Naval Air Section. Pop was flying in 743 squadron, prior to joining 825 Firefly squadron, and was a close acquaintance of Ken Birtwhistle the First Lt. at *Stadacona*, who being from Charlottetown, P.E.I., was invariably asking Pop for a ride to the island. In July, Pop weakened and took Ken for a ride to Charlottetown in a newly acquired Firefly. Pop's account is as follows, "What got into me I don't know because I never did such a thing before or after, but I did a job on Charlottetown. Standing on one wing, I went down between the spires of the basilica, then down the main street so low that that witnesses said they could smell the fuel. One citizen owned the radio station and the local paper and there were half-hour announcements for the next couple of days, asking for anyone who could identify the aircraft. By the time I got back to 743 squadron, all hell was breaking loose! I told Shep (Don Sheppard) the whole story and said I was prepared to go to Johnson (Cdr Johnson, the Officer in Charge) and come clean. Shep said he had already been queried and had said it could not have been any of his aircraft. (I had not signed out for Ch'town and he didn't know where I was going). He persuaded me to keep my mouth shut which I was happy to do. *Warrior* at the time was in the Gulf and naturally denied having anyone in the area. I found to my horror that Ken's father, whom I had met years before and who was the Chief of Police in Ch'town, had been advised before we ever took off that Ken and I would be coming over! He kept his mouth shut - God bless him! After some days, the aircraft was positively identified as an Anson!! and the affair gradually died down. It had all been completely lost on Ken in the back seat who was terrified throughout and kept his head down between his knees!"

There was a personnel change that took place in September, with the appointment of LCdr. J.N. Donaldson, RCN who assumed command of 743 FRU, and the previously mentioned Cdr. Johnson, now in command of the Naval Air Section. Johnson was a large, hard-drinking, morose and lonely Yukoner who had already been dubbed "The Ogre". He dwelt, in what was loosely described, as a suite in the officers quarters, and it was soon evident that his erstwhile peaceful lifestyle was being seriously disrupted by the large number of young single officers, also in residence. Most of these individuals, not having much to keep them occupied in the evening, other than whooping it up at the bar, usually continued partying in the officers' quarters. That the poor man was lonely, and unable to cope with such activities surrounding him, was obvious, and all soon learned to shun his end of the building. He did however, manage to trap the unwary at the bar, where he was regularly established and once snared, one would be subject to an endless barrage of complaints from the Ogre as he brooded over all his problems. Dick Bartlett recalls one evening when he and Tats were careless enough to pass the Ogre's den, who upon spying them, insisted they join him inside for a nightcap. Dick said, "The aroma inside the cabin was breathtaking". Apparently the Commander was very fond of salt cod and sardines, both which he kept in his quarters, and as Dick relates, "The place smelled like the bottom of a tiger's cage". The partying in the officers block was almost out of control on occasions, and Deke Logan recounts one rather boisterous evening, with an exuberant George Marlow making a great din, singing and carrying on in the wee hours. The Ogre told George to "Shut up - Now!". George's reply was "You will have to catch me first." This resulted in a hilarious chase throughout the barrack block with George egging on the Ogre with taunts, while the occupants of the building formed cheering sections for the two participants, watching George scampering gaily, and the Ogre lumbering madly, up and down the corridors. George finally made a racing dive down the emergency fire chute, but his successful escape to freedom was short lived by a "lengthly stoppage of leave" and extra duty punishment awarded the next day by the Ogre.

Also in September, there occurred the arrival of a small group of Royal Naval personnel bound for the RCAF Winter Experimental Establishment at Namao, Alberta. This event was of some significance to the RCN since by arrangement with the Admiralty, three RCN officers were to be included in the program together with two Seafires and one Firefly loaned from the RCN. The three aircraft plus a 743 FRU Anson piloted by Lt. Tommy Coultry departed from the Air Section on 23 September with a detachment of personnel and spares provided from FRU 743. This initiated what was to become a long standing participation in winterization trials for Canadian naval aircraft, which over the years was exceedingly valuable in the development of winter aviation equipment and cold weather aircraft modifications. Lts. Hal Fearon and Mike Heyward (an RN engineer/ pilot) each flew the Seafires while Lt. Robby Lavack flew the Firefly. Hal recalls the 30 degree below F. temperatures, and the fact that the cartridge-fired starters failed miserably in cold weather tests since the cartridge propellant would just not fire with any kick if exposed to the cold. He remembers thousands of test firings with little remedial success in overcoming the problem. Although the Griffon engines worked well, the pneumatic and hydraulic systems were also subject to failure with the seals breaking down in the frigid weather. As it finally worked out, the only way the Seafires and Firefly could be reliably started in the sub-zero weather was to pre-warm each starter cartridge, and insert them one at a time in the five chamber rotating breech. If more than one cartridge was inserted in the breech, the remaining ones cooled almost immediately and lost their "urge". This lack of a reliable starting procedure in cold weather was obviously a major operational limitation that never was satisfactorily resolved, and had not been fully appreciated by the RN and RCN prior to the trials.

One of the more interesting and unusual events that occurred in September, was the activation of the Swordfish aircraft for transit to various Naval Divsions. This plan was in part, a response to the approval for an RCN Reserve air arm to be formed at four Naval Divisions with the provision of Harvard trainers for the planned reserve pilots. The Swordfish were to be supplied to various Reserve locations for training reserve air maintenance personnel. The aircraft were selected and flown to several Naval Divisions across the country, namely Windsor, Toronto, Kingston, Lakehead, Winnipeg, Saskatoon, Calgary and Edmonton. All aircraft arrived safely with the last one arriving at Edmonton after almost 40 hours of flying, encompassing ten days and covering 2400 miles.

The flights were not completely without incident. Knobby Westwood recalls himself, Mike Wasteneys and "Abby" Byrne with "Windy" Windover navigating and two crewmen, LAM Smith and AM/E Anderson, in the three Swordfish, sedately chugging over the endless Saskatchewan prairie at 60K, when Byrne's aircraft experienced complete engine failure, lobbing into a plowed field by Neepawa in a great cloud of dust, only to emerge unscathed in an adjacent stubble field. Westwood and Wasteneys elected to join Byrne and landed alongside him. The trouble was found to be a broken fuel line, so Mike took off with Anderson for Winnipeg where a Swordfish had just recently been delivered. In the meantime, the remainder of the party were royally entertained at the Legion Post at Neepawa until Wasteneys returned from Winnipeg the following day with the replacement fuel line. Then heading westward, deliveries were made at Saskatoon, then Calgary and Edmonton. It was at Calgary that the Swordfish arrival attracted the most attention when Wasteneys elected to fly the aircraft from the airfield at #10 Repair Unit at Calgary (where Westwood had parked and gone on leave) to the parade square at Tecumseh, the Naval Division. This flight was the basis for wild rumours of a serious crash, with police cars roaring up, sirens screaming, following the arrival of the venerable Swordfish as the aircraft, barely clearing the telephone wires, touched down and came to a halt on the parade square. By the time the police arrived, Mike and Windy were quietly relaxing at the bar, marvelling at all the excitement. Mike, now being an old hand at direct delivery to Reserve Divisions, decided that this was also the logical way to get the next aircraft to HMCS *Nonsuch*, the Edmonton Division. Here, he had the assistance of Tommy Coultry, the Anson pilot, who was waiting to take the three Swordfish pilots back to Dartmouth. Tommy, acting as the DLCO (self taught) and enthusiastically waving a pair of makeshift bats, directed Mike, who was clattering in from the river flats, then up over the power lines and houses onto the baseball diamond across from the Naval Division, once again attracting the attention of the local populace. The aircraft landed safely, and was pushed across the road into the drill hall, finally ending the epic Swordfish cross country expedition.

Meanwhile back east, the modifications to the supercharger clutch on the Seafires of 803 squadron, unfortunately were proceeding somewhat slowly at Montreal, and it was questionable if even a detachment of the aircraft would be modified in time to join *Warrior* for the planned October cruise to the West Coast. This question was quickly answered by a rather freakish accident that befell the first two modified aircraft. The two Seafires had taken off from Montreal for Dartmouth, and while en-route became somewhat unsure of their position, (pilots are never lost), so Lt. "Whitey" McNicol leading the section, on seeing an airfield strip ahead, called up to his number two Lt. Norm Eversfield, and said "I will go in first", and he peeled off to land. Eversfield, who mistakenly thought his leader had said, "You go in first", veered off in the opposite direction, to approach from the other end of the strip. Whitey had just landed, when he heard the chilling and ominous comment over the radio, "I'm down." Well, they were both down and rapidly approaching each other from either end of the airstrip. They collided in the middle of the field! Fortunately neither were hurt, but the aircraft were badly damaged and out of service. Whitey carried the can for this one, and was given a severe sentence at the resultant court martial primarily because he was the senior of the two. This created a degree of animosity among the other pilots at the time, and although his punishment was subsequently reduced to a loss of seniority in rank, it was still considered punitive.

With 803 squadron definitely out of the immediate picture for any further carrier work, the squadron undertook in September the task of providing a naval aircraft display team during the annual Canadian National Exhibition at Toronto. This role was to continue for a period of over ten years, and the high standard of flying and precision aerobatics demonstrated by the various squadrons over the years provided the Naval Air Branch with an excellent on going opportunity to publicize and demonstrate its little known existence to the Canadian public.

It was recognized that the lack of the necessary alterations and additions (A and A) to winterize *Warrior* was a problem that could only be immediately resolved by transferring the carrier to the West Coast during the winter months. Since the earlier Cabinet decision of the previous March called for the retention of two Light Fleet Carriers, it made sense for *Warrior* to transfer to the warmer climes of the Pacific coast, and be based at Esquimalt.

Lt. A/E Bill Maxwell, who after leaving *Warrior* in the summer, recalls the continuing manning problems being experienced in the air maintenance trades, which were still actively seeking recruits. As a consequence Lt. A/E Jack Ratcliffe was sent on a recruiting tour to seek additional maintenance personnel. He located, amongst others, a number of ex-RCAF aircrew, who expressed interest in such a career in the Naval Air Branch, many whom had been decorated for air operations during the war. Maxwell, in the capacity of an instructor at the Mechanical Training Establishment (MTE), HMCS *Stadacona*, was assigned as a Basic Training officer for these budding air mechanics. At one inspection by Admiral "Buck" Taylor, the Commanding Officer Atlantic Command, the Admiral spied the ex-RCAF aircrew and said, "What are those things these men are wearing on their uniforms?" The reply by Capt. Hart, Commanding Officer of the establishment was, "Those are wings Sir, these men are ex-RCAF aviators, some of whom have had distinguished flying careers, those wings are a service badge award." Buck glowered and said, "I suppose if they were ex-Horse Marines you would have them wearing spurs, would you?" The wings came down! This particular episode underlines the degree of ignorance and lack of experience of some of the RCN officers about aviation in general, and Taylor's disparaging remarks were inexcusable. Most of the men involved soon left the service, since many of them were secretly hoping for a flying career in the RCN, rather than employment as aviation mechanics. The Admiral's degrading remarks certainly did nothing to encourage the remainder to stay.

825 squadron flew aboard in early October, for additional carrier workups off the coast of Nova Scotia, concentrating primarily on advanced crew training. The actual number of flying hours achieved by each crew was not significant, averaging perhaps 18-20 sorties during the month, most flights lasted only about one hour, so the

pilots averaged less than 15 hours per month during Sepember and October.

On 5 November, *Warrior* and *Nootka* sailed for the long trip to Esquimalt, heading for the Panama Canal , with 17 Fireflies of 825 squadron embarked, one additional aircraft aboard being a Swordfish for delivery to the Pacific Command. This left the Air Section flying activities to 803 fighter squadron and 743 FRU utility squadron. The FRU had increased the scope of its activities and aircrew strength considerably over the past few months, with additional pilots and observers being appointed to the unit for general flying refresher, instructional duties or utility flying duties while awaiting appointment to an OTU or other air training courses. Veteran pilots continued to return from the Pacific, having served with the British Pacific Fleet, and were now in the process of being assimilated into the new Naval Air Branch.

For *Warrior*, the three week flying period in November started out with a howling gale, which lasted for three days and gave all and sundry aboard the carrier the dubious experience of a 30 degree roll in heavy seas. Once in the Bermuda area however, flying got under-way, and for 825 it was probably the best to date, with good flying weather and an excellent opportuniy to conduct dive bombing, rocket firing and general air strikes against the fleet units. The first, and somewhat doubtful honour of being catapulted while still weighing anchor, also took place in Kingston harbour, Jamaica, with six Fire-flies in the launch. Dick Bartlett and Darkie Lowe both remember this episode, which probably was both a first and last for the RCN. All the aircraft sank off the bow, and the only saving element appeared to be the ground air cushion, which helped to provide additional lift as the aircraft dropped from flight deck level. No wind and high air temper-atures did not help! By the time the three week flying period was over, the aircraft serviceability had steadily improved and crews had averaged about 20 hours for the month of November. It was soon apparent from the point of view of general habitability however, that *Warrior* was almost as unsuitable in hot weather as in cold. In the Canal Zone, the sticky and humid weather was particularly bothersome for the men in the mess decks and even worse in the hangar, where the stifling heat, lack of air circulation and the long working hours required to keep the aircraft serviceable, all added to the general discomfort. Transiting the canal was a first for many of the ship's company, and it was rather surprising for many to learn that the overall width of a Light Fleet Carrier, which included the gun sponsons, was in excess of one of the canal locks and the outboard section of the sponsons had to be unbolted and removed. Even so, this only left a few inches clearance on either side, as the ship scraped through. Looking at the concrete sides of the lock one could read the scrawled names of the many warships of the USN which had passed through the canal over the years, including some of the Pacific Fleet battleships sunk at Pearl Harbour, and other long gone fleet units lost in subsequent Pacific War battles.

Flying re-commenced once through the canal, and *Crescent* along with the cruiser *Uganda* from the Pacific Command, joined *Warrior* and the three units proceeded to Acapulco, which was a welcome respite for all to get ashore and away from the hot confines of the ships. Acapulco in 1946 was an almost unknown and undeveloped port, completely unspoiled, with only one major hotel. One could walk the complete length of the sparsely used and beautiful beaches, and the friendly young Mexican children were a delight, happily selling beer and hamburgers for a few pesos. Even the dare devil La Quebrada divers plunging dramatically from the cliffs into the now famous swelling and swirling tidal pool, were completely unaware of the value of their prowess, also charging a few pesos or even cigarettes for their death defying performances. A couple of rather unusual incidents took place while the ships were at Acapulco, one concerning the local General, who dwelt in a lofty, but somewhat ramshackle fort on top of the hill. Apparently, he was in a bit of a snit about the Inauguration on 1 December, of the new President of Mexico, (maybe he wasn't invited) and in any event he refused to recognize, on behalf of the Mexican Government, the usual courtesy of exchanging credentials and calls with the Canadian ships. There was also a fairly rough justice being exercised at Acapulco in those days, which was vividly brought to our attention in no uncertain manner. It concerned one of the Canadian Shore Patrol jeeps which was stolen, and the local police located it with a young Mexican man leaning against it. There were no questions asked, they just shot him dead on the spot. The general

Group of 803 Squadron pilots from Seafire Exhibition Flight, 1946. L-R Monk Geary, Hal Fearon, Bob Falls, and Clunk Watson. Credit Beatrice Geary

RCN pilots under training in UK 1946. Front L-R Ken Learmouth, Ken Hunt, Jack Beeman, and Al Carter. Rear L-R George Hopkins, Alec Cupples, Roy de Nevers, Joe MacBrien, and Tom Murphy. Credit R. de Nevers.

RCN Officers undergoing Observer Training. Credit M. Page

825 Squadron Firefly taking a late "wave off", Warrior 1946.
Credit DND G373

DLCO Ted Davis and "talker", Warrior, 1946.
Credit DND G648

Firefly of 825 Squadron just about to engage wire, Warrior 1946.
Credit S.E. Soward

HMCS Warrior in Esquimalt Drydock, 1946-47. Credit DND G903

Firefly going down into hangar, Warrior in Caribbean during cruise to Esquimalt, 1946. Credit PA141261 G. Salter

Firefly taxiing forward for catapult launch, Warrior 1946. Credit PA141268 G. Salter

behaviour of all Canadian naval personnel was unusually good, during the visit which could no doubt be directly related to this incident. There was one minor misdemeanor which took place and could not help but be noticed by grinning bystanders on the carrier. This was the tardy arrival alongside *Warrior* at 0800, of Lts. Jack Lewry and Marc Favreau just as the ships company were being mustered. It was their mode of transport which attracted the most attention, namely a "borrowed" native canoe, which was the only available means of returning to the ship, the pair having missed the last ship's boat back to the carrier the previous night. Their luck ran out since Cdr. Ken Dyer, the eagle-eyed Executive Officer, was intently watching this unscheduled, somewhat unseaworthy craft, duly coming alongside.

During the trip around from the East Coast, as was to become customary, the squadron officers were also integrated into the ship's routine, by standing watches both ashore and afloat. Lt. G.H. "Skinny" Hayes was the genial Senior Watchkeeper, and the officers of the squadron usually acted as second Officer of the Watch during off duty flying or more often during the night watches. I recall one late watch, when Cliff Gavel and I were both on the Compass Platform, and since the Captain (Houghton) had left for his sea cabin, Cliff assumed temporary charge and established himself in the captain's seat (high chair). Cliff had a very clever Lou Costello type of balancing act which he did with his cap, flipping it forward by the visor, twirling it with his finger, then deftly flipping it back on his head, giving a somewhat comic saluting effect. He was busily practicing this little pantomine, from the comfort of the Captain's chair, when a voice behind him said, "How do you do that?" Without turning, Cliff said, "Its a piece of piss", and proceeded to demonstrate it once more. It was only after a few extra twirls that he turned around with a big Costello grin on his face, to recognize with dismay that it was Captain Houghton who had slipped back in the dark and had been observing this performance for some time. Houghton, being a magician of some renown himself appeared more interested in Gavel's act than the lack of propriety being displayed.

Another aspect of indoctrinating the aviators in seamanship, was the use of correct terminology. I was on the platform as second OOW, one evening and was acknowledging the reports of the lookouts stationed above in the Air Defence Position (ADP) with the usual airmens' "Roger". Cdr. Dyer happened to be within earshot, and taking me aside, informed me that the correct response to a lookout's report was always the reply "Very good." It became the subject of some humour among the new watchkeeping squadron officers, as we con-jured up such fictitious lookout reports as "Iceberg dead ahead", "Incoming torpedo to Starboard", "Rocks on port bow" or some other equally catastrophic situation report. This was always acknowledged by seriously intoning, "Very good", which seemed such a passive, disinterested response. We decided something like "Oh Migawd", "Uh Oh" or "Sheeeit" was a much more instinctive and appropriate acknowledgement. We also idly wondered what reply the officer on the bridge of the doomed Titanic made in response to the lookout's iceberg report.

As the ships headed north to Esquimalt, flying resumed and continued for the first two weeks of December. One particular exhilarating flight took place shortly after leaving Acapulco, when some of the aircraft carried out a high altitude radar calibration for the surface units. The weather was superb, with ceiling unlimited, and in the cool clear air at 25000 feet the whole splendorous California coast and mountains were in bright relief for a hundred miles. On 7 December, it was decided to give personnel of the ship's company some carrier familiarization and short flights of fifteen minutes were carried out, (usually a tail chase and low flying ie. beating up the fleet), this was a bit of a jolly and a quick way to grab a few deck landings. I remember on my second launch that day I was following Doug Peacocke in a loop, and somehow he ran low on airspeed at the top, and next thing I knew, I veered past him a few yards away, both of us still upside down. Meanwhile, his passenger Cdr. Eric Boak, with his eyes the size of golf balls (as were probably mine), gaped in utter astonishment as my inverted aircraft, mostly out of control, unexpectedly tumbled by.

It was recalled by Sid Britton, that on this part of the cruise a rather unusual confrontation took place between Cdr. Mortimer, the Air Commander and one of the flight deck CPO's. Apparently there had been bad blood between the pair for some time, and finally Mortimer decided to have it out with his antagonist. It was settled in

825 Firefly after barrier crash, Warrior, July 1946.
Credit PA141239 D. Forgie

825 Squadron Firefly starting up while based at Patricia Bay, BC.,1946. Credit Don Fox via Moore

the traditional Royal Navy manner, by staging a grudge boxing match, which was held in the after lift well. This was something new for most of the Canadian crew, and everybody was suitably impressed to see the Commander and the Chief manfully whaling away at each other. Mortimer was eventually awarded the decision, (not necessarily a popular one) mostly for his left jab which seemed to keep his burly opponent at bay. It was agreed by all, that this was a novel and sporting way to make the cruise more interesting.

On 15 December 1946, after a great visit to San Diego, the first phase of the trip to the West Coast terminated at the entrance to Esquimalt Harbour, with a twelve plane launch off Beacon Hill Park, Victoria (in snow flurries), followed by the short flight ashore to the nearby RCAF Station at Patricia Bay, where the squadron was warmly welcomed. There was a very pleasant friendly atmosphere at the Air Station at Pat Bay, and the facilities and general amenities were a great improvement over those at Dartmouth. The squadron was allocated a well-maintained hangar with more than adequate space for offices and stowage of aircraft spares. Accommodation provided for all ranks was comfortable and the overall reception and co-operation from the RCAF was excellent. There was reduced squadron activity for the rest of December, with leave at Christmas and over the New Year. The Firefly squadron was now emerging successfully from the extended flying workup, morale was high, with everybody eagerly looking forward to increased flying and more carrier operations in the coming year.

Chapter Two

AIRBORNE

In January 1947, on the West Coast, 825 Firefly squadron now augmented by two new pilots, Lts. Al Woods and Fred Townsend, recommenced a full flying program at Patricia Bay, concentrating on refresher Airfield Dummy Deck Landings (ADDLS), advanced formation tactics, instrument flying, and navigation exercises for the observers. The sailing date for *Warrior*'s return to the East Coast had now been established, with the ship departing from Esquimalt mid-February and arriving Halifax at the end of March.

At this time, most of the 825 squadron pilots were RCN(R) officers recruited under the two year service commission which terminated in September 1947. As a result, most of us were in the throes of deciding our future and whether a permanent commission and a career in the RCN was a valid option. My own future was solved rather neatly in a somewhat unexpected manner. I was one of a group kicking a football around on a Friday afternoon, when LCdr. Tattersall, the CO, leaned out his office window and yelled to me, "Soward are you going or staying?" I looked at my watch and since it was only about 3 PM, said "I'm staying!", meaning that I would hang around for the rest of the afternoon until secure, assuming perhaps a test flight might be required. It was only some months later, when my permanent commission came through, did I realize that Tats had meant, was I going to stay in the service or go when my commission expired?

Meanwhile, as *Warrior* was undergoing the minor refit at Esquimalt Drydock, there were important considerations being given to the future disposition of the carrier and the planned commissioning of *Magnificent*. The original plan to man two carriers was now impossible due to the manpower ceiling imposed on the RCN, and only one carrier could be manned while this ceiling was in effect. The decision was therefore reached to pay off *Warrior* in October 1947, place her in reserve, and commission *Magnificent*. Regretfully, further financial cuts, outlined for the forthcoming fiscal year, made the retention of *Warrior* in reserve impractical, which was further complicated by the fact that the carrier without being "arcticized" was not suitable for year round operations in the Canadian environment. The situation was finally resolved with an approach to Admiralty by the Canadian Government proposing to return *Warrior* to the RN, when *Magnificent* was commissioned by the RCN. In January, change of command of *Warrior* also took place with Commodore H. G. DeWolf, CBE, DSO, DSC, RCN, replacing Captain Houghton who had completed his appointment in command.

Flying intensity increased as the departure date neared, but on Friday 31 January, disaster struck 825 squadron in a most unexpected and tragic accident, for which I always felt a degree of guilt. It was noon and Cliff Gavel and I, both being from Vancouver, were going home for the weekend. The only means of travel was the late night CPR boat, and since neither of us were scheduled to fly that afternoon, we asked if we could be flown over to Vancouver in squadron aircraft. Tats gave the OK and he and Doug Peacocke said they would take us over on the twenty minute trip. The weather was marginal VFR, in snow, as Tats took off with Gavel in the observers seat, and as Doug and I waited for takeoff it appeared as though the weather had suddenly deteriorated. We lost sight of the other aircraft in blowing snow on takeoff, but off we went after it cleared, and Doug headed for Vancouver via Active Pass transiting the pass about 200 feet just below the overcast. We heard Tats on the radio, asking Vancouver airport for a homing but unfortunately this had to be delayed due to a CPA airliner letting down over Vancouver Island on an approach to Vancouver airport. That was the last transmission that was heard from Tats. Apparently while orbiting below the overcast, waiting for the homing, he must have lost his horizon in the snow squall and flown into the sea.

Doug and I arrived at Vancouver airport, not without some difficulty, in blowing snow and low cloud. The weather quickly worsened, and the airport closed down once we had landed. It was our wretched task to inform Gavel's parents in Vancouver of the accident, while over at Pat Bay the search went on. Other than a few floating loose pieces of aircraft equipment, and an oil slick, nothing further was found. It was about 25 years later that the wreckage of the old Firefly aircraft was located in deep water by detection gear off Portland Island, a few miles to the north east of the airfield, but the fuselage broke when being brought to the surface and recovery was never again attempted. This accident was more than a squadron loss of two pilots, but a fine Commanding Officer, and Tattersall as one of the few experienced and leading aviators in the post-war RCN Aviation, would have most certainly played an essential leadership role in the development of the new Air Branch.

Morale was pretty low after the crash and it took a while for the squadron to get back into a normal operating spirit, but with the ship sailing in two weeks time, the need to prepare for flying back aboard the carrier quickly took precedence. A degree of emphasis was placed on additional instrument flying practice, and following the normal preparations for re-embarking, 825 squadron flew aboard on 13 February, under command of Lt. Dick Bartlett. *Warrior*, with *Uganda* and *Crescent* in company, then commenced the long voyage back to Halifax.

There was the occasional minor deck landing accident as the carrier headed south and the workups continued, but perhaps one of the more spectacular prangs took place on 20 February involving myself. I had just received the "cut" from the batsman (DLCO) and all was seemingly well as far as I was concerned. However, upon looking ahead, it became immediately apparent that my aircraft rushing up the deck was headed straight for the port side of the ship where the barrier stanchion was located. Being well off the centre line, the wires were low off the deck, the aircraft's hook failed to engage and I was clearly en route to a barrier engagement. The two second period between touchdown and hitting the barrier although short, does concentrate the mind wonderfully, and when a five ton aircraft moving at 50 knots engages an immovable object, something has to give way.

In this case the port wing of my Firefly was immediately torn off as the aircraft came to a grinding halt against the barrier port stanchion. Simultaneously, the propellor plowed into the barrier cables spraying around hot coolent from the shattered radiator. After all the debris and excitement had settled down, one comic amongst the flight deck aircraft handlers approached, and gravely expressed his appreciation to me for having saved them considerable work, because there was only one wing left to fold on my aircraft (always a labour intensive operation). Much to my relief and surprise I was subsequently cleared of the blame for the accident since the powers that be decided that the ship was still turning into wind when I came aboard, with the stern of the carrier drifting to starboard as I was lined up by "Bats." The barrier stanchion did not escape damage and was badly bent, but continued to operate quite normally, until *Warrior* went into refit in the Royal Navy.

The flying intensity was relatively low on the return trip due to a number of factors, including a shortage of spare parts which resulted in a reduced availability of aircraft, visits to foreign ports such as San Pedro and Havana, Cuba, and bad weather in the Bermuda area, which cancelled the rest of the scheduled flying program.

There was one rather humorous accident on the return journey which occurred one day as Al "Woody" Woods was landing aboard. He made a good landing, but on impact the aircraft hook somehow locked back up in the retracted position, and was unable to engage any arrestor wires. With quick thinking, Al immediately applied the brakes, skilfully managing somehow to stop the aircraft undamaged just short of the barrier. He was commended for this prompt action by Cdr. Flying with a Green Endorsement (Good) in his log book. Only a day or so later, Al landed aboard, and mistakenly believing that the hook had once more retracted, and he had missed all the arrestor wires again, he instinctively applied full brakes. This time however, the hook engaged the wire, and the aircraft ended up on its nose, with the propellor busily chewing away at the deck. Woody received an immediate Red Endorsement (Bad) for his second but erroneous example of quick action.

As was the custom, Naval pilots were being assigned to various ships for watch-keeping duties, and one such officer was Lt. Dave

Blinkhorn who at the time was aboard the RCN cruiser *Uganda*. Apparently Dave was the Officer of the Watch (OOW) on a quiet sunny day with the ship steaming serenely through the Pacific waters on a steady unchanging course. Since all was quiet, Dave thought a little sunbathing was in order, so apparently left the bridge and camped up on a quiet open warm spot up on the next deck. Unfortunately for him, the Commander came to the bridge and was horrified to find the control position vacant, and the ship proceeding under self-supervision. This little anecdote was enhanced by the additional report that Blinkhorn as OOW also took that occasion to take a few souvenir photos of the cruiser from the bow position, showing the vessel proceeding in all majesty without a soul on the bridge. It never came to light just how long it took Dave to qualify for his Watch-keeping Certificate, but he must have surely earned points for independent initiative!

From 13 February until arrival at Halifax on 27 March, and mainly due to the poor weather in late March, the average flying per pilot was less than ten hours, including only 8-10 deck landings. For a carrier-based squadron, this is far below the minimum level of 25-30 hours per month considered necessary to maintain proficiency. Indeed, over the twelve month period ending in March 1947, the average per pilot totalled only about 125 hours.

During the period 825 had been away, 803 squadron had been active, their Seafire fighter aircraft had all been modified, and with the arrival of 825 squadron, the two squadrons were formed into the 19th Carrier Air Group (CAG). The aircraft were lightered aboard *Warrior* the middle of April 1947, then departed for Bermuda. Six aircraft of 825 squadron flew ashore to Kindley Field, Bermuda for night ADDL practice and exercises with the fleet units, while 803 Seafire squadron carried out deck landings and fighter exercises.

Meanwhile, at Naval Headquarters (NSHQ), the subject of Hellcats was still being examined. On 16 April 1947 Naval Board considered a recommendation from Naval Staff to procure 20 Hellcats at a cost of $5000. each, in order to form an operational training squadron. Otherwise it would be necessary to reduce the unit establishment of 803 and 883 squadrons to 12 aircraft each, and allocate squadron aircraft to meet the operational training squadron establishment. This recommendation is rather puzzling insofar as the recollection of most is that the fighter squadrons always did operate with a unit establishment of 12 aircraft each. It may well have been that the proposed operational squadron establishment originally had been 15 or 18 aircraft, but this was never achieved and the reduction of 3-6 aircraft per squadron actually did provide aircraft for the Operational Training Unit (OTU). It would also appear that the need for an RCN OTU was the result of the earlier response from the RN, that they would be unable to undertake this commitment.

As the new year progressed, the overall situation at the Air Section at Dartmouth was improving slowly but the working conditions during the previous winter months had done little for morale, with the forced evacuation of the squadrons from 108 and 109 hangars due to faulty heating systems. 743 Fleet Requirement squadron was steadily expanding its activities with new pilots arriving and RCAF refresher instructor and instrument courses being given to pilots as they rotated from 803 squadron. Bob Falls, Smokey Bice, and Bill Rikely were three such officers appointed to 743, where a nucleus of experienced pilots was now being formed to provide operational training in the unit. They joined veteran operational carrier pilots including the previously mentioned Lt. Don Sheppard, DSC, who had become the first Canadian Corsair ace in the Pacific War, flying aboard HMS *Victorious*. Another returning "Pacific Ace" was Lt. Bill Atkinson, DSC, who achieved fame flying Hellcat night fighters aboard HMS *Formidable*.

Meanwhile, as the weather in the Bermuda area continued to improve, the flying intensity aboard *Warrior* increased, and during the month of April the flying average for 825 increased to about 20 hours per pilot and crew, with the emphasis on night flying from Kindley Field and night ADDLS, preparatory to conducting deck landings. This night carrier work also entailed modifying the engine exhaust by the bolting of lengths of stainless steel exhaust shields above the engine stacks on each side of the Fireflies in order that the pilots would not have their night vision lost in the exhaust glare. It was a definite improvement but, like most Fairey Aviation modifications, did not inspire much confidence. I guess it was at this point that we all finally realized that somebody was deadly serious about us doing night

Aircrew of 826 Firefly Squadron at RCN Air Section, 1947.
Credit J. B. Fotheringham

Wing folding a Seafire aboard Warrior, 1947. CreditPA141250

Pilot Course at OFTS, RCN air Section, 1947-1948.
Credit George Westwood

Pilots of 883 Seafire Squadron at RCN Air Section, 1947.
Credit R.V. Bays

RCN pilots undergoing refresher flying, Central Flying School Trenton, Ont. 1947. Front row L-R Lts. Jack Hartle, Derek Smith, and Roger Harris. Rear row L-R Lts. Ken Nicolson, Hal Welsh, D.M. Macleod, and Gerry Quarton. Credit H.R. Welsh

Seafire maintenance at RCN Air Section, 1948. Credit HS 5569 SAM P3085

deck landings on this cruise.

The night carrier landings for 825 squadron started at the end of April, with five of us eventually qualifying. It was not exactly a roaring success, since it was really a question of whether we would all qualify before we ran out of aircraft, because late wires, barrier engagements or propellors hitting the deck all took their toll of Fireflies. It was late, probably on the last night, that Pop Fotheringham, as Senior Pilot was accosted on the flight deck by the Head of the Air Dept, Cdr. Mortimer, who pointedly inquired as to the number of serviceable aircraft still remaining. Pop also remembers his unease during his own night landings, because he was consistently picking up No. 1 wire, which he was steadfastly trying to avoid at all costs, while still giving the impression of following Hunter's signal to go lower. Pop's view was no doubt based on the premise that a barrier entry is far less serious than flying into the stern.

I remember during my qualifications, (second night) on the first pass I couldn't even find the DLCO (Jim Hunter), and on the second pass I actually thought I saw him standing in the middle of the flight deck (maybe he was) waving his little dimly lit paddles. In any event, I realized on the third pass that the deck lights were so bright that I couldn't see anything! We were using HF radio in those days and it was so noisy that the ship could not hear me asking for the lights to be dimmed. In the meantime, unbeknownst to me during this stalemate, Cdr. Mortimer had made the decision to send me ashore to Bermuda after my next pass, if I didn't get aboard. The ship finally figured out what I was trying to tell them, the deck lights were dimmed, and lo and behold there was "Bats" giving me a "Roger", so all was well, and I completed my quals with no further trouble. It was rather unnerving on the free launch however, because at full power on takeoff, the engine exhaust was still very bright, playing hell with one's night vision. I can remember receiving an "RCN Well Done" from the Captain, when I finished, which might well also have been interpreted as his way of saying,"Thank God that is over!" It was some 40 years later, as I was chatting briefly with Admiral DeWolf at a CNAG gathering, that I asked him if he remembered the night landings we carried out. His answer was dryly humorous, because he said, "I didn't even want to look and see what was going on back down there, but I certainly remember the occasion." In actual fact, other than a degree of individual pilot satisfaction, it really was a waste of time and aircraft, since the Firefly was neither operationally suitable nor effective in a carrier night role. I doubt if any other navy, anywhere else, in peacetime, had ever seriously bothered to pursue this particular form of entertainment, with this particular aircraft; certainly the RCN never ventured to do it again. Perhaps it was all an ambitious (and dubious) attempt by Mortimer to make himself look good before returning to the Royal Navy. But still, as Brian Cartwright recently observed, "Looking back on those night qualifications, it was rather fun!" Brian was no doubt basing his comment on the airmens' light-hearted philosophy "If you have the aircraft available, I have the time."

There was one rather embarrassing, but laughable episode that took place later in May, when *Warrior* was working with the British West Indies Squadron off Bermuda. Vice Admiral Sir William Tennant, the Commander-in-Chief of the squadron requested that *Warrior* provide an aircraft to take some aerial photos of his two heavy cruisers, *Kenya* and *Sheffield*, while underway with the squadron fleet units. Jack Steel and myself were elected, so off we went loaded with an F24 camera. Jack was busy clicking away from the observers compartment while I was engaged in sideslipping the aircraft to keep the wing out of the picture. After so much of this Jack asked me to tell the squadron to do a 180 turn and proceed on the opposite course, to avoid the sun shining on the camera lens. The ships obliged and the whole squadron continued under my dubious control. Feeling very important with my new found authority, I ordered the required headings and course alterations. We ended the sortie shortly after, with profuse thanks from the flagship, and with our promise to expedite the processing of the film, we departed. About an hour later, Jack came back from the photo section with a long face to inform me that after all that fleet steaming around, not one inch of film had turned over, because the camera had jammed from the outset. Much to our embarrassment another crew had to repeat the exercise the next day.

On 14 May 11 Fireflies and 1 Seafire, flew ashore to the Air Section at Dartmouth as *Warrior* approached Chebucto Head, terminating the sea time for the two squadrons. As the 19 CAG departed *Warrior*, a light-hearted summary of the flying activities over the past year for the two squadrons was presented by the flight deck engineer as follows:

- Aircraft have flown for 1300 hours, consuming 54,738 gallons of petrol (gas), enough to take a jeep around the world on the equator 44 times.
- Aircraft have been catapulted 141 times and have landed on the deck 1063 times.
- The popular wires are numbers 3 and 4 which have been hooked up on 210 occasions. Number 10 wire has had, (fortunately) only 10 extensions.
- 9 aircraft have entangled themselves in the barrier, always seeming to get there ahead of the Fire Rescue Party.
- Altogether 26 aircraft have pranged on the deck involving the preparation of 16 lbs. of Forms A-25. (Accident Reports)
- Only 1 aircraft has been written off charge (in the sea).
- 331520 litres of oxygen have been used, which the Air engineer Officer claims is sufficient to service a Firefly at cruising speed to the moon and halfway back again.
- The Aircraft Handling Party have run 6750 man hours up and down the deck.

Although this summary of some of the flying activities aboard *Warrior* is only partially complete, it is worthy of mention that during the year aboard, only one aircraft had been lost and there were no fatalities while aboard. Considering that 825 squadron, although primarily in an Operational Training status during this workup period, had also managed to carry out night deck landings, indicates a high level of accomplishment, and reflects well on the aircrew proficiency, the ship's Air Department and the excellent support provided by the maintenance staff. While acknowledging that there were 26 Firefly and Seafire deck landing accidents, this total still compares favourably with Royal Navy Firefly and Seafire squadrons operating under similar conditions. Sid Britton claims that *Warrior* actually did establish a Royal Navy record insofar as over 680 consecutive landings had been carried out without an accident. He thinks the record was terminated when Deke Logan landing his Seafire, hit the ship's crane on the starboard side (along with the tip of one of L/S Fred Lucas' fingers).

On 15 May 1947, there was an occasion for celebration with the long awaited re-activation of 826 and 883 squadrons, reforming as 18 CAG. Pop Fotheringham assumed command of 826 squadron, with Bob Monks taking command of 883 squadron, both officers being given the rank of Acting LCdr. These two squadrons commenced operating with the Seafires from 803 squadron and the Fireflies of 825 squadron (19 CAG). They in turn were now preparing for re-equipping over in the UK with the new Sea Fury fighters and Mark IV Fireflies. The other personnel change that took place was assumption of command of 803 squadron by Acting LCdr. H.J. Dickie Bird from LCdr. C.G. Clunk Watson.

In June there was a first for Canadian Naval Aviation with the presentation of naval pilots wings to Surgeon LCdr. E. Alford. The doctor had been undergoing pilot training at 743 squadron since January, and was the first medical officer to qualify as a pilot in the RCN.

On 6 June 1947 there was another Naval Board Meeting, which was obviously a follow up to the one of April concerning the purchase of Hellcats. At the June meeting, Naval Board noted that the cost of Hellcats had risen to $8000 each, and the procurement would mean the addition of a third type of aircraft with the added problem of supply and maintenance. It was decided that no further action would be taken regarding Hellcats.

This definitely put an end to the Hellcat proposal. The reasons given however, are suspect. First, the USN price from all accounts included virtually new aircraft with a full support package of aircraft parts. This would have resolved the spares problem being encountered with the British aircraft, and the maintenance load would not necessarily be increased by a third type, since the Hellcats would have formed the complete OTU inventory. The price of $8000 per aircraft was a steal, particularly when one compares them to the newly received Sea Furies, which not only had a price tag of over $80,000 per aircraft, but also being a new aircraft would encounter considerable operating and initial maintenance problems. One cannot help but be curious of the role played by Capt. G.A. Rotherham, DSO,

Air Mechanics and Air Handlers of 883 Squadron, Nov. 1947.
Credit PA183112

LCdr. Jim Hunter accepting Sea Fury for 803 Squadron from
officials of Hawker Aircraft Company. Credit R. Monteith

Classic trio of RCN Seafire Mk.XV's October 1948.
Credit PA136657

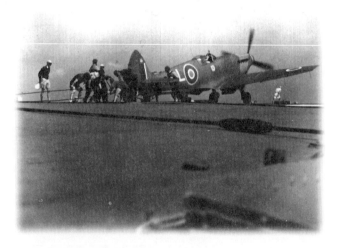

Seafire deck landing Warrior, April 1948.
Credit PA 131215

Servicing teams of 19 CAG Fury Squadron, Eglington, 1948.
Credit P. Wiwcharuck, J. Anderson.

19 CAG Furies in close echelon formation, 1948
Credit PA116627

19 CAG officers and wives at wardroom gathering, Eglington, 1948.
Credit R.E. Bartlett.

OBE, Royal Navy at this juncture. He had served in his position of Director of Naval Aviation since the previous January, and as a matter of course had a clear mandate from Admiralty to serve as a strong advocate of British aircraft. By his own admission, he had on previous occasions dealt directly with the British Board of Trade and Admiralty to expedite allocation of production Sea Furies to the RCN. Observing that a year earlier by Naval Board direction, the Admiralty were informed that the RCN were considering the purchase of USN aircraft, Rotherham was certainly in a position to be well informed and provide his advice on the ramifications of the aircraft situation.

In June, command of the Air Section also changed with the appointment of Acting Captain H. S. Rayner, DSC & Bar, RCN, replacing Cdr. Johnson in command. The appointment of an officer of Captain's rank boded well for the Air Section and squadrons, and was an indication of the growing importance of the Air Branch and the support now being provided as the Naval Air Section expanded and consolidated its operations and activities. At the end of June, the Air Section was visited by The Honourable Brooke Claxton (Babbling Brooke) the Minister of National Defence, who toured the establishment and was given a display of ADDLS in honour of the visit. This was followed in July with the additional aviation appointments of Jim Hunter as 19 CAG Commander and Fred Bradley as 18 CAG Commander, both being given the rank of Acting LCdr. Bradley who had earlier left the service and took up farming, decided the pastoral life was not for him, so he re-entered the RCN and was promptly made a Group Commander. It would appear from this appointment that he had re-thought his earlier views about working with a group of ex-RCAF pilots with little naval aviation background.

With the ongoing increase in the scope of Naval Aviation two new sections, the Operations Centre and the Ground Instructional Centre were formed, in addition the 1st Carrier Borne Army Liaison Section (CBALS) was established under the command of army Major, "Red" Johnson. This formation was to remain in existence for many years, serving in a liaison capacity both ashore and afloat, working with the operational squadrons in joint exercises and with the Canadian army both locally and at Rivers, Manitoba. As Major Charley Barter, OIC of one unit recounts;" The formation of the CBAL unit was significant in a sense because during the last two years of WW2, Army air liaison officers who formed part of the ground control team, played a major role in exercising control of the RAF tactical support aircraft in Europe. They also participated in the air cover organization in the Salerno landings in Italy which marked the first use of naval air power by the Royal Navy to support such landings. In the immediate post-war period there was an Army Air Liaison Group with the RCAF at the Joint Air Training Centre at Rivers, Manitoba, but this was only marginally supported by the small RCAF detachment of Mustang fighters, and for practical purposes, the RCAF had virtually given up supporting the army in this important and well proven role. It was the newly-formed RCN Air Branch that enthusiastically assumed this task of tactical air support and the formation of # 1 Air Liaison Group with headquarters at the Naval Air Section, comprising three army Sections, became an integral formation in the Navy's tactical air support role."

During the summer months, additional personnel changes took place, with various pilots being sent on aviation courses in the UK. Three such officers were Lts. Don Knox, Bill Munro and Doug Peacocke who were appointed for DLCO training. Upon arrival, however, there was a delay in commencing their course, and since they were living in London they were rapidly running out of money. They cunningly (and surreptitiously) signed on as temporary help at a local London brewery. This work had one considerable fringe benefit, namely unlimited free beer, which they happily quaffed as they did odd jobs and sloshed paint and beer around the establishment. This novel moonlighting employment however came to an abrupt end when somebody on the London staff jokingly mentioned their participation in the work force, inadvertently "ratting" on them, the Canadian Naval Member, London, Commodore Agnew getting wind of their clandestine labours.

Lt. Deke Logan who was also on duty in London that summer, recalls with amusement a hilarious London traffic episode involving Doug Peacocke. Deke just happened to spy Peacocke heading toward a busy West End traffic cross walk. Doug, observing the known hazard that traffic drives on the left, looked to the left before venturing across the road. He was promptly clobbered by a slow-moving cab coming from the right. After picking himself up unhurt, and levelling unprintable imprecations at the driver, Doug, who by this time had landed halfway across the intersection, looked carefully to the right to ensure he was in the clear, and blithely walked into another cab approaching from the left. It took him more than a few ales at the nearest pub to regain his usual composure!

Deke also recounts a conversation he had with Commodore Agnew about naval aircraft. The Commodore had questioned Logan about the merits of the Firefly IV and the Barracuda. Deke obligingly responded to the Commodore with both barrels, by saying that the "Barra" was the worst aircraft he had ever flown, and it was a blessing for it to be taken out of service. On the question of the Firefly IV, he was equally scathing in saying that it was not as good as the Mark I and was a waste of money. For good measure Deke also said that the purchase of a Light Fleet carrier was of dubious value, since it was too slow and had no place in the future of Naval aviation. These blunt remarks were hotly disputed by the Commodore, who harking back to his wartime days as an Escort carrier captain, considered he was in a much better position to judge what was good for the RCN, than was a junior airman.

It is pertinent to record that on 3 June 1947, after a two year struggle, the Royal Australian Navy (RAN) had finally obtained Government approval to purchase two Light Fleet carriers from the UK and form their own Naval Aviation. The strongest opposition to the formation of an Australian Naval Air Branch naturally came from the Australian Air Force (RAAF). It is significant that the Air Force argument (based on the belief the RAAF could provide their personnel for loan to the Navy) was thoroughly rejected by the Australian Naval Board, insofar as the RAAF approach claimed advantages which did little but benefit that service and did not further the efficiency of naval aviation. It is further revealed that both the Air and Naval Staffs in their joint study actually concluded that the naval plan (establish their own Naval Air Arm) would provide the more efficient weapon for current naval purposes. In spite of this, and in a final vain effort to compromise, the Chief of Staff of the RAAF proposed that naval officers be seconded to the Air Force. In response, the Chief of the Naval Staff stated that he could see no reason to adopt a system in Australia which had already been discarded elsewhere, ie. in the UK in 1937. These overall comments are clearly outlined by Ross Gillett in his History of Australian Naval Aviation, "Wings Across The Sea."

It is revealing to note that the problems being encountered by the RAN over the two year period in attempting to form their Air Branch, mirror those being met in forming our own Canadian Naval Aviation. It is disturbing to see the RAF, RCAF and RAAF expound their outdated common view and demonstrate their determination to prevent any other military organization venturing into the sphere of aviation. It clearly indicates their appalling lack of understanding the unique expertise required in performing the role of naval carrier aviation in the maritime environment, and the fact that air operations at sea is an essential and integral component of naval warfare.

While the Naval Air Section at Dartmouth was expanding and establishing the various support facilities, the formation of a Director of Air Engineering at Naval Headquarters was underway with a small nucleus being formed. Lt.(E) A/E Rolfe Monteith was the first to join the Directorate in July 1947, under LCdr. A/E Neil Smith. Rolfe had just recently completed his conversion courses to Air Engineering, and prior to that served extensively in the highly organized and tightly disciplined environment of a Royal Navy cruiser, arrived at NSHQ just in time to be immersed in the confusion of a post-war naval staff trying to re-organize itself and also create its own Air Branch. He was greeted warmly by Smith upon assuming his new appointment as Deputy Director, but was somewhat nonplussed later when Neil handed him the keys to the office and filing cabinets and departed upon a previously arranged extended annual leave. Since the section only numbered the two of them, Rolfe, as Acting Director, subsequently found there was little "directing" to do.

From the Air Engineering perspective at the RCN Air Section, there were problems being encountered with regard to the overhaul and major repairs required for crashed aircraft, particularly those which had occurred aboard *Warrior*. Under the RCN/RCAF Agreement, the RCAF had the responsibility for the transport and recovery of all military crashed aircraft. Since the nearest major repair facility was at Canada Car and Foundry Montreal, this meant that all naval aircraft suffering major damage had to be shipped via rail on a flat car. As LCdr. A/E John Doherty, who was AEO of the Air Section, recounts, often the damage incurred in the process of transporting the aircraft was as great as the aircraft had initially received. In one case he remembers a Firefly being shipped that was fully repairable, but by the time it was unloaded at Montreal, the aircraft had to be written off. This method of transporting damaged aircraft was obviously unsatisfactory and the lack of a convenient overhaul facility for RCN aircraft was of major concern. It was mainly because of this, Fairey Aircraft of Canada was formed and shortly after in 1948, purchased the disused wartime aviation plant at Eastern Passage, hence then becoming the permanent prime civilian aircraft overhaul contractor for RCN aircraft, a service they would provide for the next 25 years.

At the Air Section, the flying intensified in 18 CAG as the squadrons worked up. This was was sadly marred on 17 July 1947 when the first fatal crash for the Air Section took place. An 826 squadron Firefly piloted by Lt. Jack Lamon along with his observer, Lt. Bob Gailbraith, unfortunately crashed into the sea off Musquodoboit, killing both occupants.

Warrior sailed 2 August 1947, for the UK, primarily in a ferrying capacity with 27 officers and 179 men of 19 CAG aboard for air training courses and re-equipping with new aircraft. This move to the UK for 19 CAG was to be for an extended period, during which the conversion and a thorough workup on the new Sea Furies and Firefly IV's would be undertaken prior to returning to Canada aboard the newly to be commissioned *Magnificent* the following spring.

Upon arrival at Eglinton, three 803 squadron pilots, Lts. Pat Whitby, Deke Logan and Jeff Harvie, were sent to 778 squadron at Ford for conversion to the new Sea Furies, which would shortly be delivered to the squadron. At Ford, the three Canadians were engaged at the Trials Unit, primarily flying the new Fury in an extended program to determine whether or not the Centaurus engine would perform satisfactorily in the new fighter. This was done by attempting to fly the aircraft under a wide range of conditions and hopefully putting 300 flying hours on the engine (and also waiting to see if the engine would keep running). The honour of actually being the first to fly the new Sea Fury however, belongs to Lts. Rod Lyons and Bob McKay, who were serving at the RN Ferry Flight at Culham, engaged in flying the new aircraft away from the Hawker Aircraft factory.

As far as Deke Logan was concerned, the flying carried out at the Trials Unit served them in good stead, as they in turn began checking out the other members of the squadron. Logan in recalling the period, believes that the engine handling course provided to all the pilots in August by Bristol Aircraft, the Centaurus engine manufacturer for the Sea Fury, was largely responsible for the minimum engine problems encountered in the initial working up of the squadron. He also considered the quality of Fury squadron maintenance was good, particularly observing the lack of proper engineering publications available for the new fighter. LCdr. A/E Dennis Foley and Lt. A/E Art Geraghty deserve great credit for their supervisory role in achieving the high level of maintenance that was provided during this difficult introductory period of the new Sea Fury. In spite of the usual flying restrictions imposed by the winter weather, flying rates in 803 squadron were satisfactory, each pilot averaging nearly 15 hours per month.

One Fury was lost when Lts. Bob Mckay and Jimmy Pulfer were carrying out a "tail chase" and their Furies came together so to speak. Jimmy made it back to the airfield but Bob's aircraft was sufficiently damaged to be uncontrollable, so he was forced to bale out. This he managed to accomplish, but only with major difficulty after considerable efforts to kick himself free of the aircraft. In doing so, he permanently injured his arm and shoulder. He safely parachuted into the sea and was rescued by an Irish fisherman. Bob had the dubious, and rare distinction, of being the only Canadian naval pilot to successsfuly bale out of a Sea Fury.

Dick Bartlett, 825 squadron commander, recalls the Eglinton 19 CAG workup period in some detail. He considered the group a generally happy lot, who for the most part put up with the not always minor irritations of poor accommodation and working conditions with typical good humour. This, coupled with a high degree of ingenuity improved overall conditions considerably as time passed. The flying rate in 825 squadron steadily increased as the maintenance crews under the capable supervision of Lt. A/E Al Brown, became familiar with the new Fireflies. Initially, the individual monthly flying rate in 825 squadron averaged about 12-15 hours in September 1947, but increased substantially to 20-25 hours by January 1948.

Back in Canada at the Dartmouth Air Station, 18 CAG with their

Seafire XV and Firefly I aircraft were busy with advanced armament training consisting of dive bombing and rocket firing. This was a short but intensive work up, for what was intended to be a combined multi-ship and aircraft attack on the surrendered German submarine *U190*. This operation dubbed Exercise Scuppered, took place in a position about 50 miles south-east of Halifax, where the submarine had torpedoed and sunk HMCS *Esquimalt* on 16 April 1945, the last Canadian ship to be lost in WW2. The order of battle for the exercise scheduled for Trafalger Day, 21 October 1947, started with the Fireflies of 826 squadron attacking the surfaced submarine with rockets, followed by 4.7 inch gunfire from the two Tribal destroyers, *Haida* and *Nootka*. Then a bombing run by 883 squadron Seafires with 250 lb. bombs would take place, the exercise culminating with an A/S mortar attack by the frigate *New Liskeard*. Like many grand schemes, it did not go as planned. The event was observed and monitored by no less than Capt. "Herbie" Rayner, supported by LCdr. Mac Leeming and "Kam" Maxwell, (then a Midshipman of three weeks seniority), all airborne in a Canso piloted by the commander of the Dartmouth Air Station, Group Captain West. The sinking honours went without question to 826 squadron Fireflies, which plastered the sea and the wallowing U Boat with rockets, the submarine first tilting, then quickly going down by the stern.

The Firefly pilots were actually fortunate to have achieved this, since as Lt. Jim Burns, one of the 826 pilots involved, stated, "The rocket attack was so screwed up by the Group leader's approach that the remainder of the rocketeers could barely line up on the target, resulting in virtually all the projectiles of the first flight overshooting the sub." Fortunately, those in the second flight had time to correct, and eventually, Lts. Jim Burns, Doug Ross and Freddy Rice were credited with being the successful marksmen. As Ross was to sub-sequently relate, his final manœuvering had all the aspects of an aerobatic display until he and Fred Rice managed to get in position to fire their rockets, Ross claiming four hits and Rice two. All this of course, taking place to the discomfiture of Cdr. Hugh "Von" Pullen of *Nootka*, who barely got a missed salvo away. The final humiliation was the message from Rayner to the destroyers which said, "Sorry, my bird."

Perhaps one of the funniest 'Keystone Comedy' type of incident took place about this time. As previously mentioned there was the weekly Musquodoboit "Bullet" train which rambled through the lower half of the air station. On one particularly fateful morning, S/Lt. Art Bray, the duty officer, was peacefully carrying out his varied duties whilst driving a jeep, and somehow he managed to stall his vehicle on the railroad track crossing the main station road. Attempts to restart the vehicle were singularly unsuccessful. Much to his dismay, at this critical point in time, he heard the ominous whistle of the approaching train as it chugged around the bend into the base. Art, now galvanized into activity by the urgency of the situation, leaped from the jeep and pelted frantically down the side of the tracks toward the oncoming "express". As he neared the approaching engine, he began waving his arms, cap in hand, and yelling to attract the attention of the engineer. The sight of this wildly waving apparition now apparent to the train engineer must have made his railroading day! Not being used to such an enthusiastic reception from an excitedly screaming railroad fan, the engineer graciously acknowledged Art's desperate signalling with the railroad version of the "Royal wave", and a friendly toot of the train whistle. This genial greeting was quickly abandoned when the engine driver on getting back to the business at hand, spied much too late, the abandoned jeep ahead on the single track. The train then ploughed resolutely into the vehicle, carrying the wreckage effortlessly along the right of way in front of hapless Art Bray's disbelieving eyes.

In the fall of 1947, recognizing the requirement for a separate and identifiable unit to conduct operational pilot training, 743 squadron was re-organized into two separate flights, one being the Fleet Requirement Unit (FRU), which had a primary role to provide utility and communication flying for the Air Section and the fleet. The other flight was formed to conduct pilot flying refresher, advanced flying tactics and conversion to operational aircraft.

Also in the fall of 1947, several pilots were temporarily attached to various Naval divisions for recruiting purposes. I, as one, was sent to HMCS Nonsuch Edmonton, and while there I had the occasion to meet the retiring Chief of the Naval Staff, Vice Admiral H. E. Reid. In a brief conversation, I took the opportunity to ask his opinion of the role and future prospects for Canadian Naval Aviation, assuming I would hear how rosy an airman's future would be. His answer was hardly inspiring, when he stated, "I consider the aircraft merely as any other weapon such as a gun or a torpedo." This was rather disturbing to hear. Recognizing the significance of such classic WW2 naval aviation triumphs as the attack on Taranto, the brilliantly executed Japanese carrier air strike on Pearl Harbour, and the tremendous and critical carrier battle of Midway (which forever doomed the pre-eminent role of the battleship), it is not difficult to reach the conclusion that Admiral Reid did not really understand what naval aircraft were all about. The fact that carrier aircraft are a manned, mobile, independent and multiple use weapons system, capable of sinking any ship afloat, seems to have been lost on the Admiral.

Warrior now back from the UK, was next operating in mid-November 1947 with 18 CAG Fireflies and Seafires, carrying out deck landing training, fighter tactics and navigation exercises for the new crews of 826 squadron. Deck landings went well with 183 being carried out the first week. The usual foul winter weather off Halifax however, reduced flying and the short workup terminated on 21 November. This was *Warrior*'s final flying commitment, and for the rest of the year the carrier was engaged in storing and provisioning with supplies and equipment for the forthcoming transfer to the yet to be commissioned *Magnificent*. Again due to a lack of winterization, *Warrior* was forced south to the Bermuda area to carry out the cleaning of ship and preparations for paying off. *Warrior* departed for the UK on her last RCN voyage on 12 February 1948, and on arriving in the UK, she was met with a salute off Belfast by eight Sea Furies of 803 squadron. On 23 March 1948, following the transfer of the main party of officers and men to *Magnificent*, the Broad pennant of Commodore DeWolf was struck, and *Warrior* reverted to the Royal Navy.

In January, as the new year was ushered in, there was the usual rotation of squadron commanders, Acting LCdr. Terry Goddard DSC. a veteran ex-FAA observer taking over 826 Firefly squadron from Pop Fotheringham. He in turn assumed command of 883 Seafire squadron from Bob Monks. Dawgface Monks, was a colourful character who did more than his share to enliven the somewhat spartan party life in the early days of the Naval Air Section. Probably his greatest claim to social fame was his successful recruitment of local Dartmouth females to provide some spice to the various mess activities. He successfully rounded up nine young and enthusiastic members of the opposite sex, who were all a great source of pleasure to the somewhat isolated aircrew officers. From that point thereafter, the girls were known as "Dogface's Baseball Team", and for several years, whether singly or as a team, they were invariably present and accounted for at the regular mess parties.

Meanwhile at Eglinton, on 28 January 1948, LCdr. Jim Hunter, the CAG Commander, had a close call when he experienced a propellor overspeed, as the constant speed unit failed while conducting a flying display in his Sea Fury. He managed to skilfully force land close to the airfield, but was badly shaken in the crash and lucky to be alive, the aircraft being a write off.

LCdr. Dennis Foley, recalls that overspeeding of the propellor was becoming a vexing problem with the Sea Fury. The major difficulty was establishing the initial cause. It transpired after extensive investigation that under certain negative "G" conditions the oil pumping rate was erratic, causing oil exhaustion in the Constant Speed Unit. This in turn allowed the propellor to overspeed against the fine pitch stops, causing excessive RPM. This often resulted in a progressive breakdown of the engine as the sleeve valve gears broke, jamming the gear system, followed by the ultimate destruction of the engine as the cylinders started to fly off.

All was not smooth sailing with the group maintenance and Hunter, being a tough task-master, believed some of the senior maintenance personnel were not carrying out their responsibilities effectively. This resulted in a major purge, with a number of supervisory rates being sent back to Canada or returned to the Royal Navy. Petty Officer John Turner remembers there was a considerable degree of hostility resulting from this action, since many of the men thought that some of the banished supervisors were unfairly being made scapegoats. John felt that Petty Officer Morris McCubbin was one such victim. McCubbin was responsible for the maintenance of the Coffman Starters, and since he had no suitable place to work, he set up shop in the Chief and Petty Officers hangar crew-room. Since he was always noticeably present there, McCubbin was considered to be a malingerer, which in Turner's opinion was an erroneous perception.

Turner, as an armament Petty Officer, most definitely recalls the major lack of armament tools and equipment, (which were supposed to have been supplied by the Royal Navy). In many cases the CAG armament personnel had to improvise by actually fabricating their own tools and using alternate sources of material. In one such improvisation, there was no varsol available to clean the aircraft armament components, forcing the armourers to use dangerous high octane aviation fuel in order to get the work done and meet the flying commitments.

Ron Heath, a member of 803 squadron, however, recalls a kindlier side of Jim Hunter when Ron had occasion to prang on takeoff. He selected the gear up on his aircraft, but a loose throttle tension allowed the throttle to slide back, losing takeoff power and impacting the Sea Fury on the runway. (Also known as a wheels up takeoff). Ron was convinced his flying career would be terminated and he would be sent ignominiously packing back to Canada. Heath waited with considerable trepidation to get his just punishment from the CAG Commander for this rather expensive error of judgement. He remembers hearing the measured footfalls as Hunter approached, then stop, followed by silence, and a long, hard, look. Then to Ron's immeasurable relief (and astonishment) heard "Big Jim" say, "Dont worry Ron everything will be alright".

While on the subject of incidents, Deke Logan recalls a somewhat similar episode involving Pat Whitby, who completed what Deke humorously described as a "nose-down landing". Pat managed to get the aircraft in an abnormally tail high position while landing (maybe a little brake?). The five-bladed propellor blades, in their 13 foot arc, immediately commenced a buzz saw attack on the runway during the Fury landing. This incident naturally became the subject of the usual light hearted and invariably unsympathetic bantering among the pilots.

Anti-submarine instructional courses for 825 aircrew reduced flying for about six weeks in February and March, but April was a very good month, which averaged in excess of 30 hours per crew, which also included participation in an RN strike force of 5-6 squadrons over various parts of England. The resulting favourable comments by senior Royal Navy officers was good for morale, and the fact that most of the crews were now well experienced, kept the overall squadron efficiency at a high level. During the Spring, one Firefly was lost when the pilot, Lt. Vince Murphy, was unable to recover from an inverted spin (not many do) but he was fortunately successful in baling out. Regrettably his passenger, squadron Steward James McDonald, was unable to escape from the plunging aircraft and died in the crash. In 1990, some forty three years later, it was a pleasant surprise for Dick Bartlett to be notified that the Garvach Branch of the Royal British Legion, Women's Section, had kindly marked the crash site with a memorial cross dedicated to McDonald, a most thoughtful and compassionate mark of respect in memory of the young Canadian.

On 15 March, one Sea Fury was lost in a hangar fire, caused by a falling portable maintenance lamp. The RN were very quick to blame the incident on the Canadian CAG personnel, and this caused a fair degree of bickering. Fortunately, it came to "light" soon after, that the bulb in the RN-supplied fixture was not the prescribed safety type, it thereby exploding in the fall. The matter was apparently eventually smoothed over, quietly forgotten and a new aircraft provided by the RN. However, the incident created a fair degree of bad feeling and both Jim Hunter as CAG Commander and Dennis Foley as AEO were logged. Dennis to this day, claims he was never informed that the RN later repented their hasty attempts to throw the entire blame on the Canadian squadron personnel.

There was also a bit of humour that took place at the fire scene. Apparently Petty Officer "Moose" Warnock became a bit of an unsuspecting and unlikely hero during this incident. Moose was on duty elsewhere that day, issuing the tots as Rum Bos'n, and, as custom dictates, was benefitting from the available "sippers". He returned to the hangar via the back door in a jolly frame of mind just in time to witness the burning Sea Fury and the personnel frantically pushing aircraft in an attempt to evacuate the hangar. He promptly roared into action and no doubt spurred on by his extra rum issue, galvanized the rest of the hands as they successfully cleared the remainder of the aircraft from the now fiercely burning hangar.

There was some comic relief provided by the station fire teams in their attempts to save the building from the rapidly advancing flames.

As Pat Whitby recounts, "The remote area of the hangar meant the firefighters were dependant on a small creek for their water power. The crews roared into action, pumps commenced pumping, and the men at the nozzles were at the ready. It unfortunately transpired that the hoses and connections were in such poor shape that virtually all the water was dissipated by a multitude of fountains en route to the nozzles. All was not lost however, because by this time the heavy foam-making fire vehicle had growled its way to the scene. The intake hose was quickly plunged into the creek, pumping commenced, foam generated, and the command given to turn on the hose, the end of which had been briskly manned and run out to the hangar door to quell the inferno within. Foam issued in copious quantities, but it was the truck which was quickly foamed over-somebody had neglected to connect the truck end of the hose! Shortly after, the village fire department team arrived and the fire was quenched."

Although the building had been quickly evacuated of aircraft, it was soon readily apparent to the CAG personnel, that the hangar itself was doomed, no doubt partly due to the questionable efforts of the station fire crews. Just as the flames were at their peak, the NAAFI tea wagon wheeled on to the scene, so the CAG members decided to "stand easy", with a cup of tea in front of the fire. Over the previous weeks however, the female operator of the van had been hassled daily by some of the Canadians who, anxious to have their tea break, were invariably trying to speed up the serving arrangements, passing the line up and crowding in the rear door (thirstily led by Chief Dunn of 803 squadron). The young Scottish serving girl finally blew her top and warned all and sundry that the van was out of bounds, and the first one to attempt to access by the back door would get a cup of hot tea thrown in his face. It just so happened that the CAG Commander, Jim Hunter, having been airborne, had just arrived on the scene only to be roundly chastised by the Royal Navy station brass for having his CAG troops on a tea break, while the fire was still roaring away. He quickly went around to the rear of the serving van and opened the back door to tell the NAAFI girl to stop serving and clear out. The unsuspecting Hunter was promptly deluged with a cup of hot tea for his efforts! Needless to say, that particular tea server was not seen around the CAG for some considerable time.

Guy Laramee, as a CPO Air Artificer in the CAG, while awaiting the delivery of the Sea Furies, recalls the cold, wartime accommodation at Eglinton, consisting of buildings heated by a stove one cubic foot in size, with a days ration of 2-3 lumps of coal, augmented with a half dozen little sticks of wood. Fortunately, being located in a rural dispersal area, the buildings were surrounded by farms. With food (for extra BTU's) constantly on everybody's mind, there was the inevitable "foraging". Guy remembers Chief Hoare running in excitedly one night saying,"Look fellows, an egg!" Since eggs were virtually non existent (except powdered), this was indeed an important find. The joy lasted only a few minutes, when it was discovered that Hoare's discovery was a plastic "laying egg".

The surreptitious "acquisition" of additional food, ie. chickens, did not continue unnoticed, and the local farmers naturally began to complain. Dick Bartlett recalls one irate midnight call from a farmer to the Station Duty Officer and they proceeded to one hut that was suspect. Dick relates, "There were chicken feathers everywhere, and the story was that the occupants had been having a pillow fight, and the pillows had burst. The fact that there were also feathers under the hut, was casually dismissed by the occupants as being attributed to the resident rats. The strong smell of fried chicken in the air was notice- ably left unexplained. The next morning I mustered the squadron, explained the problem, and left a collection tin for donations. This was generously oversubscribed, providing enough money for 50 chickens, which was twice the amount of the farmers claims, so everybody was happy".

Dick also remembers the CAG attempts to resolve the heating problems, by the introduction of "oil-fired stoves" heated by used aircraft engine oil. This worked a treat, but left the Fire Marshal singularly unimpressed. The matter was subsequently settled as Dick recalls, "By modifications to the stove and modifications to the Fire Marshal's thinking."

Fortunately, the Canadian CAG in spite of their good-natured but somewhat audacious pilfering, did leave Eglinton with a good feeling with the local populance. Indeed, several members of the group married local girls, but as Guy Laramee recounts, "The constabulary remembers the departure of the Canadians with mixed feelings. When

I was there some four years later, and walking along the small village road near Eglinton, I was stopped by the local policeman who commenced a conversation with me as follows, "Canadian eh?" "Yes Sir." "Are the Canadians coming back?" "No Sir." "Thank the Lord", and he walked off."

The purchase of the Sea Fury as a replacement aircraft after the short tenure of the Seafire XV, warrants some discussion. In a major sense, the RCN was breaking new ground by accepting the first production Sea Furies, as long as 7-8 months in advance of the regular RN squadrons. This meant that the 19 CAG personnel would be facing the brunt of the teething problems inherent in a new aircraft entering squadron service. There was no doubt that the Sea Fury was the ultimate single engined naval fighter, and had an outstanding performance. This unquestionably provided the RCN with an excellent opportunity to fly a first class state of the art fighter, and in doing so, achieved operational parity with the RN and USN in the employment of front line carrier borne fighter aircraft.

It was neither generally known by the Canadian public, nor adequately publicized by the Department of National Defence, that the two Sea Fury squadrons of the RCN flying the most advanced piston powered fighter aircraft, were the only post-war Canadian operational fighter squadrons in existence. This would continue until the RCAF commenced flying a few Vampire jet fighters at Chatham N.B. in 1950. Even so, under certain conditions, the performance and weapon load carrying capability of the Sea Fury was superior to the Vampire. The lack of a comparative operational fighter during this post war period, continued to be a considerable source of embarrassment to the RCAF.

The overall high performance of the Sea Fury was unfortunately offset to a degree by the considerable engine difficulties which were increasingly encountered over the next two years. They were eventually resolved after the aircraft had undergone considerable squadron service, the problems identified and the engine modified. One major difficulty was "coring" caused by circulating cool oil congealing on the honeycomb of the oil cooler. This caused a gradual build up of congealed oil restricting the flow until it ceased, starving the engine of oil, which in many cases resulted in the engine seizing or breaking up internally. An additional factor associated with the slow progress in assimilating the aircraft, was the shortage of qualified maintenance personnel, lack of adequate tools and incomplete documentation and servicing instructions.

LCdr. Dennis Foley, in his capacity as CAG AEO, makes the following interesting comments on this aspect of the Sea Fury initial operations: "The new CAG concept of maintenance from the previous individual squadron system resulted in quite a change. Due to maintenance personnel shortage, the CAG was only manned to about 64% of its established strength, and in the junior ratings less than 50% were qualified to sign the Form 700 (Inspection log) since they were fresh out of maintenance school. For the Sea Fury air trade personnel, no proper maintenance courses had been arranged other than a 10 day course at Worthy Down by instructors who had never seen a Sea Fury and had made up lessons from handbooks that were not up to date. I eventually arranged a manufacturers course during the Easter break. Trying to work up a CAG with new aircraft, especially the Sea Fury, with a shortage of trained maintenance personnel, in the conditions they had to work under in the winter in Ireland left much to be desired. I never felt the maintenance personnel received the recognition they deserved, considering everything."

Following the return of *Warrior* to the Royal Navy in March 1948, it is important to summarize and comment on the flying activities carried out by the carrier during the 2 year period of service with the RCN. Although her flying career with embarked squadrons was of relatively short duration, it brought out many valuable lessons for the operation of subsequent Canadian aircraft carriers. More important, the individual flying experience that was gained by the aircrews greatly broadened the very limited aviation expertise that previously existed in the fledgling air branch.

In 825 squadron, the total hours flown ashore and at sea during the 14 month period averaged less than 150 hours or a total of 11 hours per month, day and night, per pilot. Total deck landings were in the order of about 70 per pilot. Included in the deck landing total was the night qualification of five pilots, yet actual hours flown while aboard ship during the period, averaged less than 80 hours per pilot, which translates into about one deck landing per hour of flying while at sea (including deck landing qualifications). This is a miserably low total and the flying rate was so inadequate that by today's standards, it borders on the dangerous. The fact that there were no fatalities, and only one aircraft lost during the entire operating period at sea, is quite remarkable, and the personnel involved during this period, many who were inexperienced, deserve considerable credit. In the RCN, operating a single carrier complicates both the flying program and ship workup schedule to a major extent. The flying time allocated to the squadrons while at sea is, of necessity, often very limited. Ship refits, self maintenance periods, ship exercises, courtesy visits, protocol considerations, weather problems, fleet requirements and aircraft availabilty, all take their share of available time, leaving surprisingly little opportunity to get on with the main function of a carrier, which is to fly aircraft with operational efficiency and safety.

In 825 Firefly squadron, many of the maintenance personnel aboard were virtually starting from scratch, just as were the air department and aircrew, even though there was a nucleus of experienced personnel. The number of times the AOG (aircraft on ground due to lack of parts) situation occurred was excessive, partly due to a sheer lack of operating experience with the level of aircraft spare parts required, which was particularly aggravated by a source which was both distant and tenuous. This entailed both frustration and extra work for the maintenance staff, whose overall performance and ability to improvise was excellent, working long and hard hours to keep the aircraft flying. This was accomplished with a ship's routine that was often quite inflexible, allowing little deviation, which inhibited the planning, workload and continuity of the squadron maintenance schedules. The operating limitations imposed therefore, in the first RCN peacetime carrier, were unique when compared to the RN and the USN. They, in such circumstances (more particularly the USN), when working up a new air group, would assign a specific carrier for the task, manned with experienced personnel and supported with a complete aviation infrastructure. This ensures that scheduled flying commitments are achieved, and the work ups follow the required syllabus. We, in the RCN, had to get by with what little was available, using very limited resources and our own relatively inexperienced personnel. In doing so, we still managed to achieve a comparable standard of operational flying, which under the circumstances was highly commendable.

The overall operating period of 803 Seafire squadron aboard *Warrior* was unfortunately very limited, due to the supercharger defect which virtually wiped out any opportunity for the squadron to work up with the ship and 825 squadron. It would be reasonable to suggest however, that if both squadrons had been aboard simultaneously for the main period at sea, the operating difficulties would no doubt have been greatly increased while working up with the two types of aircraft aboard. It is more than likely that the flying hours achieved by 825, low as they were, would have been even less with the Seafire squadron aboard during this period.

On the general subject of flying hours, Stan Wood recalls his early period when flying as a Lt. in the Royal Navy, commenting as follows:

"The most detrimental effect on the Air Branch in the early years, was the lack of flying time. It was difficult to regain the confidence that I had earlier felt from my RCAF training days, when I flew a concentrated number of hours, averaging 33.2 hours per month. During my flying time with the RN, from January 1946 to March 1947, I flew an average of 11.3 hours per month. During my time with 18 CAG, May 1947-November 1948, I flew an average of 7.3 hours per month. This was hardly sufficient to develop the feeling an aviator must develop, to wit, that he and the aircraft are as one. I note that my flying ability had gone from above average in the RCAF, where I had been a runner up for a flying trophy, to low average ratings during my early naval flying career. There simply is no substitute for flying time to gain experience and confidence. It was not until I got back to an RCAF station at CJATC Rivers, where I had Chipmunks, Harvards, Austers, Norseman, DC3's (Dakotas) and P51 Mustangs at my disposal, that I regained complete confidence in my flying ability and fell in love with flying again. When I returned to *Shearwater* in 1953, I was pleased to see we had got our act together and that we were becoming professionals. I believe that many of the problems in the early days were a result of our maintenance personnel being treated as though they were irresponsible, illiterate ditch-diggers when, in actual fact, they were for the most part intelligent, willing individuals who wanted to be part of the team, but were hamstrung by a navy with a 19th century outlook".

The foregoing comments of Stan Wood concerning his flying training experience in the RN from January 1946 to March 1947 are interesting. His operational training on Fireflies and a Seafire conversion, included deck landing training on both types. His flying rate average was only 11.3 hours per month, including periods between courses, where no flying took place. From this it can only be surmised that the deep manpower cuts and reorganization of the wartime FAA, seriously affected the flying intensity of the advanced aviation training courses and the availability of the facilities being provided by the post-war Royal Navy. The considerable drop in the flying rate is all the more remarkable when one compares it with the 40-60 hours of day and night flying per pilot the peacetime FAA squadrons had averaged while operating aboard carriers in 1938-39.

At the Naval Air Section, the first pilot OFTS course providing conversion to Seafire XV's for subsequent employment in 18 CAG, warrants discussion. During this nine month period, commencing February 1948, the pilots including Ken Gibbs, Shel Rowell, Knobby Westwood, "Doc" Schellinck, Stan Berge and "Sandy" Warren averaged only about 68 hours on Harvards and Seafires, or about 7-8 hours per month. Initially the main problem was attributed to low Seafire serviceability, and the usual takeoff and landing accidents, which in most cases although minor, reduced aircraft availability. Later in October, Sandy Warren was unfortunately killed climbing away after taking off in a Seafire and somehow losing control at about 800 feet of altitude, crashing to the ground. This accident resulted in the students being given additional hours in Harvards, no doubt as a somewhat futile safety check precaution, following Warren's fatal crash. As Ken Gibbs notes, the number of hours flown toward the latter part of the course did increase to about 15 hours/month per pilot, but this was still well below the minimum level considered necessary to provide proficient flying. An operational training course, to be curtailed in flying an operational aircraft (Seafire) and forced to revert to Harvard trainers to supplement the training, was not of comparable benefit. It can be readily seen that the immediate post-war period was certainly undergoing major manning and organizational problems for

RCN Aviation, and the situation in the RN did not appear to be much better.

The year 1948 opened on a sad note at the Winter Experimental Establishment (WEE), with the fatal crash in January of a naval aircraft at Namao, Alberta. Lt. Gerry Quarton RCN, formerly of 803 squadron, was demonstrating at an air display what was intended to be a high speed pass in a Sea Fury, followed by a steep climb and a half roll off the top. For some reason he kept his aircraft on its back at the top of the manœuvre and failed to initiate the roll, the nose dropped, then Quarton appeared to attempt to pull through to complete a loop, but by this time he was too low! He almost made it and although the aircraft was actually in a level attitude, it was still mushing down. The big five bladed propellor clipped the runway, and the Fury travelling at a tremendous forward speed, virtually disintegrated. Experts subsequently examining the accident, estimated the aircraft was travelling at over 400 mph. when it struck the runway, the engine itself impacting a considerable distance away from the initial point of contact. It was suspected unofficially, that the aircraft seat may have become dislodged while the aircraft was inverted, and the subsequent disorienting effect on the hapless Quarton, may well have been the major cause of this unfortunate accident.

In April 1948, at Naval Headquarters, the post of Assistant Chief of Naval Staff (ACNS) (Plans), was assumed by Acting Commodore H. N. Lay, OBE, thereby providing for the first time, a degree of aviation background input to the Naval Board. Lay was a strong supporter of Naval Aviation and had already expressed his preference for USN Aviation and American naval aircraft. Due to a lack of a senior aviation specialist, he also assumed the additional position of Assistant Chief of Naval Staff (Air), thereby serving on Naval Board in a dual capacity.

7 April 1948, was a red letter day, with the commissioning of HMCS *Magnificent* at Belfast, North Ireland. The new carrier proceeded to sea for acceptance trials under command of Commodore DeWolf. The Executive Officer was Cdr. D.W. Piers, and Commander Flying was Cdr. "Cocky" Reed. On 15 April, after steaming to Portsmouth, flying trials were carried out, then in mid May, the carrier returned to Belfast coming alongside the airport jetty at Sydenham,

Sea Fury at Winter Experimental Establishment, Namao, Alberta.
Credit Roy Budesheim

Scattered wreckage of Sea Fury piloted by Gerry Quarton at Namao
following fatal accident, January 1948. Credit Roy Budesheim

803 Squadron maintenance personnel, Eglington, 1948.
Credit J. Knowles via P. Moore

RCN Sea Fury being hoisted aboard Magnificent, Eglington, 1948.
Credit PA16887

Magnificent alongside jetty at Eglington, loading 19 CAG aircraft in summer of 1948. Credit R.E. Bartlett

Magnificent underway from Ireland en route Halifax with 19 CAG embarked. Credit DND MAG 114

Flight deck air maintenance crew, Magnificent, 1948.
Credit D. Foley.

826 Squadron Firefly undergoing maintenance at Rivers
Manitoba, 1948. Credit PA141915

Belfast, where the aircraft of 19 CAG were hoisted aboard. A flight of two Sea Furies, two Sea Hornets and a Sea Vampire from 806 Royal Navy Aerobatic Team under command of LCdr. Dick Law DSC, RN, were also embarked for transit to Canada, 806 squadron being scheduled as one of the star participants in an aerial display to celebrate the opening of New York Idlewild Airport.

The carrier sailed on 24 May, arriving off Halifax on 1 June, but poor weather cancelled the planned flight ashore of the CAG, with only two Sea Furies making it through to the Air Section at Darmouth, the remainder having to be tediously lightered ashore to the small boat marine jetty at the air station. This inefficient and time-consuming method of having to barge or lighter aircraft back and forth from the carrier and the Air Section at Dartmouth, would continue to be a vexing transfer problem, emphasizing the long term need to provide a carrier jetty at the air station, as was customary at similar USN and RN air bases.

It is of interest to note following the period that the newly commissioned *Magnificent* was completing trials and loading aircraft for the return to Canada, there was a small team of Canadian Naval Air officers visiting at the USN Air Test Centre at Patuxent River, Maryland. This group consisting of Lts. Hal Fearon, Marc Favreau and Art Geraghty were examining the newly developed Douglas AD Skyraider carrier aircraft. This aircraft in addition to its designed role as an attack bomber, was also being considered for Anti-submarine duties and as an Airborne Early Warning (AEW) aircraft for the USN fleet. The AD had an excellent built in versatility and from 19-23 April 1948 was test flown by Fearon, with Favreau conducting basic tests for its suitability in the ASW role. This particular evaluation was significant for two reasons, the RCN did not yet have an ASW assignment for its forces since NATO had yet to be formed, and the policy of buying British naval aircraft had been emphatically made clear at the Naval Board level. That this policy was continuing was evident by the recently purchased, marginally useful, Firefly Mk IV now in 825 squadron service. It was at least encouraging to note that there was a degree of independent initiative being shown at the Air Staff level in examining USN aircraft, in spite of the "buy British" policy. It would be interesting to know to what extent this visit to the

USN was supported by the Director of Naval Aviation, Royal Navy Capt. G.A. Rotherham.

In any event nothing ever came from this brief study, since the USN did not develop the ASW AD concept any further. The aircraft was however, subsequently used extensively by the USN and the Royal Navy in the important role of Airborne Early Warning (AEW) for the fleet.

On 4 June, just after 19 CAG and the RN 806 squadron had returned to the Air Section, a most unusual and never fully-explained, fatal accident took place. Lt. Nigel Fisher, RN, of 806 squadron and a member of the famous Royal Navy Fisher family of both World Wars, had taxied out for takeoff in a Sea Hornet. The weather was poor that day, with a ceiling of about 400 feet. Due to the low cloud base, the only flying activity was an ADDL session with Seafires by the OFTS. Ken Gibbs, standing by the DLCO position on the runway, recalls seeing Fisher preparing his Hornet for takeoff, and noticed what appeared to be a considerable flow of fuel leaking from the aircraft. Ken immediately ran toward the aircraft waving his hands, but Fisher, misinterpreting the signal, merely waved back in greeting and commenced his takeoff, climbing very steeply up into the overcast. It was just a moment later that Ken was horrified to see the silver Hornet in a momentary flash, diving vertically out of the low overcast, crashing into the sea just to the south-east of the airfield between the shore and Macnabs Island. The aircraft being made of wood, disintegrated completely. One speculative explanation for this bizarre accident, was the likelihood that Fisher, while climbing steeply into the overcast, failed to break out of the top of the cloud as anticipated and became disoriented, losing complete control of his aircraft. This was a tragic day for the elite 806 squadron, a small, close knit group of outstanding pilots.

In July 1948, change of command of the Air Section took place with Cdr. A.B.F. Fraser-Harris, DSC RCN, taking over from Capt. Rayner. In the same month, the Air Section held the first naval aircraft display in Canada, which was attended by over 15000 people. It was an excellent opportunity for the public to view all the naval squadron aircraft in aerial and ground displays and the entire presentation was very well received. This was a particularly outstanding show, with 806 squadron making their final dress rehearsal prior to their New York demonstration. Since the world's two fastest piston engined aircraft, namely the Sea Fury and the Sea Hornet were performing, it presented the local public with a quality of air show that had never been seen before in Canada. One of the most impressive displays was that given by the Sea Hornet, with the pilot doing a complete loop over the airfield, alternatively feathering the two engines, culminating in a loop with both engines feathered. (To save fuel as the announcer would glibly explain). A particularly impressive, but completely unplanned and unrehearsed incident took place, when the solo Sea Fury of 806, squadron having just completed a loop, experienced a propellor overspeed which was accompanied by the ear-splitting noise of the big Centaurus engine winding up to excessive RPM before the engine failed. Fortunately, since this manœuver took place right over the airfield, the pilot skilfully landed the aircraft without incident.

It was also the summer of 1948 that LCdr. Gerry Daniel was appointed to the Air Section, to set up the Naval Air Maintenance Training School. He was most ably assisted by Lt. (A/E) Jack Ratcliffe, without whose remarkable talents to locate and scrounge/ expropriate the necessary materials and equipment, the school opening may well have been delayed. The initial staff was shortly augmented by four Royal Navy Chief Petty Officer Air Artificers on loan to the RCN, who in addition to their high standards of discipline, did exceptionally valuable work, preparing diagrams and fabricating the various engine and hydraulic system components for the instructional display examples at the budding school. Two Tiger Moths were also "acquired" from RCAF sources, one being made serviceable from parts of the other, and since these aircraft were of little use for aircraft maintenance training, the one little Tiger Moth was retained for local flying, having its maiden flight on 29 October 1948. About the only buildings available to set up the school were the two oldest hangars, previously occupied by the squadrons, and they were in poor shape requiring a considerable degree of work to make them habitable for classroom use.

Stan Conner, then an Air Mechanic Second Class, (AM2) was involved in this initial phase, and much to his disappointment, was told that instead of going to the UK, as had been the previous arrangement, he would be taking one of the first courses right here at the Naval Air Section. There were two classes of airframe mechanics and two of air engine mechanics. Included in their syllabus was a basic tool training course at the Mechanical Training Establishment (MTE), at the main naval base at Stadacona. The overall period of instruction lasted for nearly one year, providing a thorough grounding in the basic air trades. One of the RN instructors that Stan remembers particularly well was CPO Pitt, who later transferred to the RCN. Since the original instructors were all English, the school was quickly labelled by the students 'The Kipper Kollege of Aircraft Knowledge'. On the other hand, Ed Janusas recalls that his class, called the school 'SNAM Quentin' because their RN CPO instructors were perceived to be so strict. Stan's recollections include the discomfort of sitting in the draughty cold hangar, in makeshift classrooms. Virtually all the naval personnel were occupying buildings with a similar low standard of comfort, so there was little point in complaining and little sympathy to expect. As Stan was later to comment, "It was this kind of struggling to survive that made our branch so unique, and the esprit de corps was 'something else', because we had to make do and improve it on our own."

As the Air Section expanded and personnel increased, it was inevitable that the occasional weird character would surface. This happened one day to Lt. Windy Windover as he crossed paths with a matelot in front of the Administration Building where the Captain and Executive Officer (XO) were located. The sailor did not oblige with the customary salute, so Windy fearing this oversight would be spotted by one of the senior officers, and he would be in hot water for not enforcing rules, called the man back saying, "Do you not pay your respects to a passing officer?" The man replied, "I salute no one excepting the Lord God and his son Jesus Christ, who in fact I am." Concerned that the 'Second Coming' may be imminent, Windy cautiously conducted the sailor to the Master-at-arms. Because the case was rather unusual, and the man continued to insist on his identity, more senior authorities were alerted and it was arranged for the man to be immediately brought before the Captain. The man's story remained unshakeable, so Fraser-Harris sent for the Medical Officer, who recommended the man be taken across the harbour to

HMCS *Stadacona* at Halifax. "OK," said the Captain. "Send him over to *Stadacona*, but maybe he won't need a boat. Take him down to the jetty and point him to Halifax. If he sinks, rescue him and provide a boat. If he walks, FOR CHRIST'S SAKE, let me know right away!"

In the fall of 1948, the first Canadian Football team was formed at the Air Section, where it was enthusiastically supported by the air personnel. Included in this first team were Lt. "Springer" Bob Greene, the Physical and Recreational Training Instructor, who assumed the coaching position and aircrew players such as Lts. Duke Wardrop and Chuck Elton who were joined by the Captain's Secretary "Scratch" Lt. Harvey Cocks. An additional player was L/S John "Red" Allan who subsequently went on to Admirals rank. This first team competed in the Halifax and District Canadian Football League, with opposing teams from HMCS Stadacona, Dalhousie University and the Halifax Wanderers Athletic Club. This initial formation of a football team at the Air Section was the beginning of a long and illustrious career for the fledgling club which later became officially known as the Shearwater Flyers when the Air Section was commissioned as HMCS *Shearwater* later in the year.

Flying activities in August, continued with an attachment of two RCN Sea Fury pilots, Lts. Smokey Bice and Jack Sloan, to 806 Squadron to join in their naval flying display at the CNE Airshow, which was augmented with a Sea Fury and a Firefly as a static ground exhibit. The overall flying display was an outstanding success, with an aerobatic performance by 806 squadron Sea Furies and the Sea Hornet that was brilliantly performed.

Continuing with operations, *Magnificent* embarked 19 CAG in August and conducted deck landing qualifications, with 171 deck landings carried out during the ten day period. Two aircraft were ditched, but the crews were recovered. On completion of the short cruise at the end of August 1948, the Broad Pennant of Commodore DeWolf was struck. The Commodore was a popular Commanding Officer, having shown both his interest and concern for the welfare of the ship's company and the embarked squadrons during his tour in both *Warrior* and *Magnificent*. Commodore G.R. Miles OBE, RCN, then assumed command of *Magnificent*.

During the on-going squadron workups, there were the usual

individual flying problems and incidents, (often with unsympathetic, irreverent comments) and on one particular day at the air station, Lt. Ed Gigg encountered engine difficulties while flying his Griffon-powered Mk 1 Firefly. He was actively engaged in a determined effort to make it safely back to the airfield, and in so doing, was keeping all informed who cared to listen, with a running commentary which went something as follows, "It's stopped again - I'm not going to make it - No she's picking up again - Maybe I'll make it. There it goes again - I'm going to have to ditch - I'm OK again, I might make it!" At this point, the bored voice of Duke Wardrop broke through the excited commentary saying, "Just keep flapping Ed, You'll make it." And he did!

On 16 August, 18 CAG consisting of 9 Seafires and 9 Fireflies left the Air Section for a two month training period at Rivers, Manitoba, where they were to engage in joint exercises, armament training, and gunnery spotting with the army at Shilo. This mass transit across Eastern Canada was not without its problems. Bad weather held up the group at Ottawa, where the squadrons made three attempts to get through to North Bay. On the second attempt on 19 September, the 9 Seafires in three sections headed west out of Rockcliffe airport, on a visual flight rules (VFR) Flight Plan. Cloud was soon encountered, which rapidly thickened and the trip quickly became an instrument flight. As Hal Welsh recounts. "I was flying #2 on the group leader and while formating on his wing light, began to realize we were rapidly penentrating heavy and dark cumulo nimbus cloud (thunderstorm type) and shortly after the order was given for the nine plane formation to turn port 180 degrees. Losing sight of the leader's wing tip while turning, I increased my rate of turn and before I knew it, I was in a spin with all sorts of problems, with the altimeter unwinding like an express elevator and airspeed winding up towards infinity. At this point I decided to put into action my oft practiced spin recovery, only this time it was for real! On breaking out of cloud I saw the ground rushing toward me at an alarming rate, and had no option but to yank back hard on the stick. This was followed almost immediately by a great eerie silence, like no engine noise! I had been running on the drop tank which had deserted me on the pullout. I finally managed to reselect my main fuel tank, the engine caught, but now here I was with a 300 feet ceiling and nowhere to go except up into cloud and make my way back to Ottawa, by way of a VFR flight in cloud on instruments." Hal recalls making it to Rockcliffe airport which was fortunately in the clear. Naturally, being the last to arrive, he was bombarded with mundane questions like, "Where is your drop tank, and why are the wings on your Seafire all wrinkled?" As Welsh recounts, the Air Engineer Officer volunteered the cheery information that he estimated it took 12-14 G's to pull off the tank and wrinkle the wings. The aircraft incidently, was a write off!

Lt. Mike Considine, flying an 826 squadron Firefly also had his problems. He experienced a very rough running engine and finally, after a few anxious moments and various manœuvers, made it in to Rockcliffe airport. There was good reason for the engine malfunction, because as Lt. Jim Burns relates, "There was a hole in the side of the engine in which you could stuff your fist." Mike's troubles were not yet completely behind him. After a new engine was installed, he headed for Rivers and on arrival had a landing problem. Apparently the runways were being rebuilt, and a grass strip was in temporary use. This was not the easiest to see or land on for the first time, and Considine much to his embarrassment ended up with his aircraft in a nearby ditch.

The trip for the Seafires was finally completed by landing at Rivers on 20 August, this auspicious arrival also had its dramatic overtones. Prior to departing Winnipeg for the last leg to Rivers, the CO, Pop Fotheringham, remembers reminding everyone of the need for accuracy in timing the fuel consumption of the drop tank. At the cruicial moment approaching the break in the circuit at Rivers, he suffered the ignominy of having his own engine quit as his drop tank ran dry. Welsh continues the story. "When he drifted back through the formation, we all peeled off, port and starboard, and took up our positions for a carrier landing sequence. The Pongos (army) and Air Force types were impressed, they thought it was all planned."

At the Rivers Joint Air Training Centre, the Naval squadrons were warmly received, by the other two services, and fortunately, as in most cases, the policy problems between the top echelons of the RCN and RCAF did not penetrate to the operating level. Stan Wood recalls that all the naval aircrew took part in parachute training up to the point of a live jump, which was prohibited by the concern of naval authorities that somebody might suffer an injury. On the other hand, Stan Wood always maintained the view that the stag party games in the officers' mess turned out to be probably more hazardous to one's limbs than a live parachute jump ever would have been.

There was one incident took place with a bit of humour, (albeit black) involving an instructional foulup while rehearsing training from the practice jump tower. As Hal Welsh remembers, "The army Sgt. providing the dummy jump demonstration, sternly ran through the sequence of orders which were, 'Stand up', 'Hook up', 'Close up to the door', 'JUMP'! On that final order, the Sgt. made a grand exit, leaping dramatically off the jump tower stand. But he had forgotten the one most important sequence - 'Hook up'. He fell 30 feet and broke his leg!"

By mid-summer of 1948, the perceived unsatisfactory terms binding the original RCN/RCAF Agreement had so seriously affected the station sharing arrangements, that a decision regarding the future of the rapidly expanding Naval Air Section could no longer be ignored. Over the past two years, various submissions had been made at the local level to have the Agreement revised to a realistic arrangement that reflected the actual situation. Nothing had been done about these submissions, in part because the Naval Headquarters Staff had certain reservations about Dartmouth as a future Naval Air Station. This was primarily due to the fact that the RCN was not comfortable with an air station that required the sharing of facilities with the RCAF, and the servicing requirements of two civilian airlines, namely Trans Canada Airlines and Maritime Central Airways. Other airfields were certainly investigated, but logic, and the practical need to have a naval air station with access to the sea, and close to the naval base at Halifax, effectively made the Dartmouth location the only viable option.

As far back as July 1947, the Naval Board had recommended that transition to full naval control be initiated and spread over a two year period. This had resulted in the RCAF Search and Rescue Squadron moving to RCAF Station Greenwood three months later, but also leaving the RCN saddled with this additional commitment which was still the responsibility of the RCAF under the original Agreement.

Another transfer of power of control had taken place in April 1948, with the signing of an agreement for the establishment of a Naval Air Stores Depot at the Air Station. In spite of these added naval commitments and the practical need for the RCN to achieve independent control of its own activities, the RCAF continued to be completely unresponsive to any further suggestions that they relinquish the actual control of the air station. The situation was now quite ludicrous. The RCN Air Section now consisted of 11 hangars out of the 14 on the station, and was operating 56 aircraft when all units were ashore. The RCAF on the other hand, used only 2 hangars and operated two aircraft in a small Composite Flight. RCN personnel totalled 900, while RCAF personnel numbered only 250. It is very difficult to understand the objective of the selfish stand the RCAF had assumed in this wrangle, through deliberately refusing to relinquish to the RCN, a run down wartime airfield that they the Air Force did not use, and obviously did not want to maintain. It most certainly smacks of sheer obstructionism, and it is all the more revealing that the only way the RCAF was eventually forced to hand over control, was through the authority of a Cabinet Defence Committee meeting in September 1948, which arbitrarily decided that the RCN would take over the air station. This very situation points out just how determined the RCAF was to hinder the growth of Naval Aviation. Subsequent events proved that this attitude was well entrenched and would continue.

LCdr. Dick Bartlett who joined the air staff at Naval Headquarters in August 1948 was made quite aware of the antagonism existing at the higher levels of the RCAF when he was instructed to make arrangements with the RCAF to provide an aircraft to transport a replacement engine for a Seafire grounded at an airport in Maine, USA. This he did with a long time friend, who was a senior Wing Commander in charge of the Transport and Communications Division at RCAF Headquarters. It was a simple straightforward request, so the necessary instructions were issued to the local RCAF transport section at Dartmouth to stop off in Maine on the next regular transport flight to Ottawa and unload the engine. About a week later Bartlett went over to the Wing Commander's office to express his appreciation for the timely assistance, and was very much taken aback to be told that the Chief of the Air Staff, Air Marshall Curtis, had heard of the incident, and was annoyed to the point that he issued a directive which stipulated all such flights to the USA would in future require his personal approval. Although little was said to Dick Barlett about the incident by the embarrassed Wing Commander, it was quite clear that Curtis was more concerned about the assistance being provided to the RCN, than he was about the actual visit to the USA. The final outcome was that the Wing Commander was shortly after posted to a station up in the Yukon.

On 2 September 19 CAG re-commenced flying aboard *Magnificent*, with 825 Firefly squadron under the temporary command of Lt. Doug Peacocke (succeeding LCdr. Dick Bartlett), while command of 803 Fury squadron was assumed by Acting LCdr V.J. Wilgress. Unfortunately, the weather was poor in the local area allowing only three days of flying. Later as the ships headed to the Gulf there were major air operations undertaken, including a full scale air strike by all available aircraft on the Magdalen Islands, followed by joint exercises with the RCAF. Unfortunately, the flying activities came to a complete halt with the contamination of the aviation fuel from water in the ship's fuel tanks. This, unfortunately resulted in the loss of two aircraft which were forced to ditch with engine failure, another two narrowly escaped the same fate.

In addition, several other aircraft suffered from rough running engines. It was at this point that Dennis Foley took the necessary action to temporarily ground the aircraft until the problem could be resolved. Commander "Cockie" Read, who was Commander (Air), took exception to this and a major disagreement occurred, revolving primarily around the jurisdiction and responsibility for the ship's aviation fuel. Foley, rightly took the view that his responsibility as Air Engineer begins when he receives the fuel for the aircraft and if there is any fuel contamination, he, as AEO, would have to ground the aircraft until the situation had been rectified by the ship's Engineering Staff. Special filtering precautions were taken with chamois filters and it was established that there was salt water in the ship's aviation fuel tanks. Further investigation determined that this was caused by an excessive pressure in the pumping system (believed originally set incorrectly by the manufacturer) which emulsified the fuel and salt water mixture. The purpose of pumping of salt water into the fuel tanks was to displace the aviation fuel with salt water, providing the basic pumping pressure for delivery of the aviation fuel, which in the RN was a commonly used system. Once the pressure setting on the salt water pumps was correctly set, the problem of contaminated fuel was eliminated.

During this short period of no flying, *Magnificent* continued on with the cruise, entering Hudson Strait and anchoring at Wakeham Bay, with the two escorts in company. Flying recommenced en route to Halifax, exercises again being conducted with the RCAF. The carrier then returned to Halifax prior to being placed in dry dock at Saint John, New Brunswick, with all aircraft and maintenance personnel proceeding to the Naval Air Section at Dartmouth.

It was about this time that Lt. "Smokey" Bice, with established credentials as a Seafire and Sea Fury solo aerobatic star, experienced a real downer. Having just undergone his routine annual aircrew eye medical with the civilian practitioner Dr. Glenister, Smokey was dumbfounded to say the least, when the good Doctor proceeded to issue a prescription for glasses. (Girls do not like passes from boys wearing glasses). To cap this blow to Smokey's ego, the Doctor's dead serious parting remark was, "I hope you don't drive a car!" Lt. Harry Swiggum was to later fire his shot commenting, "It looked as if the glasses had been manufactured by the Coca Cola Company". Smokey however, did survive this ordeal and continued flying glasses and all!

In spite of all the problems associated with the RCN assuming control of the air station, there was a general boost in the morale for the Air Section, knowing that the shoddy accommodation and generally run down facilities at the air station could now be given the required attention. Although it would take considerable time and funding, at least a base development plan could now be established by the RCN for the entire air station. It was in late September after disembarking from *Magnificent* that 19 CAG disbanded and reformed. This on-going disbanding, reforming and combining of the operational squadrons into CAG's was becoming a headache for all concerned. Establishing the most efficient and operationally suitable system for the peacetime organization of squadrons was rendered particularly difficult by the constant changes, leaving little opportunity for suitable evaluation. There were proponents that believed the two fighter squadrons should form one CAG and the two Firefly squadrons form the other. This it transpires, had limited success. CAG maintenance, with similar aircraft while ashore, certainly offers an advantage from a centralized point of view. At sea however, to provide the carrier with a balanced operational capability, a squadron of each type of aircraft should simultaneously operate aboard in their respective roles. This requirement automatically precludes a centralized squadron maintenance system. To compound the problem, the re-equipping with new aircraft at short intervals, places a heavy burden on both air and ground crew. One over-riding consideration which was always present with four operational squadrons, was the requirement to share the very limited time aboard the single carrier. This invariably resulted in a lack of sufficient carrier flying time, so essential to achieve squadron operational first line proficiency. Similarily, the carrier's air department constantly integrating new squadron personnel, suffered from a lack of continuity, slowing the development of established operating standards which are essential for safety and efficiency.

At the end of September a dreadful, near-fatal accident at Dartmouth occurred in 19 CAG when Lt. George Hopkins had one Sea Fury wing fold on him just as he was reaching takeoff speed. The aircraft skidded inverted down the runway, and came to rest with Hopkins terribly injured with massive near fatal facial and head injuries suffered from abrasive contact and being battered by the folded wing. He lost an eye and was to undergo extensive reconstruction of his head and face with plastic surgery for many years. It was only through his excellent youthful stamina and ongoing remarkable courage that he lived to survive the crash. George subsequently completed a degree in Electrical Engineering, continuing his naval career as an Electrical Officer. The cause of the crash was a fault in the wing locking indicator which apparently, under certain circumstances, only appeared to be locked. It was only after subsequent modifications to the system and an ongoing visual check by the line personnel, that the matter was resolved. Unfortunately, this rare type of accident was bound to occur in the process of teething problems with new aircraft first entering squadron service. It was inevitable that 19 CAG would continue to encounter more problems as the aircraft

Representative RCN aircraft at Shearwater, December 1948. Credit DNS 3264, SAM P3086

Magnificent entering Halifax harbour for the first time, June 1948. Credit HS 4484, SAM P3133

flying rate intensified.

In October 1948, as 18 CAG was returning from Rivers, a regrettable accident happened in 883 squadron, a repetitive type of accident which seemed to occur all too frequently in the Seafire squadrons. Lt. Tom Murphy crashed and was killed, flying over Michigan, when the fighter squadron ran into marginal weather. There is nobody more vulnerable than a pilot who is flying formation on another aircraft in poor visibility and cloud, who, if losing sight of his formation leader, is abruptly forced to depend on his own aircraft instruments. The Seafire XV was not an easy aircraft to control under such marginal conditions, and as the lead aircraft proceeds into the cloud, a very dangerous situation often developed, resulting in the individual pilot encountering considerable difficulties.

Lt. Rod Bays who was leading the second flight of three Seafires with Tom Murphy as his number two and Harry Swiggum as number three, recalls this unfortunate accident. Rod elected to commence a turn to starboard as they entered the cloud to avoid the possibility of closing on the first flight of aircraft led by Don Sheppard. Rod got in difficulty and lost control of his aircraft whilst in the turn and ended up in a spin. Fortunately he broke through a hole in the cloud and regained control. Harry Swiggum recalls seeing Murphy's aircraft flick to starboard in the turn and disappear. Swig then found himself also in a spin, and just managed to obtain control of the aircraft before breaking out of the overcast.

Back at the air station, flying intensity increased as the new Sea Furies actively worked up following the CAG reforming. It was on 14 October, that the first fatal Fury accident befell the CAG. I was the air controller in the tower that day, and Lt. Stan Berge reported himself in difficulties, with the engine cutting out intermittently. He was not visible from the tower, did not have time to give his position, but reported he would try and make the field. About the same time, the Group Commander, Jim Hunter, was in the landing circuit and approaching the runway. Somebody in the tower pointed out a Fury approaching the field from the north, which I identified to him as Hunter. In actual fact it was later believed that it was probably Stan Berge's Fury the observer had seen in the same general area as I had simultaneously sighted Hunter's aircraft. Shortly after, the transmissions ceased, the Fury was obviously down and a major air search was initiated, but with very little information available as to where the aircraft had crashed. Later that night, Ken Gibbs and Joe McBrien were in Operations when a phone call came in from a farmer reporting that he had seen an aircraft in difficulty earlier in the afternoon to the north of the airfield. They grabbed a jeep, went to the area and came upon a telephone lineman replacing a severed line which had been reported early in the afternoon, apparently by the same farmer. It subsequently transpired that the farmer had seen the aircraft go very low over his farm, slash through the wires to the sound of a crash seconds later after disappearing over a clump of trees. Gibbs and MacBrien following the trail of broken trees in the dark, which was accompanied by the strong smell of gas, located the missing Fury inverted, but virtually intact. Stan was still in the cockpit, dead of a broken neck, his head having been struck through the open canopy by a protruding stump as the aircraft flipped over and hit the ground. As it happened, Stan died instantly. It is mind boggling that a witness had seen the aircraft obviously in trouble, heard it crash, yet took no reporting action until he heard it on the news later that night. He claimed to be too busy at the time of the crash to call the air station, but he did find time to go to a neighbour to complain to the phone company about his line being down. We were all pretty bloody minded after encountering that incredible bit of stupidity, which in the view of many, bordered on criminal negligence.

A subsequent accident, as 18 CAG was returning to Dartmouth, occurred to a Firefly of 826 squadron, piloted by Lt. Freddy Rice, fortunately with happier results, involving a degree of humour. Stan Wood recounts the incident as follows: "We Fireflies flew directly over Lake Superior from Fort William to Kinross. I was flying #3 in a four plane formation, when Fred Rice's aircraft developed engine problems. I was detailed to accompany him south to the American lakeshore where we were to proceed east following the shoreline in case he ditched. He did ditch, and very nicely done, particularly since it was in a howling gale and a 300-400 foot ceiling."

Note - There was also an anonymous cheeky comment heard over the radio, following Fred's announced ditching intentions, namely, "Are you going down for a coke, Fred?" This was in reference to

Wayward B17 bomber at RCN Air Section, November 1948. In
foreground Lts. Shel Rowell and Stan Berge. Credit K.L. Gibbs

Training Air Group "Smoker" RCN Air Section, 1948.
Credit Stan Conner

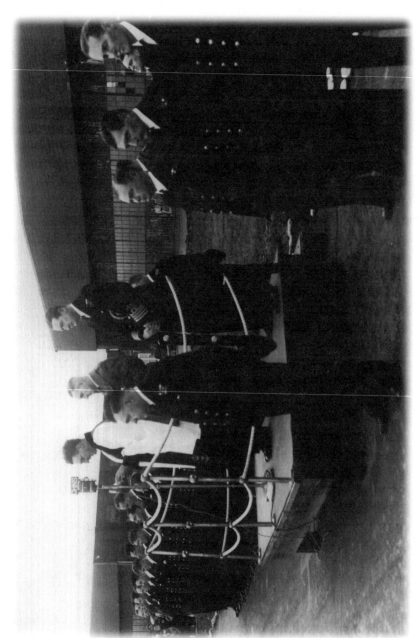

HMCS Shearwater commissioning ceremonies. December 1, 1948. Credit DNS 663, SAM P2441

Fred's well known penchant for coca cola, which he normally kept in good supply in his cabin, and sold as mix. "Fred ditched so close to the shore that he and his mechanic hardly got their feet wet. They then walked south towards a highway, but got lost in their direction and ended back close to their downed aircraft. Fred waded out to the aircraft, ripped out the standby compass, and using that, proceeded in a reasonably straight line to intersect the highway. Upon reaching the road, the pair attempted to flag down east-bound vehicles, but nobody was about to pick up these two weirdly dressed and bedraggled creatures, particularly since it was night and pelting with rain. Finally, ever innovative Fred pulled out his large Verey Pistol, and on seeing a truck bearing down, fired a blinding red flare down the highway. The truck stopped, and the driver, no doubt greatly impressed by the calibre of Fred's artillery, drove the pair to Sault Ste. Marie, where the rest of the Firefly crews were all huddled around a bar." As can be imagined, Fred was royally welcomed by the rest of the aircrew for a variety of reasons, not least of which was the fact that he was the cash officer and carrying the travel funds for the entire group who were at this point virtually penniless.

There was a sequel to the ditching. Fred being a quiet, resourceful, but somewhat ornery rebel, loved to shock the fisheads (non-flying naval officers). Upon returning to the Air Section, following his ditching, he was appointed to a frigate. Since Fred had supposedly lost all his gear in the ditching, he reported aboard his new ship in battle-dress (believed to be ex-RCAF issue-dyed navy blue). He was promptly sent back to the Air Section and instructed not to re-appear until properly dressed in uniform. Fred stayed at the air station for some period of time, until eventually the paybobs provided him with an advance of funds for a new uniform, so finally with great reluctance, he joined his frigate. Fred's independence of character was also reflected in another dress discrepancy. He invariably wore a pair of thick crepe cushion-soled shoes, in the fervent belief that pounding the pavement with hard leather soles, jarred the brain, and incurred lasting cerebral damage. (Gunnery Officers take note!)

A rather unusual incident with an international flavour took place late in the year involving a WW2 B17 Flying Fortress which un-expectedly landed at the air station. The aircraft was rather oddly painted with no identifying insignia, other than a crudely hand painted NC number on the tail fin. The pilot of the aircraft identified himself as a member of a navigation flying school from the United States, and claimed they had lost their way (some navigation school!) and elected to land at *Shearwater*. Although air station authorities were suspicious of the story, Canada Customs could find no reason to hold the aircraft, and so fuel was provided as requested by the pilot, which was paid for with cash. There was some supposed engine defect with the aircraft, so a test flight was undertaken the next day, and other than the loss of part of an engine cowl, which did not seem to bother the crew, the aircraft made a normal return to the airfield. About the same time, the United States Consulate office in Halifax was a bit uneasy about the strange aircraft and requested that the B17 be held at the airfield. There was no legal way this could be done by the *Shearwater* author-ities, but there was still some fiddling being done on the engines by the crew, so the aircraft remained another day or so. It was during one of the following nights that the aircraft taxied out to the more isolated runway button by Macdonald Lake, along which was an access road. After some delay, the pilot requested takeoff for a test flight. This was denied since test flights were not allowed from the field after dark. Minutes later, the aircraft suddenly took off without permission and disappeared into the night. Susequently, we heard the aircraft arrived in the Azores, and when searched by the US authorities, was found to be loaded with contraband guns and ammunition illegally bound for Israel. Their "accidental" trip to *Shearwater* had obviously been care-fully planned, and the load of armament had apparently been taken aboard the night the aircraft was at the remote runway button, under the guise of a test flight. The crew, although claiming to be Florida residents, were apprehended and returned to the USA, and apparently subsequently charged.

Following the reorganization of the air groups, the two fighter squadrons, 803 and 883 squadrons formed up in November 1948 as 19 CAG. At the same time 883 replaced their Seafires XV's with the new Sea Furies, and command of the squadron was assumed by Acting LCdr. Ray Creery. Command of the 18 CAG squadrons consisting of 826 (Firefly I) and 825 (Firefly IV) changed in December, following the re-organization, with Acting LCdr. Jack

Stokes, a veteran ex-FAA observer, taking over command of 825 squadron and Acting LCdr. John Roberts taking over 826 squadron from Acting LCdr. Terry Goddard.

After the formation on 29 November, of a local RCAF-RCN Board, chaired jointly by Cdr. J. Plomer, RCN and W/C. R.O. Shaw, RCAF, the final transfer arrangements were quickly and harmoniously completed for the control of the air station to the RCN. On 1 December 1948, the air station was commissioned as HMCS *Shearwater*, which was indeed a great day of celebration by the Air Branch, with Acting Capt. A.B.F. Fraser-Harris, RCN, assuming command.

Unfortunately in early December another fatal accident occured in the OFTS, with a midair collision between two Seafires. In this accident, Lt. J.M. "Marsh" Stewart was killed when the tail of his aircraft was severed by the second Seafire piloted by Lt. "Rocky" Campbell, who managed to make a successful dead stick forced landing at the air station. Marsh, being at a low altitude, had no opportunity to bale out and his aircraft plunged into the harbour. Stewart was an experienced pilot, who having served in the Pacific War, had recently been appointed to 743 squadron as an instructor.

After the assumption of the air station by the RCN, the RCAF withdrew most of their personnel, the exceptions being the small Composite Flight, and #102 Marine squadron, consisting of high speed launches, operating out of the Marine Base at Baker Point. Since the navy did not yet have sufficient numbers of trained control tower personnel, the RCAF continued to provide some air controllers and a small number of airmen for tower duties. The actual transfer of control to the RCN generally went very smoothly and this was no doubt largely due to the close co-operation and genuine attempts by the RCAF/RCN Committee personnel to achieve a reasonably untroubled transition. This spirit of endeavour was encouraging and displayed once again the fortunate ability of the services to work together at the local level.

In spite of winter gales and snowstorms, which made working conditions difficult, and the still sub-standard living conditions, the morale and spirit of the personnel at HMCS *Shearwater* remained high. The fact that for the first time Canadian Naval Aviation was now well-established at its own base, was probably the most significant event to date in the short, often frustrating, but steady development of the Canadian Naval Air Branch.

There was, however, on-going concern about the operation of the new Sea Furies, which although having impressive performance, were continuing to encounter a variety of unexpected problems, which appeared to revolve primarily around the reliability of the Centaurus engine.

Chapter Three

FORMING UP

With the advent of the New Year in 1949, changes and improvements continued steadily at *Shearwater*. One very significant addition to the air station was the approved construction of permanent married quarters, which would considerably alleviate the desperate housing shortage in the Dartmouth area. An additional and important improvement to the facilities of the station was the repair and rebuilding of the accommodation provided to the men. These buildings on the station had long been neglected, but with the repairs now underway, morale improved considerably, although any sports facilities available to the ships company were still very limited and somewhat primitive. There was however, one popular recreational activity that unexpectedly materialized, although not obtained through "normal service channels". This particular "sport" was detected one evening quite accidently by LCdr. Chris Mitchell, the Station Electrical Officer, while he was making a pre-occupancy inspection of his newly assigned married accommodation in one of the many "Emergency class" temporary buildings on the station. Much to his surprise he found his building, although listed as vacant, fully occupied by a group of enterprising females from the nearby town of Dartmouth, who were industriously plying their trade in the "oldest profession" with the enthusiastic embracement of the naval occupants (the second oldest profession) of the nearby mens' barrack block. This surreptitious, and highly popular activity however, once uncovered, was short-lived much to the disappointment of all the participants.

The first months of 1949 were particularly cold, with the usual maritime blizzards blasting through Nova Scotia. After one heavy snowfall, the air station tractor section was busily engaged in clearing roads and trying to open various driveways. Gerry Daniel recalls one midnight incident involving the clearing of the driveway to the Staff House residents. LCdr. Les Kniffen being an occupant, requested the tractor service and Gerry was glad to approve the snow removal. The snow clearing efforts by the bulldozer operator were being partly hampered by one of the garages adjacent to the driveway, so the operator neatly solved the problem by "dozing" the entire garage back several feet, thereby clearing away the obstruction. He then continued on clearing, finished the job and went on his merry way with grateful thanks from Kniffen. The next morning Cdr. Eric Boak, the Executive officer, also a resident of the Staff House, was unfortunately not as appreciative, mainly because the newly shifted and battered garage not only happened to be assigned for his personal use, but his car was still parked inside! As Gerry recalls, Les Kniffen's status with the Commander was immediately downgraded to "persona non grata".

A/B Ed Janusas also very clearly remembers the cold, windy duty on the aircraft line in winter, and in particular the shortage of winter jackets for the crews who were working outside refuelling and servicing the aircraft. There was such a general lack of winter gear that as the watch rotated, it was necessary for each man to hand over his jacket to the on-coming line crewman. When the naval crew members saw the generous supply of winter clothing issued to their opposite numbers in the RCAF servicing personnel, the comparative dress standards became markedly obvious.

About this time another change that took place was the re-organization of 743 squadron into a Training Air Group (TAG), with subsequent reforming of the maintenance personnel. This altered the TAG to the status of a self contained unit similar in organization to the two operational air groups. At the same time the Seafires were withdrawn from service, requiring the current OFTS pilot class to complete their training on Harvards. This was a retrogressive step, which certainly emphasized the general unsuitability of the Seafire as an OFTS aircraft unless properly maintained and supported in adequate numbers. Additional problems were also being experienced with a lack of suitable aircraft for observer training, so in order to meet the requirements for additional aircrew, the next observer and pilot operational flying training courses were re-scheduled to be conducted in the UK.

At *Shearwater* in the spring of 1949, the air station activities were becoming more varied and Gerry Daniel recounts an amusing incident that took place whilst he was airborne in the station Tiger Moth. He was happily clattering around in the local area, when he noticed a decided restriction in the stick movement of the aircraft with an attendant loss of elevator control. Not being equipped with a radio, and concerned about his control problem, Gerry prudently elected to make an emergency landing on the nearest runway, and since there was no other immediate air traffic, he landed with no difficulty. He re-checked his controls and noticed that all the ball bearings had fallen from the bottom of the joy stick, and were rolling around the cockpit floor, thus causing the problem. As Gerry recalls, he was stopped on the runway and the duty controller, (he believes it was me) came alongside in his car and said "Gerry what the hell do you think you're doing?" Gerry explained the reason for the sudden emergency landing, then said, "Well, what would you do if the balls came off the bottom of your joy stick?" He clearly remembers that particular rhetorical question terminated the need for further discussion.

In all the various trade branches in the RCN, the need for shore billets to allow the rotation of personnel from sea positions was essential and the Aircraft Handlers Branch (A/H) was facing a situation where there was little employment ashore in the same labour intensive numbers as required aboard the carrier. At sea, the branch was actively employed in all the flight deck operations including crash/fire rescue, movement of aircraft, security of aircraft, catapult launches, and aircraft recovery. Ashore, other than the manning of the crash/fire rescue vehicles, the number of personnel required was markedly less. To provide a level of employment for the branch at the air station, somebody came up with the bright idea of using these men in the control tower, in an assistant controller capacity, referred to by the previous RCAF staff as 'B Stand Operators'. This was approved, and once implemented, not only provided an excellent opportunity for the Handlers to advance their trade grouping, but also serve in an aviation capacity ashore, which was both challenging and interesting. The group of men in the Air Handler Branch were by and large a bright and capable lot, and after taking a slightly amended and abbreviated flying controllers course, which was taught by the off duty naval tower controllers, they proceeded to fill this essential duty. As the years went by, and the all-weather facilities of the air station were later established, the branch's role was further expanded to include the function of Ground Control Operators. This duty involved manning the Ground Control Approach (GCA) Radar, by the higher trade groups and rank levels, and was an equally successful application of their services.

On 1 February 1949, Lt. Tom Coultry now serving in 803 Fury squadron, was flying about 30 miles east of the air station when he experienced an engine failure. Tom elected to bail out, but even under ideal conditions, this was a difficult task in a Fury. He did manage to get clear of the cockpit, but his parachute fouled the tail plane and Coultry was killed in the crash as he went down entangled with his Sea Fury. It was becoming apparent that engine malfunctions with the Sea Furies were increasingly worrisome and altogether too frequent, causing major concerns regarding their reliability when flying in the stringent role of an operational fighter.

With the on-going difficulties with the Sea Fury Centaurus engine, there was a natural build up of concern among the fighter pilots and morale suffered following the deaths of Stan Berge and Tom Coultry, both accidents having been clearly attributed to engine malfunction. There was a reluctance among some of the Fury pilots to continue flying the aircraft, which in a few cases prompted subsequent requests for a transfer. In rare instances there was an outright refusal to accept an appointment to a Sea Fury squadron. There was no doubt that the squadron pilots were losing their confidence in the Centaurus engine. Jim Hunter the CAG commander fully recognized the problem, and in an attempt to partially dispel the unease, contacted Cdr. Ted Edwards, the senior airman at Naval Headquarters and successfully prevailed upon the naturally somewhat reluctant Edwards to come to the air station and fly the Sea Fury. It was Hunter's hope that this example of a senior aviator from a non-flying position piloting the Fury would have a positive effect on the low morale problem. This Edwards did later in February, and after a quick cockpit check, he took off and flew the aircraft. It was generally agreed that Edwards deserved considerable personal credit for this somewhat unorthodox effort. By

RCN aircrew at NAS Ream Field California, for ASW course with USN, Feb. 1949. Credit E.M. Davis

Armament crew re-arming Firefly aircraft 20mm. cannon, Magnificent,
March 1949. Credit PA142015, J. Ward

his own admission, he was basically an ex-Swordfish pilot, had never flown fighters, and over the past year flown less than ten hours in training aircraft, flying even less in 1947. Many years later, he questioned the wisdom of conducting the flight with such dubious qualifications. The expression "more guts than brains" does come to mind. Edwards also had occasion to wonder if the flight had ever achieved its purpose.

While the operational squadrons were shore-based and undergoing normal personnel changes, *Magnificent* was returning the Mk IV Fireflies to the UK and replacing them with the Mk V model. This was neither a major change, nor much of an improvement. Other than a form of power wing folding, the only external difference between the two aircraft was the addition of racks beneath the wings on the Mk V's to carry sono buoys and the installation of sono buoy receiver equipment in the observers compartment. This addition resulted from NATO's recognition of Canada's recent decision to change-over the role of the RCN to that of specialized Anti-Submarine Warfare. This rather pathetic attempt by Fairey Aviation to classify the Mk V Firefly as an ASW aircraft through the installation of such limited, basic equipment, was fairly typical of the current lack of progressive ASW aircraft development by the Royal Navy. It did little for the RCN other than to saddle us with another expensive aircraft, limited in endurance, and poorly equipped for all-weather day and night operations. The payload was so minimal that the observer, who could observe but little, was given a weight limitation, otherwise the aircraft's weight and balance limits were compromised. As a weight saving measure, the four 20mm. cannon were removed and the ports blanked off, which did help the situation somewhat, while also improving the handling qualities of the aircraft.

This imposed weight limitation had a humorous aftermath as Acting LCdr. (E) (A/E) Wally Tuck, RN recalls. Originally this weight limitation was outlined in a message from Naval Headquarters, so in turn he arranged for several of the new Mk V Fireflies to be weighed, and found that they all exceeded the prescribed limitation. He decided to take matters in his own hands and in his capacity as Senior Air Engineer at *Shearwater*, unilaterally ordered that the aircraft be grounded. A great scuffle then ensued with Commander Air and Captain Fraser-Harris complaining bitterly to the Air Staff at Naval

Headquarters. This caused an additional furore because the Air Staff then had a row with the Director of Air Engineering, Cdr. J.B. Caldwell, who was a Marine Engineer, brought in as the Director of Air Engineering to supposedly inject some discipline in the branch. As Wally Tuck whimsically recalls, Caldwell who was unaccustomed to being chewed out, then leveled a blast his way, almost as though Tuck had created the problem in the first instance. Apparently at one point, Caldwell was so fired up, he was on the verge of packing the innocent Tuck back to the RN.

It should be noted that the foregoing weight restriction also affected the Firefly V's operational performance. In a tactical role, the Firefly's strict limitation in ASW external droppable stores was so critical that on some occasions the Sea Furies had to be fitted to carry extra sono-buoys, which were dropped where necessary, to hopefully expand the small sono buoy search patterns being set up by the Fireflies.

The aircrew of 825 squadron, while re-equipping with the new Fireflies, were also taking anti-submarine courses at the Royal Navy school at Londonderry. This training culminated in an exercise with four "enemy" submarines and the newly arrived *Magnificent* with her escort. In spite of the inadequate equipment, the squadron gave a good account of itself, with Lt. Bill Babbitt and his observer Lt. Hal Pickering actually claiming and getting the credit for detecting and attacking three of the subs, one which they caught on the surface. At the subsequent de-briefing, the four submariners all denied that any of them had actually surfaced during the encounter. Finally one, the captain of HMS *Alcide*, did admit that he had inadvertantly broached during the exercise and didn't report it and he was the one caught on the surface, the alert Firefly crew having read the name of the submarine during their attack.

Magnificent returned to Halifax with 825 squadron equipped with the new Mk V Firefly aircraft on 25 February 1949, and the squadron disembarked. The carrier remained alongside for a short period prior to embarking 19 CAG Sea Furies of 803 and 883 squadrons, the latter now under command of Acting LCdr. R.A. Creery who had taken over the squadron the previous December. Also on this cruise was 826 squadron (Mk I Fireflies) under command of Acting LCdr. J.W. Roberts. *Magnificent* then proceeded with the squadrons aboard, for a working up cruise to the West Indies in the first week of March. At the same time 825 squadron was reforming ashore with their newly arrived Mk V Fireflies. It should be noted that the separate tranfer of 826 Firefly squadron from 18 CAG to operate aboard *Magnificent*, along with 19 CAG Sea Furies, was a not uncommon event. In this case, the additional squadron provided *Magnificent* with a more balanced aircraft complement, enabling both a degree of ASW capability and the flexibility of the carrier to participate in a more varied series of fleet/air exercises.

Magnificent arrived for deck landing training in the Bermuda area with *Haida* and *Micmac* in company. The weather around Bermuda was unsuitable, so the ships proceeded to the Kingston Jamaica area. During the ensuing flying operations, a Firefly was ditched and a Sea Fury (Lt. "Doc" Schellinck) went in the drink on takeoff. Thankfully the two pilots and the observer were safely recovered. Later in March, another aircraft was lost when Lt. Joe MacBrien torque stalled in his Fury on final approach to the carrier, he too was rescued unhurt. Flying continued en route to the Canal Zone and with HMS *Jamaica* as a target, fighter strikes were carried out by the Sea Furies as general squadron workups with the surface units continued. At Colon the Halifax-based fleet units were augmented by three west coast based ships, the cruiser *Ontario*, the destroyer *Athabaskan* and the frigate *Antigonish*. The planning for the next phase of the cruise was carried out at Colon, which involved additional much-needed carrier air search and strike exercises. The RCN ships were then formed as Task Force 215 sailing to rendezvous with the America and West Indies squadron of the Royal Navy still under command of Admiral Tennant.

It was on 20 March 1949, that the "mutiny incident" aboard *Magnificent* occurred, which followed previous similar "incidents" aboard the other RCN ships *Athabaskan* and *Crescent*. These events, which were thoroughly examined by the subsequent Mainguy Report investigation, resulted in a welcome and permanent improvement in the thinking, general service conditions, attitude, and overall RCN officer/man relationships. The situation aboard *Magnificent* should never have been allowed to deteriorate to the extent it did, and the role of the Executive Officer, Commander D.W. Piers, bears close scrutiny.

In brief, 32 Aircraft Handlers, (usually a high spirited and happy go lucky group) staged a temporary "sit in" in their mess and refused to go to work. By and large, they were simply just plain fed up being continually jerked around, and deeply resentful of the manner in which they were generally being treated. The paramount objective of an aircraft carrier is to operate aircraft efficiently and safely. To achieve this, the ships' routine must have the required degree of flexibility, and full co-operation between the Executive Department and the Air Department is essential. This obviously requires an understanding and appreciation of the ship's primary role by the Executive Officer. The inflexibility of *Magnificent*'s ships routine, the lack of understanding of Commander Piers to adequately recognize this requirement, and his perceived shortcoming to intelligently manage his subordinate officers and men, was made abundantly clear.

Louis Audette, one of the three Commissioners of the Mainguy Report, describes the conditions aboard *Magnificent* in his chapter "The Lower Deck and the Mainguy Report of 1949", in the book The RCN in Retrospect. Audette states, "A salient cause which led to eventual insubordination was the unsuitability and irresponsibility of the Executive Officers and their apparent inability to engage either officers or men to follow them. There were many cases of the injudicious assignment of men to tasks which more enlightened superiors would have been reluctant to assign them: Aircraft Handlers were forced to clean up after officers' cocktail parties. During a "make and mend" or afternoon off duty, just before sailing for Britain, a number of Aircraft Handlers (the future mutineers) were detailed to secure automobiles brought on board by ships' officers. This assignment was so deeply resented even by some of the officers, that it had to be cancelled before completion of the task, making the initial error even more apparent to everyone."

When discussing the implicit order for all HMC ships to institute Welfare Committees, Audette writes, "The Executive Officer of HMCS *Magnificent* (Piers) was aware of this clear and unmistakable order but because in his own words he 'Did not believe in the desirability of Welfare Committees,' there was no Welfare Committee in the ship. The only reason we (the Investigating Commission) could not classify this officer as a mutineer was that he lacked the co-operation of another insubordinate accomplice, although the passivity of the ship's captain (Commodore Miles) might perhaps have been likened to complicity."

As Audette further relates, "In all three ships, the men were aware of their officers' disobedience of orders on this score (to establish Welfare Committees) and resented having no forum in which to plead. It never seems to have occurred to the officers involved that their own defiance of orders led their men down the path toward collective insubordination." It is significant that one of the conclusions of the Mainguy Report stated, "If Welfare Committees had been properly constituted and allowed to function, it is probable that none of the incidents would have happened."

Serving air officers aboard *Magnificent* at the time, fully recognized that *Magnificent* was an "unhappy ship" and the obvious antagonism between the newly appointed head of the Air Department, Commander Bruce McEwan, RN (on loan to the RCN) and Cdr. Piers was well known, even down to the level of the flight deck crews of Air Handlers. They in turn on several occasions expressed their opinion of the Executive Officer in no uncertain terms, and at times this was even done within earshot of officers of the Air Department.

Perhaps some of the most illuminating testimony presented to the Mainguy Inquiry in the month following the "incident" was that of LCdr. Clunk Watson, who was LCdr. Flying and second-in-command of the Air Dept. to Cdr. Bruce McEwan. Audette was impressed with Watson's testimony and described him as "Interested in the men, straightforward, intelligent and well balanced." Clunk in answer to a question asking if inter-departmental bickering was confined to the Executive Officer and the Air Dept., replied, "There was no consideration of any other Department by the Executive Officer at all." Watson also describes the feeling of futility expressed by Cdr. McEwan who had several times gone to the Captain expressing his concern about the lack of consideration being shown primarily to the Aircraft Handlers and their working conditions. In another instance, Watson detailed the differences between the officer-man relationship in the RN and the RCN, pointing out that the "RN troops will put up with a lot more than our people, from the mere fact they expect it. Their ships are uncomfortable and their messing facilities and sleeping facilities as I remember, are pretty bad. The Canadian lad, too has had a much better education, comes from a better home than his equal rank in the

RN and his lifestyle before the Navy was on a higher scale, whereas as a rule, the life in the RN is better than most of the RN troops have been previously used to."

On the subject of RN officers serving in the RCN Naval Aviation Branch, Clunk was very explicit, "First of all in dealing with the Canadian Navy, we are dealing with Canadians as such and Canadian officers should be employed in the Air Arm - we are now over-borne or over burdened with RN Officers, who in my opinion, and as a rule I have known most of them before, are not the RN's best and they don't know how to handle Canadian troops and Canadian officers. The quicker we get rid of the RN the better!"

In answer to the question, "Is your objection to the RN because they are RN, or because they have been sending out what you consider to be their second best?" Clunk's response was brutally frank! "One is that most RN officers take jobs which young Canadian officers, if given the chance, could handle but never get the experience because they are never given the chance. I would like to see a young Lt. given a chance to do a job and get promoted and obtain more experience. If he can't cope with it, remove him, but let them have the opportunity! There are one or two exceptions, but most of the RN officers we get are LCdrs., who couldn't do their job in the RN and who know nothing about handling aeroplanes as a rule. One or two of them have an idea. Some of the exceptions are in fact, LCdr. Hemsley who is an excellent clued up character and also Cdr. McEwan. These are the two people in my opinion who are invaluable to us, but throughout the Air Arm there are a lot of others that are doing a lot of harm rather than a lot of good." Watson, who had five years wartime service in the FAA, and had also served in six different aircraft carriers, including Warrior, obviously had the background and experience to substantiate his opinions.

It is significant to relate that in spite of the major criticism directed by the Mainguy Report at specific officers, these same officers were almost without exception subsequently promoted, one almost with indecent haste. In a sense, this indicates their own non compliance of orders was being condoned by the highest naval authority, ie. the Chief of Naval Staff, and their promotions perceived as a gesture of disdain toward the Mainguy Inquiry itself. Piers himself eventually became a Rear Admiral, and many years later when the "incident" aboard *Magnificent* was aired on CBC television, upon being interviewed, Piers loftily suggested that he had been vindicated in his actions by having achieved Rear Admiral's rank. Cynics on the other hand, have suggested that the officers involved may well have been kicked upstairs or promoted, to keep them "out of harms way".

In the meantime, there was mounting concern among the Aviation Staff at Naval Headquarters about the current reliability level of the Sea Fury engine. But with no immediate equivalent operating experience in the Royal Navy to make valid comparisons, and the general lack of experience of the Air staff at Naval Headquarters with the new aircraft, it was difficult to come up quickly with the proper course of action to resolve the problem. It was becoming rapidly apparent, however that a major decision would have to be made soon by the RCN Directorate of Air Engineering to identify and satisfactorily resolve the mounting problems with the engine.

It was about this time that discreet inquiries were made directly to the USN by members of the Headquarters Air Staff, probably at the USN Naval Attache level, to determine whether Hellcats were still a viable option. The purpose being the formation of at least an operational training unit of Hellcats, which could help fill the gap until the Fury engine problems could be satisfactorily resolved. Hellcats were still being used extensively by the USN in the advanced operational training role, and were particularly valuable for carrier training until such time as their replacement, the new F8F Bearcats, were available in greater numbers. Apparently, Royal Navy-trained Chief of Naval Staff, Admiral Harold Grant heard about the inquiry to the USN. As Cdr. Ted Edwards was to recall, all the Naval Air Staff officers were ordered to assemble in the "Crowsnest" at HMCS *Bytown* Officers Mess, and were read the riot act by Grant, who directed them to cease trying to circumvent Naval Board policy decisions. He made it very clear that the RCN would continue to remain in the Royal Navy camp, by continuing to buy British aircraft, and under no circumstances would he allow the RCN to become dependant in any way upon the USN. He also suggested that he thought it was about time the aviators started thinking like Canadians in the interests of Canada. This was an ironical comment, because it was apparent to the assembled group of air officers that in Grant's view, a Canadian should think Canadian by being pro British and accordingly buy British aircraft. Most damaging to Grant's concept of a Canadian was the revelation that, when he was being interviewed earlier at the Mainguy Inquiry, he angrily rejected the much sought after proposal to adopt "Canada" shoulder flashes, by saying "I had always refused to wear them in the past and would never wear them in the future, regardless of any contribution it might make to morale." In any event, the Admiral's angry confrontation with the Air Staff, killed once and for all, any further attempts to procure USN Hellcats.

On Monday afternoon of 28 March 1949, one of the most tragic and inexplicable accidents took place at *Shearwater* which shocked the entire Canadian Naval Air Branch. I was duty controller in the air station control tower, and two of the off-duty controllers, Lts. Whitey McNicol and Jimmy Pulfer, were airborne, engaged in proficiency flying as part of a flight of Harvards. The other two aircraft were piloted by Lts. Glenn Hutton, an ex-Pacific War Corsair pilot who had served aboard the British carrier *Victorious* with McNicol and Roger Harris, who was attached to the OFTS. LCdr. Bob Monks, the Commanding Officer of the OFTS had taken off in a Sea Fury for a routine acceptance test flight and was airborne that afternoon. The four Harvards had been practicing formation flying, and were heading south to cross over the airfield. McNicol, the leader, had called for and received permission to pass over the airfield, and the flight disappeared from my field of view as he led them over the station.

Lts. Ken Gibbs and Ken "Big Nick" Nicolson had just taken off in a Firefly Trainer, when suddenly Nick said to Gibbs, "Look there's a mid air collision!" Gibbs looked up just in time to see two Harvards spinning down on the shoreline to the south of the station Marine Section, one with no tail and the other with a wing missing. They then crashed into the shallow water off Macnab's Island. At the same time, they saw the Fury pass quite close, heading south-east over the harbour entrance, with white smoke trailing from the engine, flying in level flight at an altitude of about 1000 feet. The Fury was then observed to suddenly push over into a steep dive, then crash into the sea by Macnab's Island. Nicolson stated that when he first noticed the Fury it appeared that Monks was attempting a barrel roll around the flight of Harvards, but something went horribly wrong as the Fury hurtled through the formation.

As the tower air controller, I neither saw the Fury, nor did Monks ever request the necessary permission to enter the control zone. Neither was it customary to make an unauthorized pass at a flight of aircraft. It could never be established what went wrong, but Bob Monks, although a very experienced and a capable pilot, had very little flying time on the Sea Fury and the aircraft will certainly tend to momentarily flick over when flying at high speed if the control column is not handled carefully.

As Ken Gibbs relates, "In my view, Monks was close enough to the airfield after the accident, to have turned in and made an emergency landing. I believe he deliberately dove into the sea and committed suicide". It is quite possible that Ken Gibbs' assessment is correct, and Bob Monks, once he had realized the enormity of what he had just done, may well have taken his own life. The outcome of this shocking accident, was the deaths of Glenn Hutton, Jimmy Pulfer, Bob Monks and Able Seaman J. Cambray, a passenger in one of the Harvards.

The effect of this terrible accident went out like a shock wave. Lt. Jim Burns recalls that all naval flying was temporarily suspended at the air station. Meanwhile, the news of this major accident hit the Aviation Staff at Headquarters like a thunderbolt and at a most unfortunate time. Already there was considerable talk at the Naval Staff level, concerning the problems being experienced by the Sea Furies, the excessive accident rate, and the overall negative image that was unfortunately being projected by the on-going teething problems of the new branch. Additionally, the fatal Seafire crash, some four months earlier, involving Marsh Stewart, who had been C.D. Howe's son-in-law, of necessity had brought the Naval Aviation Branch flying operations very much before the senior Federal Government officials. Indeed, there was some serious speculation amongst the Naval Staff as to the certainty of the future of naval aviation. There is no evidence to suggest that the subject came officially before Naval Board, but the survival of Canadian Naval Aviation was at a most crucial stage, and rumours penetrated to the air station that the air branch may even be abolished. Fortunately, the tension eased, and recognizing the need to persevere, flying operations quickly recommenced. As it subsequently turned out, this particularly disastrous episode appeared to be the low point in the development of Canadian Naval Aviation and steady progress followed.

Magnificent, in the meantime as part of Task force 73, having joined forces with an RN squadron of ships, participated in convoy exercises with the Fireflies, while continuing on to Guantanamo Cuba, the big USN naval air base. The Sea Furies of 803 and 883 squadron were busy in the strike role in March, carrying out attacks on the surface forces comprising the cruisers of the RN and HMCS *Ontario.* The fighters conducted a long range search on one exercise, locating the "enemy" cruiser force through a fortunate break in the clouds at a distance of over 200 miles from *Magnificent,* following this with a strike of nine aircraft.

As Lt. Mike Page was to recollect, "It was necessary in this case for the Sea Furies to conduct the long range search, because the Fireflies had been flown ashore to the USN base at Guantanamo Cuba, in order to carry out compass check swings on the aircraft." This requirement was precipitated by the fact that Lt. Harry Sutcliffe, one of the observers, having got hopelessly lost on one of the exercises, in turn had blamed his aircraft compass. The check swings subsequently established that the compasses were faultless, but in the meantime from 25-29 March, the Firefly crews ashore had the benefit of four days lolling around the officers swimming pool, until *Magnificent* arrived in the area. On 29 March, the Furies also carried out strikes on the big USN carrier USS *Coral Sea* and the British cruiser HMS *Glasgow.* This was an excellent working up cruise for 19 CAG, with good flying weather and several opportunities to carry out their prescribed strike role.

On 25 March 1949, one near miss occurred at *Shearwater* in 825 squadron as Lts. Shel Rowell and Bill Babbitt were carrying out the popular "Tail chase" which was not only good fun but also provided excellent training in following an aircraft through various aerobatics. Shel was leading, and as he passed over on the top of a loop, he decided to carry out an aileron roll to complete a figure eight aerobatic manœuver. Babbitt, who was overtaking him, suddenly found himself upside down veering past Rowell, and staring at his leader's propellor, which seemed inches away. Shel also recalls this little chase, because he swears that Babbitt was so close he could hear the other aircraft's engine. He also claims that his own rear view mirror mounted above the windscreen, was tilted by the powerful prop wash from Babbit's passing aircraft. The two finally did rejoin, formating rather gingerly on their way back to the base.

Flying continued at the end of March from *Magnificent* for a brief period after departing from Guantanamo, then following a short visit to Bermuda, the three squadrons launched in a fairly heavy pitching deck from the carrier on 7 April and flew directly to *Shearwater* some 225 miles away, carrying out a strike on the air station upon arrival.

One change of senior air personnel took place at Naval Headquarters, Ottawa, with the assumption in April of Commodore C.N. Lentaigne, DSO, RN, to the position of Assistant Chief of Naval Staff (Air) from Commodore H.N. Lay. Lentaigne had previously been serving as a Captain in the position of Director of Naval Aviation, having replaced Captain G.A. Rotherham, in January 1949. This promotion augered well for Naval Aviation since Lentaigne had been most supportive of his Canadian Naval Aviation staff. There was also one additional change of command which took place at *Shearwater* in April, with LCdr. L.R. "Tan" Tivy, RN taking over the Training Air Group following the tragic death of Bob Monks.

With other on-going changes of aircrew officers in the various squadrons, there was also the occasional unusual situation that seemed to crop up as air personnel changed and departments were expanded to meet the growing needs of the station. One rather intriguing story came from Deke Logan, who by virtue of having undergone a Safety Equipment course in the UK, suddenly found himself at the orders of Commander (Air), in charge of the station Safety Equipment Section, relieving Lt. Art Bray who had decided to transfer to the Supply Branch. Deke was immediately approached by his two Safety Equipment technicians, CPO's "Radio" Macdonald and "Knobby" Clarke, who volunteered some advice on the status of the inventory of equipment which must be examined and assumed by each relieving Officer in Charge. The two Chiefs assured Deke that there would definitely be no shortages in equipment such as flying clothing items, because they kept the inventory balanced by a most ingenious scam. The system they employed was to take the usual bundle of returned (unusable) worn flying clothing such as mae wests, helmets, gloves, flying suits etc. to the Air Stores building where they would be replaced by new clothing items. The discarded material was then put outside at the back of the building for subsequent destruction. The enterprising pair would later surreptitiously drive to the rear of the building and load the discarded items in their vehicle and return them to the Safety Equipment Section, thereby always ensuring an adequate supply of redundant material for exchange with new items. The system worked beautifully! There was however, one missing equipment item on the inventory, for which the Chiefs had no solution. It is hard to believe, but Art Bray had somehow been conned into accepting a bulldozer on his inventory, the whereabouts of which was completely unknown and had seemingly disappeared. There was no way that Deke was going to sign for that particular item, and it took considerable persuasion for Captain Fraser-Harris to write off that major piece of machinery from the inventory. As a matter of record, Ken Gibbs actually recalled being assigned to fly a bulldozer search mission in a Firefly with no success whatsoever. Bulldozers obviously held a great fascination for the local pirates!

Magnificent sailed again in late May, this time with 826 and 825 squadrons embarked, the flying emphasis for 825 squadron initially being on deck landing familiarization for the pilots with the new Mk V Fireflies. This had entailed a very intensive flying period ashore for the squadrons and in May with both groups ashore, over 2600 sorties had been flown, the concentration being on ADDL's and crew training. The intended cruise was scheduled for over three weeks, but the entire program was abruptly terminated when *Magnificent* ran aground at the entrance to the harbour at Port Mouton, Nova Scotia on 4 June 1949. Fortunately there was little damage and the carrier was refloated four hours later with the assistance of tows from the destroyers. *Magnificent* was forced to proceed to Saint John, N.B. for a hull inspection, and the aircraft were lightered ashore to *Shearwater*. Flying from the carrier had been minimal during this abbreviated period, the aircrews averaging only about 7 hours and 8 deck landings. With *Magnificent* out of service until October, a completely new program had to be prepared for the two Firefly squadrons of 18 CAG. In one sense, the grounding of *Magnificent* precipitated a series of events, which in the long run, were to be a blessing in disguise for the Naval Aviation Branch and would result in a permanent change in the aircraft procurement policy of the RCN.

With *Magnificent* out of service, an alternative flying schedule was improvised, and in early July 1949, both 825 and 826 Firefly squadrons formed up as 18 CAG and were detached to the large USN naval

Sea Fury crash landing, Shearwater, Summer 1949.
Credit PA168845, W. Blakely

19 CAG Fury pilots briefing, Shearwater, Summer 1949. L-R Ken
Nicolson, Knobby Westwood, Mike Wasteneys, Pat Whitby.
Credit PA145683, C. Polischuk

18 CAG Fireflies at NAS Quonset Point Rhode Island, July 1949.
Credit PA140264, E. Colbert

1000 lb. bomb being mounted on Firefly. L-R CPO Whitely AB
Sandilands. Credit PA 136506, C. Polischuk

826 Firefly Squadron at Shearwater, July 1949. Credit R.O. de Nevers

826 Squadron Firefly doing FCLP at Charlestown, RI., August 1949. Credit PA 140290, J. Colbert

air station, at Quonset Point, R.I. Here, plans had been prepared to cross-train the pilots of the two squadrons to the USN carrier landing signals and landing technique. This was definitely a practical requirement, since there was an increasing emphasis on hemispheric co-operation. Operating with the USN and adopting standardized carrier operating procedures was the obvious key to integrated naval air operations between the two navies. Of additional importance was the need to establish the compatibility of the equipment involved, and it was important to determine if the British built Fireflies were suitable for the USN carrier landing technique. The standardization of signals was one consideration, but whether the British aircraft could stand up to the greater rate of sink used on landing in the USN system, which required a strong undercarriage with oleo legs designed accordingly, was a completely different matter.

The training program under USN supervision was extensive, lasting from 7 July to 24 September. The two Canadian DLCO'S who had been trained originally using the British signals, were Lts. Doug Peacocke and Bert Mead, who worked throughout the period with their opposite number, the USN LSO. (Landing Signals Officer). It was soon apparent that the Firefly was generally unsuitable for carrier operations using the USN landing technique, which called for pushing the nose over at the "Cut signal", then flaring out in the three point attitude. The British-built aircraft were not designed to accept the high rate of sink resulting from this technique, and even if a three point landing resulted, the consequences were invariably a bounce, a burst tire, and in more extreme cases, a broken oleo or undercarriage assembly. Bert Mead recalls the older and more heavily used Mk I Fireflies had more undercarriage failures than the Mk V's , but later on, the newer aircraft began to show stress damage, with skin wrinkles being transmitted through to the wing centre section. Almost the entire two and a half months were spent training on the USN technique with pilots averaging 50 hours during the period. Regretfully, the pilots did not have as much confidence in the USN LSO as they did in Peacocke and Mead, and the general view was that the American was unsure and uncomfortable working with the British aircraft. In spite of the difficulties, serviceability remained quite high, considering the number of broken undercarriages that occurred with the Mk I aircraft. The final day of reckoning took place the third week of September when the pilots were all given a final briefing before going aboard the USN carrier USS *Saipan* for deck landing training.

Perhaps the one remark that really shook up the already nervous USN LSO, was at this briefing just prior to going aboard, which took place after ten weeks of exhaustive flying on field carrier landing practice (FCLP) involving thousands of landings. When asked if there were any final questions, Ken Gibbs glibly asked, "Would you mind just running through the signals one more time?"

Another discussion and subsequent incident that comes to mind was made aboard the *Saipan* just prior to the first landing of the Mk V's. This was a conversation that ensued between the USN Flight Deck Chief and Lt. Don Knox, the Senior Pilot of 825 squadron. Apparently Knox made the observation that, "Those barriers don't look all that strong compared to the ones we have on British carriers". The Chief condescendingly replied, "Don't you worry Sir, there's not an aircraft you people are flying that can get by those barriers of ours!" Knox, as befitting his status as 825 senior pilot, made the first approach and landing. His Firefly aircraft bounced, missed all the wires, went under, over and through the barriers and skidded virtually all the way to the forward part of the flight deck before grinding to a halt, minus a complete undercarriage. As Bert Mead laughingly recalls, Knox stepped out of the wreck with a big grin and an "I told you so expression" on his face.

The trials mercifully ended after a day or so with the captain of *Saipan* considerably on edge after watching his beautiful teak-covered flight deck being chewed up and splintered by what appeared to be a never ending series of deck landing accidents. Although some landings were accomplished without difficulty, it was painfully obvious that the British aircraft were just not rugged enough to take the stress on the undercarriage required by the USN landing technique. The American-built carrier aircraft on the other hand, were specifically designed to accept the high rate of sink, and with their strong undercarriage and long stroke oleos were built to operate under extreme deck movement and accordingly suffered virtually no operating problems.

Doug Peacocke, as DLCO/LSO also felt that there were other contributing factors. He recognized that the British aircraft did not stand up as well as American naval aircraft to the heavy impact of the USN type landing, but did feel that some of the pilots had not

825 Squadron Firefly being ranged on flight deck USS Saipan, September 1949. Credit PA 140293, J. Colbert

825 Squadron Firefly deck landing aboard USS Saipan, September 1949. Credit PA140276, DND

826 Squadron Firefly taxiing aboard USS Saipan, September 1949. Credit PA 140270, DND

826 Squadron Firefly aboard USS Saipan September 1949 after undercarriage collapsed on landing. Pilot Lt. Les Peaver. Credit PA141121, J. Colbert

825 Squadron Firefly being hoisted after deck landing accident aboard USS Saipan, September 1949. Credit PA 140266, DND

completely mastered the actual landing technique of the USN system. There may well be a basis for this comment, because subsequent landings aboard *Magnificent* by the same pilots, showed the Fireflies could cope, albeit with a modified landing technique. This differentiated from the standard USN landing method by bringing the Fireflies to the "cut position" at a lower height above the deck, followed by a more gentle easing forward of the stick. Consequently, a lower rate of sink occurs with less severe impact by the aircraft on the deck. One design feature of the Fireflies, which had contributed to the problems associated with the USN landing system was the forward-mounted fuselage V frame of the hook, which brought the hook point itself much closer to the aircraft's centre of gravity. This, on occasions, created a see saw effect which actually pulled the aircraft out of the air before the main wheels or tail reached the deck. In turn, this tended to slam the aircraft on to the deck, either main wheels first or tail wheel first. There was no doubt however, that the Fireflies even flown by an experienced pilot, were not built to accept heavy deck movement caused by rough seas, thereby incurring a higher deck landing accident rate than the USN.

Although the deck landing objective was not achieved, due to the discontinuence of the carrier landing phase, the conversion of pilots to the USN signals had been generally successful. Moreover, the close co-operation between the two navies and the hospitality of the USN personnel and their generous sharing of all their facilities, was most pronounced, and all the Canadian personnel enjoyed the benefits of sharing the services of the well equipped air station. From the officers point of view, the comfort and overall conveniences of the Batchelor Officers Quarters (BOQ) was indeed a great improvement over the still sparse facilities at *Shearwater*, and the extra-curricular activities of the base and the local area after hours, were particularly enjoyed by the Canadian personnel. One innovative modification instituted by the Canadians living in the Batchelor Officers' Quarters at the base, was the substitution of beer for coke in the vending machine. This worked like a charm and became a popular (and believed permanent) modification for both the RCN and USN residents.

The carrier's unexpected grounding in early June, had also altered the balance of the year's flying program for 803 and 883 fighter squadrons of 19 CAG. They departed for Rivers, Manitoba, in June for an alternative extensive armament program and joint operations with the army. The departure for the two squadrons, with the aircraft fitted with extra fuel tanks, began with an impressive flypast, but the trip soon turned into a shambles. Of the 17 Furies in the transit flight west, only 11 arrived without incident. The remaining 6, all experienced various engine-associated, forced or emergency landings en route. Indeed as one cynical wag remarked, "You don't have to navigate to reach Rivers, just follow the trail of Sea Furies pranged on the way".

Lt. Jack Runciman was one of the six luckless pilots who experienced an engine failure, force landing his Sea Fury in a farmer's field near the old WW2 airbase near Ste. Eustache, Quebec. After leaving a trail of destruction as he skidded through the field, he hurriedly vacated the smoking wreck of his aircraft. Rather shaken from his experience, he was despondently contemplating his situation, only to be accosted by the angry farmer who was not only completely unsympathetic about the pilot's personal well-being, but demanded to know why the hell Jack didn't land at the nearby airfield, rather than in the prized field of grain.

Jim Hunter, the CAG Commander, was in the awkward position of having to make the decision to continue flying, or ground all the Furies. From the perspective of the Group, there was considered to be a fair amount of foot-dragging on the part of Naval Headquarters Air Technical Staff. Initially, there was a reluctance on their part to believe there was anything specifically wrong with the Centaurus engine. Hunter, sensibly, but reluctantly chose to ground the aircraft and flying ceased for 19 CAG in late June of 1948. Improvised training, however took place with the pilots engaging in tactical reconnaissance exercises with Harvards and artillery spotting exercises using army Auster aircraft. Additional time was spent in simulated parachute jumping and other army exercises.

Meanwhile, the engines were being inspected and stripped to identify the engine problems and the modifications required. As it turned out, the Centaurus required various design changes to the oil filter system, oil pressure system and the hydraulic controls for the constant speed unit.

Lt. Bill Maxwell, the Group Assistant Air Engineer Officer, recalls a brief conversation he had with Jim Hunter, as he was agonizing over a decision to ground the aircraft. Bill made the light-hearted comment that since the United States aviation industry had just grounded a world-wide fleet of 300 Constellation commercial aircraft with technical problems, the implications of a couple of dozen Sea Furies being put out of service shouldn't upset things too much.

It is not surprising that the Fury Centaurus engine was experiencing operating problems, since it had been originally designed for the Bristol Brabazon, the big new transport aircraft intended to spearhead the post-war British efforts to achieve leadership in the commercial aircraft field. Engine handling in a transport aircraft is completely different from that of a fighter aircraft, which often requires extended periods of full power, with sudden maximum throttle changes, to met the operational fighter role. The Rolls Royce Griffon engine, designed for fighter use did not suffer from such rough engine handling techniques, nor did the radial engines produced by American manufacturers Pratt and Whitney, and Wright, which powered virtually all USN aircraft.

Initially, there was a degree of protective scepticism shown by the Bristol engine representatives regarding the validity of the engine problems being encountered by the RCN fighter squadrons. They did however, move fairly quickly designing the necessary modifications, once satisfied that a problem existed. This view was no doubt considerably strengthened when Frank Murphy, the Bristol Aircraft test pilot, arrived at Rivers, took his first test flight and promptly ran into engine difficulties. When it became obvious that the engine problems would be somewhat lengthly to correct, the pilots returned to the air station and commenced flying in the remaining Seafire XV's which had been re-activated for the months of September and October.

While the naval personnel at Dartmouth were getting acquainted with the air station that summer and becoming more aware of their immediate physical surroundings, most evident to the east of the airfield was a small scattered settlement generally known as Eastern Passage. Among the residents were some of the most enterprising and resourceful group of thieves one could imagine, and aptly referred to as "Eastern Passage Pirates." They most surely lived by the doctrine that "If it belonged to the Government it belonged to the public." ie. them.

One of their earliest and most daring escapades took place in early

1949, shortly after the navy assumed control of the Radar Unit, located a mile or two east of the airfield. On commencing work one Monday morning the Officer in Charge noted that he had no power for his building and radar equipment. It did not take long to establish that the copper main power line had been dug up over the weekend and the cable completely removed and sold through a convenient outlet. This was a major project by the pirates, involving several hundred feet of the heavy cable. Following this escapade, and to provide a semblance of security around the sprawling base, Ed Janusus recalls the Air Maintenance School trainees were assigned to security patrols. Issued with .303 rifles, safely loaded with blank ammunition, they trudged wearily around the perimeter of the base at night following completion of their normal working hours.

Gerry Daniel remembers another partially successful heist the pirates undertook, which brazenly took place in broad daylight. Gerry was down in Z2 Hangar in a meeting with LCdr. John Doherty, the Station AEO. While looking out the window of Doherty's office, Gerry happened to glance over at a number of surplus Swordfish aircraft parked off the side of the nearest runway, still awaiting disposal. He was surprised to see that the engines were being dismantled by some industrious labourers equipped with a truck mounted gantry (crane). Gerry said, "John why are you removing the engines from the Swordfish?" John replied, "We're not taking those engines out." Gerry then pointed out the activity going on, and to Doherty's consternation the engines were indeed being removed and in full view of anybody that cared to watch! A group of the "pirates" had already trucked off with some of the engines, selling them for scrap to an accomplice in the junk business, and were still busily engaged in the removal of the remainder. I think we were all concerned about the accuracy of the intelligence gathering conducted by this nefarious group, and it was obvious that they had good access to what went on at the air station, since many of the civilian workers on the base had been recruited from their own kin and neighbours from Eastern Passage.

Perhaps the most audacious but fortunately unsuccessful theft was "The case of the purloined bulldozer." One particular day, the Officer of the Watch (OOW) on duty at the main gate adjacent to the highway, noticed a bulldozer operator heading down the road toward the highway. On approaching the barrier, he stopped, waved cheerily and proceeded across the highway to the Marine Section. Sometime later he re-crossed the road and headed back up the hill toward the airfield. This little parade was repeated several times during the day and eventually the operator being readily identified, was waved through the gate each time. As the work for the day was ending, the bulldozer operator was once more heading down the hill to the main exit, only this time he was towing a large grading machine. He almost made it through the gate. Fortunately for us, the duty watch personnel had just changed at the gate and the operator's procession was unexpectedly stopped by the new watch personnel. In spite of great protestations of innocence, he was apprehended. It was subsequently established that the cagey rascal was not only making off with the towed grader, but was also stealing the bulldozer!

One particular unit at the air station that appeared to be involved in a number of dubious activities, was the civilian-manned Works and Bricks Section, responsible for the building maintenance and general repair of all utilities and services. By virtue of this mandate, there was the usual gossip about misuse or the absconding of government material and equipment under the control of the Manager of the section. This gentleman, by the name of Cyril Lemon, was a past master of the technique of getting something done for nothing, but he finally came to grief in a most unexpected manner, at a most inopportune time. This took place while his section was being given a routine inspection by the Department Head from the Halifax Dockyard.

As Gerry Daniel recounts, "I was in the mess just prior to lunch, and received a most agitated call from Mr. Lemon, informing me that his car was immersed in the muddy pond adjacent to the Air Maintenance School hangar. Upon investigation, it transpired that Lemon had taken his car to the Maintenance School and prevailed on one of the ab initio mechanical trainees to conduct a free tune up on the vehicle. This the young lad commenced, but his efforts were short-lived. Apparently, he successfully started the engine from the under the hood, but the car, having been left in gear, then proceeded on its own, lurching over the bank ahead and down into the pond. When Lemon finally arrived to pick up his vehicle, only the top was visible above the water's surface. As can be imagined, there was a considerable degree of activity involved in recovering the vehicle with a mobile crane, which in turn generated a sizeable crowd of snickering goofers. I never saw the car on the air station again, and come to think of it, I don't believe I ever saw Lemon again."

The RCN was pretty well established in all sections of the base now, and as the support infrastructure was being studied and developed, there was the usual number of senior officers visiting from Naval Headquarters. The shortage of suitable aircrew flying clothing was still evident, so the subject was invariably brought to the attention of anybody that would care to listen. One day, a senior Supply Branch Captain was conducting his familiarization tour of the station, and ran across Lt. Harry Swiggum who was then working in the Link Trainer Section. The Captain innocently asked, "Well, how is everything going Swiggum?" Swig's reply came back like a dart. "Things are going just great Sir. Today it's my turn to wear the aircrew watch." Swig possessed the rare gift of inserting an instantaneous humorous response or a comment in a joking vein and it was usually much later (after the laughter) that the impact of any applicable barb was felt for what it was worth. It is amusing to look back on our penchant for the aircrew watches, because they were big, ugly, very seldom worked when most needed, were always being repaired and because the source of supply was the UK, the demand was never satisfied. But our attitude was that they were an aircrew entitlement and we were damn well going to claim them.

While all the various squadron flying activities were taking place on the East Coast, there was a somewhat unusual flying episode that occurred during the summer at the Winter Experimental Establishment (WEE) flight, Edmonton. This involved Lt. Ron Heath who had joined the unit the previous year. Heath in his capacity as Officer-in-Charge of Flight Test, reveled in this job which provided a great opportunity to fly the twenty odd aircraft in the unit, these included the WW2 Lancaster bomber through to the current British piston and jet fighter aircraft in service.

This particular day, he was participating in an air show at Edmonton, flying a Sea Fury as a follow-on to a high speed pass by a Vampire jet fighter piloted by an RCAF colleague. Not to be outdone by the jet, Ron gave it "his best shot", flying before the crowd at the maximum speed he could wring out of the Fury, followed by a violent pull up and a series of vertical upward "twizzles". He com-

This cartoon is the product of the pen of Lt.-Cdr. (P) C. G. "Clunk" Watson and was drawn shortly before his death in an air accident at Toronto on August 23. Lt.-Cdr. Watson was poking a little gentle fun at the RCN (R) pilots who took refresher flying courses at HMCS Shearwater last summer. The cartoon is reproduced by permission of the RCN publication, "The Crowsnest."

Cartoon sketch by Clunk Watson, depicting Seafire first solo by RCN(R) pilot, Summer 1949. Credit "Crowsnest" publication

Mock Crest of Seafire Exhibition Flight, August 1949.
Credit Clunk Watson

pleted his flight, landed and was disconcerted to be accosted by the maintenance engineer, who took him to the Fury and showed him a series of popped wing rivets together with a pair of well wrinkled wings. In short, the aircraft had been stressed well beyond allowable limits. Ron was nonplussed with this revelation of damage and sturdily denied any wrongdoing, insisting that he had merely carried out his normal high speed pass and vertical climb. In any event, the matter was considered unusual and required further investigation, which involved a visit by Ron to the Institute of Aviation Medicine at Toronto. There he was rigorously examined in the Centifruge to determine his tolerance to the effects of "G". After several tests it was established that Ron Heath possessed not only a remarkably high tolerance of seven and a half "G's", but he could absorb it for about 20 seconds without blacking out. This was an unusually high tolerance figure, but after reviewing the results, they were confirmed as being correct. Ron, as a consequence was cautioned to exercise prudence whilst engaged in high speed manœuvres involving excessive "G" forces. As far as can be determined, he may well be the only pilot to have flown the rugged Sea Fury to such a wing bending degree and lived to tell about it.

On 23 August 1949, a shocking accident befell the specially formed group of 10 Seafires known as "Watson's Circus" under command of LCdr. Clunk Watson. This team had been selected for the RCN aerial display at the Canadian National Exhibition, Toronto and upon arrival at Malton airport commenced rehearsing, with the lead flight busily polishing their aerobatic act. The number two in the flight, Lt. A.C. "Chuck" Elton, struck the aircraft tail of the leader Clunk Watson with his Seafire wing while they were executing a low-level formation barrel roll, a difficult aerial manœuvre, requiring considerable practice and skill. There was no opportunity for either occupant to bale out, and the two aircraft crashed near the Malton airport, instantly killing both pilots. It is ironic to note that highly experienced Seafire pilot, Cdr. Mike Crosley, RN, some 35 years later discusses in his book, "They Gave Me A Seafire" the stability problems the Royal Navy encountered with the Seafire Mk XV when it entered service. He specifically describes the lateral controllability difficulties and associated instability of the aircraft which occurred at high speed, and during major throttle changes. Co-incidently, he goes on further to state that the only Seafire in which he would carry out a formation barrel roll, was in the earlier and much more responsive and docile Seafire Mk III.

Crosley, as a matter of interest, spoke well of his wartime Canadian Seafire squadron pilots in his book, and mentioned both their skill and enthusiasm. One of the four Canadians serving in the squadron was twenty-one year old S/Lt. Glenford "Bid" Bedore, RNVR, from Arnprior, Ont. He was unfortunately killed on 24 July 1945, when the wings of his Seafire tore off as he pulled out of a dive during an attack on Japanese targets at Suta, Japan. In 1949, the remaining three Canadian fliers, ex S/Lts. P.H. Stock and W.J. Losee and, now Lt. Neville Geary, RCN, thoughtfully dedicated a memorial to their lost comrade at the Anglican Church at Arnprior.

The Malton accident impacted heavily on Canada's Naval Aviation, not only with the death of two pilots, but with the significant loss of Clunk Watson, one of the most capable, brightest and promising leaders of the fledging Air Branch. It was a sad, ironic ending for Watson, as it had previously been for Tattersall. Each had survived the many operational hazards of the FAA at war, serving with distinction, only to be struck down in peacetime flying accidents. At that particular time, other than Jim Hunter, there were no other perceived leaders with equivalent flying experience and stature to assume an active leadership flying role in RCN aviation. In spite of this tragic and upsetting accident, the Seafire Flight continued with their airshow for the duration of the National Exhibition, under the able leadership of Lt. Bill "Chiefie" Munro. This act reflected great credit on all those involved, and was an outstanding example of the gung ho spirit of endeavour currently prevailing in the young Air Branch.

Personnel changes again took place, with the command of *Shearwater* being assumed by Captain E.W. Finch-Noyes from Capt. Fraser-Harris in August 1949. Command of 19 fighter CAG also changed in September, passing to Acting LCdr. V.J. Wilgress the CO of 803 squadron. He replaced Jim Hunter who had led the CAG since first forming up in July 1947, having gone through the difficult startup and workup phases with new aircraft. Acting LCdr. N. "Nibs" Cogdon assumed command of 803 squadron.

Also in September, after some 18 months of protracted negotiations between the RCN and the RCAF, approval was granted by the

Naval Board for the formation of an Air Accident Investigation and Prevention Section (AIPS) at Naval Headquarters. This proposal had first been made in March 1948, by Lt. Ted Davis and Lt. A/E Adrian "Ade" Phillips, who had perceived such a requirement for the expanding Naval Aviation Branch. In an unfortunately justifiable sense, a cynic might say that the initial high accident rate of Canadian Naval Aviation was in itself justification for creation of such a section.

In practice, the type of flying being conducted by the RCN was far more readily identifiable to that of the USN and the RN, and it was both logical and appropriate that such commonality would be better served by establishing a separate naval air Accident Investigation and Prevention Section (AIPS), modelled along the lines of the other navies. This would enable the RCN to exchange similar naval flying statistics and operating data, which could be much more readily compared and applied, than that provided under the auspices of the RCAF Accident Investigation Branch. This is not to suggest in any way that the RCAF unit was not capable and efficient in its assigned responsibilities. It was evident however, that it was naturally orientated for the specific requirements of the RCAF, which in many ways had little knowledge of, or interest in, naval air operations. More specifically, the RCAF was not yet engaged in flying first line operational aircraft, and had no knowledge of the specialized type of carrier air operations currently being exercised by the RCN. This in itself more than adequately justified such a separate Naval Section.

This proposed separate unit was strongly opposed by the senior ranks of the RCAF, which naturally did not wish to see any erosion of their overall aviation jurisdiction and responsibilities. Fortunately, common sense and the utter logic of the proposal prevailed, and the new section was established. Davis and Phillips spent nearly six months sorting out the many details of their new assignments, working closely with their opposite numbers in the RCAF. The job specifications were highly detailed and included: investigating accidents; writing up modifications to aircraft and equipment; revising operating procedures; introducing safety regulations; analyzing accident trends with accompanying statistics; and not least of all, the publishing of a quarterly magazine dealing with accidents and their prevention.

After the AIPS was in full operation, the staff was eventually doubled to two pilots and two engineers, with the status and title being changed to the Directorate of Flight Safety. The value of such an organization soon became readily apparent at the squadron level, where safety publications from both the USN and RN commenced to be regularly distributed, and Flight Safety Officers were established in each squadron. Although the Naval Flight Safety Directorate remained separate from their RCAF counterpart, the two groups worked closely together over the years in analyzing and investigating aviation problems of mutual interest and concern.

There was a humorous anecdote involving Ted Davis on one occasion when he was involved in an accident investigation, which required him to remain overnight in a small town in one of the New England States. Apparently there was little in the way of accommodation at the location, so he arranged to spend the night at a private home. The next morning, Ted paid a modest sum for his overnight lodging to the lady who owned the house, and as service custom dictates, he asked for the required receipt. To his great amusement, his duly signed and dated receipt read: "Received from Mr. E. Davis, $5.00 in payment for sleeping with me one night."

On 11 October 1949, an accident took place with the ditching of a naval aircraft, which had some subsequent humorous twists. Bill Munro and Harry Swiggum were each delivering an Anson (twin engined WW2 trainer) from Saint John, N.B. to *Shearwater*, and encountered bad weather which closed in on them, both ahead and behind, in spite of a more encouraging forecast. They were forced to climb on top of the cloud, but were still faced with the eventual problem of having to get back down through it and hopefully pinpoint their position. After becoming visually separated, they each experienced a series of problems too numerous to mention. Swig finally made it into RCAF Station Greenwood just as it was getting dark. He does recall cheerfully piping up to Munro, saying he could see car lights and familiar landmarks, namely the welcome sight of the Bay of Fundy and that he was going to land at Greenwood. Swig always remember Munro's disgruntled reply was, "You lucky bastard!" Munro obviously not so lucky, running short of fuel, facing deteriorating weather, darkness, and running out of options, elected to carry out a night ditching in Lunenburg harbour, about 50 miles short of his destination. This, he skilfully accomplished in spite of all the unfavourable conditions involved in such a dubious venture.

The ensuing Court Martial will always be remembered as one of the more hilarious on record. Bill Munro was the lone Defendant - primarily because his Anson was sitting in Lunenburg harbour and Swig's wasn't. There were four charges involved: violating visual flight rules (VFR); flying without due care in the face of deteriorating weather; hazarding Her Majesty's aircraft; and carrying a dog aboard the aircraft. This last one was the real tickler, because Lt. Harrington, a pilot on leave with his cocker spaniel, had bummed a ride in Munro's aircraft. (Which Harrington no doubt later regretted). There was only one parachute in the aircraft, which, when they were obviously getting into big trouble, Bill Munro graciously offered to his passenger. This was declined by Harrington, presumably because he wasn't too keen on jumping out of an aircraft in the dark of night, (and he didn't want to leave his doggie).

At the Court Martial, the Prosecutor was Captain Finch-Noyes, assisted by whom he thought was his prize witness, Commander M. "Boogy" Johnstone, an RN aviator on loan, and the Commander (Air) at *Shearwater*. The counsel for the Defendant was Roland Ritchie, whose ability and reputation for successfully defending errant airmen was well established. He immediately tore the prosecution's case to shreds by quoting from the Station Flying Orders, issued by Johnstone, which on examination proved to be so contradictory and confusing in selected passages, that they completely undermined the prosecution's case. Captain Finch-Noyes, seeing his arguments going down the tube, rallied somewhat by concentrating his prosecution efforts on the fourth charge - the doggie. Ritchie ran away with that one by saying that there was nothing in the Flying Orders that said a dog could not be carried in an aircraft. The Prosecutor however, did locate an obscure section in the Flying Orders stating that livestock shall not be carried in Her Majesty's aircraft. Ritchie skilfully countered with the argument that no evidence had been presented to the Court to suggest that the dog was dead or alive. (Alive it was, because it too arrived ashore in the rescuing fish boat following the ditching.)

Bill Munro well remembers that part of the trip, because he heaved the dog aboard the fish boat from the half submerged aircraft. He also recalls that the terrified animal dived deep into a pile of fish to hopefully get away from all the undue stress and excitement. As

Bill stated some forty years later, he knew there was going to be a bit of a stink about the ditched Anson, but he hardly needed the fishy smell of the dog all night in the motel to remind him of it!

In any event, the prosecution's case was now in tatters, and the Members of the Court had no option but to dismiss all charges, albeit mainly on technical grounds. Swig, in the meantime had passed the proverbial hat around the assembled audience at the Court Martial, collecting the princely sum of $500. This was enough to pay Ritchie's fee, and we all happily adjourned to the bar. Roland Ritchie incidently was subsequently elevated to the Supreme Court of Canada, serving as a member of that distinguished body for many years.

It was mid October 1949 that *Magnificent* cleared the dry dock at St. John, and as part of her refit, an alternative DLCO/LSO platform had been fitted, in order to effect the transformation to the USN landing technique. As an interim step, it was decided that the 18 CAG Fireflies would operate using a modified British approach technique, suitable for the British aircraft, while utilizing the standard USN signals.

A change of command of *Magnificent* also took place in October with Commodore K.F. Adams taking over from Commodore Miles, the Executive Officer Cdr. Piers having been replaced by Cdr. A.G. (Gus) Boulton in the previous June. The carrier sailed from Halifax 17 November, and deck landing training commenced. Although there were minor deck accidents, the landings went much better, using the American signals and the modified British approach/landing technique, but the carrier qualifications were interrupted by the receipt of a signal directing *Magnificent* to carry out a search for a missing B29 aircraft.

On that particular day there was a heavy pitching deck, and since the Fireflies were doing a free deck takeoff, the critical timing of the launch of each aircraft into the swell was not always easy to predict. Shel Rowell, and Bert Mead, who launched him, both recall the unnerving view of the carrier's bow unexpectedly dipping down into the swell instead of up, as Rowell's accelerating Firefly trundled downhill on the takeoff. The weather was also generally poor in the search area, and the limited endurance of the Fireflies was an additional problem. Bill Babbitt recalls the visibility was quite bad on returning to the carrier, and was having difficulty locating the ship. Lt. Jack Beeman, the observer suddenly announced he could see *Magnifi-*

cent, so Babbitt wheeled around at wavetop level as directed, and lined up for a landing approach, only to find to his chagrin that Beeman's carrier was a scruffy old tanker. They finally found *Magnificent*, but by this time the sea state was much higher and getting back aboard was a problem. The trick was to find a short period when the pitching deck briefly steadied up, and Doug Peacocke, the LSO had his hands full trying to get everybody aboard. This was further complicated by three landing accidents, and this took time to clear away the wreckage. After several wave off approaches, the last aircraft finally managed to get aboard and flying was cancelled for the rest of the day.

Rowell, flying a Mk V Firefly, also remembers that on the second day, the eight plane Firefly searchers spent so much time forming up before setting out on a time-consuming search pattern, that considerable valuable time and fuel were wasted. In actual fact, the aircraft unknowingly flew right over the downed survivors who were frantically waving at the passing searchers. After a fruitless two hour sortie, the aircraft were low on fuel, and returned. It was only after the last aircraft had landed that the plane guard *Haida* was detached a distance of some 14 miles to an area where an orbiting B17 had since sighted the survivors. The diversion of the aircraft for the search and the subsequent rescue although necessary, and was of some training value, did restrict the work up of the CAG flying program, and for the month at sea from 18 November to mid December, the average flying per crew was less than 12 hours with only 7 deck landings. The longest sortie, which occurred during the search for the B29, was no more than 2 hours and 45 minutes. Lt. Bert Mead recalls a rather disquieting incident that took place prior to the carrier sailing in November, which no doubt had an adverse affect on the servicing of the new Fireflies. Now that the Mk V Fireflies were embarked, the provision of adequate aircraft spares and gear was essential to keep the aircraft properly supported. Bert remembers seeing Lt. Mike Patterson, one of the CAG Air Engineers, watching despondently as the carrier sailed, adhering to a rigid departure time, leaving a significant load of late arriving spare Firefly parts sitting on the jetty, which could not be hoisted aboard before sailing. It would appear that overall importance of operating aircraft, was not yet being fully recognized, and a tendency still existed on the part of the carrier's executive to maintain an inflexible and established ship's schedule, regardless how it affected the ability to fly and maintain aircraft.

Air maintenance trainees were now joining the Air Branch in a regular stream, and one such member was Ordinary Seaman Roger Campbell who had previously joined *Shearwater* in July, but as his Air Rigger course was delayed, he ended up temporarily in a "manual party", a squad which basically spent their time cleaning up around the air station. He was later attached to 825 squadron employed for odd air jobs within the squadron, and was aboard with them for the cruise in November. His assignment was cleanup work in the scullery section (dish washing area) of the main galley, and he most vividly recalls a neat little scam that was being operated by the scullery workers. This involved the dumping of unclaimed surplus rum issue, which once mixed with water, must by regulation be discarded. It was customary to do this by chucking it down the sump under the dish washer. The scullery staff had modified the dumping process, by installing a freshly scrubbed bucket in the sump covered by a similarly well cleaned grate over the sump. As the rum was dumped through the grate, it was neatly intercepted by the waiting bucket. To forestall any danger of detection, the dishwasher was flashed up, just prior to the rum disposal, effectively screening the area with clouds of steam. The waylaid rum was later appreciatively consumed by the artful scullery staff.

In November 1949, the 19 CAG pilots having returned to Rivers, commenced ferrying their recently modified Furies back to *Shearwater*. The Centaurus engine modification program was extensive, and yeoman work was carried out by the maintenance staff under the hard-working and capable supervision of Chief Petty Officer Wiwcheruck. Lt. Hal Fearon who had been detached to Rivers from the Winter Experimental Flight, was assigned the responsibility to conduct the test flights and acceptance of the modified aircraft which involved considerable flying tests and close liaison with the Bristol Company engine representatives.

It was during the period that the Furies were grounded, that Peter Wiwcharuck had some rather interesting moments with the CAG Commander Jim Hunter, which also had a humorous side. As Peter recalls, "We were given approval for a squadron-level test flight following the engine modifications. The ground crew were excited over what we had accomplished and worked hard to get all the aircraft ready for test flights the next day. Just at "Secure" time, Jim Hunter came and said he wanted to test fly his aircraft THAT EVENING! I couldn't believe it! Everything was set up for the next day. In spite of protest ... more silent than open, Jim's aircraft was rolled out ... He climbed in and took off 'into the blue'. He did his basic test at the safe altitude ... then apparently decided to show the Army how the Navy flies. He put on quite a 'one-aircraft' air show! After he landed we pushed the aircraft into the hangar and closed the door. Jim no doubt knew that all the oil filters would have to be pulled and cleaned...and the oil changed. The engine would need a complete inspection, oil checked for metal particles and the aircraft grounded until the checks were done. Jim walked away without saying anything. I thought it would be a terrible situation if the next day all the pilots could take-off, except the Group Commander because his aircraft was grounded -BY HIM. I called my faithful crew together, we went into the hangar and spent the rest of the night completely servicing Jim's Fury. Thinking back a bit to incidents in Ireland and *Shearwater*, I figured I owed Jim a bit of 'stress'! Here was my opportunity to square away some anxious moments in a peaceful manner. We parked Jim's aircraft the next morning away from the flight line and opened up all the cowlings...placed a 45 gallon drum under the engine clearly indicating that the oil was being changed. When Jim arrived he examined the aircraft log book and it recorded the aircraft was unserviceable for oil change and filter inspection. Jim changed colour a couple of times, said nothing and commenced walking up and down like a caged tiger. I was bursting inside, both with pity for his agony and with joy over the fact that he was dancing to MY music. Shortly after, when all the other pilots were getting ready for start up, Jim came in and asked rather meekly, 'When will my aircraft be ready?' I pretended to be busy and answered 'I'm not sure'. In the meantime we had got the aircraft all cowled up, moved the aircraft to the flight line and then presented Jim with the signed log book. He looked at it for a minute, then obviously emotionally touched, said 'I knew you wouldn't let me down.' Suddenly I became aware that Jim Hunter was still the CO and I was still a Chief, and he ultimately had the last word!"

There was obviously a considerable degree of hidden mutual

respect between Jim Hunter and Peter Wiwcharuck because Hunter subsequently made arrangements for Peter to go to school full-time and complete his grade 12 as a prelude for being recommended for commission in 1950. Peter always felt that Hunter in spite of his officially austere manner, was a kind and rather emotional man and loved and respected him for that.

One trip back for the Furies from Rivers had its moments of excitement, when on 4 December, a group of 5 Furies with Vic Wilgress leading, were approaching Greenwood, N.S. The weather had started to turn sour around Saint John, NB. and the conditions were rapidly deteriorating upon approaching Greenwood. Without warning, the leader suddenly made an abrupt turn to starboard, his 4 wingmen were caught off guard, and all were forced to scatter, (every man for himself). One of them, Lt. Doc Schellinck, elected to climb and finally broke clear at about 25000 feet, and all five of the aircraft were forced to fly either over, in and under the cloud, until finally making it individually into RCAF Station Greenwood. The Sea Fury had only minimal navigation aids fitted at that time, so encountering instrument flying conditions as a formation group, was decidedly hazardous. The pilots' overall lack of instrument flying experience on the aircraft and the fact that this flight of aircraft was unable to maintain visual flight, had penetrated cloud illegally in a controlled airspace without clearance or an instrument qualification, was just begging for trouble. The lesson resulting from the previous unfortunate experience of the Seafires while returning from Rivers did not appear to have been absorbed. It is no wonder that the commercial airline pilots landing at *Shearwater* were getting a bit twitchy, as they made their standard instrument approaches, being more than somewhat concerned about the possibility of encountering naval aircraft milling around in marginal weather.

In spite of the run of bad luck and problems with the Sea Fury engines, there was the occasional bit of good publicity concerning the aircraft. One in particular, was a flight of two Sea Furies flown by Ray Creery and Eddy Myers from Toronto's Malton airport to *Shearwater*. They made the 825 mile trip at 20,000 feet in a record time of 1 hour and 54 minutes, averaging a ground speed of 435 miles per hour, which was duly recounted in the Halifax Chronicle-Herald newspaper.

Although the Naval Air Branch was expanding and developing steadily, the year ended generally on rather a flat note as a result of the number of fatal accidents; the various incidents resulting from the 19 CAG engine problems and the deck landing fiasco with the Fireflies aboard the carrier *Saipan*. All these factors adversely affected morale and reduced the flying intensity, together with the overall effectiveness of the squadrons' workup programs. Nobby Westwood recalls that following completion of his Operational Training on Seafires, he only flew a total of 58 Fury hours from May 1949 to December 1949, during his tour as a pilot in 19 CAG. The Firefly CAG fortunately fared better during the year, averaging about 170-180 hours per pilot in each squadron, but regrettably with only a limited amount of the all important carrier operational flying time.

On 13 December 1949, the first Naval Aviation Officers' Conference was held at Naval Headquarters. The Conference was opened by Commodore C.N. Lentaigne, the Assistant Chief of Naval Staff (Air), (ACNS Air), and he optimistically described an encouraging year ahead for Canadian Naval Aviation, summarizing the state of the Branch in the Conference Minutes, which were highlighted as follows:

"There has been a definite strengthening of the position of Naval Aviation during the past year. Headquarters organization has been changed to include ACNS (AIR) as a full time member of the Naval Board. In addition to the Director of Naval Aviation (Capt. H.C. Rolfe, RN) has been added the new Director of Air Logistics. The Air Supply Directorate is now a separate unit and no longer a part of a larger Supply Directorate. This should result in an improvement in the stores situation at an early date."

Accident statistics since 1947 showed there has been a steady increase in flying hours accompanied by a decrease in the accident rate:

Year	Flying Hours	Accident Rate per 1000 Landings
1947	3,800	5.6
1948	6,555	4.7
1949	7,208*	3.9

*This figure indicates that the total for 1949 will be approximately 9010 hours.

Air station improvements include a new control tower to be commenced in 1950.

A new barrack block for the men will commence building in the spring of 1950.

Clarification of the relationship between civil aircraft companies and the RCN is being hastened."

The foregoing summary was encouraging for Naval Aviation, particularly with regard to the approved new construction at *Shearwater*, which was still very short of adequate facilities. The comparative summary of flying hours and the accident rate was particularly significant, observing that over the three year period, the flying intensity had tripled while the accident rate had dropped by one third. These figures bear out once again, the importance of the direct relationship between flying hours per pilot and proficiency, resulting in a reduced accident rate. The already improved flow of spare aircraft parts and the increased numbers of trained maintenance personnel obviously also played a large part in the dramatic changes over the three years.

A rather depressing summary of aircraft availability was also presented during the meeting, which estimated that only 8 Mk 1 Fireflies and 10 Mk V Fireflies would be available on the first line squadron establishment basis, with the Mk 1 Fireflies actually at the point where they were becoming uneconomical to repair. Encouragingly it was mentioned by ACNS (Air) that the proposal to purchase USN Avengers would be coming before Cabinet shortly, which must have raised spirits considerably.

A rather significant observation was made by the Staff Officer Air Personnel to the effect that there was already a shortage of trained air personnel which was aggravated by an ongoing tendency to accept new commitments before the approval had been given to increase the aviation complement. The fact that already 11% of the total naval complement was now composed of aviation personnel, indicated just how unrealistic it had been in 1945 to assume that Naval Aviation could simultaneously meet the manning requirements of the air station and the carrier, while being restricted to this percentage level.

Planned flying for 1950, was to commence with a major carrier air training program for 18 CAG, consisting initially of a cruise to Bermuda with the Fireflies. 825 squadron, outfitted with 10-12 of the new Mk V Fireflies was at a reasonable strength with 12 pilots, but 826 squadron equipped with the old Mk I Fireflies, many which had

18 CAG Fireflies on line at Shearwater, Winter 1949. Credit B. McArther

Three of RCN Winter Experimental Establishment personnel at
Watson Lake Alberta, January 1950. L-R Bert Mead, Don Jones, and
Hank Arnsdorf. Credit E.M. Davis

19 CAG Sea Fury pilots at Shearwater, Spring 1950.
Credit George Westwood

been in service since 1946-47, had a maximum of only 8-10 aircraft, with about 10 pilots. Indeed, the reduced aircraft complement of 826 squadron was mentioned in passing by Cdr. Boogy Johnstone at a general aircrew meeting discussing the proposed operating schedule for the new year. Johnstone, in answering a question from me about plans for replacement aircraft, described 826 as a "lame duck squadron" which unduly miffed John Roberts, the squadron Commanding Officer. Roberts was even more put out, when I identified myself as a member of 826 by blurting out, "Yes Sir, I know. I am in it." Needless to say I was "really in it" with Roberts after that innocuous little exchange.

Flying intensity increased as the month of January went by, which was highlighted by a combined 18 Group strike on RCAF Station Greenwood on 6 January 1950, which commenced with a moment of temporary confusion. Captain Finch-Noyes, the Captain of *Shearwater*, a kindly man who showed great interest in the station flying activities, had expressed his desire to go along on the air strike, so he was placed in the observers seat of my aircraft. Just before the Group began the mass takeoff, Terry Goddard the 18 CAG commander called me on the radio, which was very garbled and said, "Your passenger is on the button." I could not contact the Captain on the radio, so my first thought was that he had inexplicably managed to climb out of the rear seat of my aircraft, and was now standing on the runway button where we were all lined up. Not being able to see him, I was just in the throes of climbing out to see what the hell was going on back there. Meantime, Goddard had climbed out of the back of his aircraft and was running my way making frantic motions toward the observer's cockpit. Only then did I realize that Finch-Noyes had unknowingly put his foot on the floor transmit button in the rear seat, and in so doing had blanked all radio transmissions, thereby preventing the mass take off and delaying the grand departure for the strike.

The rest of the month for 18 CAG was spent on ADDLS, and general tactical training for each squadron. The 18 CAG squadrons in their assigned role of fighter reconnaisance aircraft, also spent a considerable part of their flying time carrying out aerobatics, low flying and formation flying.

It was about this time, that Lts. Don Knox and Bob Cocks of 825 squadron had a close call. As Shel Rowell remembers, Cocks was flying formation on Knox, and lost sight of the aircraft in the sun while changing flight positions. The first inkling Knox had that something was amiss, began as his Firefly propellor commenced sawing away on something obscured under the front of the aircraft. And indeed it was! It was the fin and rudder of Bob Cocks' Firefly. Apparently Cocks had inadvertantly pulled ahead and taken the lead from under Knox's nose, thereby having his tail thoroughly chewed up for his efforts. Both arrived safely back at *Shearwater*, but there was a lot of "Ooohing" and "Ahhhing" from the CAG bystanders at the "near miss" graphically evident by the badly damaged rudder on Bob's aircraft.

On 13 January, all aircraft of 18 Firefly CAG were lightered aboard *Magnificent* and the first phase of the workups commenced with the operating period off Bermuda, where the group flew ashore to Kindley the US Air Force base on the island. This was an excellent field from which to operate, and provided the pilots with a final opportunity to complete their ADDLS before going aboard for initial deck land-ings. The US Air Force personnel were co-operative hosts during our period ashore, but our low-level flying over the airfield early one Sunday morning unfortunately bothered the sleeping residents, creating a bit of a stir. This was aggravated somewhat when Lt. Hal Welsh pranged during an ADDL and wrote off the undercarriage of his aircraft. The subsequent deck landing qualifications however, went fairly well, all the aircraft flying aboard from Kindley, the carrier then departing for Halifax, arriving there on 2 February. Although the limitation of the 25 knot maximum speed of *Magnificent* had not yet posed a specific restriction, it was evident that in conditions of no natural wind, the operating of the Mk V Fireflies would be marginal under some sea and aircraft weight conditions. Under similar wind conditions however, it was obvious that the Sea Furies would continue to experience problems with their higher approach and landing speeds. A no natural wind situation in southern climes is quite prevalent and on later cruises as the Furies began more concentrated carrier flying, the inadequacy of the ship's speed was very much in evidence, necessitating the cancellation of a number of Sea Fury sorties.

The carrier sailed again on 13 February 1950, this time for an extended two months operating period in the Caribbean. The flying initially concentrated on completing the deck landing training (DLT), then shifted to instrument flying, aerobatics, fighter interception training and navigation exercises. Then additional sorties were carried out shadowing the fleet, followed by squadron strikes on the ships. This was all planned as part of the workups to concentrate on more advanced ship-air exercises and tactical use of aircraft prior to working with the USN Task Force and their carrier aircraft later in the month.

On 18 February, the first RCN peacetime carrier fatality occurred when Lt. Les "Crash" Peever of 826 squadron was killed when taking off on a normal free launch. Peever was a likeable, carefree type, but with an unfortunate inclination to have a somewhat reckless attitude to his flying. This particular accident was very much avoidable, but there was an ongoing personal flying competition between Lt. Hank Utting and Peever, and the name of the game was to see who could get airborne from the carrier deck in the shortest distance. Utting was a loner, a very determined and over-aggressive type of pilot who had already achieved a certain notoriety. For some strange reason best known to himself, he periodically engaged in an aerial game of "chicken" by making unorthodox, sometimes head on passes at the other naval aircraft. In January of 1949, he had been involved in a minor mid-air collision when four Sea Furies carried out a mock attack on two Fireflies. Utting flying a Firefly was reprimanded for what was described as "carrying out a dangerous manœuvre" and Doc Schellinck, one of the Fury pilots, was admonished for "not keeping a sufficient lookout". Luckily both aircraft were able to land safely, but from all accounts, they came so close that the rear view mirror was knocked off the Firefly. Ironically, Hank Utting would die seven years later, seated as a passenger in an RCAF Mitchell bomber which spun in out of control near Ottawa, while being flown in instrument conditions by a senior RCAF officer.

The particular type of reckless horseplay going on between Utting and Peever was not easy to curb unless quickly detected. In this particular case, Peever pulled his Firefly up very quickly off the deck, reached a very nose high attitude, the aircraft torque stalled to the right then crashed nose first into the sea, sinking inverted alongside the starboard side of the carrier. Lt. Roy de Nevers, the Senior Pilot of 826 squadron, remembers this accident clearly. Roy happened to witness Peever's take off, and noticed as the aircraft's tail wheel passed over the after edge of the forward lift, that the tail elevator of the aircraft made a sharp upward movement, the tail wheel then hitting the deck, as the already airborne aircraft climbed steeply away.

Peever, obviously knocked unconscious, went down with the aircraft. His observer, Chief Petty Officer Peter Arnoldi miraculously survived, and clearly remembered his traumatic experience. Peter, who had a dry sense of humour, later in a whimsical vein, described regaining consciousness, but by that time, he was so deep and it was so dark that he could neither see the surface of the water nor even know which way was up. He managed with difficulty to extricate himself from the observer's cockpit of the rapidly plummeting aircraft, but he then literally did not know in which direction to swim. He did know however, the downward path of the aircraft was most certainly not the right one. The floatation in his Mae West gave him some guidance and he began the agonizing journey back up to the surface. Peter claims he was down so far, that he had to stop from time to time on the way back up to rest his arms. I was airborne at the time of the accident and was directed to search the sea surface for possible survivors. I had completely given up hope, when all of a sudden, a figure popped to the surface, and there was Arnoldi! We do know that he was underwater for several minutes, and it was only his remarkable ability to hold his breath and his hobby of underwater swimming that saved him. This unfortunate accident cast a pall on the ship and squadrons, and could not help but bring to mind the airmans' age old saying, "Flying itself is not inherently dangerous, but it is terribly unforgiving!"

A social visit to Charleston, South Carolina was a brief but pleasant respite, and on departure the two squadrons had a CAG flypast of 14 aircraft over the city. Light winds later prevailing in the area, curtailed flying to a degree with the Mk V Fireflies until heading further south we picked up the NE Trades at Mona Passage. A good day of flying took place on 1 March when we launched 14 aircraft to carry out a photo reconnaissance of the islands off the south coast of Santo Domingo. This exercise organized by our army CBAL detachment, turned out to be more interesting than we had anticipated, when we spied a small coastal gunboat anchored in a secluded cove in one of the islands. This promptly attracted the attention of most of the pilots who responded with a series of enthusiastic simulated rocket and strafing attacks. This action must have created some uneasiness amongst the gunboat crew, because in no time at all they had gone to "Action Stations", uncovering machine guns and manning their deck cannon. We lost interest in them at that point and carried on with the exercise. As the cruise continued, the overall flying intensity increased dramatically with the good weather and excellent serviceability of aircraft, the number of sorties increasing often to two per day for each crew.

Following this period of intensive flying, we then had a welcome rest and recreation stop at Havana, Cuba, which although under the corrupt President Batista regime, continued to be the liveliest and most popular city in the Caribbean. A very attractive place to visit was the Bacardi Rum factory outlet in downtown Havana, where, as a consequence of a large purchase of rum by the carrier's wardroom (at fifty cents a bottle), unlimited rum drinks were provided all day long "on the house".

The best flying of the cruise commenced on 16 March, when the Canadian ships now formed as Task Group 22.1, commenced Caribex 50 with an aerial search for the USN ships of Task Force 21. This heavy force was a fairly impressive array of seapower, consisting of the Essex class carrier *Philippine Sea*, the battleship *Missouri*, five cruisers and a screen of 16 destroyers. The fleet exercise was the first opportunity for us to engage a major group of ships in simulated combat, and was the highlight of the cruise. The exercise commenced with 825 squadron conducting a series of low level search patterns for the "enemy force", while maintaining radio silence. Aboard the *Philippine Sea* were upwards of 60 aircraft comprising squadrons of the speedy little interceptor, the Grumman Bearcat (Hellcat replacement) and the new Douglas Skyraider dive bomber. The Skyraider was particularly noteworthy because it was the first naval aircraft to have the awesome capability of being able to carry it's own weight of external stores. Opposing this powerful concentration of aircraft were the 22 somewhat dated Firefly aircraft of *Magnificent*.

Lt. Shel Rowell, flying with observer Jack Stokes, the CO, claimed the first sighting of the USN ships which were well protected from surprise attack by the dispersal of their destroyers as picket ships well on the outside of the screen for the major units. Flying at wave top level, the crew of the Firefly could however, see the superstructure of the fleet units several miles away on the horizon. Flying so low, the crew avoided radar detection and using a difficult to detect morse code transmission, disclosed the USN fleet position, which was in excess of 100 miles distant from the Canadian ships. Receipt of the message was the 'go' signal for the Fireflies of the small strike force of eight aircraft from 826 squadron.

Lt. Bruce Torrie was aboard *Magnificent* in his capacity as Fighter Direction Officer (FDO), but since the fighter squadron of Furies were not available for this particular cruise, due to the delays caused by the Centaurus engine difficulties, Bruce had considerable spare time on his hands. Just prior to the exercise, he was fiddling with the radio frequencies in the Fighter Direction Room and noted the callsign "Onionskin", of the *Philippine Sea* controlling the Combat Air Patrols (CAP) in protective air cover over the USN force. After listening for some time, Bruce, now familiar with various USN callsigns and procedures, proposed to his Section Head that he initiate some diversionary radio commands from *Magnificent* to confuse the USN "enemy" fighters. This worked like a charm.

Our small strike of 826 Fireflies were not aware of Torrie's activities, since his instructions were being executed on another radio frequency, but as our force approached the US fleet, we were very surprised to see a large swarm of Bearcats turning away from us. Apparently the USN fighter CAP leader queried his controller, and even asked whose directions should he follow, since he was in receipt of contradictory instructions. Bruce in a firm voice directed that all CAP aircraft obey his instructions only - and they did!

This simplified our attack considerably and with all enemy fighters demoralized and heading elsewhere, we attacked. Undetected, I headed for the *Philippine Sea*, flattened out of a dive at 400 knots and roared down the length of the crowded flight deck of the carrier at about 50 feet. It was a naval pilot's dream to conduct a simulated bombing and strafing attack on a large slow-moving carrier with her flight deck crowded with aircraft in various stages of refueling. Our attack took place about 8 AM and we later understood that the American Admiral was just partaking of his breakfast when we raced through his fleet. He was incensed because he initially thought it was his own aircraft beating up the ships, and there had been no warning of an imminent air attack. After the strike, for the 826 Fireflies, it was every man for himself since by that time the Bearcats were all over us like a bad smell. I remember high tailing away right on the deck at full throttle and saw a Firefly flown by Lt. Mike Sandes slightly ahead of me at wave top level, frantically jinking and turning as three Bearcats buzzed around him. We carried out another attack later in the day, which unfortunately did not achieve the same success, since the sky was black with Bearcats as we began our high level attack.

It was about two years later, when I was attending an LSO course at Pensacola, Florida, that I met a USN Lt. by the name of Hal Marr, who had been aboard the *Phillipine Sea* in one of the Bearcat squadrons. When I mentioned being aboard *Magnificent* on the strike exercise, his comment was priceless. He said. "Oh yeah, you were the guys in those Fireflys that were making all those head on passes when we finally caught up with you." I hastened to clarify his comment by indignantly interjecting, "Jeeze when you only have seven or eight aircraft and there are twenty or so Bearcats coming at you, they were all head on passes, because every time we turned to get away, there was always another Bearcat dead ahead coming at us!" He laughingly agreed, saying, "It sure was a hell of a lot of fun."

In the next strike, the Skyraiders with an escort of Bearcats made an impressive attack on the Canadian fleet units. I was flying as part of the CAP for *Magnificent*, in a flight of Fireflys at about 25000 feet and we were vectored by our FDO to intercept the incoming strike of American aircraft. We were given a good intercept vector, but it was all to no avail, because the Skyraiders and escort cruised serenely by us at over 300 knots, and even at full throttle we could not even match their speed. The Americans then successfully carried out a heavy dive bombing attack on *Magnificent* with about 30 Skyraiders and their fighter cover of Bearcats. It was a pity that the Sea Furies could not have been aboard with us for these exercises. It would have been an excellent opportunity for them to form the escort of the strike forces of *Magnificent* against a large carrier, and to have the chance for the Furies to mix with the Bearcats and carry out interceptions against the long range Skyraider strikes. The relative performance of the Sea Fury compared to the two new American aircraft would have been interesting to establish. By and large though, we did luck out flying the obsolete old Fireflies, which performed surprisingly well under the circumstances.

The remainder of the exercise shifted to a combined RCN and USN force, which mounted an air strike against Guantanamo naval base. This was a good exercise in combined operations with the carriers of each navy controlling the other's aircraft. The emphasis then shifted to a simulated overseas movement of carrier forces, which involved RN, RCN and the USN ships including a hunter killer anti-submarine group and a logistic group. The number of sorties for the two squadrons then diminished as the fleets went their separate ways, the Canadian ships proceeding to New York for a recreational stop the first week of April, before heading for Halifax.

This intensive flying period was probably the most rewarding to date for the carrier-based squadrons. Perhaps the most significant contribution to the improved flying rate was the outstanding service-ability, which through hard and dedicated work by the maintenance teams, averaged over 90% aircraft availability for the most important flying phases. Deck landing accidents were minimal, and the greatly improved flying standards achieved, proved without question the importance of planning and maintaining an intensive and sustained flying period in good operating conditions. This was the first requisite to developing a high level of combat readiness.

In summary, the two squadrons had logged over 550 hours and 365 deck landings over the two month carrier embarked period, ending on arrival at Halifax on 14 April. Individually, the crews logged in excess of 30 hours of carrier flying in March alone, and for the first three months of 1950, 826 squadron pilots achieved the greatest increase, averaging over 50 hours of embarked carrier flying. This was a considerable improvement over the individual flying times previous-ly achieved aboard Warrior in a similar time period, and was an encouraging sign of progress in the conduct of air operations at sea.

While those of us in 18 Firefly CAG were enjoying the worldly pleasures of New York in April 1950, a welcome message was received from Naval Headquarters that the Cabinet had approved the acquisition of 75 Avengers from the USN to replace the Fireflies now in service in the RCN squadrons. This decision to purchase American naval aircraft had a major positive impact on the future of the RCN air squadrons, and marked the first step in the shift by the RCN to USN aircraft from the previous "Buy British" policy. As previously mentioned, it had been well recognized that the Fireflies were generally unsuitable in the anti-submarine role and the conduct of all weather day and night carrier operations. Moreover, the $80,000 price tag for the Mk V Firefly was excessive, observing that it was an aircraft with virtually no potential to expand its anti-submarine capability. This alone precluded the aircraft as a viable alternative.

The Avenger on the other hand, had a proven all-weather carrier capability, and its ability to accommodate a crew of three, equipped with the necessary electronic equipment for the ASW role, provided the RCN with the best aircraft currently available. A final clincher was the remarkably generous financial terms offered by the USN, which provided 75 aircraft complete with a full package of spare parts, tools and equipment. The entire cost including all the spares worked out to about $5000 per aircraft. Since the Avenger was also in full operational service in the ASW squadrons of the USN, the Canadian purchase provided an opportunity to establish for the first time, not only a commonality of equipment for carrier operations, but also the opportunity to develop a standard ASW doctrine between the USN and the RCN air squadrons.

LCdr. Dick Bartlett, who was on the Naval Air Staff at Headquarters, recalls a bit of a last minute dither at the Treasury Board level regarding the purchase, as the fiscal year end approached in March 1950. Apparently under the regulations in effect, the Canadian Commercial Corporation, as the purchasing agent, required someone in authority to actually sight the aircraft being purchased and confirm as having done so. With only a couple of days left before the end of the fiscal year, Dick was sent post haste to Washington, where he was ordered by Commodore Lay to proceed immediately to San Diego. There he was met by a staff car and, in company with a USN team of officers, went directly to the Naval Air Station where numerous Avengers were parked in a cocooned status. He had time to open up two of the sealed Avengers, write down the serial number, then scurry to the next commercial flight for Washington to meet the year end deadline. A quick meeting was then held in the Pentagon about two hours before the fiscal deadline, and the serial numbers of the seventy five Avengers "Sighted and accepted" by Bartlett were received and solemnly recorded. Dick laughingly recalled that as he left the meeting, one of the USN officers mentioned in passing, "I hope you realize it is most unlikely that the serial numbers and aircraft you just checked are the ones that the RCN will eventually receive."

The news of the Avenger purchase was a happy announcement for 826 squadron, and five pilots were detached the first week of April from New York to San Diego, California, to temporarily join two USN ASW squadrons currently flying Avengers at the Naval Air Station, North Island. Lt. Harry Swiggum and myself went to VS 25, while 826 squadron CO designate, LCdr. Norm Donaldson, and Lts. Roy de Nevers and Hank Utting proceeded to VS 26. We were there for a three week period, and the hospitality and genuine goodwill of the USN squadron personnel was outstanding. The conversion flying on the Avenger consisted of about 25 hours, including general aircraft handling, formation flying, coupled with rocket firing in the desert air range at El Centro, California. This was all valuable and interesting flying experience, providing us an excellent introduction to the Avenger prior to coming into service in the RCN.

It was also in April of 1950 that a sombre warning came from Naval Board addressed specifically toward naval aviation accidents and flying discipline. The message read as follows:

"The Naval Board views with concern the number of aviation accidents which have occurred in the last year.

2. The evidence is clear that NAS (Naval air station) air discipline is the cause of many accidents and the heavy toll of lives.

3. All pilots are to be informed of the above by their Commanding Officer. He is to impress upon them that rigid air discipline is essential to the safety of personnel. He is further to stress to the senior air specialists their responsibilities in this matter.

4. It is to be emphasized to all officers that it is their duty to report cases of disobedience of Flying Orders and that failure to do so is an offence under Article 96 of The Naval Service Act 1944.

5. Addressees are to ensure that Standing Orders are so framed that they prohibit irresponsible flying, and all infractions of these orders shall be dealt with as serious offences."

The serious tone of the foregoing message, was duly digested, but there was always one wag around to indulge in an inevitable humorous reaction. One particular comment heard was that since the message had clearly meant "There Will Be No More Accidents", then in order to conform and to be "Obedient Servants", we had better stop flying!

There was no doubt that the need existed to tighten up flying discipline, and the quality of Squadron Standing Orders, Air Station Flying Orders, and general Air Doctrine at *Shearwater* left much to be desired. The problems being encountered however, went much deeper than that, and also involved overall command and control, leadership, airmanship and aviation expertise.

Since the formation of Canadian Naval Aviation in September 1945, a tremendous number of problems had to be overcome, and it should be borne in mind that an entire aviation organization had to be created simultaneously, in many instances without adequately trained and experienced personnel. This applied to virtually all air departments, including engineering, electrical, training, logistics/supply, administration, personnel, operations and planning.

LCdr. Wally Tuck, on loan from the Royal Navy, had been the Senior Air Engineer at *Shearwater* since December 1948. He recalls those difficult times during the establishment of the Canadian Naval Air Branch. He considered that many of the problems he encountered were quite predictable, taking into account that a new Branch in any service will experience growing pains.

With his strict Royal Navy background, Tuck found it difficult to accept the familiarity he encountered between the Canadian officers and men. He also felt that there was a general tendency to "run before learning to walk", although he noted that there was no shortage of enthusiasm. He also believed there was a casual, "devil may care" attitude amongst some of the aircrew which resulted in unnecessary casualties in the air. Although he perceived a degree of relative slackness in maintenance procedures, he also noted a positive willingness to learn amongst the air technical trade personnel. He was aware that the logistic system in place left much to be desired, and the lack of commonly used spare parts occurred frequently. The experience of actually running out of aircraft tires and hydraulic fluid was troublesome and he spent considerable time personally seeking suitable alternatives to minimize the AOG (Aircraft grounded) situation.

Tuck's comments were no doubt valid, and a good indication of the problems of having to support operational aircraft flying both afloat and ashore, from a supply source over three thousand miles distant. His points about the relative familiarity between the officers and men are interesting and once again emphasizes the attitude differences between the RN and the RCN, as clearly outlined by Clunk Watson in his testimony at the Mainguy Inquiry. To a certain extent, the areas of perceived slackness in maintenance procedures could be justified because the individual technician often had to improvise, due to a lack of parts and equipment, in order to keep the aircraft in a flying status. Initiative, if properly applied, was in many cases the only way to get the job done and Canadians, generally with their more varied background, did tend to perhaps display more initiative and versatility than their more strictly disciplined Royal Navy contemporaries.

The policy to second Royal Navy fliers to the RCN for senior positions in aviation, was no doubt initially justified to a degree through sheer necessity, since there was only a handful of experienced Canadian naval aircrew who remained in the post-war service, with sufficient seniority and the background to provide adequate leadership. But as Clunk Watson stated at the Mainguy Inquiry, the quality of air personnel selected for loan from the Royal Navy was not only inconsistent, but in some instances it was clearly inferior. This was regrettable, but in the Royal Navy the FAA was going through major cutbacks and many wartime aircrew officers were redundant with no career prospects. Consequently, when an opportunity arose to go to Canada and serve at the higher RCN rates of pay, with a promotion to an acting rank, it provided an attractive incentive for such officers. The problem was further compounded by the difficulty of working with RCN non-flying officers who were not only often ignorant of aviation matters, but also invariably outranked the temporarily assigned RN officers. Observing that the loan period was only for a year or two, there was a natural inclination by the officers involved to avoid "rocking the boat" and maintain relations at a comfortable level during their short period on loan. There were a few in the group who attempted with limited success to exert their proper authority, but if they ran afoul of their opposite RCN officers, it was inevitable that the working relations would deteriorate. In short, it was usually a losing game, and often the course was to choose to try and get along and enjoy the brief tour of duty.

An additional problem was the requirement to create and administer new and comprehensive flying orders which would properly reflect the peacetime requirements of RCN aviation, and also conform to the regulations governing flying in Canada, as prescribed by the Federal Department of Air Services. An up to date and complete set of Station Flying Orders and a well organized air department were both major and immediate requirements. The Commander Flying position at *Shearwater,* filled by an RN officer whose sole experience was gained in the wartime FAA, where such flying procedures and air station organizations had little or no relevence to peacetime naval flying in Canada, further aggravated the situation.

Another difficulty was being encountered at the Senior Pilot, Squadron Commander and Group Commander level. In the peacetime RCN, seniority in rank reigned supreme. Executive officers were encouraged to sub-specialize in aviation as pilots and, following their wings graduation and operational training, were quickly appointed to an RCN air squadron. In some cases after a short squadron tour, with minimal flying experience, they would in many instances be promoted to an Acting rank and then appointed in command of a squadron. With such limited flying experience and often lacking the necessary aviation leadership qualities, this posed decision-making problems, particularly when leading a squadron of pilots, who in many cases had greater experience and proven flying ability. In some instances such hastily promoted officers would as a matter of course be quickly re-appointed to the position of Group Commander. They would finish their tour of flying in a minimum time, then transfer back to pure executive duties, often completely severing their ties with Naval Aviation. Others would emerge much later after being promoted, and actually be appointed back to more senior aviation positions, while all the while lacking the necessary sound aviation background and ability.

On this subject, many years later, Pop Fotheringham stated, "I personally felt a twinge of guilt at being quickly promoted and serving in command of several pilots who, though junior in rank, had considerably more flying experience. However, since the policy was inflexibly controlled by 'the Fishheads', one could only live with the system until the matter resolved itself a few years later." Fotheringham's personal misgivings were unwarranted, because there were a few notable exceptions such as himself and Don Knox, who were able to fully justify this particular type of fast tracking in aviation career planning. They each remained primarily in Naval

Aviation, working their way up through the various aviation levels, taking air courses, gaining valuable flying experience and progressively advancing in key aviation appointments, thereby retaining a close involvement in the branch as it developed. In the years ahead their experience was of considerable value in serving and promoting the cause and future of Naval Aviation.

The determined emphasis on seniority was in the main, a form of direct discrimination against both the ex RCAF pilots and the wartime Canadian RCNVR and RNVR FAA pilots. Often such officers had excellent operational background and considerable flying experience, but lacking seniority in rank and "proper naval background", they were required to serve under squadron commanders whose main qualification for command was seniority.

There was in addition, a degree of recklessness and poor airmanship being displayed by a small number of the pilots, which is to be expected from a large group of adventuresome young men who were the product of expedient wartime training and experience. The fact that they would form part of the nucleus of a newly formed air branch was inescapable, but their lack of overall aviation discipline was not effectively contained, mainly due to the previously described problems, which obviously contributed to the initially high number of avoidable accidents. Fortunately, these difficulties were now beginning to be resolved as the branch evolved, overall flying experience gained, and the more highly qualified Canadian aviation personnel were attaining the seniority level to be appointed to more responsible positions.

At the end of April 1950, there was the usual rotation of squadron command appointments. LCdr. Dick Bartlett assumed command of 18 CAG from LCdr. Terry Goddard and Acting LCdr. Don Knox assumed command of 825 squadron from LCdr. Jack Stokes. In 826 squadron, Acting LCdr. Norm Donaldson assumed command from LCdr. John Roberts. Meanwhile in 19 CAG, Lt. Bill Munro took over command of 883 Fury squadron from LCdr. Ray Creery. Munro was the first officer to be given squadron command while retaining the rank of Lt., and was a classic example of an officer with the necessary flying skills and required leadership qualities to be given the responsibility of command, but, who in the eyes of senior RCN executive non-flying officers, did not hold sufficient rank or seniority to be promoted to the rank of an Acting LCdr.

During the absence of *Magnificent* on the 1950 Spring cruise, the Fury squadrons at *Shearwater* were undergoing extensive advanced workups prior to embarking for carrier operations. From January through to May the squadrons concentrated on flight drills, air to air and ground attacks which included advanced fighter tactics, air to air firing at towed drogue targets, night formation and radar controlled interceptions. Concentration upon simulated carrier landings ashore, using the USN signals, began in February and continued into March. This was an interesting and challenging phase, necessitated by the change to the flying pattern and approach technique of the American carrier landing system.

Lt. O'Rourke, one of the USN Landing Signals Officers seconded to *Shearwater* during the transition phase, was certain that the Fury could approach at an 85 knots airspeed, while still maintaining the constant altitude required by the USN technique. This was about a 5 knots slower speed than that used in the descending British system. There was a fair amount of disagreement on this point, since the Canadians were equally sure this was too slow a speed for the Fury, and uncomfortably close to the aircraft's stalling speed. To the surprise of many, O'Rourke, who had never even flown the Fury, offered to personally demonstrate his theory, which he did much to the surprise and admiration of the other pilots. He skilfully flew around in the pattern literally "hanging on the prop" at 85 knots, as he brought the fighter in for a practice carrier landing. Although he proved his point by his impressive demonstration, it was subsequently agreed that the Sea Fury came down too heavily at the 85K speed, since there just wasn't enough control to flare out for a good three point landing. The undercarriage of the Fury was not built to absorb that high rate of sink, and on impact often bounced or suffered damage. The landing technique finally evolved was an approach at about 88-90 knots with a slightly lower altitude at the "cut" position, the pilot then easing forward on the control column and (hopefully) flaring out into a three point landing.

Although the flying rate of the 19 CAG Sea Fury pilots was still on the low side, it was steadily improving and by the end of May the pilots had averaged between 80-90 hours since the year began.

In August 1950, as part of the on-going exchange of anti-submarine training between the RCN and RN, two Canadian crews, consisting of pilots Lts. Bill Atkinson and Doug Ross with observers Peter Grady and Jack Lewry, were assigned to 815 Royal Navy squadron based at Eglington. This was an advanced tactical unit, testing for the first time, radar detection of transiting snorkelling submarines, using the various radar equipments then in service. Over the three month period, the Canadian crews flying Barracudas, gained excellent experience in detecting the British target submarines in all kinds of weather and sea states. A great rivalry developed between the RN submarine commanders and the searching aircrews, and often considerable controversy arose whether or not the subs had actually been sighted and attacked, the submariners invariably disclaiming any possibility that they had been detected. On one such de-briefing, the captain of one sub vehemently denied they had been sighted and attacked. The decision in this case was most decidedly awarded to the aircraft, when Doug Ross pointedly asked the captain of the submarine in question, if he had been wearing a red sweater at the time of the alleged sighting. The captain finally reluctantly confirmed this was indeed his wearing apparel as the submarine dove to escape detection.

Magnificent sailed on 15 August, with the two Fury squadrons of 19 CAG and 825 Firefly V squadron embarked for a 14 week voyage to Europe, for what was described as a "Diplomatic Cruise", the object being to make visits to specific NATO countries in consolidation of friendship and to establish operational ties with the other NATO navies. From the point of view of a social/diplomatic cruise, the trip was a resounding success involving 12 separate port visits by *Magnificent* and her escorts *Micmac* and *Huron* to ten different countries. As was the usual custom when a good cruise by RCN ships to exotic foreign ports was undertaken, there was a great clamouring of other officers to get in on the deal. *Magnificent* was quickly overcrowded with surplus and unnecessary bodies, and the old seniority game once again came into play, to the extent that Bill Munro as a Lt. was required to give up his assigned cabin as CO. of 883 squadron and bunk in with his squadron pilots.

In comparison to the concentrated flying conducted earlier in the Spring, this Fall cruise was singularly unsuccessful for the embarked squadrons. As it transpired, the majority of the flying was mainly confined to carrier qualifications followed by some limited exercises

803 Sea Fury Squadron aboard Magnificent, Fall 1950. Credit George Westwood, Alex Fox

Group of 18 Firefly CAG aircrew aboard Magnificent Spring
cruise 1950. Credit via Norm Donaldson

826 Squadron pilots at acceptance of first Avenger by RCN,
from USN at NAS Quonset Point, RI. L-R Harry Swiggum, Stu
Soward, Hank Utting, Norm Donaldson, and Roy de Nevers.
Credit via Norm Donaldson

Group of 18 CAG pilots at Shearwater in Summer of 1950, after re-equipping 826 Squadron with newly arrived Avengers. Front row L-R Bill Blatchley, Hal Welsh, Stu Soward, and Charley Bourque. Rear row L-R Fred Townsend, Ken Gibbs, Norm Donaldson, Shel Rowell, and Harry Swiggum. Credit via Norm Donaldson

825 Firefly Squadron aboard Magnificent in Fall of 1950. Credit via Norm Donaldson

Sea Fury being waved off, Magnificent circa 1950.
Credit Alex Fox

Newly arrived Avenger and formating Sea Fury. Note
Avenger still in USN paint and with gun turret fitted.
Credit PA168850, R.E. Quirt

conducted en route to the UK prior to flying off to Eglington.

On 29 August, Lt. Shel Rowell of 825 squadron, provided one of the more "arresting" carrier arrivals. On landing, Shel's Firefly hit and bounced on the main gear, then once more landed, bounced, and then the situation immediately started to deteriorate. Aware that his aircraft's hook had missed all the wires, Shel stuffed the nose down and charged determinedly at the two barriers. As he went over/through them, various aircraft components, ie. the undercarriage and radar dome, were quickly torn off. The aircraft then continued, skidding relentlessly up the flight deck to the forward deck park, where the previously landed Fireflies were being secured. Don Knox who had just landed, was being taxied forward of the barriers when suddenly the eyes of his flight deck director popped wide open. This was followed by a frantic brake signal to Knox, then the man made a precipitous departure and quickly disappeared. Don being somewhat taken aback by the directors unorthodox disappearance, glanced up at his rear view mirror just in time to witness Rowell's trail of unstoppable wreckage heading his way. A lot can happen in five seconds! The final and humorous outcome of this frantic deck activity, was Knox strapped in his Firefly, (where else?) waiting to be parked, staring with anxious disbelief as Shel and his sliding Firefly slowed, and with the benefit of considerable friction, parked alongside him. As it turned out, the only space left on the flight deck was where Rowell's aircraft ended up, and no doubt where he would have been parked anyway. Albeit, admittably in this instance, the aircraft was precariously at rest on the edge of the flight deck with the port wing hanging over the carrier's side.

Flying recommenced aboard *Magnificent* on 19 September with simulated strikes against the Australian carrier HMAS *Sydney*, but the flying intensity dropped considerably as the ships proceeded through confined waters and began making their diplomatic calls on the Scandinavian Countries. The Firefly pilots averaged less than 12 hours and 10 deck landings in the month of September. In October it was even lower, being less than 5 hours and 1-2 deck landings each. The flying totals achieved by the Fury pilots were equally disturbing, each pilot averaging about 11 hours in September, which was mostly ashore, and with only 4-5 deck landings. In October, the results were also discouraging, averaging only 7 hours per pilot and 1-2 deck landings. By this time, there was considerable concern being expressed by the air officers, that the proficiency of some of the less experienced pilots was becoming dangerously low.

Following the visit to the Scandinavian countries the fleet units visited Lisbon the first week in November, where a non-flying disaster occurred aboard *Magnificent* that was a real hoot. Apparently the officers' laundry arrived aboard from the local launderer just before the ships sailed. It was always a favorite ploy of such cleaning establishments in foreign ports to bring the clothing back just before sailing, this way the quality of work done, cannot be detected until after the ship has sailed. In this case at least the laundry was clean, but the entire load for the 120 officers was done up in three big boxes, one labelled collars, one shirts, and the other socks. This load was hoisted by the ship's crane from the jetty and unceremoniously dumped on the flight deck, much to the amusement of the flight deck crew. There were no names on any of the clothing, so all the officers involved had to frantically scrabble through the enormous piles in a futile effort to find something in a familiar size. Perhaps the most luckless one was 825 squadron commander Don Knox, who made the serious error of sending his best wool doeskin uniform to the laundry for dry cleaning. It had been thoroughly washed, dried in the sun and returned in a size that would have been a tight fit on a small chimpanzee!

On 5 November, the pilots were assigned to carry out FCLP's on the runway at Gibraltar. This procedure consisted of flying around "The Rock" (a major obstruction) in a vain effort to get some simulated carrier landing practice. It was hardly rated a success since most of the time, LSO Doug Peacocke was out of sight, his position on the runway well hidden by the enormous hill, until each aircraft came around the corner on final approach.

By now, the pilots of the Fury squadrons were experiencing great difficulty in trying to maintain flying proficiency on their high performance fighters, which were tricky to deck land under the best of conditions. On 9 November, the sensible decision to ground the Sea Fury pilots from further scheduled flying was reluctantly implemented, after several "hairy passes" were made in attempts to get back aboard the carrier. Perhaps the most prophetic indication of the deteriorating situation, was a comic pantomine of the LSO's signalling actions by

Lt. Duke Wardrop, who before being launched, satirically waved through the sequence of "high", "low", "fast", "slow" signals. The forecast of his yet to come landing, was "bang on" in a manner of speaking, because that was the combination of signals he was given on his landing approach, which abruptly terminated when he piloted his Fury straight down the deck and slammed into the barrier.

On a lighter note all was not completely lost, since the hazards of flying had obviously necessitated a few Centaurus engine changes, and by regulation the damaged engines had to be carefully re-sealed in their large metal containers. These were prominently marked "QUARANTINED ENGINE - DO NOT OPEN." Through the generosity of their European hosts, coupled with additional discreet purchases, several privately owned bottles of Mumms Champagne were also carefully stowed in the containers prior to sealing. The combined shipment was then peacefully transported back to *Shearwater* free of any unwanted official tampering.

In summary, the average number of 40 hours flying achieved by the Fury pilots achieved on the cruise, resulted in only about a dozen landings each, which was unacceptably low for the 14 weeks the squadrons were embarked. The Fireflies did fare better in November with good weather, and the flying rate improved considerably during the transit between the Azores and Bermuda where they participated in Exercise Maple Leaf. In this exercise, 825 squadron carried out anti-submarine patrols and rocket firing, ending the flying on a higher level, averaging between 18-20 hours for the month before flying ceased on 17 November, when the Canadian ships came to anchor at Bermuda. The decision was then made to cancel the remainder of the flying on the return leg, prepare the aircraft of the three squadrons, and launch when the carrier neared flying range of Halifax.

The cruise ended with a fly off of the embarked squadrons on 25 November 1950, culminating in a combined strike on arrival at *Shearwater* which completed the embarked flying for the year. There was one important lesson to be learned from this cruise, namely the folly of attempting to carry out a mixed bag of activities with the carrier, without ensuring that an adequate flying program can be maintained. Although it was important for Canada to "show the flag" to the various NATO countries and stress the diplomatic ties with Western Europe, an aircraft carrier in this role is virtually wasted from the flying point of view, and such primarily social activities could have been far better served by a cruiser and a flotilla of destroyers.

While *Magnificent* was at sea on the extended cruise with the three squadrons of aircraft, 826 squadron had been busy ferrying the newly acquired Avengers from Quonset Point, RI. to *Shearwater*. Already, the Avengers had shown their worth by the greatly increased flying rate being achieved. In September, following initial conversion to the aircraft, flying intensity increased dramatically to nearly 30 hours per crew. Included in the schedule were advanced ASW exercises with the RN submarine HMS *Andrew*, and the commencement of FCLP's prior to going aboard in the New Year. For the first time, the ASW squadrons were equipped with a well proven, easy to maintain aircraft, fully capable of meeting foreseeable requirements. Moreover, the Avenger's superb day and night carrier landing capability and all weather instrumentation, considerably enhanced the overall confidence of the squadron crews in their aircraft.

Perhaps the best test of the Avenger's performance took place on 24 November, completing a very intensive month of advanced tactical flying. This was 826 squadron's participation in Exercise Homecoming. Eight aircraft equipped with long range fuel tanks, departed from the air station for a night torpedo strike on *Magnificent*, reported to be some 600 miles south, proceeding north from Bermuda. The total flight time involved was nearly 9 hours, of which 7 were at night. The carrier was detected after conducting an extensive square search. To simulate actual wartime conditions, radio silence was maintained, other than half hourly C/W position reports from the lead aircraft. A successful simulated night torpedo attack was carried out on the ships, the aircraft finally landing back at the air station about midnight.

There were a few anxious moments on the trip, particularly when changing tanks as the last fuel drained out of the external tanks. This procedure was a bit tricky because the only indication of the tank being empty was a drop in the fuel pressure, or the engine to cough (stop). Watching the gauge, while simultaneously trying to fly formation at night, required considerable concentration. On the long flight back to *Shearwater*, fuel did become rather critical, since our not-so-trusty navigator in the lead aircraft made our landfall about halfway between Yarmouth and Halifax, which was about 80 miles in error. This ran us all a bit short of gas and by the time the welcome lights of *Shearwater* appeared, we only had about 15 minutes fuel remaining. The next morning we took off again, completing a five and a half hour sortie to the carrier which culminated in a simulated rocket attack. Total flying in the 24 hour period was over 14 hours, amply demonstrating the reliability and flexibility of our newly purchased Avengers. This was a great morale booster for the aircrews involved, and for the industrious ground crews who worked around the clock to meet this particular flying commitment.

The annual Naval Aviation Conference took place at Naval Headquarters on 14 and 15 December, with several items on the agenda, the major ones being described as follows:

One important subject discussed was the need to maintain continuity of operational crews aboard the carrier for a sustained period, thus ensuring a high degree of combat readiness. The new concept proposed that 826 squadron equipped with 15 Avengers and 883 squadron with 10 Sea Furies form the permanent operational carrier group. 825 squadron with an initial 6 Avengers and 803 squadron with 7 Sea Furies would provide the function of a supporting air group, work up the crews and pilots to an operational level, then feed them into the first line squadrons at established intervals.

Another topical item tabled at the Conference, concerned accident prevention, which was initiated by Lt. Ted Davis. He emphasized the need for longer periods of embarked time for the squadrons, thereby reducing the embarked accident rate, which was naturally higher than that ashore. He was followed by Cdr. Gratton-Cooper, RN, the capable and popular Cdr. Air aboard *Magnificent*. In a letter of May 1950, he had emphasized the importance of intensive embarked flying periods and categorically stated that the proposed European Cruise as planned would result in twice as many accidents as were being experienced by the RN and the RAN (Royal Australian Navy). He then read off the related statistics which bore out his prediction, suggesting a contributory cause of such accidents should be defined as "Command Error". Commodore Adams in the discussion that followed, fully agreed, pointing out that the cruise was "almost useless" from the flying point of view. He further stated that *Magnificent* had almost been excluded from exercises with the RN due to the low flying intensity being achieved by the Canadian crews.

A final point of operational interest was brought up by LCdr. Ray Creery, who stated that the RCN intended to introduce night fighters with an all weather capability, crew training for this would commence in the Support Group in 1952. Commodore Lentaigne expanded on this subject, stating that the right aircraft for this role was yet to be identified, but he did indicate that the two seat jet Venom (British) appeared suitable, although it would not be available until 1954.

The overall tone of the Conference had been positive, as other aspects of Naval Aviation were discussed in detail, with good progress being made in the areas of the most urgent priority.

The 1950 year ended on a quiet note, as the air squadrons settled in at *Shearwater*, and *Magnificent* went to the drydock at St. John in December, for a short refit. Although the all important carrier flying in 1950 had been inadequate for satisfactorily progressing the operational capability of the squadrons, the welcome addition of the Avengers, the apparent resolution of the Sea Fury engine problems, and the successful adoption of the modified USN landing technique, did provide a positive base to build upon in the coming year.

Chapter Four

CLIMBING AWAY

As the 1951 New Year was ushered in, there were a couple of bizarre incidents that took place at *Shearwater* involving both *Magnificent* and air station personnel, which to this day have neither been discounted nor explained. These activities were officially reported radar contacts, believed to be caused by Unidentified Flying Object(s) (UFO), which in the first instance was detected by the radar operators manning the air warning and approach radar system at #16 Radar Unit at *Shearwater*. Cdr. Terry Burchell, then the Electrical Dept. Head aboard *Magnificent*, recalls certain aspects of these events. Following the *Shearwater* reports he spent two nights at the air station radar unit, while at the same time having the radar operators aboard the carrier man the radar in unsuccessful attempts to again detect the objects. In one instance, the contacts under investigation had been reported as radar blips detected coming in to the air station from seaward, then passing quite slowly over the airfield. Burchell recalls that the two operators were quite shaken by their experience, and absolutely convinced that UFO's had done a dummy run over *Shearwater*. On the other hand there was also the inevitable weather pundit present, saying that the weather during the nights concerned, was perfect for "temperature inversion and ionized little puff balls of clouds".

Cdr. J.V. "Rusty" Steele also recalls this incident. He was on the staff of the Director of Naval Intelligence at Naval Headquarters and was assigned temporarily to *Magnificent* in order to investigate the reported UFO incidents. He does recall that one report stated that the object had appeared on radar, tracked in from the sea and then, moving extremely rapidly, had proceeded westerly over the harbour and disappeared. These particular incidents were not necessarily isolated, since similar radar contacts had also been reported along the United States Atlantic seaboard.

On a more humorous note, and with UFO's still in mind, LCdr. A/E "Spike" Morris, one of the engineering pilots at *Shearwater*, was airborne one night in a Harvard when he was directed by the tower controller to investigate a bright light to the east of the airfield. Morris was unable to detect anything out of the ordinary, so requested more details as he climbed eastward in his trusty trainer. The tower controller in acknowledgement gave him an approximate heading to follow and Morris continued chugging away in his climb, but again failed to close the unidentified light. After some time had passed Spike finally told the tower he had reached his maximum height, had indeed sighted the bright light, but in view of the fact it was the planet Venus that he was trying to intercept, he proposed discontinuing the chase since he would be unable to proceed further without oxygen.

The tale of the suspected Russian submarine was another unusual incident that should not pass without mention. This event took place about roughly the same time during which the "cold war" was an ongoing major concern. Apparently an early morning fisherman sighted a submarine well into the Bay of Fundy near the entrance of Chignecto Bay. The craft was aground in the morning fog and quite close to shore. The incident was promptly reported to the local RCMP, who in turn alerted the naval authorities in Halifax. They responded by detaching two frigates at top speed (18 knots) to intercept the unknown intruder. In the meantime the maritime aircraft at RCAF Station Greenwood were launched to carry out a sono-buoy barrier patrol to hopefully prevent the submarine from escaping. Needless to say, the tides are extreme in the Bay of Fundy and it was apparent that the intrepid Russian captain had, while no doubt carrying out a reconnaissance of coastal shipping and navigation routes, managed to ground the sub on the mud flats at low tide.

While the ships were en-route there were messages back and forth between them and the Flag Officer Atlantic Command, eg. "What do we do when we get there?" Answer, "Escort submarine to nearest port!" Question, "What do we do if it wont come?" As it transpired, the question was academic since the onrushing tide was obviously going to arrive much faster than the plodding frigates. The submarine finally managed to pull itself free of the mud bank on the rapidly rising water, eluded pursuit and disappeared once and for all. It will probably never be known if the sub's captain ever admitted his grounding to his superiors, but he certainly should get marks for initiative in penetrating so deeply in such treacherous Canadian waters. Then again, maybe he was just plain lost in the fog.

At Naval Headquarters during January 1951, the 8th Annual Senior Officers Conference took place, and one agenda subject brought up by Commodore Lay was of particular significance to RCN Aviation.

Lay, who had long supported the concept of Naval Aviation, opened with some telling comments about the Maritime Air role being carried out by the RCAF. His main point was that the RCAF while having taken on major NATO commitments in Europe with the new Sabre fighter Air Division, had badly neglected their Maritime Air Command. Suggesting that the RCAF were not truly interested in supporting the Maritime Air role, Lay proposed that it would be in the best interests of the RCN to take over this commitment, basing his argument on the following factors:

1 That greater efficiency in anti-submarine warfare would result from the integration of all weapons and techniques into one service.

2 That longer "pilot life" would result from expansion of the Service in this manner, with consequent overall economy.

3 That expansion of the Naval Service would give a more favourable balance between the three services than now exists.

4 That the question of command in maritime warfare would be simplified.

5 That combined operations with other navies, particularly the USN, would be facilitated since the latter is organized along similar lines.

6 That expansion of RCN Aviation would simplify "career planning" providing for greater advancement with continued specialization.

Following discussion on Lay's proposal, it was agreed by all those present that the RCN should take over this commitment and Commodore Lay was directed to conduct further studies on the proposal.

On 15 January, at *Shearwater*, and as outlined at the previous annual Aviation Conference, the two air groups underwent the planned major re-organization, with 18 Carrier Air Group (CAG) changed to consist of 826 and 883 squadrons equipped with Avengers and Sea Furies respectively. 803 Sea Fury squadron and 825 Firefly squadron now designated as 19 Support Air Group (SAG), were now the shore-based backup unit to the CAG. Employing this latest concept was a good move, ensuring aircrews would be appointed to the SAG, convert to aircraft type as necessary, then proceed to the CAG which would remain the operational embarked air group. At the same time, LCdr. Nibs Cogden assumed command of 19 SAG from LCdr. V. Wilgress.

An important addition to the aviation facilities at the air station was also made in January 1951, with the opening of the new Chezzetcook Firing and Bombing Range to the east of the airfield. The availability of the new air firing range was immediately put to use with a rocket and cannon firing display by the CAG prior to their departure on 5 February to Quonset Point, RI, where the aircraft were to be hoisted aboard *Magnificent* from the air station jetty. This method of getting the aircraft aboard the carrier was much more quickly accomplished than the time consuming transporting of the aircraft by barge in Halifax harbour, particularly during the inclement maritime winter weather.

This was the first embarked period aboard for the Avengers of 826 squadron, and due to the need to work up aboard, the Avengers, although sporting the RCN roundels, remained in their midnight blue USN colours, with the gun turrets still fitted. The USN stores and spare parts provided were very substantial, so the operating of the Avengers was greatly simplified with such a complete supporting package. CPO "Taff" Hullah on loan from the Royal Navy, was the squadron chief, and with his dogged Welsh personality and considerable expertise, quickly established the modus operandi for the maintenance teams. A/B Jack Moss who had just been drafted from SNAM, recalls going aboard *Magnificent* carrying his hefty British tool kit full of spanners and hammers, only to be informed that he might as well chuck the kit since he would be working on the American built Avengers.

At the same time a major change in the aircrew structure for the ASW squadrons took place. Now that the Avengers were coming into first line service, there was both the space and operational requirement for a third crewman. Designated as Observers' Mates, the new branch comprised initially of Able and Leading Seamen ranks, were as the name suggests, trained to assist the observer in the operation of the additional detection and communication equipment being fitted to the Avenger. The aircraft with its large interior space easily accommodated the third crew member, and the Observer Mates played an increasingly important role in the improved anti-submarine capability of the modified Avengers.

Magnificent with the CAG aboard arrived off Bermuda on 10 February, where the aircraft flew ashore to carry out final field carrier landing practice, and various training sorties. The carrier qualifications started out badly on 28 February 1951, when Lt. Bill Munro, the Commanding Officer of 883 Fury squadron, stalled and crashed in the sea after taking a late wave off, narrowly missing the port side of the carrier.

Everybody breathed a sigh of relief as "Chiefie" Munro bobbed to the surface shortly after, shaking his fist. Those watching, assumed that Munro was expressing his anger at the late wave off, but this was not the case. Munro was incensed that the ship's ejectors ie. sewage outlets, were not closed off and he was, to put it as politely as possible, literally "paddling in pooh". Then the day's flying went from bad to worse, when Lt. Jack Hartle of 883 squadron was unfortunately killed on takeoff from the carrier, when his Fury stalled and crashed into the sea. The third accident of the day took place in the afternoon, when Lt. Roger Fink of 826 squadron splashed into the sea with his Avenger as he was approaching the carrier for a landing. This accident did have a humorous twist, since Roger obeying the well known directive to get clear of the aircraft, did just that, and ran out on the wing of his sedately floating Avenger, and prepared to dive into the sea. Noting that his aircraft was still bobbing quietly on the surface, he then walked back along the wing and retrieved his pilot dinghy from the cockpit. Again he did his wing walk, threw his dinghy into the sea and in a classic pose with hands over his head, dived into the sea, inflated his dinghy, climbed aboard and waited to be picked up, all this while his aircraft slowly subsided into the water.

All this activity was closely observed by the ship's goofers, including some of the squadron pilots, who were greatly impressed with the buoyant qualities of the reliable Avenger. When Roger later returned to Kindley AFB, he was nervously met by his aircraft maintenance team consisting of A/B Gus Salkus and A/B Jack Moss. Salkus hesitantly stuck out his hand and gravely shaking hands, formally greeted Roger with, "Glad you are well, Sir!" The pair needn't have had any qualms about the serviceability of Fink's Avenger however, because it was generally agreed that the engine failed due to fuel starvation, by running a fuel tank dry.

This rather disastrous day mercifully ended, albeit somewhat early, as Commander Gratton-Cooper, the Air Commander sensibly cancelled flying for the rest of the day. There was somewhat of a negative reaction to the unexpected series of accidents. Two of the newly arrived ex-RCAF pilots in 826 squadron decided that carrier flying was no longer their first choice in an aviation career, so they departed post haste. In an amusing aftermath, Lt. Dave Etchells, one of the pilots in 883 squadron, remarked to Lt. Pappy Macleod that at a rate of a dollar a day flying pay, each deck landing was working out to be worth about twenty five cents apiece, which was hardly enriching. Dave was obviously more concerned about the monetary value involved than most, he having had a rather unorthodox career in the past. Etchells vaguely described himself as an ex-flying soldier of fortune, ie. wars fought, ambushes arranged, etc., one of his more lucrative post-war activities being the clandestine and illegal ferrying of Messerschmitt 109 fighters from Eastern Europe to Israel.

The CAG squadrons, successfully completed their deck qualifications over the next few days, the carrier remaining in the Bermuda area on general flying training exercises for a short period then returning to Halifax for ten days. On 20 March 1951, *Magnificent* and her escort with the CAG embarked, then sailed for an extensive flying period commencing in the Bermuda area then proceeding on to Trinidad.

Avengers of 826 Squadron over Magnificent, Feb. 1951.
Credit N. Donaldson

Flight of 826 Avengers flying in Bermuda area, Feb. 1951.
Note gun turrets still installed. Credit N. Donaldson

First modified ASW Avengers of 826 Squadron flying off coast of Cuba
in April 1951. Credit R.E. Quirt via DND PA140240

On 27 March, the first fatal accident at *Shearwater* since 1949 took place in 803 Sea Fury squadron. The CO. of the squadron, Lt. Doug Peacocke experienced complete engine failure while exercising with three other Sea Furies flown by Lts. Ron Heath, Mike Turner and S/Lt. Jack Morehouse and was forced to ditch in nearby Wright's Lake. This he successfully accomplished, although suffering a bone jarring impact resulting in injury to his back. The other aircraft in the meantime were summoning help by radio, and a local amphibian aircraft responded to the call and flew to the scene. Morehouse was directed to dive low over the crash site to provide assistance to the amphibian, while Peacocke, although in considerable pain, had escaped from his ditched Fury and was in the process of being picked up by a local fisherman. Tragically, Morehouse in concentrating on trying to lead the amphibian to Peacocke's location by flying low over the spot, inadvertently flew into the trees around the lake and was instantly killed in the crash.

Down in the Caribbean, during March and April, *Magnificent* was engaged in a heavy flying program, which with good weather provided the two CAG squadrons with an excellent opportunity to progress their individual workups. There was a dramatic improvement in the hours flown by the 826 Avengers, and most important, the sortie lengths, invariably averaging in excess of two hours of more productive airtime, achieved excellent training results. During the two month period the total embarked flying time for each crew was averaging in excess of 60 hours, involving close to 35 deck landings. 883 Fury squadron also posted an impressive increase in flying activity with each pilot obtaining close to 35 hours and 25 deck landings during the same embarked period.

As expected, there were a few accidents on this cruise, perhaps the most spectacular was when Bill Munro had a bit of bad luck as the hook of his Sea Fury pulled out. The hook went zinging back over the stern of the carrier, while Munro and his Fury went barreling up the deck, ran through two barriers and then slammed upside down by the forward lift in the inevitable smoking heap. Pappy Macleod, who was in the goofers position, ran down to help lift the Fury tail to extricate Munro who was trapped in the cockpit. Much to Macleod's surprise, he bumped into Munro who was already coming through the island hatch door from the flight deck. Later even Munro saw the humour of the accident, because as he stopped to speak to one of the squadron chiefs who was running by to the wreck, the chief said, "I can't stop now Sir, we have to get the pilot out of the aircraft." There was no question Bill Munro must have set a blurring speed record escaping from the inverted Fury, which had practically no ground clearance even with the little side hatch jettisoned.

The overall flying rate achieved on this cruise was obviously a considerable improvement over the dismal flying achieved during the previous one in the Fall, proving the point that a well planned schedule is essential to meeting the primary task of concentrated air operations. The maintenance teams in the CAG performed sterling work during this cruise in the Caribbean. Although working many hours under very hot conditions in the hangar deck, they achieved a high rate of serviceability, which was well exemplified as the two squadrons launched 22 aircraft to fly ashore to *Shearwater* when the cruise ended on 27 April.

At Naval Headquarters there was a timely change of senior air personnel with the arrival of Commodore C.L. Keighly-Peach, DSO, OBE, Royal Navy, who in March 1951 assumed the position of Assistant Chief of Naval Staff (ACNS) Air from his predecessor, Commodore C.N. Lentaigne. The importance of Keighly- Peach in the position at this particular time, was due to the need for continuity over the next two years, since there were major aviation policy decisions now in the process of being formulated. Not least of these was a replacement fighter for the Sea Fury commencing in 1954, and a requirement to establish a suitable aircraft to supersede the Avengers now in service. LCdr. Dickie Bird in his appointment as Staff Officer Fighters, was already investigating USN sources for an all-weather fighter which was required in the role of air defence of the fleet. One aircraft which appeared to be the most suitable for the RCN was the new USN F2H3 Banshee, a twin-engined fighter. Bird's preliminary study estimated that 60 aircraft would be required during the period from 1954 to 1959, based upon a complement of 16 aircraft in each squadron, with 100% reserves ie. 16, and an attrition allowance of 28 aircraft. This figure was calculated upon the attrition rate experienced by the operation of the Sea Fury and the USN predictions for the

F2H3. The selection of a new jet-powered generation fighter was obviously also very much tied to a replacement aircraft carrier for *Magnificent*, capable of operating such aircraft.

On 1 May 1951, all the RCN air squadrons were re-numbered to give them a Canadian identity within the Commonwealth numbering system. This would be representative and provide commonality for block numbering of additional squadrons and groups in the event of expansion. The old numbers were therefore relinquished and 803 and 825 squadrons were changed to 870 and 880 respectively and 19 SAG changed to 31 SAG. 883 and 826 squadrons were renumbered to 871 and 881 squadrons, while changing from 18 CAG to 30 CAG.

Flying intensity remained at a high level during the month of May at *Shearwater* as the CAG squadrons operated ashore, while the two squadrons of 31 SAG embarked for flying aboard *Magnificent*, the pilots carrying out refresher deck landing qualifications. An intensive night flying period then followed for 881 squadron as the crews prepared to conduct night deck landings scheduled to commence in June. There was one accident in May when Lt. Bill Rikely experienced an engine failure in an Avenger while carrying out night Field Carrier Landing Practice (FCLP). He managed to force land his aircraft successfully in the middle of the airfield with the wheels up. Fortunately, rather than an engine malfunction, which could well have caused an investigative delay, it turned out to be a case of fuel starvation by running on an empty tank.

June started as planned, with 881 Avenger squadron carrying out night deck landing qualifications aboard the carrier in local waters, and conducting advanced ASW day patrols, while the Furies of 871 continued with day operational fighter tactics. By mid-month the squadrons were once more ashore at the air station, but it is worthy of note that the night qualifications completed by 881 squadron were the first night deck landings carried out by an RCN squadron since the brief attempt made by 825 squadron in the spring of 1947. The introduction of the Avengers, and the crews now qualified for around the clock flying operations, was an important milestone, and the reality of achieving this capability with such a reliable and proven aircraft gave the RCN Avenger squadrons, for the first time, a professional level of ASW operations comparable to both the USN and Royal Navy.

Meanwhile at Naval Headquarters, the unqualified success of the Avengers had prompted the Air Staff to determine the possibility of purchasing an additional number of the aircraft. This was successfully negotiated with the USN and an additional 50 aircraft were subsequently purchased at a price of $9500 each. Cdr. John Doherty who was involved in the negotiations, recalls that there were some additional non aviation naval funds tucked away, which were available if spent before the end of the fiscal year. He contrived to allocate them to an aircraft modification allowance and was able to use these funds to include eight Airborne Early Warning (AEW) converted Avengers in the purchase. These aircraft called "Guppies" subsequently played an important role in the RCN as the "eyes of the fleet", employing their powerful long range radar equipment for surveillance duties with the added capability of vectoring Sea Furies and Avengers toward unidentified distant contacts.

Also in June there was a change in command of air personnel, as LCdr. J.G. "Garn" Wright, DFC, a wartime RCAF pilot, took over command of #1 Training Air Group from LCdr. Tan Tivy, RN. Tivy was a popular and respected airman who thoroughly enjoyed his two year stint with the RCN at *Shearwater*. Probably the time he recalls best, although perhaps a bit ruefully, was rather humorous and involved flying a Firefly trainer from the TAG with a young novice passenger in the rear seat. Apparently the youngster was a bit chilly, and inquired if there was a heat control in his rear cockpit. In response Tan gave him instructions to locate and select the prescribed lever. This was followed immediately by a horrendous silence as the engine stopped, and all voice communication ceased. Apparently the lad had inadvertently selected the Master Air/Ground Switch in lieu of the heat control. It certainly must have been the mother of all master switches, because everything was turned off. Tivy's only recourse was to make a forced landing in the nearest clear space he could find, which he successfully accomplished with no damage to himself or his passenger, although the Firefly's overall condition left much to be desired.

On 7 August, 30 CAG aboard *Magnificent* with a full complement of 871 squadron Sea Furies and 881 squadron Avengers, sailed on a major cruise to the Mediterranean encompassing an eleven week intensive operational flying period. The prevailing wind, as the carrier headed across the Atlantic, was sufficient for the Furies and flying was intense for both squadrons, with 881 Avengers concentrating on navigation training and the Furies continuing with fighter direction exercises. During one such exercise on 10 August, Lt. Mike Turner had a close call. He was flying in a group of 4 Furies about 70 miles from the carrier when he experienced falling oil pressure followed by a complete loss of power and was forced to ditch. Mike was unable to retrieve his pilot dinghy but remained afloat with his Mae West. The rescue operation went remarkably well, with an Avenger arriving at the scene in about 45 minutes, and dropping a partially inflated dinghy right on the target about 20 feet from Turner. He was picked up shortly after by *Micmac*. Duke Wardrop who was in the same flight with Turner, also experienced engine power loss, barely making it back aboard the carrier. There was a fair amount of concern about the two incidents, which were caused by an almost complete loss of engine oil, and it was suspected that the same mechanic had worked on both the aircraft. It was fervently hoped that whoever had been involved had seen the error of his ways, but in any event fortunately no further engine oil pressure problems occurred.

By mid-August *Magnificent* was operating in the Med, but shortly after a suspected outbreak of polio occurred aboard and we were all quarantined, thereby being denied any of our scheduled port visits. The planned flying programs were not that adversely affected, other than night flying for the Avengers, which was temporarily cancelled on medical grounds. The Fury pilots fared better than those of us in the Avenger squadron, because during the periods when there was insufficient wind to bring aboard the fighters, they were allowed to proceed to the Royal Naval Air Station at Hal Far, Malta. Lt. Pappy Macleod remembers that the RN personnel were very careful about approaching the Canadian pilots, and when supplying them with lime juice, (what else) they carefully distanced themselves at one end of a twelve foot pole, the other end having a bucket of juice attached.

There was one amusing episode during these diversions to Hal Far that took place, when 8 of the 871 squadron Furies forced to fly ashore, were in the process of landing at the air station. It seems that the Captain of the station had grandly bestowed on himself the imposing title of "Air Commander Mediterranean", and as such he established a little protocol procedure when airborne from the airfield, which on return, consisted of a radio announcement to the Mediterranean in general, using his self-appointed title, ordering all aircraft to clear the area as he commenced his landing approach. Apparently the 871 Furies were well into their stream landings when the exalted announcement was made to clear the area, which of course was disregarded since the Canadians were unaware of any such procedural nonsense. Once again, the imperious order was given, again the same negative result. Finally, the Commander now completely exasperated, ordered, "Sea Fury on final approach, go around again." This just happened to be Duke Wardrop, who seldom at a loss for words, responded with, "Sure as my name's Etchells, you can kiss my ass!" Well that really tore it, and shortly after there was a swarm of RN personnel surrounding the landed 871 Fury pilots _ although at a respectful 'polio safe distance', demanding to speak to a pilot by the name of Etchells. Dave Etchells, innocently standing in the group had enough sense to keep mercifully silent.

There were some good combined RN and RCN flying execises conducted during the period from 20 August to 11 September, and one in particular was a complete success for *Magnificent*. The FAA torpedo squadron at Hal Far equipped with their new Firebrand aircraft, had requested and received approval to carry out a dawn strike against *Magnificent* on 21 August. Commodore Adams, not to be caught napping, approved a long distance air intercept by 871 Sea Furies, which took off before dawn and were vectored out by *Magnificent*. The carrier's fighter direction radar was working particularly well due to an unusual anomaly in the atmosphere, and the inbound strike of Firebrands was intercepted over 100 miles away. The first inkling they had of the successful Sea Fury action, accurately guided by LCdr. Art McPhee aboard *Magnificent*, was when the Firebrands lumbered through the slipstream of the attacking fighters. The planned attack petered out after that, the Firebrands returning to Hal Far, with the RN more than somewhat miffed, suspecting some underhanded trick on the part of the Canadians. Following the interception, the Furies continued the week carrying out fighter direction exercises with RAF Vampire jets from the RAF station at Takali, and participating in combined exercises with the British army.

On 24 August 1951, a not-so-routine Sea Fury ferry trip for Lts. Mike Wasteneys and Hank Leidl took place. Being on duty in the UK., they were assigned to fly two replacement Sea Furies from England to Malta for 871 squadron. The pair, with Wasteneys in the lead, took off in less than optimum conditions from Lee-on-Solent ie. a 300 foot ceiling and visibility 1/2 mile in heavy rain. Shortly after takeoff as they were climbing to 21,000 feet, Mike experienced radio failure, so passed the lead to Leidl. Wasteneys noticed that the aircraft were icing up rather badly and they were adding more and more power, but Hank Leidl, pre-occupied with flying on instruments did not look out of the cockpit until they leveled off at their assigned 21000 foot altitude. Mike detected a look of horror on Leidl's face even partially hidden as it was by the oxygen mask, as he glanced over at Mike's aircraft which looked more like a winged icicle than a Sea Fury. Mike later recalled that he had never encountered so much ice before, noting that Hank's aircraft bore a strong resemblance to a snow-laden Christmas tree. They were still in cloud, so obtained permission to climb higher, finally breaking clear at 32000 feet. Just beginning to relax somewhat, Mike then unhappily noticed that all the remaining elecrically operated instruments in his cockpit had failed, and the engine oil pressure was now reading dangerously low, invariably a warning of more trouble on the way. Other than increasing RPM on the engine, which fortunately appeared to alleviate the problem, Mike could do little else except mutter away to himself. They finally broke into the warmer Mediterranean air over the French Alps, and at this point Mike duly considered landing at the French Airbase at nearby Toulon. With the lack of communications and associated complications, he decided, "What the hell" at least now the engine is working fine and Malta, surrounded by good weather and warm water, was less than two hours away. The remainder of the trip proved to be quite uneventful, other than the canopy of Wasteneys' aircraft fogging up with condensation rendering conditions less than ideal for landing. If nothing else, this particular experience, although harrowing, certainly established that the Fury with its powerful Centaurus engine was capable of flying through any icing condition.

During August over a three week period, 881 squadron Avengers were very busy with anti-submarine exercises, working with RN submarines and surface units, carrying out sonobuoy exercises and ship/air homings. The weather although excellent for flying, was creating some very uncomfortable conditions aboard the carrier, which was not unexpected when one considers that approximtely 1000 bodies were for a large part mainly confined to an equivalent of a hot steel oven for hours at a time. Everything possible was done to alleviate the enforced restriction to the ship caused by the polio threat, not least of which was periodically stopping the carrier, with all hands at liberty to swim in the warm blue Mediterranean sea. One additional, but somewhat unorthodox diversion which captured everybody's attention, was the dropping and detonation of a heavy depth charge astern of the ship one late afternoon. This produced immediate results in the form of hundreds of stunned fish, which were quickly scooped up by the waiting ships' boats, providing a fresh fish dinner for all aboard.

The polio quarantine was finally lifted and in mid-September 1951, the ships entered the Grand Harbour of Valetta, Malta, the target of some of the heaviest German and Italian bombing attacks of the war. The damage was still very much in evidence, and in the inner core of the city, the living conditions were bad, much of the wartime destruction remaining unrepaired due to the desperately poor economic conditions prevailing. The respite ashore however, after over a month at sea, was still very welcome, and I recall Bill Munro and myself had a run ashore the first night. We conspired to go along with the Executive Officer and the Principal Medical Officer (PMO) with the object of visiting some of the RN listed "Out of Bounds" establishments to confirm their unsuitability, and also to investigate a few other exotic night spots. That evening was a real eye opener, which was spent mainly in the infamous section of Valetta known as "The Gut". We visited one particular notoriously sleazy place called the 'New Life Cafe and Bar' in which, for obvious sanitary reasons, only carefully opened bottled beer should be consumed. The next morning we noticed that virtually all the names of the various establishments we visited the previous evening were prominently displayed throughout the ship as being particularly "Out of Bounds".

After a few days the carrier left for Naples on 24 September, with the Avengers working en-route with an RN frigate and submarine, while the Furies continued flying with tactical fighter sorties. Although

Naples was lively and offered a considerable variety of entertainment, probably one of the best features of Naples was it's close proximity to Pompeii and Capri. On a visit to the excavated Pompeii, one of the more attractive souvenirs to be found was a lapel-sized bronze flying phallic symbol, quickly renamed a "winged dink" which could be purchased for a package of cigarettes. Also while at Naples, Jack Stokes, Bill Munro, Bill Rikely and myself gained access to a car and driver, and on a weekend took the trip from Naples to Sorrento, thence by ferry to Capri. Our driver was a cheerful character named Joseph who regaled us with considerable trivia on the journey. At one point he went to great length to sorrowfully point out a nondescript building that had apparently been struck by allied bombers during the war. He quickly got off the subject however, when I asked him if he had visited Malta lately. Capri was delightful, with balmy weather, uncrowded and completely relaxing, providing a marvellous break from the previous heavy flying task and the hot living spaces of the ship. It is not often that one can arrive at a destination for the first time and discover it is as lovely as had been anticipated. Capri was without question, a place that met all our expectations.

Meanwhile at *Shearwater*, a particular gap was filled in the aviation organization, with the formation of #1 Helicopter flight equipped with three Bell HTL 4 helicopters which were delivered to the air station on 1 September 1951. The initial requirement for helicopters in the RCN had been originally stated for the newly commissioned ice breaker HMCS *Labrador* for use in the role of aerial ice reconnaissance and light utility support and transport. It was logical that the unit be established at *Shearwater* to meet this requirement, and LCdr. Darkie Lowe was appointed Officer-in-Charge. At the same time, LCdr. Dennis Foley was appointed as both the Air Engineer Officer and a pilot for general flying duties. Air maintenance personnel had in the meantime prepared for the introduction of the helos, by having undergone specialized training at the big USN base at Lakehurst, New Jersey, followed by additional training at the Bell Aircraft factory at Fort Worth, Texas. The recognition of the rotary winged aircraft in this initial role for the *Labrador* was most timely, since it also expanded the role for helicopter operations in the air branch for many subsequent important applications including photography, air rescue, air transport, ship support, spotting for torpedo firing and other utility roles.

Additional developments were also taking place at the policy level with a planned air liaison visit to Washington in September by Commodore Keighly-Peach from Naval Headquarters. His primary objective was to discuss with senior USN officers the suitability of the F2H3 Banshee and the S2F-1 ASW aircraft for possible use by the RCN. It was also an opportunity for the Commodore to be fully briefed on various aspects of the greatly increased co-operation between the two navies in aviation matters. This was already very much in evidence with the current training by the USN of Canadian pilots for LSO duties and helicopter operations, with ongoing discussions for basic pilot training. Already with the introduction of the Avenger, the shift to American air stores, and the procurement of associated anti-submarine aviation equipment, was providing a steady flow of material, considerably simplifying the logistic support for the American aircraft.

Aboard *Magnificent* flying operations re-commenced 2 October, after the week in Naples, and the carrier proceeded to the French port of San Raphael in company with the RN carrier HMS *Ocean*, during which the aircraft of both carriers participated in mutual air strikes and shadowing exercises. On 4 October, the NATO exercise Symphonie Deux began with ships of the French Navy, RN and RCN participating in sea/air operations over the next two weeks. Over 35 ships participated in various phases of the exercise, with both squadrons from *Magnificent* flying throughout the period, which included strikes on a component of the fleet at anchor in Salins d'Hyeres and an escorted convoy.

Following the completion of the exercise on 12 October, and while the NATO ships were at anchor, a 'spirited' group of officers from *Magnificent* launched a clandestine, night aircraft dinghy assault on the newly painted HMS *Ocean* at anchor nearby. From the Canadian point of view the attack was a complete success, with smoke generators strategically placed to disperse their fumes through the air intakes of the British carrier, and a large red maple leaf sprayed on the glistening side of the ship. The Brits did not share the encounter with the same enthusiasm as the Colonials, and huffily responded with a nasty message of complaint. Nobody really seemed to be too concerned about the prank however, and since we were leaving the next day, there was little retaliatory action that could be launched. Flying was pretty well curtailed for the next ten days as *Magnificent* headed into a howling gale on reaching the Atlantic, so the majority of the time was spent by the squadrons preparing all aircraft for launching on 24 October as the Canadian ships neared Halifax.

This first Mediterranean operational training cruise was an outstanding success for both squadrons, not only for the high flying rate achieved, but also for the opportunity to participate in joint exercises with other NATO navies, providing the carrier and the squadrons an opportunity to make direct comparisons with the other NATO fleets. It was very clear that close co-operation and the hard work carried out by all departments aboard *Magnificent* had achieved excellent results, and the standards of flying accomplished were certainly equal to or superior to those of the other navies involved. Even considering the scheduled time spent in port, or the occasions when flying was necessarily curtailed, the results achieved were impressive. The crews of 881 Avenger squadron on this eleven week cruise averaged in excess of 110 hours both day and night, with each pilot realizing close to 60 deck landings. The Sea Furies of 871 squadron although sometimes curtailed by a lack of wind, also had a significant total with each pilot averaging in excess of 60 hours flying and over 35 deck landings. The maintenance support was excellent during the entire trip, with virtually all the flying commitments being met.

The clear blue waters of the Mediterranean, the storied islands with their historical background, and the sombre beauty of the African coast, all graced the scene. Coupled with this was the sharp contrast between the cool, clear, dawn sorties and the stifling mid-day launches. By then, the aircraft metal was too hot to touch, as chockmen lying on the scorching deck draped themselves around the wheels, engulfed in the blast of running engines and the acrid fumes wafting over the flight deck from the carrier's stack.

LSO and Flight Deck Officer, Lt. Bob Cocks on this cruise, and reminiscing many years later, graphically brought back those days when he eloquently wrote, "Can we not all remember the Fury range at dawn. Shadowy hands clutching the chocks, exhaust stubs rosy in the rising light, dustpan lights spilling pools of white over the gray gritty deck. The wands beckoning, right wheel on the centre line, left hand forward, right hand back, fingers clenched, all the needles pointing up. The green wand circling, circling. 'I'm at max power now you clot!' Dawn breaks; off, tail up a bit, fog streaming from the propellor, airborne at the lift, jink, lift the gear, suck up the flaps, 130 knots, 20,000 feet, seven Furies behind, the wind out of Tripoli, the sun rising over Cyprus. Below is Malta, Lampedusa, Sicily, and off to the east, USS "*Wasp*" with a belly full of Bearcats who are going to catch hell if we get them at the right altitude. God it was fun!"

Warrant Engineer A/E Gordon Cummings, who spent his wartime service with the RCAF, fondly described carrier flying from a different perspective, when in 1951 as an air technician he penned his feelings while participating for the first time in the maintenance side of carrier flying operations. He had previously sensed that the true romance of flying had died as maintenance systems changed in the RCAF and elsewhere. He perceived the attitude of the individual air mechanic alter, from a feeling of pride and of taking loving care of his assigned aircraft, to the more remote impersonal involvement in the "centralized maintenance" system now generally in use. This is where the specialization became a detached and oft thought thankless task to "keep-em-flying."

Cummings wrote as follows, "Thus it had become for me, until I first stood on the deck of a carrier and took part in the preparations to fly off the ship's aircraft. What an engaging picture! Aircraft being ranged on the flight deck, to all appearances too closely bunched together by the Aircraft Handlers. Mechanics each giving their aircraft a last minute check. Final orders from the bridge come over the loud speakers. "Aircrew man your aircraft". "Start up". The roar of several thousand "horses". Propellors dissolve into silvery discs, inches away from rudders and wing tips, wind lashed chockmen lying on the deck at the wheels - the "thumbs up" from "Bats". The ship turns into wind. The final check of wind speed over the deck by "Wind", our nickname for the control room assistant with his hand held anemometer, momentarily holding the stage and enacting his little drama, legs braced against the wind, his outstretched arm, the spinning cups of his instrument. Then after a seemingly long delay, the green light flashes on from the flying control bridge. "Fly off aircraft". The batsman gives the signal, the roar of the engines become thunder and one by one in quick succession the aircraft take off and are away on their mission.

The immediate thrill of watching the aircraft take off was replaced by our thoughts of the pilots and crews as their aircraft rapidly disappeared from view. How did they feel, miles from the ship, over a seemingly endless expanse of restless sea, with no familiar landmarks for comfort or solace? How dependant they are on their aircraft and on the men who keep them serviceable. "They are, at any time," you say. True of course, but how much more important and responsible the aircraft mechanic's job seemed just then.

Finally the aircraft reappear. First as specks in the distance, then quickly growing larger, to zoom past the ship, sometimes in a fast "beat up". The speakers blare, "Standby to receive aircraft." Trained deck crews take up positions. The ship is ready for the final act, and what a performance! Carefully choreographed, all the drama and tension of a high trapeze act can be felt as the batsman and pilots culminate hours of practice to bring the aircraft safely back, often to a rolling, pitching deck. One is gripped by the amazing surety of an arrestor hook as it picks up a wire and brings the aircraft to an abrupt, singing stop; the coordination and split second timing of the landing routine; hook disengaged, wire snaking back, barriers down, the aircraft taxiing forward, flaps up, wings folded, barriers up, wires reset. In seconds, the next aircraft is in the landing "groove" over the ship's stern. The keen-eyed mechanics watch for any sign of trouble with their aircraft: the puff of "smoke" of a propellor "pecking" the deck, or a bursting tire. The happy relief when all aircraft are safely back on deck. The performance is over.

But work on the aircraft is not over. While some are in the air, others are in the hangar being readied for their turn to fly. The men are on the job, working long, tedious hours in cramped quarters, under an artificial light, some with stomachs which never get used to the unpredictable movement of a ship at sea. Yes, taking part in the "Play" requires a lot of hard work from one and all. By now though, the initial impressions of confusion have been distilled into a realization of the integrated effort and vigilent attention to detail which has been demanded of everyone and which has welded individuals into a compact, efficient group working toward a common end.

Flying from an aircraft carrier is an exciting operation, filled with tension, born of danger. Yet for those who play a part, it is a demanding and enriching experience in teamwork and team spirit, seldom found elsewhere to the same degree. All the hard work, sweat and trials are forgotten in the knowledge of achievement and a job well done, culminating in a glowing feeling of pride and satisfaction for all participants; a feeling of well being; a rich reward for labour. For me, at least, these were necessary ingredients. The romance of flying was reborn"

In October 1951, following Canadian Privy Council approval, the Admiralty was informed that Canada would be prepared to pay for major alterations to *Magnificent* in order to modernize the ship. These improvements included strengthening of the flight deck, and improved lifts, arrestor gear and safety barriers to accommodate anticipated newer and heavier aircraft. Although this proposed modernization was not expected for another 2-3 years, *Magnificent* while under this refit would be out of service for as long as two years. To resolve this problem the Admiralty proposed three alternatives:

(a)   Borrow a carrier temporarily during the refit period.

(b)   Exchange *Magnificent* for a modernized Light Fleet Carrier.

(c)   Purchase one of the partly completed Light Fleet Carriers upon which all work had ceased at war's end, then complete and modernize the ship.

During a visit to London in November, Mr. Brooke Claxton, the Minister of National Defence, discussed the matter of *Magnificent* further with British officials, then reported back to Cabinet to arrive at a decision regarding the future replacement of *Magnificent*.

Meanwhile after discussions in Washington, although initially not of major significance, there was a change in the RCN pilot training program when the USN approved flight training for four RCN Midshipmen, commencing 28 October 1951. This was the first departure from the current policy of training RCN pilots with the Royal Navy and reflected the shift of emphasis to the USN. The training was to cover the full pilot syllabus including advanced training specialization, for both carrier borne fighter and anti-submarine aircraft. The four Canadian students to undergo this first pilot training course were Midshipmen J.H. Birks, A.F. Cottingham, G.J. McMillen and J.A. MacKay.

Magnificent still had one more trip to make in 1951, with senior officer changes also taking place as the Broad Pennant of Commodore Adams was struck at sunset on 29 October and Captain K.L. Dyer, DSC, the previous Executive Officer of *Warrior*, assumed command. Commodore Ken Adams was a popular figure, and there was no doubt he was instrumental in bringing back a strong sense of purpose to *Magnificent*. He most definitely achieved his vow when assuming command of the carrier, when he stated, "The purpose of an aircraft carrier is to fly aircraft, and that is what we are going to do." *Magnificent* sailed at the end of October after embarking the officers and men of RCAF 410 squadron, the ship then proceeding to Norfolk, Virginia to pick up 47 Sabre jets for the NATO assigned squadron.

It was a rough trip to the UK, with heavy seas causing an excessive roll to the ship, requiring the carrier to heave to for securing of extra lashings for the wind swept Sabres. The jets were off loaded at Glasgow where another batch of new Sea Furies was hoisted aboard, the carrier arriving a week later at Halifax, then proceeding to Halifax Shipyards for a six month refit. In a sense, it was an ironic situation for the RCAF to prevail upon the RCN to transport their squadron personnel and jet fighters to the UK. One cannot help but wonder how they could have made the move without the use of *Magnificent*, which some senior RCAF officers eg. Air Commodore Guthrie, considered to be an unnecessary, obsolete and expensive toy.

In November, there were air command changes with LCdr. W.H. (Bill) Atkinson, DSC, taking over 881 (CAG) squadron from LCdr. Norm Donaldson, and Lt. E.M. (Ted) Davis, taking over command of 880 (SAG) squadron from LCdr. Don Knox. The appointment of Ted Davis to a squadron command responsibility while in the rank of Lt. was the third such case where the lack of seniority precluded a promotion to LCdr. The other change was in 871 (CAG) Fury squadron, as LCdr. D.H.P. (Pat) Ryan replaced Lt. Bill Munro as the Commanding Officer. There was a rather amusing tale related by Ed Janusus about Pat Ryan, following his appointment as Commanding

Spray-swept RCAF Sabres during Atlantic storm en route
UK. DND HS 47415 and HS 47416

AB Hughes of 881 Squadron carrying out an engine check on Avenger aboard Magnificent, Fall 1951. Credit PA140241

Group of 871 Squadron officers at Mess Dinner aboard Magnificent, circa 1951. Credit A.E. Fox

Officer of the Fury squadron. Apparently Pat decided that the squadron should be given a thorough pep talk on the role and purpose of Canada's naval fighter squadrons, placing emphasis squarely on the fact that the enemy was "The dreaded red menace", namely the USSR. Following this stunning revelation, the squadron maintenance group in a tongue-in-cheek decision, stoutly declared that they would henceforth be known to one and all as "Ryan's Red Raiders."

Lts. Bill Munro, Pappy Macleod and Duke Wardrop were all re-appointed to the 11 month long Junior Officers Technical and Leadership Course (JOTLC). This course, as the name suggests, was designed to indoctrinate junior officers with all the major specialization subjects in which an RCN officer should be knowledgeable. There was no question that it was essential for the air officers to undergo such training in order to be able to compete professionally with their non-flying contemporary officers whilst serving in executive appointments. This was particularly important observing that in the RCN, all aircrew officers were classified as General List Officers with their pilot or observer qualification considered a secondary specialization. This perhaps was a mixed blessing insofar as the Air Branch was currently not sufficiently large enough to offer a full flying career for aircrew officers. Aviation officers were simultaneously handicapped by virtue of the fact that to serve competitively in Executive seagoing appointments and command positions, they must be in possession of an upper deck watchkeeping certificate and be professionally qualified for command of a ship by passing the Destroyer Command exams. To achieve this, while still striving to be a currently active and fully professional aviator, was often difficult and unproductive for many. The situation was further complicated by the fact that promotion to the rank of Commander, although inconsistently applied, was in many cases unofficially predicated upon passing such examinations.

It is perhaps worth noting that the subjects taught on the JOTLC, which included, Torpedo anti-Submarine, Navigation Direction, Gunnery and Ordnance, Communictions, Marine Engineering and Ship Construction, Electrical, Supply and Administration, Damage Control, and Leadership, disregarded completely the major subject of Naval Aviation. Yet aviation not only represented numerically the largest single branch, but also was allocated about 10% of the RCN annual budget and the prime justification for the only RCN aircraft carrier. This in retrospect was a disturbing situation, since by omission it suggests that every General List Officer should be professionally knowledgeable about the duties and activities of each and all branches with the exception of Aviation. This certainly did result in many junior General List RCN officers being woefully ignorant of the role and scope of their own Canadian Naval Aviation. Subsequently this fostered in many officers an attitude of benign neglect or even antipathy, which in many ways tended to parallel the attitude displayed in the Royal Navy toward their own Naval Aviation at the outbreak of WW2.

In November, as the year drew to a close, additional changes in personnel and re-assignment of responsibilities took place at *Shearwater*, as the RCAF relinquished occupancy of the Marine Section and various associated buildings. The responsibility for search/rescue duty and the manning the three high speed launches (HSLs) and other miscellaneous small craft was now assigned to the RCN. Associated commitments also included the patrolling of the Cow Bay and Chezzetcook air firing ranges and local ferry service at Eastern Passage. One additional but less desirable duty the HSLs crews also assumed, was that of transporting the pregnant spouses of the station personnel across to Halifax late at night, when the wives invariably went into labour. On occasions, this was one of the more onerous tasks, particularly in the oft prevalent fog, the craft proceeded slowly in low visibility across Halifax harbour and the crew facing the prospect of an imminent birth. Fortunately, the nurses attached to *Shearwater* were often able to assist, their presence aboard being a welcome comfort.

One of the buildings vacated by the RCAF was E Block, a large well-built prewar building which was designated to be the new Naval Air Maintenance School (NAMS). With its large classroom spaces, separate facilities and adjacent drill square, it was a great improvement over the previously used derelict hangars. As Gerry Daniel remembers, the building transfer was not exactly a smooth turnover from the RCAF to the RCN, because due to the usual bureaucratic delays, the building was unfortunately left unoccupied for a period before the

RCN were allowed occupancy. When the block was finally taken over, it was discovered that the 'Eastern Passage Pirates' had struck again, and in a commando type night sea raid had crept ashore and in a short space of time had liberated all the plumbing fittings, and anything else of value that could be easily transported.

In December 1951, the Annual Aviation Conference convened in Ottawa under Commodore Keighly-Peach. His opening remarks were enlightening for many, particularly with reference to the fact that he personally felt that the RCN fleet composition was lacking in operational balance with only one carrier and two air groups. He did inform the Conference that his opinion had been made known, and the matter was now in the hands of higher authority. With regard to the need for replacement naval aircraft, he hoped to have the Furies replaced by 1954 and the Avengers by 1955. These dates were to a degree predicated on the date that a modified carrier, capable of operating faster and heavier aircraft, would be available. The Commodore also mentioned the need for the provision of plane guard rescue helicopters for the carrier, and noted that 3 Sikorsky HO4S helos were now on order. He also recognized the growing importance of Airborne Early Warning (AEW) surveillance aircraft and stated plans were underway to obtain more such aircraft.

During later discussions at the Conference, it was interesting to note the divergence of opinion with regard to maintenance procedures. The technical staff were very much in support of a group maintenance system which was more centralized, while the airmen considered that control of maintenance should be at the squadron level. This was particularly applicable, observing the frequency that detachments of aircraft were being moved about the country.

In discussion opened by Captain Raymond, the Commanding Officer of *Shearwater*, he disclosed that the air station was increasingly being assigned more and more responsibilities, resulting in overworking personnel. In a detailed study he outlined 14 major tasks assumed by the air station, which he believed exceeded that of any other air station in the country. In support of this contention, LCdr. Les Kniffen pointed out that the Naval Air Maintenance School under his command was now the largest technical school in the RCN. There was certainly growing evidence that the commitments assumed by

Naval Aviation were exceeding the personnel resources assigned for the task.

There was encouraging news for construction projects for 1952, which in addition to the requirement for essential technical buildings and hangars, included the approval for planning the long-awaited deep water jetty and a new runway to accommodate jet aircraft.

Perhaps some of the most gratifying news divulged at the Conference was the fact that total flying hours for the year had increased by over 50%, while the accident rate had again improved, this time by dropping nearly 15%. The disembarked rate had now dropped from 38.9 accidents per 10,000 hours flown in 1950 to 25.8 per 10,000 hours for the first 9 months of 1951. The carrier embarked rate had also shown a considerable improvement, dropping from 295.6 accidents per 10,000 landings to 134.4 in 1951. The latter half of 1951 had dramatically improved with statistics for the Mediterranean cruise indicating the rate had dropped even lower to 85.7 accidents per 10,000 landings. The introduction of the Avenger, the increased flying intensity and the CAG/SAG organization, were all instrumental in achieving these improved accident statistics.

Commander Gratton-Cooper in summarizing the flying operations of *Magnificent* during the year, observed that the most productive level of flying could best be achieved by a three month intensive flying cruise with rest and relaxation for the personnel by periodic long weekends in port. This comment made good sense and was fully supported.

There was some interesting data concerning the Royal Navy presented to the Conference which showed the Royal Navy had approximately 21.7% of their manpower specializing in naval aviation duties. By comparison, it was becoming increasingly obvious and worrisome that the current strength of Canadian Naval Aviation locked in at 11% of the total RCN strength was becoming a marginally economic proposition.

For the first time, it was divulged that the RN concept of the mirror landing aid was reaching a level of development where it was envisaged that the benefits of such a system would soon replace the LSO control system, reducing the error due to reaction time, thus allowing the aircraft carrier to effectively accommodate the increased landing speeds of jet fighters.

The year 1951 ended overall on a most positive note, with the flying operations maintained at a high level both ashore and afloat, and the consolidation of the air station facilities now under RCN control, providing a suitable base upon which to plan and expand for the years ahead.

In January 1952, the 9th Senior Officers Conference took place at Naval Headquarters. The agenda item of major significance to Naval Aviation was a revision and expansion of the original proposal introduced by Commodore Lay in the previous year's Conference. In this paper, titled 'Transfer of RCAF Maritime Air Responsibility To the RCN', Lay introduced additional factors for consideration which would significantly affect the future of Canadian Naval Aviation. Lay pro-posed a modification in the method adopted to attain the main objective. Details were outlined as follows:

1 - "In the sphere of command in maritime warfare, the RCAF is questioning naval supremacy and wants co-equal status with the RCN.

2 - Development of anti-submarine devices indicate a trend disposed in favour of airborne detection and weapons. These include dunking sonar, Magnetic Anomoly Detection (MAD) gear, infra-red detection and various homing weapons.

3 - Shipborne developments have by comparison, remained somewhat static and no solutions appear imminent, due to the following problems:

   (a) how to maintain an attacking run against a submarine capable of counter attacking with pattern running torpedos;

   (b) how to increase speed and detection range in order to provide adequate protection against the very long range torpedos in the immediate future;

   (c) how to provide expensive and complex ships in sufficient numbers from the resources that are likely to be available in peace or in war.

4 - Civil authority is most anxious to reduce the cost of defence, a circumstance that can be exploited by the RCN.

5 -   Responsible Canadian military authority has more than once suggested that Canada cannot afford a Navy and would buy more security per dollar by concentrating upon the RCAF. It is known that some political circles have listened to this idea with favour."

In his presentation, Lay elaborated further upon some of the foregoing factors, emphasizing the need for the RCN to take advantage of the new air weapons and sensors becoming available for anti-submarine warfare by applying them to Naval Aviation.

At the same time he cautioned the conference members that it will take very little time for the RCAF to take advantage of such new techniques. By so doing, he suggests that the argument may well be subsequently presented by the RCAF that the surface units of the RCN are both expensive and marginally effective in the ASW role. This in turn would politically enhance the attractiveness of Maritime Air Command at the expense of the RCN.

Lay summarized his presentation with two recommendations:

(a)   that future naval policy should emphasize more strongly the growth and development of Canadian Naval Aviation, and that,

(b)   this policy should concurrently include planning for the absorption of all maritime air operations by the RCN, which will involve the exploitation of public relation factors inherent in (a) above.

Commodore Keighly-Peach, no doubt called before the conference for comments in his capacity as Assistant Chief of Naval Staff (Air), supported Lay, and outlined the discussions in the UK in connection with Maritime Air, which was still very much of an RN/RAF hassle. He went on to caution the conference members that the RCAF were now taking a greatly increased interest in Maritime Air and recognized the unsuitability of their present aircraft.

This was an inevitable development, because now that the RCAF had set up their NATO Air Division, they could now concentrate on their proprietry but neglected Maritime Air Command, and commence to publicize and politically exploit the need for them to switch to a large maritime aircraft. If nothing else, this would open the door for the RCAF to again become involved in four-engined aircraft operations, which in the post-war years had been denied to them, since there was no Canadian Bomber Command role to justify such heavy aircraft.

The overall implications of Lay's recommendations, if accepted, would have been dramatic for Canadian Naval Aviation, but in spite of his strong argument to actively support and expand the branch, his recommendations obviously fell upon deaf ears.

In a disturbing rebuttal, Admiral Mainguy, the Chief of Naval Staff, stated that under the present circumstances it was the task of the RCN to convince as many as possible of the importance and place of Maritime Air, and to encourage the RCAF to put more effort into this place, rather than some other air task. It was essential for the two services to work together and for the RCN to back the RCAF.

After this astonishing statement, which completely ignored Lay's first recommendation to support and develop Canadian Naval Aviation, Lay persevered by stating that the subject of Maritime Air had been introduced at various war colleges, including the National Defence College, and the consensus was that Maritime Air should be controlled by the Navy. This was discussed by the conference members, and in the usual method of delaying a controversial matter, it was agreed to seek more information on the subject. In final summary, the members agreed that the proper course for the RCN under existing conditions, was to assist, support and push the RCAF in every way to enable them to build up an efficient Maritime Air Arm. Significantly, the recommendation by Lay for Naval Aviation to be supported and expanded further, did not appear to have been discussed.

It is difficult to understand the rationale behind Mainguy's statement and the subsequently strong endorsement of RCAF Maritime Air Command. At the 1951 Senior Conference, the decision had been made by all present that the RCN should take over the Maritime Air commitment, calling for further investigation. Mainguy's outright rejection of Lay's eminently sensible and pragmatic follow-on recommendations at the 1952 Conference, showed a disturbing change of policy planning and an apparent lack of understanding of the implicit ramifications of the Maritime Air situation. His obvious rejection of Lay's proposals for the RCN to expand and support Naval

Aviation and assume the role of Maritime Air, must have subsequently been sweet music to the ears of the adroit, politically astute planners of the RCAF. It is doubtful if the deliberations concerning Naval Aviation at the Senior Officers Conference were ever openly divulged, so perhaps it was unknown to the airmen generally that a golden opportunity to prepare for an expansion of the Naval Aviation role had not only been ignored, but a chance to forge a meaningful career in Canadian Naval Aviation had also been denied.

One final matter of concern to Naval Aviation was an additional paper originally prepared by Lt. Vince Murphy in his capacity as Staff Officer (Air) to Commodore Lay. The paper discussed the proposed application of ASW helicopters in the UK, where such helicopter operations were to be carried out jointly, the RAF operating them in a Coastal Command type of shore-based role, and the RN responsible for the ship-based element. The subject of ASW helicopters in the RCN had been proposed as an agenda item for the 9th Senior Officers Conference, but it is unclear if the matter was ever tabled for discussion. Lay however, in his paper, clearly spelled out the on-going difficulties of joint control of forces in the maritime role being experienced by the RN and the RAF. Based on the assumption that the encouraging development by the USN of "dunking sonar" from a helicopter had the potential to be a major advance in ASW sensor detection, Lay proposed that this system, because of it's anticipated effectiveness, could best be exploited by helicopter in the naval ship-based role, which was now being actively pursued by the USN. This proposal made considerable sense, since it was unrealistic to visualize any need for ASW helicopters operating from Canadian shore bases, ie. RCAF, in a coastal patrol role. Lay correctly perceived the application of helicopters in an ASW role was an entirely new concept. It was therefore important to ensure that any future role of the helicopter in maritime operations was properly assigned to the RCN as part of the overall ship-based ASW detection and weapon systems.

At *Shearwater*, the flying activities commenced in January 1952 with the arrival of a detachment of USN P2V Lockheed Neptune long range patrol aircraft for combined fleet drills. 881 squadron participated jointly with the USN aircraft, carrying out combined ASW exercises with 17 USN ships and three submarines off the Nova Scotia coast. Additionally, the RN submarine *Alcide* participated for a nine day period, offering a further period of intense ASW exercises for both 881 and 880 Avenger squadrons. The Sea Furies of 871 meanwhile continued with fighter tactics which were followed by a strike against the Swedish cruiser *Gotland* after her departure from a Halifax visit.

In Washington and Ottawa, the initial co-operation established between the RCN and USN was steadily increasing as pilot exchange tours were arranged. In addition, the USN had approved the assignment of Canadian pilots to other facilities. Lt. J.C. Sloan was appointed to the USN Naval Air Test Centre at Patuxent River, Maryland, while LCdr. John Roberts proceeded to the USN Experimental squadron (VX1) at Key West Florida.

Landing Signal Officer (LSO) training for RCN aviators was also continuing, now that the standard USN signal system was fully adopted by the RCN. Lt. Bob Williamson, was the first to undergo the course, and he had been followed by Lt. Bob Falls in the summer of 1951. I was the third to take this course, arriving in January 1952. The RN and USN training course for LSO's differed in one main respect, insofar as the UK system employed experienced pilots both ashore and afloat to demonstrate the correct carrier landing technique. Using this concept, the pilots became so expert (called clockwork mice) that they were literally training the novice LSO's by repetitiously flying the approaches in the proper manner. The USN technique was to train the LSO's employing student pilots, who were in advanced training and preparing for their carrier landings. They commenced with hundreds of Field Carrier Landing Practice (FCLP) approaches, then advanced to deck qualifications aboard the training carrier. It was a well organized program with the students initially carrying out deck landings using the venerable Harvard trainer, complete with an arrestor hook, then advancing to additional deck landings, flying in the operational aircraft currently in use. One major outcome using the USN technique, was that a novice LSO saw just about every mistake in carrier landing practice that a student pilot could possibly make.

An interesting part of the USN course was that several NATO countries had arranged for their pilots to be trained by the USN. Some of the foreign students relied very heavily on their short basic English language course and on occasions experienced a time lag while methodically going through the stages of translation, comprehension and reaction to the signals from the LSO.

One graphic example of this occurred when a young Italian student was carrying out field carrier landing practice in a Skyraider (AD). All was seemingly well on the approach except he was a bit too high, so was signalled by the LSO to descend. This he did, and as he reached the correct height, the LSO gave him the "Roger" signal indicating he was now at the prescribed altitude. Rather surprisingly, the student continued descending, so was then given a low signal, requiring corrective action. This was again ignored. By this time the aircraft was dangerously low, so the LSO gave him the mandatory "Wave off" signal to apply full power and go around again. The next thing we knew, the big Skyraider had hit the ground well short of the runway, bounced, then headed directly our way, barreling across the airfield at about 80 MPH. The three of us scattered in all directions, I obviously went the wrong way initially, but managed to scuttle back across the runway just in time, passing under the wing of the aircraft as the big propellor blades whistled by my head. In short order, the aircraft undercarriage collapsed and the young Italian and his Skyraider ground to a fiery halt, he quickly vacating the burning aircraft unscathed. After the excitement had waned somewhat, the LSO being more than somewhat curious, asked the student why he had not acknowledged the "Roger" and "Low" signals and made the necessary response. The youngster looked a bit puzzled for a few seconds, then with disarming frankness said, "But Sir, I was still answering your high signal."

There were inevitably accidents aboard the training carrier, which although not excessive in number, did result in fatalities. One such occurred with a Bearcat, the speedy little Grumman fighter, when the young pilot, during his deck qualifications, got slow in the approach and torque stalled, crashing into the sea and going down with his aircraft. The same day, a Skyraider also stalled and crashed into the sea, the pilot fortunately being recovered. Being an involved eye-witness to such accidents, was always a sobering experience.

In March 1952, there were air group command changes with

LCdr. Ray Creery taking over 30 CAG from LCdr. Dick Bartlett and LCdr. Pop Fotheringham taking over 31 SAG from LCdr. Nibs Cogden.

On 2 April, Lt. Jack Sloan while carrying out his duties at NATC Patuxent River, experienced a harrowing flight from which he was lucky to have survived. Jack, with a chase plane in company, was carrying out a routine flight in an F9F jet which involved monitoring air flow characteristics. The two aircraft leveled out at 30,000 feet, and shortly after Jack experienced difficulty in maintaining accurate flight, he then became weak and found he required both hands on the control column to keep the aircraft stabilized. He became progressively weaker, then decided to reduce power and descend in a gentle dive. He was very disoriented by this time and other than trying to contact his chase plane pilot Cdr. Elder, Sloan only recalls difficulty in keeping the aircraft in the dive, and passing through layers of cloud. His next recollection was flying in level flight at about 3000 feet near Andrews Air Force Base. Shortly after this, and unable to contact Cdr. Elder, Jack then vaguely heard a radio transmission from Elder to Patuxent River tower informing them that he, Jack Sloan, had dived into the ground near Andrews Air Force Base. Following this rather shock reviving announcement, and with voice assistance from the tower at the Test Centre, Sloan groggily managed a landing with the added help of 100% oxygen.

Cdr. Elder flying the chase plane had a very clear version of the event and his concise report read as follows: "Sloan began an initial dive to about 27000 feet, followed by a gentle climbing turn which ended in an inverted attitude at almost stalling speed at 32000 feet. The aircraft commenced to dive in an inverted spiralling motion, with jerky movement of the wings. Visual contact was lost when Sloan's aircraft was seen to be diving slightly past the vertical through clouds at 12000 feet. At this point I contacted the tower and reported Sloan had gone straight in."

Two additional Canadian appointments to the USN that were of operational significance took place in April 1952. Lt. J. J. (Joe) Mac-Brien was appointed to a USN jet fighter squadron at NAS Miramar near San Diego, California. This was probably the most challenging appointment to date for a Canadian pilot, since his assigned squadron

(VF781) as part of Air Group 102, was a reserve unit activated to serve in Korea, and scheduled for operations aboard the recently renovated attack carrier USS *Oriskany*, a Boxer Class carrier. The second appointment was Lt. Doug Ross, who had been assigned to VS 22 an ASW squadron. This squadron was one of the east coast units based at Norfolk, Virginia, and was equipped with the new ASW aircraft, the Grumman AF Guardian. This was a large single-engined multi-crew configured aircraft, designed as an interim replacement for the existing Avenger. VS 22 operated aboard the USS *Mindora* one of the small 500 foot long 17 knot CVE Jeep type carriers.

In April 1952, the Canadian Cabinet Defence Committee, after examining the previously described proposals from the Admiralty regarding the future of *Magnificent*, came to the decision that it would be best for Canada to acquire an aircraft carrier to replace *Magnificent*. Accordingly, a Naval Headquarters team was formed to negotiate with the Admiralty for the purchase of a mothballed, incomplete Light Fleet Carrier identified as HMS *Powerful*.

Cdr. John Doherty was a member of this team, and the only one with an aviation background, albeit technical. John remembers a considerable degree of financial dickering ensued when it came to discuss the return of *Magnificent* to the Royal Navy. The Brits apparently took the hard-nosed view that since the RCN was responsible for bringing *Magnificent* up to the latest Alterations and Additions (A's and A's) standard for that class of ship, the RCN would be required to incorporate in *Magnificent*, such new and major modernization items as an angled deck, steam catapult, landing mirrors, together with a host of minor improvements. Doherty incidently does recall during those technical discussions, that the Admiralty team also inquired whether the RCN Staff Requirement for a carrier included the angled deck for *Powerful*. This was the first he had heard of the concept, so the decision was made to hold the matter in abeyance pending clarification by the RCN Air Staff. With regard to the Admiralty interpretation of the "A's and A's", the RCN team rightly disputed this view, arguing that the items under discussion were modernizations and in no way could be considered as A's and A's. Doherty recalls the Canadian position then hardened somewhat, making it very clear that if the Canadian Government purchased the incomplete *Powerful* on an "as is" basis and paid for completion and modernization of the ship to Canadian standards and specifications, then the Admiralty would have to forego any similar such claim on *Magnificent*.

The Admiralty finally accepted this condition and as Doherty recalls, the Canadian team later had a well earned celebration since they estimated that they had saved the Canadian Treasury about five million dollars. The British argument was actually rather unrealistic in insisting *Magnificent* be brought up to such a truly modernized state, because it would then follow that *Magnificent* would end up in the same category as the modernized *Powerful*. Conceivably Canada might just as well have purchased *Magnificent* for subsequent modernization and borrow a carrier during the period involved. So why bother with *Powerful* in the first place?

On 17 April 1952, a most tragic, difficult to accept, fatal mid air night collision took place off the coast of Nova Scotia. This was a training exercise by a flight of Avengers from 31 SAG consisting of a night illumination sortie on the cruiser *Quebec*, followed by a simulated torpedo attack. Pop Fotheringham acting as the illuminating aircraft led the flight out to the area, then detached to drop the flares to light up the cruiser. Apparently at the briefing, the use of navigation and formation lights during the attack was brought up, and Pop recalls telling the pilots that the lights were to be left on. Some confusion must have subsequently arisen between the other pilots, because during the attack run, inexplicably the lights were off and just after Lt John Murphy, the flight leader, banked into the attack run, his aircraft was struck by the number two aircraft piloted by Lt. Bill Hutchison. Pop recalls hearing only a fragmentary garbled radio transmission at the time of the accident, which sounded like a voice saying "I'm ditching," or "I've ditched", then silence.

The death toll was horrendous with seven crew members killed, which was the first fatal *Shearwater* accident to take place in over a year. Thankfully, this was the last such accident to befall Naval Aviation which would take such a toll of life. The confusion regarding the navigation and night formation lights was no doubt the major contributing factor, since without lights upon which to concentrate, in a simulated attack of this type, the ability of a pilot to maintain an adequate separation between aircraft is severely compromised. Killed in the accident were: Lt. John Anderson, Lt. William Hutchison, Lt. John Mason, Lt. John Murphy, S/Lt. Phillip Plotkins, A/BOM William Hunter and A/B OM Douglas Moffatt. Although an intensive search was carried out by ships and aircraft, only a few pieces of aircraft wreckage was ever found.

Magnificent, having undocked on 12 April following completion of the refit, was at sea on 24 April conducting the solemn memorial service for the crews killed the week earlier. 30 CAG then embarked with the pilots of 871 Fury squadron and 881 Avenger squadron carrying out deck landing qualifications. Ship drills and evolutions for the carrier were conducted, together with CAG workups for the next three weeks while operating off Bermuda. These operations were enlivened somewhat on 15 May by Lt. Mike Turner of 871 squadron, who on being recalled to the carrier during heavy deck movement, missed all the wires on landing as the stern dropped away. The resulting accident was spectacular, his Fury going through the barriers and ending inverted on the forward part of the deck. He walked away unhurt. *Magnificent* returned to Halifax on 17 May, but two days later was at sea as part of a major armament display by the CAG and the shore-based SAG aircraft, coupled with an air strike against the ships.

Meanwhile at *Shearwater*, another aviation milestone was reached with the arrival of the first Sikorsky HO4S-2 helicopter, the aircraft being flown by LCdr. Darkie Lowe and LCdr. Dennis Foley, from the manufacturers plant at Bridgeport, Connecticut. This was the first of an initial order of four aircraft, the remainder scheduled to arrive by the end of the year, becoming the nucleus for the #1 Helicopter Flight. This was a significant advance because the HO4S was an excellent well-proven utility aircraft, of primary value as a plane guard for the carrier and capable of many varied tasks. There was also a well qualified maintenance team now in place to service the arriving helicopters, the men all having taken specialized training in the USA.

In May 1952, there was increased activity by the Air Directorate Staff at Naval Headquarters with another visit by Commodore Keighly-Peach and LCdr. Dickie Bird to Washington for high level discussions with the USN. There was on-going pressure from the UK to convince the RCN that the replacement aircraft for the Sea Fury and Avenger should be British aircraft, namely the Sea Venom jet fighter and the Gannet ASW aircraft. There was also a core of diehard pro RN Canadian officers who were in support of purchasing these aircraft. This put Keighly-Peach in the proverbial hot seat, since as a senior Royal Navy officer on loan to the RCN, his mandate from the Admiralty included the promotion and sale of British naval aircraft. In his position as Chief of Canadian Naval Aviation, he likewise had a major responsibility to recommend the aircraft that would best serve the interests of the RCN. Dickie Bird was also very involved, he being the main proponent of the Banshee fighter for which cost and performance figures were now avaiable. The main purpose of the visit therefore was to determine the plans of the USN and the opinion of senior USN officers with regard to the operation of carrier-based all weather fighters on the North Atlantic trade routes. The new USN aircraft designed for this role would also be discussed.

On 5 May 1952, Lt. Vince Murphy in his capacity as Staff Officer Air to Commodore Lay in Washington, briefed Keighly-Peach on the USN view of all-weather carrier fighter operations in the North Atlantic. Murphy disclosed that the USN were virtually unanimous in the view that existing and proposed carrier jet fighters cannot be operated efficiently and economically from the CVE and CVL class of carriers in the North Atlantic. This view was predicated on the fact that the small hulls of these ships were too prone to heavy seas and suffered from excessive deck movement for an unacceptable period of time. Such a conclusion had ominous implications for the RCN, because the USN CVL Class carriers were not only considerably faster (31 knots) than the proposed modernized British Light Fleet Class (24 knots), but also had a flight deck of greater physical dimensions. The key words here in the USN comments were "cannot be operated efficiently and economically", implicitly recognizing that although jet fighters could be physically flown on and off the CVL size carriers, it would be a very marginal concept. At the same meeting, Murphy was briefed on current RCN aviation planning and it was divulged by Keighly-Peach that Cabinet approval had been given for the RCN to purchase *Powerful* for the initial sum of $15M. The plans were to modify the ship to take heavier and faster aircraft, and install the British steam catapult. No mention was made at this stage to include

Sea Fury barrier engagement, Magnificent, August 1951. Credit PA146258

RCN Acceptance team for first Sikorsky HO4S, Summer 1952.
Credit D. Foley

Sea Furies ranged prior to launching from Magnificent circa 1951-1952. Credit DND MAG 3346

881 Squadron Avenger crew briefing aboard Magnificent off Malta. L-R Lt. "Buck" Buchanan, Lt. Jack Lewry, and ABOM "Buck" Rogers. Credit PA140243

VT 40 Avenger carrying out mock attack on HM Submarine off NS coast, December 1951. Credit R.E. Quirt via DND PA133245

LSO crouches to evade incoming Sea Fury after a
late waveoff aboard Magnificent, circa 1951-52.
Credit PA115378

the newly conceived angled deck and a mirror landing system in the modernization program.

On the subject of the comparative suitability of the USN Banshee and the British Sea Venom, it was apparent that the latter, basically a two-seat RAF interceptor modified for carrier use, was unsuitable for the RCN in the envisaged role. The main disadvantages of the Sea Venom were relatively short endurance, unnecessary two seat configuration, and inferior radar performance. In addition, the aircraft was untried, had not been given a priority level of production, and being an RN adaption of an RAF fighter, did not have the built-in robust characteristics of a naval designed carrier aircraft. The F2H-3 Banshee on the other hand, met the basic RCN requirements in all respects, and being a USN fighter, not only had the distinct advantages of North American logistics and commonality of useage, but when the time came to replace the Sea Fury, the Banshee would be a well tried and tested carrier aircraft in full USN service.

One problem concerning a replacement carrier for the RCN was that the options presented by the Admiralty were of necessity restrictive, since the only carriers offered were the basic wartime Light Fleet Class carriers. Bearing this in mind, it was questionable if the Admiralty had ever considered, or had even been asked, whether the RCN all-weather jet fighter requirement would be operationally compatible with this class of ship in the North Atlantic. Observing that the Royal Navy had considerably less experience than the USN in operational carrier jet flying, it may well be that the RN did not have sufficient expertise to advise on the use of *Powerful* in this role by the RCN. The relative inexperience of the Royal Navy was borne out by the fact that the first-line naval squadrons, although performing creditably while serving in Korea, were still operating Sea Furies and Fireflies aboard the obsolescent *Colossus* class of Light Fleet British carriers, since the FAA had yet to put operational jet fighters in first line service. It is not the intention of these comments to belittle the Royal Navy's efforts in carrier aviation development, because indeed it was the Admiralty who carried out the first jet aircraft landing on a Light Fleet Class carrier in 1945. It was also to their credit that the angled deck, steam catapult and mirror landing system were conceived and developed. Unfortunately the British did not have the overall resources to quickly put such major carrier advances into general service. Thus, it was the USN with their single-minded purpose, marvellous organization and greatly superior financial resources that capitalized on such innovative carrier developments.

Of overriding concern for the RCN was the relatively long term technical planning required for *Powerful* to embody the major improvements required to operate faster and heavier aircraft. There was also the need to make major internal design and equipment changes to bring the ship up from the inferior expedient wartime design to an adequate level of peacetime Canadian habitability standards. With these factors in mind, it was doubtful if *Powerful* would be ready for service until 1957. At the same time, the naval Air Staff were working to a different deadline, since the phasing out the Sea Furies entailed a replacement with a modern jet fighter, preferably in 1954 but no later than 1955. If nothing else however, a positive result of the Washington meetings was the recognition that the Sea Venom aircraft was no longer a viable contender, and Keighly-Peach and his Air Staff could now present a strong recommendation to proceed with the Banshee as the only available and suitable fighter replacement.

On 2 June 1952, the CAG were once again laboriosly lightered from *Shearwater* aboard *Magnificent* and the carrier sailed for a four month cruise to European waters. Operating in the approaches to the English Channel, the Avengers of 881 squadron commenced night flying, with *Magnificent* later joining up with HMS *Indomitable* of WW2 fame for joint flying exercises. This flying was a prelude to Exercise Castinets which began 17 June, with the two carriers forming into a Carrier Support Group. The first two phases of this exercise consisted of convoy support, with 881 squadron flying day and night anti-submarine sorties, while 871 squadron Furies flew day fighter patrols. Phase three of the exercise continued with the aircraft carrying out offensive sorties against submarines transiting a specific area. Castinets ended on 25 June, with positive results achieved by the CAG aircraft. 881 squadron Avengers scored well with two submarine sightings and six disappearing radar contacts (submarines diving). The Furies did equally well in their air defence role, having been credited with five "enemy" aircraft shot down. The entire operation went

Magnificent resuming course after landing on Furies and
Avengers, Summer 1952. Credit J. Anderson

View of hangar deck, Magnificent, note aircraft spare parts on
bulkhead, July 1952. Credit PA140247

Fury hitting barrier after hook end broke away, pilot S/Lt. Dave Tate,
September 1952. Credit PA153034

Magnificent and plane guard destroyer coming about after landing on
Sea Furies. Credit DND DNS 5673

extremely well under closely simulated war conditions, with 30 CAG breaking their previous monthly record by flying 1032 hours, 663 by the Avengers and 368 by the Sea Furies. A significant development during this period of flying was that 881 Avengers were now flying an impressive percentage of their time around the clock as night flying increased to as much as 30% of the total.

After a short visit to Portsmouth following the completion of Castinets, *Magnificent* and her escort sailed on 1 July for Malta, then on 14 July, 30 CAG increased flying operations as *Magnificent* proceeded easterly to meet the British Mediterranean Fleet. About this time LCdr. Pat Ryan experienced increasing difficulty with his deck landings which was aggravated with problems caused by defective vision, so Pat relinquished command of the squadron. This was assumed by Lt. Ron Heath, since Lt. Deke Logan the Senior Pilot in the squadron, had, in a classic example of career planning, just departed the carrier at Malta to attend a scheduled JOTL course.

On 23 July, the carrier ran into light wind conditions after the Furies had launched, the end result was two of the aircraft had to divert to the airport at Ellenikon, Greece, one of them experiencing hydraulic problems. This complicated the situation somewhat, since *Magnificent* had a tight schedule to meet while proceeding through the Dardanelles to Istanbul with the British fleet. An Avenger with a maintenance crew aboard, therefore flew ashore, repaired the Sea Fury and the three aircraft flew on to Istanbul, Turkey.

An elaborate series of festivities had been arranged at Istanbul, which was cut short by the crisis that had developed in Egypt with the military coup d'etat on 23 July, that forced out the frolicking King Farouk. The entire British fleet sailed from Istanbul in short order much to the dismay of the thousands of visiting naval personnel, *Magnificent* departed shortly after with an equally unhappy crew who had just commenced partaking of the various Turkish delights.

Ron Heath now had the problem of getting the two Sea Furies and the accompanying Avenger and crew back aboard the Torbruk-bound *Magnificent*. International rules disallowed the landing on of aircraft in the Dardanelles and Bosphorous, so Heath and his cohorts had to remain ashore with their aircraft, manfully rising to the occasion and doing their best to fulfill the unexpended entertainment commitments left behind by the departed fleet. This ended when instructions were shortly received for the aircraft to proceed to Malta and rendezvous with *Magnificent*.

The aircraft flight plan was to proceed from Istanbul to Malta by way of Athens and Rome, but at Athens, as they were preparing for take off, wingman S/Lt. Jimmy "Shamus" Dawson suddenly announced that his Fury had a brake failure. This was an unwelcome turn of events, with the carrier now 500 miles away and no supply of spare parts immediately available. This required some impromptu action, so Ron exchanged aircraft with Jimmy, kept mum about the brake defect and they headed for Rome, but unexpected very high head winds en route forced a diversion to Naples. On arrival at the Naples airport, the control tower was unmanned since it was a Saturday afternoon, so they prudently proceeded to land on the longest runway. Ron checked his brake pressure which looked OK, and after landing, with still with no word from the tower, he elected to turn left at the end of the runway. This was when trouble really began, because the Fury obstinately turned right and promptly drove into the first three of a line of fifteen parked Italian Air Force Vampire jets. The big five bladed prop of the Fury chewed into the wings of the first, knocked it around, then getting serious proceeded to take bites out of the other two. The next thing Heath observed was pieces of metal raining from the sky like slices of bread (or salami). This was followed by Shamus taxiing by in his Fury holding his nose, a picture of dismay and horror. They shut down their aircraft amidst the carnage and silence, but nothing happened, no fire trucks, no rescue crew. Nothing!

As Heath was to recount, "About an hour and a half later a little man pedaled sedately by on a bicycle, did a beautiful double take, quickly accelerated and wheeled off. Shortly after, all hell broke loose, with the Commandant, the fire truck, photographers *et al* arriving. Curiously enough the Commandant was more concerned about the condition of Heath's Sea Fury than what was left of his three Vampires. The USN detachment at the airport were most sympathetic, proposing that the Fury be loaded on a C130 Transport aircraft and flown to Malta. By this time the 881 Avenger had arrived, and I decided it would be simpler if we just continued on to Malta, if my aircraft was still sound." (What an optimist).

On further examination, it was determined that the undercarriage "D" doors on the Sea Fury were badly bent during the destruction of the Vampires so Ron decided that they should be bashed back into shape, so to speak. Chief Petty Officer Johnny Hart, in charge of the support crew, was horrified by this proposal and refused to have any part of it. Ron finally prevailed on the crew for the loan of a sledge hammer and pounded the doors into a semblance of shape so the undercarriage could go up (and down). Meanwhile, the crew put a couple of patches on the more obvious tears in the metal skin of the Fury. As Ron was to admit later, "The Sea Fury was not really all that serviceable (surprise), what with a couple of inches of new paint showing on the tail appendage where it had been shifted while involved in demolishing the Vampires. I made the decision we would go, provided the magneto check on the engine run up was satisfactory. After doing the engine check, which appeared OK, we took off, arriving uneventfully an hour later at Hal Far air station, Malta. Understandably the engine on my Fury was shock loaded beyond limits and had to be replaced."

This rather unique tale had a comical sequel, when some ten years later while serving at Naval Headquarters, Ron Heath was passed a thick file which contained the history of the accident. The final correpondence was from the Chief of the Italian Air Force addressed to the RCAF, as was all the other correspondence. The text of the letter disclosed that since the RCAF and the Italian Air Force always had such an excellent relationship (except for WW2), the Italians, with true Roman gallantry finally decided that this incident never took place. Since the RCAF were considered by the Italians to have been involved in an accident that never officially occurred, there was no way the RCN could ever have been implicated. As near as can be determined, Ron Heath remains the RCN's leading peacetime "Ace" albeit "Friendlies".

After a week of heavy carrier flying in August, which involved a night strike on the USN fleet by 881 squadron Avengers, *Magnificent* finally left the Malta area on 18 August, and made a westward passage to Gibraltar, en route conducting day and night flying exercises. Leaving the Mediterranean, the Canadian ships set course for the UK, arriving at Belfast on 28 August, while seven aircraft of the CAG flew ashore to Sydenham at Belfast. In early September, *Magnificent* sailed with the full CAG aboard, which was the start of an intensive month's flying, reaching a peak with large scale NATO manœuvres. The first of the exercises was in the Londonderry area, and involved British and Canadian ships opposing an RN and Portugese submarine. The second exercise was somewhat disrupted on 8 September by the loss of a Sea Fury from 871 squadron, which ditched. The pilot, Lt. Brian Bell-Irving, was handily rescued by the Portugese frigate *Diogo Gomes* after about 25 minutes in the 56 degree water. Brian, wearing an immersion suit, obviously was none the worse for wear, as he was noticed exuberantly manning an oar in the ship's boat on his return to *Magnificent*.

At *Shearwater*, the Support Air Group were busy during the last week of August and early September with the annual air show at the CNE at Toronto. This involved a fairly sophisticated program for the Furies and Avengers of the group, consisting of a live armament demonstration on the lake in front of the grandstand. Rocket firing with concrete heads and strafing runs on a water target were great crowd pleasers and impressive to watch.

1952 was the first year that the RCAF demonstrated their new F86 Sabre jets at the CNE and this consisted of a high speed pass in front of the crowd, which was obviously greater than the speed normally achieved by the RCN Furies. This speed advantage however was largely offset by a plan concocted by the group commander Pop Fotheringham, and squadron commander Doug Peacocke. With a bit of subterfuge, the Furies on completion of their rocket attacks, climbed steeply to 10,000 feet while the Avengers ran through their strafing runs. The Furies then came out of a dive from the opposite direction taken by the Sabres, and with the benefit of a 15 knot tailwind, managed to whistle by the crowd at something over 400 knots, thus appearing to be as fast as the RCAF jets. Amusingly enough, some in the crowd actually thought the Furies were jets due to their distinctive whistle at high speed.

There was good news from Naval Headquarters in mid September, with the approval by Naval Board of the Banshee procurement program. A shift in pilot personnel training also took place with LCdr. Jim Hunter of the Air Staff, making preliminary arrangements to reduce the SAG Fury squadron (870) pilot strength and send selected fighter pilots to serve with USN Banshee squadrons in 1953. At the same time, pilot wings training was under review to establish the feasibility of phasing out the operational training of RCN pilots in the UK, and transferring all subsequent pilot training to the USN. This was obviously a bit tricky with two senior RN officers (Commodore Keighly-Peach and Capt. Hook) heading the directorate. However, with the RCN shift to USN aircraft, there was considerable benefit in transferring pilot training there also. In addition the fact that the Sea Fury was shortly to be phased out of service, certainly questioned the value of further post-wings operational training courses in the UK.

On 15 September 1952, commenced the largest and most ambitious NATO naval exercise since the signing of the North Atlantic Treaty Organization in 1949. This was called Exercise Mainbrace, and involved 160 ships from NATO countries. In addition to the large fleet exercises, there was a simultaneously co-ordinated large scale land force exercise underway. The main purpose of these key exercises was to reassure the Scandinavian countries that they could be defended by NATO forces in the event of an enemy attack from Eastern Europe. The role of the carrier forces in Mainbrace was to provide air strikes on the "enemy" located in Northern Norway, and then turn south to attack additional hostile forces in the Kiel area. For *Magnificent* and the RN Light Fleet Carrier *Theseus*, the exercise began with a convoy escort role with daylight air patrols provided by both carriers, then *Magnificent* would continue with night patrols in conjunction with the USN Escort Class carrier, (CVE) USS *Mindora*. The weather became very marginal as the fleet neared the Norwegian coast, and one of two fighters was unfortunately lost from *Mindora* shortly after the carrier scrambled them to intercept "enemy" aircraft. 881 squadron performed well in the exercise with three submarine sightings, one of which was rated as a "kill". Lt. Doug Ross was aboard the *Mindora* as the RCN exchange pilot of VS 22 flying the Grumman AF, and recalls the heavy flying commitments met by the carrier which involved keeping 3-4 aircraft airborne around the clock (as did *Magnificent*). During his fourteen month tour in the USN squadron he totalled an impressive 322 hours and over 100 day and night carrier landings.

It was during this period from 1952-1953 that the USN pioneered the concept of combining up to six small carriers in hunter-killer groups. This force allocation under the command of Admiral Dan Gallery, was the forerunner of the subsequent Alpha Group which, with an Essex Class carrier as the prime weapon, supported by escorts and submarines, established a roving self-contained hunter-killer group for offensive action in the Atlantic.

The next phase of Exercise Mainbrace involved *Magnificent* a few days later, carrying out close support for an amphibious group of US Marines scheduled to make a beach assault in northern Denmark. By 21 September however, the weather had deteriorated badly and gale force winds had forced the cancellation of carrier operations. The Marines eventually drove ashore at Skagen, Denmark, under better sea conditions with *Magnificent* providing air cover.

The final critique of the exercise was conducted in Oslo harbour where the carriers *Magnificent*, *Mindora* and *Theseus* gathered with the rest of the fleet. It was interesting to record the comments of Admiral Lynde McCormack USN, Supreme Allied Commander Atlantic, (SACLANT), who praised the general success of the exercise results, and the proof that the Scandinavian countries could be supported with strong backing in such a scenario. He did however also express his concern that during the course of the exercise, the remainder of his large area of operational responsibility was badly shorn of NATO forces. One aspect experienced during the exercise was the realistic conditions under which the NATO forces were operating, and it brought home to the participants, the overall risk and problems of operating naval forces in this area of ocean so often plagued with dangerous and unpredictable weather changes.

On 1 October, *Magnificent* cleared harbour to rendezvous with a Task Group including two USN carriers, the USS *Wasp* and USS *Wright*, to form the nucleus of an anti-raider Support Group for a westbound convoy en route from London to New York. This involved offensive patrols from *Magnificent* which, in one case, involved the USN battleship *Wisconsin* closing the carrier force at 30 knots. The raider was detected by an 881 Avenger, and a combined force of 80 aircraft in two strikes was launched from the carriers. This exercise continued until 9 October 1952, at which time *Magnificent* detached with the cruiser *Quebec*, entering Halifax after an absence of over four

Magnificent encountering heavy seas during Exercise Mainbrace, September 1952. Credit DND MAG 4650

Flypast of VU 32 Avengers during dedication and opening ceremony of Hampton Gray Memorial School, Shearwater, October 29, 1952. Credit Donal Peeling, PA139952

months. This entire cruise had been most productive for the CAG and with NATO exercises now becoming an integral part of regularly scheduled maneuvres, a high degree of sustainable operational readiness was being achieved by *Magnificent* and the air group.

An indication of the growing importance of RCN aviation and the overall improvement of training facilities at *Shearwater*, was the arrival in the fall of 1952, of ten Royal Navy Midshipman to form the first NATO air observers course. To meet this on-going commitment to train allied observers, the Officer-in-Charge of the school, LCdr. Jack Stokes, had his training staff augmented by three additional Officers from the Royal Navy, headed by the experienced and very capable observer LCdr. A.J. "Mac" McCullough. As Jack Stokes was to recall, in addition to the expertise provided by the RN, a considerable degree of credit for the overall organization and instructional standards established by the school, was due in a large part to Lt. Dick Quirt, who worked tirelessly to develop and procure suitable training aids and establish the classroom facilities.

A significant improvement to the overall air defence of the RCN ships took place with the arrival at *Shearwater* of the first of the eight Avenger-3W2 long range surveillance aircraft. These aircraft were to play a major role in ASW and fighter control operations from *Magnificent*, with the first "Guppy" Airborne Early Warning Flight subsequently being formed in April 1953.

In the far Pacific, en route to the Korean theatre of operations, Canadian Lt. Joe MacBrien, along with his fellow USN fighter pilots was undergoing the final preparations for combat operations. MacBrien particularly remembers at that time the comprehensive intelligence briefings provided by the USN, including a detailed account of every successful escape and evasion made by allied aircrew to date in the Korean conflict, together with procedures used by the enemy in the interrogation of prisoners of war (POW). It was revealing that he was given a special briefing as the only non USN pilot. This was of little comfort, since at the briefing, the USN officers predicted that if he was unlucky enough to become the first RCN aircrew prisoner, he could expect the full interrogation treatment. This particular interrogation process was reserved for prisoners with any unusual identity or situation such as his RCN status. He was actually offered a false ID by the USN, but was also warned that if he was subsequently forced to reveal his true identity while under interrogation, it would no doubt have dire consequences for him. Joe subsequently was to recall that the gloomy prediction of his probable fate was borne out, many years later, when he met Canadian Squadron Leader Andy Mackenzie. Andy had been shot down and taken prisoner while flying as an RCAF pilot with the US Air Force and suffered badly under the cruel treatment meted out by the North Koreans.

The final cruise for *Magificent* before the year ended was a carrier requalification cruise for the SAG pilots and crews of 870 Fury squadron and 880 Avenger squadron, the carrier sailing from Halifax on 5 November. It was a bit of a rush for me personally, having just arrived back from LSO training, and proceeding directly to the SAG Fury squadron. I just managed to obtain the minimum 25 hours on the Fury and six sessions of FCLPs before flying aboard. There was an initial rash of broken tail oleos encountered by the Furies, which on examination appeared to show the tail oleo occasionally striking the wire and fracturing. This was later rectified with a modification to the tail, and the trouble ceased.

I had the honour (during a landing demonstration for some dignitaries) of experiencing what was apparently hook bounce on one landing with the hook finally catching #10 wire, with upfront assistance from the barrier, which brought the Fury to a halt. While sitting in the Fighter Ready Room a little while later, Pop Fotheringham, with rather a mischievous grin asked, "How long do you reckon it took from the time you first touched down until you hit the barrier?" I looked at him for a minute and about all I could say was, "Oh, about as long as it takes to say shit!" Pop, a pretty smooth pilot who had managed to never experience more than a burst tire in his flying career, obviously did not understand some of the finer points of Sea Fury late wires and barrier engagements.

Magnificent conducted flying operations for three weeks with the SAG, generally north of the Bermuda area, with most pilots and crews making two sorties a day, each squadron operating on an advanced work up schedule. This was a very successful period of carrier flying for the group, with the pilots and crews each obtaining close to 25 landings and the same number of flying hours. The last two days of the embarked period consisted of strikes on the British cruiser *Sheffield* by both the Avengers and Sea Furies, with the cruise ending on 27 November 1952, terminating a year of extensive flying for *Magnificent*.

November saw yet another change to the RCN squadron and group numbering and identity system. This one was positive from the point of standardizing with the USN, and made good sense, particularly during joint operations between the RCN and USN. The change involved a two letter prefix before each squadron number, which identified both the type and function of the squadron. VF designated fighter squadrons, VS search (ASW squadrons), VH denoted helicopter squadrons and VU designated utility squadrons. The RCN operational units were therefore re-numbered as follows:

> 30 Carrier Air Group:
> VF 871 (Sea Fury) - VS 881 (Avenger)
> 31 Support Air Group:
> VF 870 (Sea Fury) - VS 880 (Avenger)

As the year ended there were some interesting figures released by the Chief of Naval Staff, which presented some illuminating financial figures outlining the expenditures on Naval Aviation from its inception. These figures, expressed in millions of dollars, were as follows:

Fiscal Year	Total Naval Expenditures	Naval Air Expenditures	% of Air Expenditures
1946-47	64.48M	6.94M	10.7
1947-48	43.72M	5.81M	13.3
1948-49	44.65M	7.22M	16.2
1949-50	73.40M	8.80M	12.0
1950-51	99.85M	11.20M	11.2
1951-52	182.37M	13.15M	7.2
1952-53-est	243.12M	18.00M	7.4
Totals	751.96M	71.12M	9.4%

The foregoing financial totals are interesting in the sense that the aviation percentage remains, on average, approximately 10% of the total naval budget. As can be seen, the percentage actually drops quite significantly for 1951-52 and 1952-53, which is largely due to the shipbuilding program underway for the fleet. Although the RCN Aviation Branch had increased considerably in both scope and operations, the actual dollar share on a percentage basis showed a steady on-going drop from 1948/49 onward, which if continued was a disturbing trend.

Chapter Five

ON COURSE

For Canadian Naval Aviation, the year 1953 ushered in a period of considerable growth and increased stability during which several important developments took place.

At Naval Headquarters, approval had been given to commence pipeline training for Canadian naval pilots with the USN. This transfer of training to the USN would not only be less costly then the existing combined RCAF and Royal Navy pilot courses, but would also provide a common standard of training with a solid naval background throughout. The change-over would facilitate the streaming of pilots to post wings operational service on Avengers, and provide a comprehensive jet syllabus for the fighter pilot graduates as they proceeded on to the planned Banshee fighter replacement for the Sea Furies. In the meantime, the remaining few Canadian pilots, under operational training in the UK, would finish their courses on Fireflies and Sea Furies and continue to be streamed into the 31st. Support Air Group onto Furies or Avengers or directly to 30 CAG if applicable.

In the United States meanwhile, the USN with typical fast tracking had expeditiously completed the conversion of an Essex Class carrier, the USS Antietam, to the canted or angled deck, as first conceived by the Admiralty. Deck landing trials were planned for February 1953. This was naturally of considerable interest to the RCN, and a team from the Naval Air Staff, Ottawa, headed by Commodore Keighly-Peach, was scheduled to witness the trials first hand, primarily to establish the feasibility of the angled deck concept to the incomplete carrier *Powerful*, now undergoing modernization and conversion for the RCN.

At *Shearwater*, change of command took place in February 1953, with Captain A.H.G. Storrs, DSC and Bar, assuming the air station from Captain D.L. Raymond. On his departure, Raymond noted that the amenities at the air station were still far from satisfactory, with over 1600 officers and men living "in a station which is still a conglomeration of old temporary buildings and grounds which have not been landscaped." On a positive note however, a badly needed new barrack block was under construction and new recreation facilities were under consideration. An additional routine command change also took place in February with the assumption of VF 870 SAG Fury squadron by LCdr. D.M. "Pappy" Macleod, replacing Lt. Doug Peacocke.

30 CAG commenced an active year of flying with both VF 871 Fury squadron and VS 881 Avenger squadrons flying to Rivers Manitoba, in February for a close air support course at the Canadian Joint Air Training Centre (CJATC). For VF 871 Fury squadron this was a highly concentrated month of advanced armament training, with the emphasis on dive bombing and rocket attacks, each pilot carrying out between two and three missions per day. As part of the work up, bomb loads of 2000 pounds (2 - 1000lb. bombs) were carried, a good indication of the Sea Fury armament load capability. This one ton bomb load also made a first hand impression on Lt Shamus Dawson, since he witnessed the imposing sight of two 1000 pounders flash by the nose of his aircraft, the ordnance being released a trifle early from the preceding Fury flown by Lt. Harry Frost.

The major concentration of the Fury fighter squadron, on armament work ups and air strike tactics, was the direct result of a delayed Canadian Government response to an official Admiralty request for the loan of 12 Canadian Sea Furies and 14 pilots for service aboard HMS *Warrior* in Korean waters. In 1951 and again in 1952, proposals had been made for *Magnificent* to be used in Korea to serve along with the Royal Navy and Australian Navy aircraft carriers. This proposal was rejected by the Minister of Defence principally on the grounds that *Magnificent* was primarily an ASW carrier, and her employment in a strike role could not be justified. In addition, if

Magnificent was assigned to Korea for fighter strike duties, it may well have been interpreted in some quarters as a failure on the part of Canada to meet NATO commitments. There was also believed to be pressure by the highest level of the RCAF to discourage this deployment, since it would put an identifiable RCN carrier and a first line naval fighter squadron in direct operations, a move which could not help but put the RCAF in a lesser light, since there were no RCAF fighter squadrons available for Korea service. The final approval to send the naval fighter squadron to Korea was eagerly anticipated by the Sea Fury pilots, and would have provided an excellent opportunity to serve in combat. The fact that Canada would have an operational naval squadron flying combat sorties in Korea should also not be overlooked from the public awareness point of view, since for the most part Canadians were generally poorly informed about the role and scope of the operations of Canadian Naval Aviation. The detachment of the CAG to Rivers however, did provide an excellent opportunity to publicize the physical existence of naval aviation with flying demonstrations carried out by the Avengers of VS 881 for the Naval Divisions at Regina, Saskatoon, Calgary and Edmonton.

At *Shearwater*, HU 21 was becoming increasingly involved in general utility duties, one particular assignment being the aerial restocking of fish for the Provincial government at otherwise inaccessible lakes in the Maritimes. Two additional Sikorsky HO4S helicopter aircraft had now been added to the squadron strength, which greatly expanded the overall capability of the air station in both the utility and search and rescue role.

The restocking of lakes must have been the inspiration for a scheme to set up a fishing camp at remote Yankee Lake for the "anglers" of *Shearwater*, thereby providing a weekend fishing diversion, no doubt justified in part by the inclusion of a degree of bush survival training. The latter occurred unexpectedly to one small group of avid fishermen, following the departure of a party headed by Cdr. Ted Edwards and Darkie Lowe, who had previously been airlifted into the remote fishing camp, dropped off with their camping supplies and enjoyed a great fishing weekend. The chopper then returned with the second fishing group led by the station toothright (dentist) Major Dave Carmichael, picked up the first team and departed in a blast of downwash. Two days later the anglers were recovered. Darkie Lowe, the squadron CO, noticed the returning group from his office and was surprised to find the party more than somewhat grungy, begrimed, certainly well-smoked and also fishless. Subsequently as was narrated, the chopper as it sped away after dropping the incoming anglers, had apparently reactivated the dying embers of the camp fire with the chopper downwash, the blaze quickly expanded and became a "camp on fire". In the meantime, the fishermen placidly casting in the middle of the lake were blissfully unaware of the ongoing drama at the camp. From that point on, they quickly became deeply involved in bush survival, spending most of their weekend fire fighting. Their efforts were eventually augmented by a volunteer team from the nearest provincial fire station who spent several hours foot slogging through the woods to the remote location. It was not a fun weekend! The story did not end there however, because not long after, Ted Edwards was more than perturbed to receive a healthy bill for "fire services rendered" from the Nova Scotia Government, which was passed to him from Captain Storrs, and penned with a cryptic "deal with this" note. It was only after frantic scurrying about and the submission of a detailed, tedious summary of all the various helicopter missions flown gratis by the helicopter squadron on behalf of Provincial authorities, that the matter of the financial obligation was quietly dropped.

During the early months of 1953, the air war in Korea was continuing unabated, following on from the heavy carrier air strikes that had taken place in December 1952. On one such raid in February, RCN exchange pilot Joe MacBrien was singled out for the award of the United States decoration, the Distinguished Flying Cross, the only RCN officer to be awarded this prestigious medal. His citation read as follows: "For extraordinary achievement while flying a jet fighter on a combat mission over Communist held North Korea on 1 February 1953, Lt MacBrien led a flight of jet aircraft against an enemy supply storage area near the town of Pukchong on the vital east coast supply route." As Kealy recounts in his History of Canadian Naval Aviation, "The mission was accomplished despite marginal flying weather and heavy anti-aircraft fire with courageous leadership and outstanding demonstration of pilot skill." MacBrien amassed an impressive 233 jet

flying hours and over 90 deck landings during his six month operational tour in Korea. His Air Group of 2 F9F-5 jet squadrons, one
F4U squadron and one AD squadron, during the same period completed over 7000 missions from the carrier with a loss of 11 pilots,
which was truly indicative of the highly intensive operational flying
being conducted by the USN carrier forces. As Joe MacBrien was to
later recount, his tour of flying with the USN on operations was an
exceptional experience, and it was truly awesome to be part of a four
carrier strike force of 300-400 aircraft. He was also pleasantly
surprised to find how valuable his air training in the RN and RCN
turned out to be, particularly the Air Weapons Course, the Joint Air
Training at Rivers, and the practical aspects of Photo Interpretation
and excellent background provided by the CBAL Army Groups
attached to both *Magnificent* and *Shearwater*.

Aboard HMCS *Iroquois* serving in Korean waters, the duty was
not all action and the drama of battle, since the life in the wardroom
was often enlivened by the ongoing rivalry between Lts. Bill Farrell
and Duke Wardrop as the two airmen served out their tour in Korea.
The pair set new highs (or lows) in the art of practical jokes upon one
another. They quickly graduated beyond the tame substitution of
toothpaste for white shoe polish and vice versa, as the jokes continued
to escalate in both rancor and somewhat questionable humour. Probably the most diabolical trick was played by Wardrop upon the
unsuspecting Farrell with the placing of a professionally crafted,
hideously life-like snake under Farrell's pillow, the result of this caper
being a horrified scream heard throughout the officers quarters. This
antic may well have terminated the contest with a truce of sorts. On
occasion they did combine their talents. One particular nefarious deed
was carried out when the ship was alongside and they were the only
officers aboard to offer advice to a naïve visiting female from the
Canadian Embassy. She had come aboard to discuss protocol details
of an official function involving Japanese guests and the ship's
captain, Landymore, who unfortunately (for him) had proceeded
ashore. The pair falsely assured the young lady that Landymore was
indeed fluent in Japanese and would not require an interpreter, they
carried their counselling even further with the mischievous and untrue
suggestion that the captain should only be allowed one social drink

because he had a problem with alcohol. It was subsequently a complete and unwelcome surprise for Landymore while attending the function, to be surrounded by a throng of Japanese, none of whom was able to speak English, while he attempted without success to attract the attention of the drink-serving waiters who were studiously avoiding him as per their instructions.

Duke Wardrop was an outwardly chippy, aggressive and complex character, who often openly displayed his contempt for various aspects of naval tradition, law and administration, by being outrageously independent. The classic example of this trait took place while in Korea. Apparently Duke's short service commission had expired with absolutely no indication as to his future disposition. Accordingly, he failed to appear on the destroyer's bridge at the required time as Officer of the Watch. After repeated pipes throughout the ship to report, with no response, and the captain becoming more incensed, Duke strolled up to the bridge in civilian clothes with a magazine under his arm. He then loftily announced, "Since I am no longer serving as an officer of the RCN, I wish henceforth to be addressed as Mr. Wardrop, and I would like immediate steps taken for me to be landed ashore at the nearest port!" Even Landymore had to eventually appreciate the humour of the unusual situation.

Meanwhile there were some interesting air staff dicussions underway at Naval Headquarters, concerning the replacement carrier for *Magnificent*. On the assumption that the RCN would be re-equipping with American Banshee and S2F aircraft to replace the Sea Furies and Avengers, Commodore Keighly-Peach and his deputy, Captain P.K. Will, USN, believed it would still be of value to investigate the possibility of obtaining a USN *Essex* Class carrier on a loan basis for the RCN. The rationale for this being that the purchase of the *Powerful* had, to a large extent, been originally predicated on the fact that the British Venom and Gannet would also be selected. Now that the British aircraft had been discarded, the opportunity for a loaned *Essex* had certain benefits. The Chief of Naval Staff approved and inquiries were made through the Canadian Embassy, Washington. The response from the USN was encouraging in one sense, because they would release an *Essex* Class carrier, the USS *Tarawa* for $1. per year. The major drawback was that the catapult currently installed could not handle the faster jets, and to modify the ship, and face the added expense of the larger crew required, did not sit well with the pro-*Powerful* group in the RCN, so this proposal was abandoned.

At *Shearwater*, an important squadron addition was made in March 1953, with the authorization to establish a separate naval experimental and testing facility, to meet the steadily increasing requirements of the Naval Air Branch. The new unit was designated Experimental Squadron 10 (VX 10) and was to henceforth assume the responsibility to test all new aircraft and equipment as it came into naval service. This move had been spearheaded by Cdr. Gerry Daniel in his capacity as Director of Air Engineering at Naval Headquarters. The need had been well recognized that a single facility was essential to test new equipment and conduct operational evaluations by naval air specialists. VX 10, being directly responsible for such activities, played a key role in the testing of the newly converted Avengers to the ASW role, together with the associated new equipments being tested and installed. LCdr. Hal Fearon was the first Commanding Officer to be appointed to VX 10, and the squadron quickly assumed its new duties with a capable nucleus of engineering officers and maintenance personnel under the guidance of LCdr. A/E Art Geraghty.

Unfortunately, flying in April 1953 started off on a bad note. The weather was generally marginal with widespread low ceilings, and the squadron programs were often limited with flying operations restricted to the local area. At night, this situation was further aggravated by reduced visibility and congested air traffic in the vicinity of the airfield. There was a generally low ceiling of about 1500 feet on the night of 9 April, and in 870 Fury squadron, Lt. Bob O'Neil having just joined the squadron after completing his operational training in the UK, was on his first night familiarization from *Shearwater*. Apparently he inadvertently flew into the cloud base just after becoming airborne, so quickly descended in order to regain visual contact with the ground. At the same time, two Avengers flown by Lts. Fred Rice and Robby Hughes were flying in formation below the overcast about 10 miles to the west of the field on a night proficiency flight. Robby, who was formating on the lead Avenger flown by Fred, was horrified to catch a glimpse of a Fury (piloted by O'Neil) suddenly appear out of the night overcast and in a blinding flash slice through the cockpit of Rice's aircraft. Fred never knew what hit him. The Avenger continued to momentarily fly on with the cockpit section literally torn away. Then it was all over in a few seconds, as the two stricken aircraft crashed out of control, the Avenger in the waters of Bedford Basin, and the Fury on a nearby hill. This double fatality was a devastating night for *Shearwater*, with the loss of long time associate Freddy Rice, while those of us in VF 870 were shocked by the loss of O'Neil our newly arrived squadron pilot. There was also the usual initial uncertainty and confusion when such an accident occurs nearby, with so many aircraft airborne, the problem being to quickly establish the identity of the aircraft and pilots, and inform the next of kin before the press got into the act and publicized the event. This accident was the first Sea Fury fatality at the air station in two years.

Regrettably, this was not the end of the bad news. An hour or so later, a group of 743 squadron Avengers led by LCdr. Jimmy Watson, were forced to descend to stay below the low cloud base around the hills south of Greenwood. S/Lt. Weldon Paton, the pilot and his crew of Chief Petty Officer "Windy" Geale, Petty Officer Paul Martin and Able Seaman M. Legare who were flying in the rear of the formation, suddenly found themselves chopping their way through heavy timber as their aircraft literally flew into the high ground. As Windy Geale was to relate, "I thought we were in trouble when the aircraft began to vibrate (as it plowed through the trees) and was getting ready to bail out." They were extremely fortunate, managing to escape quickly from the plane with little more than a severe shaking up, before the wrecked aircraft caught fire and blew up. The remarkably sturdy Avengers were to subsequently prove most protective of their crews in similar circumstances while making unplanned contact with the terrain.

Tony Storrs was to remark many years later, that he was greatly dismayed by these two serious accidents in one night, following an earlier unfortunate fatal crash of an Avenger on 3 March. Indeed, on reflection, he was wondering what he had got himself into, facing three major accidents just after assuming command. As it turned out, tragic as they were, these accidents turned out to be the last fatal ones to occur at *Shearwater* during his two year tour of command.

About the same time as *Shearwater* personnel were undergoing the trauma of the mid-air collision, Lt. Al Woods had an unnerving flight, ferrying a Royal Navy Attacker jet from winter testing at Namao to *Shearwater*, for transit back to the UK aboard *Magnificent*. Al experienced an engine flameout at 30,000 feet about 60 miles west of the Kinross airport at Sault Ste. Marie. He was unable to relight, so glided the entire distance, executing a dead stick landing at Kinross where he descended on instruments, breaking into the clear under a 2000 foot ceiling. The balky engine was examined and appeared to be serviceable after some adjustments, so Woody started off again. He experienced another engine failure and was forced to make another 60 mile glide, this time to Uplands airport, Ottawa. He was getting pretty good at 60 mile engine off arrivals by this time, so he set off once more, and other than a few more minor engine malfunctions, he made it to *Shearwater*. I had occasion to mention to Woody later, that I would have ejected out of the aircraft like a rocket if it had happened to me. Al said, "Its all very well for you to say, but I would have left my kneecaps hanging on the aircraft instrument panel if I had ejected, because the cockpit was not designed for a long-legged galoot like me!" Al, very deservedly, was later awarded the Queens Commendation for valuable service in the air, the citation stating "Lt. Woods' coolness and judgement, saved a valuable aircraft from damage or destruction and reflects considerable credit on himself and his Service." Incidently, the Attacker jet as one might surmise, was not a very successful aircraft having only limited service in the Royal Navy.

By the end of April, *Magnificent* and other ships of the Canadian Coronation squadron, headed by Rear Admiral Bidwell wearing his flag aboard the cruiser *Quebec* were preparing to join the massive naval display off Portsmouth celebrating Coronation Day, with a naval review at Spithead on 15 June 1953. Command of *Magnificent* had previously changed in March with Commodore H.S. Rayner, DSC and Bar taking over from Captain Dyer. Both the 31 SAG and 30 CAG also underwent command changes about this time, with LCdr. Don Knox taking over the SAG from LCdr. Pop Fotheringham in April and LCdr. John Roberts taking over the 30 CAG from Ray Creery in May, while Lt. Mike Wasteneys assumed command of VF 871 from Lt. Ron Heath.

Deck landing refresher for 30 CAG was carried out and then the air group joined the carrier in early May. Flying was carried out in transit to the UK but was necessarily restricted due to poor weather, but both the Sea Furies and Avengers conducted exercises in the English Channel, the Avengers working with the British submarine *Acheron*. All serviceable aircraft were later flown ashore to RNAS Lee-on-Solent in preparation for the naval aircraft flypast, while *Magnificent* and the other ships of the squadron assumed their anchorages off Spithead as part of one of the largest international display of naval ships ever assembled in peacetime.

At Naval Headquarters, the Banshee program had been approved in principle, and Dickie Bird prepared and completed the full staff proposal to the USN, which was sent with a letter of intent signed by The Chief of Naval Staff. The purchase was for 60 F2H3 aircraft at a cost of $500,000. each, with an additional $9M for spares support. The fitting of the Sidewinder air to air missile was also included in the package. As Bird was to recall, the Canadian order was planned as an add-on to the existing USN order, which was scheduled to shut down in September 1953, since McDonnell the manufacturer required the production space for their new types of aircraft such as the Voodoo, Demon and Phantom II. The acceptance of the Canadian order was actually done as a favour to the RCN, but the USN were reluctant to commit themselves to the Canadian production order until the necessary funds were fully approved and committed. At this point, the Canadian Cabinet began to question whether or not the funds could be made available during the current fiscal year which expired in March 1954. The procrastination continued, and it was only at the eleventh hour and under pressure from McDonnell, that a Canadian team were dispatched to Washington to turn over a cheque for $39M to honour the purchase agreement. All the arrangements appeared to be in place, the Canadian Embassy in Washington was preparing to process the agreement, when without any warning the Canadian Cabinet backtracked, and stated that the funds would not be released until following the end of the fiscal year. That killed the program completely, and McDonnell shut down Banshee production in September of 1953. Now the RCN was in a real bind, and about the only alternative left was to attempt to purchase used Banshees from the

USN as they became surplus in 1955. As can be imagined, there was considerable resentment on the part of the USN negotiating team, who after conducting extensive negotiations, rightly felt that they had been badly misled by the Canadian Government.

In May 1953, the on again, off again decision to implement reserve air training (initially approved in 1946) was finally put into play with the formation of VC 922 Reserve Air Squadron attached to the Toronto division HMCS *York*. This was warmly supported by several volunteers who had been former flyers, and became the primary reserve unit. Other units were soon to follow including VC 921 at Kingston, Ont. attached to the reserve division HMCS *Cataraqui* and VC 922 at HMCS *Malahat*, Victoria, B.C. Later the reserve establishment would expand to include two more squadrons, VC 923 at Quebec (HMCS *Montcalm*) and VC 924 at Calgary (HMCS *Tecumseh*). Experienced RCN pilots with instructional background were appointed to each unit, providing the means to train young pilots to a service wings status. Each unit was assigned Harvard trainers, and personnel included a small nucleus of RCN air maintenance personnel. This establishment of Reserve Squadrons commenced a long and successful period of reserve pilot training across the country, which was to eventually reach a high standard of flying training, culminating in a two week advanced period at *Shearwater* each summer.

On 15 June, 30 CAG took part in the impressive Coronation flypast of 1000 naval aircraft, co-ordinated to fly over the temporary Royal yacht *Surprise* as part of the Spithead Review. This was a very complicated flying display led by Admiral Cushman, RN in a Sea Vampire. As Mike Wasteneys recalls, "The Admiral was followed by squadrons of Sea Hawks, Attackers, Meteors, Sea Vampires, Sea Hornets, Sea Furies, Avengers and Fireflies. Squadrons converged on the main stream of aircraft from holding positions along the south coast of England. I also had a squadron of RN Sea Furies in my formation, flying directly astern of VF 871, so the sixteen Furies in my group were held in a holding position over Portland Bill. As some 500 aircraft, in squadrons in line astern came into sight, we slipped in behind them at an interval of about 50 yards. The remaining squadrons joined in and closed up behind us in a similar position. The plan was to have a continuous flow of aircraft flying over HMS *Surprise* where Queen Elizabeth and Prince Phillip were aboard observing the ceremonies. The height of the flypast was supposed to be 1000 feet passing over the Royal Yacht. By the time I reached the ship, I could not go any higher than 200 feet because all the aircraft ahead of me had successively stepped down to avoid slipstream. This practically put us amongst the masts of the various ships in the review, and the turbulence from the aircraft ahead was unbelievable. All in all, those pilots flying close formation on their leaders had a most uncomfortable flight."

As often happens, there was a small deviation to the well-planned and rehearsed massive flypast. Lt Archie Benton, USN, the exchange pilot serving with VF 871 was unlucky enough to draw the spare aircraft position for the flypast, and resigned to the fact that he would not be required in the formation, elected to fly along and watch the show from the sidelines, at what he considered a prudent and unnoticed distance. Since nobody had ever thought he would do this, he obviously had not been told not to do it. So Archie whilst engaged in picture taking and carrying out a few low level rolls, obviously attracted a degree of official attention, not least of whom was the Royal party, his presence definitely suggesting that an unauthorized aircraft was carrying out aerobatics over the Royal Review area. When Benton landed, he was greeted by two armed seamen and escorted to the Air Commander at Lee-on-Solent, where he was royally chewed out. What raised his own ire was being called a "Fucking Canadian", when he acknowledged that he was a member of VF 871. Archie, recognizing that there was a degree of hostility in the air, fortunately refrained from identifying himself as a "Yankee Doodle Dandy" and abruptly departed. However, when it was finally determined that he was a USN officer with the Canadian Fury squadron, the situation became somewhat internationally delicate. Archie gained a further degree of notoriety as he was the subject of a message sent to all ships stating that his action was in violation of all orders and caused "great consternation" to Her Majesty Queen Elizabeth II. Archie was impressed to say the least. Fortunately, it all finally blew over when Commander Abrams, the head of *Magnificent*'s Air Dept., had a little "chat" with Archie. Abrams in conjunction with Commodore Rayner

Shearwater officers hockey team 1953. Credit J. Dawson

871 Sea Fury Squadron personnel designated for carrier operations with the Royal
Navy Korea, 1953. Front row, L-R Archie Benton(USN), Jimmy Dawson, Harry Frost,
Dave Tate, Brian Bell-Irving. Rear row L-R Ben Oxholm, Mike Turner, Don McNicol,
Mike Wasteneys (CO), Bob Williamson (LSO), Dave Litle (AEO). Credit J. Dawson

Carrier row at anchor off Spithead for Coronation Review, June 1953.
Magnificent in foreground. Credit DND MAG 4588

Fireworks display by Magnificent at Coronation Review, June 1953.
Credit R. Duiven

decided that the matter would go no further and be forgotten as long as Archie promised not to do it again. Archie humbly and faithfully agreed to so promise. Abrams then pointedly remarked with a chuckle, after the meeting was over and Archie was leaving, "Of course there won't be another Coronation for some time."

Benton fondly recalls his one year tour of flying duty with 871 Sea Fury squadron, as follows, "I must say that my tour with this squadron has to rank at the top in terms of my flying assignments. I never had an assignment I did not enjoy, but the Canadian tour with 871, was certainly the most memorable. This was in the main because the officers and men were outstanding, really terrific people. The Sea Fury of course, was the last of the propellor driven fighter planes; the best that could be built. It was fortunate for me that I had come to this squadron from a previous tour with F8F Grumman Bearcat fighter planes. The F8F was the last USN propellor driven fighter airplane. So shifting over to the Fury was not too difficult for me. In fact it was better behaved, more stable, a few knots faster, definitely stronger structurally, more well proportioned and symmetrical. To sum up, it was a damn good looking fighter plane and it flew as good as it looked."

Following the Coronation ceremonies, the Canadian squadron sailed for Halifax by a southerly course in an attempt to find better flying weather. This was only partially successful, and after a limited amount of flying, the carrier and the escorts arrived at Halifax on 25 June.

At *Shearwater* there were major improvements underway, starting in May and June, consisting primarily of extensive taxi and runway repairs and the construction of a new and longer runway, which would not only eliminate the 60,000 lb. aircraft landing weight restriction at *Shearwater*, but would also provide a proper runway designed for jet traffic.

The background for the justification for the new runway is a story in itself. LCdr. Hank Leidl was the Air Staff officer who provided the impetus for getting the runway approved by Naval Staff. He went about his task in a pragmatic and business-like manner, to the extent that he solicited the expert assistance of his opposite numbers in the RCAF. They were both considerate and helpful, surveying the airfield and sending experts from their own Engineering Branch to provide detailed estimates and drawings for the proposed runway. Unfortunately Hank's plans did run into a bit of service politics when it came time to submit his proposal. Apparently the RCAF officers involved, could not simply hand over their calculations directly to Leidl. Rather, it went all the way up the RCAF staff ladders to the Chief of the Air Staff (CAS), then across to the Chief of the Naval Staff (CNS) then back down the chain to Leidl. As Jim Burns was to recount years later, when the paper reached the Naval Air Staff, there were a number of unkind comments made by senior RCAF officers, not least of which was the penned remarks by the CAS saying, "The Navy shouldn't even be flying airplanes." All of which supports our long held view that considerable antagonism was still held against Naval Aviation by some of the RCAF brass.

The overall construction on the *Shearwater* airfield restricted the movement of aircraft considerably, so the decision was made to relocate the 31 SAG with its Furies and Avengers and open up a temporary Naval Air Facility (NAF) at an unused RCAF airfield at Scoudouc NB., just east of Moncton. This transfer of all personnel and equipment required the setting up of a miniature naval air station with all supporting facilities, including a mobile control tower, crash crew and a medical team. Considerable credit for the minimal problems encountered in establishing the air facility was due to the *Shearwater* base technical personnel who worked long hours and displayed considerable ingenuity in modifying and designing mobile equipment for a separate detached air facility. This move was carried out surprisingly well, with minor upgrading and modifications quickly implemented to the service buildings at Scoudouc, and by the end of May, the entire group was well established.

Prior to shifting to Scoudouc, the flying intensity of the SAG was maintained at a high level, and in addition to the normal fighter tactics for the Furies and the ASW training for the Avengers, there was an increased emphasis on instrument cross country flying. This often involved four aircraft, with the lead pilot filing the flight on his instrument card. One such flight to Argentia, led by Pappy Macleod, involved myself, Lt. Vern Cunningham and S/Lt. Jake Birks, the first of the four original USN trained Canadian Midshipmen pilots to graduate as a fighter pilot. Our flight was to the USN base at Argentia, where we planned to refuel and of course visit the Post Exchange for "Duty Free" goods. Our purchases naturally were stowed out of sight in the wing ammunition trays, which involved taking the covers off and correctly replacing the locking fasteners. On arrival at *Shearwater*, after a formation instrument letdown and approach, we taxied in all innocence to the hangar, only to be met by the Customs Officer. To Pappy's horror, Jake bringing up the rear, blithely taxied by with his liquid purchases sticking up out of the wing, his aircraft having lost the ammunition panel cover on landing. Fortunately, the ever-alert line crew managed to remove the evidence in time, but as Pappy said later while chewing Jake out, "For Gods sake if you are going to be a smuggler look and act like one!" Vern Cunningham had rather a unique position in the squadron and remembers such humorous episodes with nostalgia. He was a teacher by profession, and as an officer in the reserves, (ex RCAF/RNVR pilot) decided he would like to fly Sea Furies and accordingly took a sabbbatical from his teaching job and joined us in 870 squadron. He remarked more than once, "It was one of the best times I ever had, they gave me an operational flying course, put me in a fighter squadron, gave me a beautiful aircraft to fly, let me carry out deck landings and zip about the country, and while doing all this, they also pay me!"

The ever increasing flying commitments of HU 21 broadened into many diverse areas as the squadron crews developed their expertise. In June, their ready capability was given public prominence by the rescue of two youngsters adrift in Bedford Basin aboard their homemade raft. Unable to hoist the pair, they were effectively blown to safety by directing the chopper's slipstream to shore.

There was gratifying evidence of further construction progress at *Shearwater* during the summer, with the completion of the new barrack block for the men, aptly given the name *Warrior* Block. The Observer School was also completed, and at the formal opening, wings were presented to the first graduating class of officers from the NATO Observer Course.

In June, at Naval Headquarters Ottawa, there was a change of personnel at the senior level with the departure of Commodore Keighly-Peach the Naval Board Member for Air, having completed his tour of duty whilst on attachment to the RCN. He was replaced by Commodore W.L.M. Brown, DSO, RN, who had an observer background. Keighly-Peach was probably the one RN officer who had done the most for the cause of Canadian Naval Aviation. He truly recognized the problems the young branch was experiencing and by distancing himself from Admiralty ties, he did everything possible to expand the scope and role of Canadian Naval Aviation by exerting strong leadership. Through keen personal interest, he gave both direction and support at the senior officer level, actively promoting the acquisition of the most suitable aircraft and equipment for the RCN, regardless of whether it was British or American built. Lt. Jim Burns was serving on the naval Air Staff when Keighly-Peach departed, and he remembers most vividly being called into the Commodore's office along with the other members. They were all dumbfounded when the Commodore unlocked the safe in the office, withdrew and showed them a personal file, which was his terms of reference from the Royal Navy whilst serving with the RCN. It was quite specific. Keighly-Peach had been directed to sell the Fairey Gannet anti-submarine aircraft to the RCN, and actively lobby wherever possible for the purchase of British aircraft and equipment by the RCN. The content and wording of the letter left no doubt in anybody's mind, that if the Commodore failed to successfully carry out these tasks, specifically with reference to the purchase of the Gannet, he could consider his future career in the Royal Navy at an end.

Perhaps Keighly-Peach's strong stance on naval aviation was best expressed in a Memorandum he directed to the Chairman of the Naval Warfare Study Group. This Memorandum focused directly upon the future composition of the RCN, dealing specifically with the five year period from 1961-1965. He outlined the already contemplated RCN fleet prior to 1961, consisting of one light Fleet Carrier, 43 escort ships with numerous miscellaneous vessels. He then made the observation that this fleet was arrived at "Without sufficient attention being paid to present and near future technical advances, vitally affecting naval warfare. The lack of emphasis being placed on aviation in the RCN is tantamount to saying that the importance of aircraft in maritime warfare is decreasing, whereas the reverse is true. It is noteworthy that the effective strength in numbers of operational aircraft has remained approximately the same over the last decade (since 1945), while during the same period, the RCN surface element has more than doubled. If plans are progressed to implement the planned composition, the imbalance will be even greater." The Commodore also took exception to the Naval Warfare Study Group premise that the planned composition of the fleet for the period 1956-60 cannot be significantly altered, contending that, "A significant change can and must be made to the RCN as soon as possible."

Keighly-Peach boldly proposed that the RCN change its present policy of concentrating on building up a sizeable fleet of Destroyer Escorts and Patrol Frigates and instead, transfer the existing or planned manpower and financial resources to a highly flexible and balanced force consisting of two Hunter Killer groups built around two aircraft carriers, one *Essex* Class, one Light Fleet Class (*Bonaventure*), and 25 Destroyer Escorts. He justified this new fleet composition by the practical need for flexibility, thereby enabling the RCN to carry out a variety of maritime roles in addition to the anti-submarine role, which would include:

A -   Support of ground forces.

B -   Offensive air operations against enemy land targets.

C -   Offensive operations against enemy naval units.

D -   Air defence of shipping.

Anticipating objections that "The Government would be against it," he went on to point out that a formal, fully supported RCN proposal for a second carrier has never been submitted to higher authority for approval. If this was done, the RCN could more effectively participate in operations until 1965; participate in a limited war if required; and could conceivably have a capability subsequent to 1965.

To counter the argument that the RCAF would be against it, he emphasized "The need to look ahead and counter the current RCAF belief that shore-based aviation is superior, by taking a view to the future when missile equipped submarines cannot be properly countered from shore bases". He went on further to state "Unless the RCN pays more than lip service to the requirement for aircraft in maritime warfare, the RCAF will take the place of the RCN as the prime authority on maritime warfare in the Canadian Defence organization". The basis for this warning was evident in the perception that the greatest advances in anti-submarine warfare has shifted to the aircraft with its obvious speed, mobility and great potential for weapon/sensor development. He also stated "Notwithstanding the previous arguments, as long as the RCN was willing to provide the personnel and funds from within existing RCN resources and manpower ceilings, the RCAF would have no legitimate reason to commence an inter-service squabble over RCN allocation of personnel and funds".

Keighly-Peach in his final remarks, went on to say that any immediate objections made within the RCN to his proposed fleet concept, purely on the basis of inadequate personnel and finances is without substance, because no detailed financial or personnel studies of the implications of a second carrier have ever been undertaken. He further dismissed any objections that his proposal would weaken Canada's naval contribution to NATO, by emphasizing the need for both quality and quantity of contribution. He zeroed in on this aspect by suggesting that "The provision of two self-contained anti-submarine carrier groups, with a reduced number of surface escorts, altbough obsolete and with a limited A/S capability, would still enable the RCN to retain an equal or greater prestige within NATO."

In his two conclusions, Keighley-Peach outlined in a financial and personnel summary, that his fleet proposal would appear to be feasible from within existing and planned RCN resources; he then emphasized that unanimity within the RCN is essential in order that a fully supported case for his ASW concept can be effectively presented. This should be able to overcome any possible objections from the Federal Government and the RCAF.

With regard to the Commodore's proposal outlining the self-contained anti-submarine carrier groups, the line of thinking he expressed, was certainly in keeping with the latest USN ASW force concept already underway, with Task Group ALPHA now formed as a self-contained and independently mobile Hunter-Killer carrier group under command of Admiral Thatch. ALPHA Group, formed around an *Essex* Class carrier, not only eliminated the previous shortcomings of small carriers, but had an extremely potent capability with newly added submarines and an increased number of ASW destroyer escorts in its force composition.

There is little evidence to indicate the degree of support, if any, that was generated in the senior ranks of the RCN by Keighly-Peach's bold and thought-provoking force concept. It can only be assumed by subsequent events and the fleet composition that evolved, namely the emphasis on Destroyer Escorts and Patrol Frigates, that the senior planners in the RCN were unable or unwilling to grasp the long term benefits of the Commodore's sweeping proposal, or even conduct a detailed study of the subject. They were obviously quite content to live with the imbalance created by a navy composed almost entirely of small ships and the inflexibility derived from such a force.

A regular change of command took place at *Shearwater* in August 1953, with LCdr. J. P. "Pat" Whitby assuming command of the Training Air Group from LCdr. Gary Wright.

Exchange tours of Canadian naval pilots with USN squadrons continued on a regular basis, and were of considerable benefit to the RCN, particularly at this time. Lt. R.L. "Robbie" Hughes who succeeded Lt. Doug Ross in exchange duties, was fortunate to be assigned, in the summer of 1953, to the first USN squadron destined to receive the new S2F twin-engined anti-submarine aircraft. His duties included a tour at Patuxent River with the Test and Development unit, working on the S2F test program. Contained in the trials were catapult launches, including regular tests with one engine feathered. This was excellent hands on indoctrination and provided the RCN access to first-hand experience on both the capability and overall performance of the new aircraft. As a result, certain changes involving the incorporation of modifications and improvements were readily identified and available to the RCN, when the eventual approval for a replacement to the Avenger was forthcoming. Hughes also was able to participate in deck landing trials with the S2F aboard USS *Mindora*, a Jeep carrier. The trials aboard Mindora were certainly realistic, with one S2F being pretty well torn apart in a partial barrier engagement, a ditching alongside the carrier, and an engine failure on takeoff. Subsequently as part of his tour, Hughes was involved in regular S2F embarked squadron deployments, including one aboard the newly modernized, angled deck *Essex* Class carrier *Antietam*.

In the summer of 1953, Lt. Bob Darlington, an RCN Supply Officer attached to the Canadian Department of Supply and Services Washington, and in direct charge of procuring air stores for the RCN from the USN, was experiencing a degree of fallout from the fiasco resulting from the Banshee cancellation. Darlington, who had been designated to be the RCN procurement officer for the Banshee air logistic support program, recalls being well aware of the fact that the USN authorities were more than miffed to have the Canadian order for the new Banshees cancelled at the last minute through a funding delay.

Cdr. John Doherty, of Air Technical Services at Naval Head-quarters was very involved in the subsequent alternative Banshee purchase plan. He recalls the extensive on-going discussions with the USN for a proposed procurement of used Banshees for the RCN. Typical of the Washington cocktail news circuit, Doherty was attending such a party in Washington, following a week of negotiations with personnel at the USN Bureau of Aeronautics (BuAer), when he first heard that the deal for purchase of second hand Banshees had actually been approved. The initial plan agreed upon in August 1953, called for the purchase of 54 used F2H3 Banshees at a price tag of $25M which included several million dollars worth of spare parts and equipment, with initial delivery planned for 1954.

Meanwhile, Bob Darlington in his position in the Air Stores Depot, notwithstanding the cancellation of the Banshee contract, continued on with his duties in charge of the overall spares support for the RCN aircraft, namely the Avenger. Pending re-negotiation of the Banshee purchase he continued to provide an extraordinary, almost custom supply service of essential aircraft parts. One particularly impressive example of prompt supply, which he will always remember, involved an Avenger aboard *Magnificent* which was unable to fly due to the lack of a critical but small fuel pump component. Upon receipt of the urgent order for the item, he was able to immediately locate the part, but the time delay in shipping it to the UK to *Magnificent* before the carrier departed was a major obstacle. He found willing assistance from two USN pilots, who took the required item, commandeered an aircraft, flew it from the Store Depot in Philadelphia to Washington, thence Darlington had it packed in the Diplomatic Bag, travelling by air courier to London, arriving aboard *Magnificent* by special arrangements shortly after. Of course, all such AOG (Aircraft on Ground) demands for parts could not be so promptly delivered, but the system worked remarkably well with such enthusiastic and dedicated efforts.

Although the delay in the Banshee program was a nasty setback, progress had been made elsewhere with the approval "In principle" to re-equip the aging Canadian anti-submarine Avenger squadrons with the new twin-engined USN Grumman S2F aircraft. Cdr. John Doherty was one RCN representative involved in these negotiations, and he recalls the USN were extremely co-operative regarding their proprietary rights to certain modifications incorporated in the aircraft. A licensing agreement with Grumman Aircraft, the designer, was required and negotiations were commenced, which when successfully concluded, would subsequently clear the way for the production of the aircraft in Canada. Canadian Naval Aviation had one strong ally in the bid to build the S2F in Canada. This was the redoubtable Hon. C.D. Howe, who was generally described in the Federal Government as being the "Minister of Everything", being one of the most powerful members of the Federal Cabinet. He had become interested in the Naval Air Branch through his daughter Barbara, who had married Lt. Marsh Stewart. Bill Atkinson had been a close friend of Stewart, and Barbara having kept in touch with her friends in Naval aviation after the death of her husband, was aware of the plans to produce the S2F in Canada. Atkinson had on occasions met C.D. Howe, and had impressed upon the Minister the excellent qualities of the Grumman aircraft, stating that it was the best aircraft with which to re-equip the Anti-Submarine air squadrons of the RCN. Howe expressed his personal support for the purchase of the aircraft by the RCN and the proposed program to build the aircraft under license in Canada. With such a strong endorsement, the approval was not long in forthcoming, with De Havilland Aircraft of Canada, Toronto, awarded a contract to build 100 aircraft which were subsequently designated as the CS2F Tracker.

The bulk of the summer operational flying activities ashore were, in the main provided by the SAG, which as an additional part of their workups, included extended flying detachments of both Sea Furies and Avengers in airshows across the country, the planned major display being the group participation at the CNE, Toronto, in September. One amusing incident took place involving our SAG Supply Officer, S/Lt.

Ed L'Heureux. Ed was not only new to the Navy, but also unacquainted with the often prankish nature of Air Branch personnel. One summer pay day, while at the Scoudouc air facility, Ed was dutifully making the necessary financial arrangements, and Don Knox and Pappy Macleod, being in exalted positions, were the first recipients. As Pappy recounts, "All the cash was lying on a chair and while I was being paid, Don was busily stuffing bundles of $20 bills in his battle-dress jacket. We both dutifully signed for our received stipend and left. Knox then briefed me on the cash situation and we went to the office window to watch the impending panic. In a matter of minutes, a somewhat rotund little figure was seen chugging across the tarmac, followed shortly after by a white-faced Ed bursting into the office, excitedly reporting the unexplained loss of $20,000. We deviously delayed matters by trying to calm him down in order to get his explanation for this poor example of the care and custody of government funds. Knox finally relented, returned the money and cautioned Ed on the dangers of leaving loose cash lying around."

This was not to be Ed's ultimate experience with cash security while acting as the SAG Supply Officer. In a later situation, he was encountering some difficulty in trying to open his safe to disburse the group payroll. The implication of this serious problem was speedily recognized by one and all, so Lt. John Burns, one of the Avenger pilots, generously volunteered to lend a hand. After putting his ear to the tumblers and spinning the combination dial for a few minutes, he successfully opened the safe. Poor Ed went away muttering, "This is definitely not the way it was taught at Supply School." Ed however, worked hard and performed well while with the SAG, invariably accepting with good humour such deviations from the true and tried system. Incidently, we never did find out what "school" John Burns had attended which had provided him with such a casual mastery in the art of safe opening.

There was one routine squadron change of command during the summer of 1953, with LCdr. Jack Beeman taking over VH 21 from LCdr. Darky Lowe in August. The helicopter squadron now operating with additional H04S Sikorsky aircraft was becoming increasingly active in the Search and Rescue role both ashore and afloat, with the on-going primary assignment of plane guard duties (Angel) aboard

870 Support Air Group Sea Furies at Shearwater prior to transferring to Scoudouc, June 1953. Credit PA137955

Wardroom officers Mess Dinner gathering Shearwater, circa 1953. Credit R. Monteith

Surplus Seafires at Shearwater Marine Section. Macnab's Island is in background with miscellaneous buildings in foreground. Credit PA153200

Sea Fury doing a free launch takeoff Magnificent, July 30,1953.
Credit PA137689

Magnificent.

Following a short annual docking, *Magnificent* was ready for the next cruise, but the month of August brought heavy fog and the CAG had to once more be laboriously lightered aboard, and it was not until 21 August that *Magnificent* and *Quebec* finally departed and commenced further flying training. By the end of August, the Canadian ships were operating under command of Commander USN Carrier Division 14 and exercising south of Rhode Island. Upon completion of working with the USN Division, *Magnificent* detached to Norfolk Virginia, for a four day period while Commodore Rayner and other senior officers attended a briefing conference for the next large scale naval exercise, the importance of which warrants detailed discussion.

This exercise, billed as "History's Greatest Maritime Manœuvres" was called Exercise Mariner and was the most important large scale exercise in which *Magnificent* and her Air Group had ever participated. Over a 19 day period, 300 ships, 1000 aircraft and half a million men from nine NATO countries took part in co-ordinated operations, ranging over immense sea areas of the North Atlantic, North Sea and the English Channel. In addition to *Magnificent* and the cruiser *Quebec*, were three Canadian ships, the destroyer *Algonquin* and the frigates *Swansea* and *La Hulloise*. The primary object of the massive exercise was to test the efficiency of the participating navies under simulated war conditions. The Canadian warships were designated part of "Blue Force" representing the NATO powers, while "Orange Force" as the enemy, consisted mainly of submarines, land-based bombers and surface raiders. The overall planning of the exercise was designed to provide maximum contact between the opposing forces.

For *Magnificent*, the exercise began on 16 September 1953, when she sailed as the senior ship of a Task Force to provide anti-submarine and air defence for a ten ship logistic force forming a "Blue Force" Iceland convoy. 881 Avenger squadron was now commanded by LCdr. M.H.E. "Mike" Page, an observer, who had taken over the squadron from Bill Atkinson, while 871 Fury Squadron remained under command of Lt. Mike Wasteneys. Flying intensity was immediately of a high order with the Avengers flying around the clock on ASW patrols, maintaining four aircraft on station. The Furies meanwhile were conducting dawn to dusk combat air patrols in air defence of the fleet and the convoy. An additional and valuable addition to the air surveillance of the fleet was provided by the flight of Airborne Early Warning Avengers (Guppies), now in service as a detachment of VS 881. Fitted with the powerful APS 20 radar, the Guppies were a most effective intercept airborne platform, providing not only radar intelligence on all surface units within a hundred miles of the carrier, but also the detection of submarine snorkel masts through the high definition characteristics of their airborne radar. With such a combination of detection modes, the Guppies also acted as an airborne controller, vectoring both the Sea Fury fighters and the Avengers to enemy targets. On 20 September, one "Orange" raider, the heavy cruiser USS *Worcester* did succeed in harassing the convoy until initially driven off by three of the screening destroyers followed by a successful simulated twilight rocket strike by the Avengers of VS 881.

On 21 September, S/Lt. Dave Tate while joining up on the squadron formation with his Fury, noticed that at the higher power settings his fuel pressure dropped and his engine wound down, obviously with fuel flow problems. He did discover that at a low power setting, he could maintain speed and altitude, but it was apparent that this somewhat unusual engine malfunction was such that it was doubtful whether he could get back aboard in the landing configuration requiring the higher power settings. After some experimenting, he was given the clearance to attempt a landing aboard, but on the approach, his decision was made for him, when even at a low throttle setting the engine would not hold power. He was finally forced down, as the aircraft stalled before he could ditch, but he executed a skilfully semi-controlled crash astern of the carrier. In a timed 32 seconds, *Magnificent*'s waiting rescue plane guard, the Sikorsky helicopter (Angel) swept down and picked up Dave unhurt. This was the first such RCN recovery accomplished by the rescue chopper, with the honours going to Lt. Ian Webster and his co-pilot Lt. Frank Harley. As Dave Tate was to acknowledge later, he was no doubt saved from serious or fatal injury by the newly issued crash helmets (hard hats) worn by the pilots at Mike Wasteneys insistence. Confirmation of the life-saving properties of the protective gear was most vividly displayed to Dave as he saw the crash helmet float away from beside

Re-spotting aircraft on flight deck of Magnificent after recovery,
July 30, 1953. Credit PA153023

31 SAG Fury and Avengers at Scoudouc NB. August 1953.
Credit PA153073

First chopper rescue by Magnificent HO4S Angel after ditching of Sea Fury by Dave Tate, September 23, 1953. Credit DND via Leo Pettipas

Launching 871 Sea Fury from Magnificent during Exercise Mariner, September 21, 1953. PA141104

him, broken in two pieces!

The 31 SAG meanwhile spent three weeks of September, primarily putting on a live armament demonstration at the Toronto CNE. This was a most impressive visual display with rocket and cannon attacks carried out against a simulated submarine moored in the lake waters in front of the grandstand. The success of the demonstration was somewhat diminished one particular day, when there was a high gusty wind blowing. Unbeknownst to us, this caused a hail of shell casings from the attacking Furies and Avengers to rain down on the nearby public parking lot, adding a touch of realism to our display by punching a hole in the windshield of a new Cadillac. It was also during this detached period that Lt. Jeff Harvie, who had temporarily joined us, achieved a degree of local fame. Apparently Jeff talked Pappy into letting him fly a Fury from the Maritimes to Toronto via his hometown of Windsor, Ont. The next day, there was Jeff as big as life, with his picture and a story in the Windsor Star, telling how he had established a world speed record flying direct from Scoudouc to Windsor. His record will no doubt stand forever, because as Pappy Macleod observed with a degree of sarcasm, "Nobody has ever bothered to fly from Scoudouc to Windsor before, and probably nobody ever will again!"

Following a special National Air Show on 19 September, the next day four Furies driven by Pappy Macleod, myself, Vern Cunningham and Jake Birks, headed west to the Pacific for a three day visit, with a faithful Avenger following along, piloted by Lt. George Noble, carrying a maintenance crew. This outward bound trip was going smoothly until just east of Medicine Hat, Pappy's Fury engine stopped, then came on again, but running very rough. After we had finally located the airport, Pappy came steaming in good and fast in case his engine failed again. In doing so, he touched down very late and had to go around again with his Fury engine coughing and farting, while the remainder of us did some rather anxious sniggering as we followed him around. We were there for a couple of days. After two failed attempts to depart caused by magneto problems in our leader's Fury, and the maintenance team had ingeniously replaced seven ignition wires they had fabricated from wire purchased in the local Western Auto Store, we again headed west. This was the first attempt to bring our renowned Sea Furies to the West Coast and in addition to the publicity, was a good exercise in cross country flying and deploying a long range detachment (some 3200 miles). The trip back was not that great! Weather over the Rockies was bad, forcing us up to 25000 feet to stay on top of cloud, then I found out my Fury had a hydraulic pump failure as we stopped for refuelling at Lethbridge. This necessitated me having to hand pump the landing gear and flaps up and down for the rest of the trip, which although time consuming, certainly proved to my satisfaction that the emergency hand pump system did work as advertised. The total flying time from Vancouver to Summerside (where the SAG had now relocated) was only ten hours and forty minutes, indicative of the impressive cruising speed of the Fury. This otherwise interesting and generally successful trip for us, was almost completely overshadowed by the tragic crash of our supporting Avenger on 4 October whilst making a precautionary landing at Kenora, Ont. Two of the crew, Lt. George Noble the pilot, and PO. George Wraith, one of the air maintenance team, were killed when the aircraft flipped over on its back. The other two occupants, although dazed and suffering from shock, were luckily able to extricate themselves from the wreckage, but fire almost immediately engulfed the Avenger. There were no fire fighting facilities to quell the inferno. Ironically, a bulldozer operator was working on the airfield, but he failed to react to the urgency of the accident and the Kenora Fire Dept. did not respond because the airport was outside their jurisdiction!

Meanwhile, Exercise Mariner completed the first phase off Cape Race and the convoy group now assumed the role of a logistic support force. Replenishment was carried out and *Magnificent* and her escorts, including the cruiser *Quebec*, were now integrated in a fast carrier force with the two *Essex* Class carriers *Wasp* and *Bennington*, designated as Carrier Division Two under the command of Rear Admiral Hugh Goodwin, USN. This Task Force (TF 218), was in turn part of a larger force of ships, designated as the Second Fleet controlled by Vice Admiral Thomas Combs wearing his flag aboard the battleship *Iowa* and accompanied by a force of heavy cruisers. The entire Second Fleet was now en route to Iceland for participation in extensive flying operations scheduled for the next phase of Mariner.

Magnificent south of Iceland during Exercise Mariner,
September 1953. Credit DND MAG 4937

Avenger with hook down preparatory to landing aboard
Magnificent, 1953. Credit DND MAG 3177

Guppy Avenger with long range radar preparing to launch from Magnificent during Exercise Mariner, September 1953. Credit DND MAF 5951

Dawn launch of Sea Furies from Magnificent during Exercise Mariner, September 1953. Credit DND MAG 4814

The fleet was transiting one of the most treacherous ocean areas, involving the combination of the Labrador Current, Greenland Current and the Gulf Stream. The ensuing mixing of these three different, overrunning sea currents of varying cold and warm temperatures, was not only subject to changing air masses overhead, but the entire region was notorious for its unpredictable weather patterns.

On 23 September 1953, a series of events unfolded around the three carrier task force, which swiftly deteriorated into a calamitous situation. A catastrophe it was feared, would result in the worst peacetime naval aviation disaster in history. The details of this incident are worthy of inclusion, with the following account provided by several of the participants. Particular thanks go to Capt. Wynn Foster, USN (Ret), who provided valuable information regarding the operations of the USN carriers and the individual pilot recollections as recounted in his article, The Mariner Miracle. The summary is as follows:

Regular air sorties were launched from *Magnificent* on the forenoon of 23 September, with 871 squadron Furies conducting fighter intercepts and combat air patrols. For 881 squadron Avengers, there was a four plane launch to conduct anti-submarine patrols, while an Avenger Guppy was airborne to conduct long range aerial radar surveillance of all surface contacts. With the Guppy was an Avenger flown by Lt. John Riley and crewed by squadron commander LCdr. Mike Page and Observers Mate A/B Ron Bosquet. Employed as a "scrapper", they were investigating and reporting the identity of all surface and submarine contacts detected on the long range radar of the surveying Guppy. Shortly after the launch, Mike Page became aware of an extensive fog bank to the southwest developing ahead of the carrier force. Indeed the fog was so heavy that it covered a large sector of the Guppy's radar, shrouding any possible Orange Force surface contacts. Both Riley and Page recall discussing the developing fog bank, with Page transmitting this significant weather information to *Magnificent*. After a two hour sortie, the Avengers returned to *Magnificent* about 1330 and were holding in the waiting position to land on, following the afternoon aircraft launch. Upon landing, Mike Page recalls he was concerned enough about the reported major fog bank, to discuss it immediately with the Operations Officer Cdr. R.A.

"Jimmy" Green, and was quite surprised to learn that the afternoon launch had taken off as originally planned. Page does remember Green saying that the decision to proceed with simultaneous launches from all three carriers was made by the OTC of the carrier force, in order to carry out the scheduled large air strike on the fleet.

The afternoon launch at 1330 from *Magnificent*, consisted of two flights of four Avengers led by LCdr. Brian Cartwright, the senior pilot. The eight Avengers were designated as part of the air strike force under control of the USS *Bennington*. A ninth aircraft also launched, was an Avenger Guppy separately controlled by *Magnificent*, to carry out an Airborne Early Warning surveillance sortie. The Canadian aircrews involved were as follows:

Pilot	Observer	Observer's Mate
Cartwright (Leader)	Smith	Merkley
Paton	Kieser	Doucette
Hilliard	Keindel	Copeland
Macnab	Johnson	McKerran
Second Flight		
Maclean	Cairney	Carlson
Hayter	Macauley	Hawthorne
Bovill	Donaldson	Bullock
Meikle	Diatchenko	Laming
AEW Guppy		
O'Connell	Schieder	Crawshaw

The strike consisted of a 52 plane force from the three carriers, composed of AD Skyraiders and F4U Corsairs from *Bennington*, additional AD aircraft from *Wasp* and the eight Avengers from *Magnificent*. The strike force was assigned to attack their three carriers commencing from a point 200 miles to the northeast of the fleet. The fleet air defence consisted of an F2H-3 Banshee squadron and an F9F-Panther squadron from *Bennington*, an F2H-2 and a F9F-6 Cougar squadron from *Wasp* and the VF 871 Sea Furies from *Magnificent*.

Aboard *Bennington*, a degree of concern had been expressed about the two degree spread between the temperature and dew point, but the aerologist believed the weather would hold, and stay reasonably clear for the remainder of the afternoon. The sea was moderate to rough with westerly winds gusting up to 40 knots. As a precautionary move, Admiral Goodwin had arranged an early launch of two AD-4W aircraft to conduct an on-going weather survey out to 100 miles to the northwest of the fleet.

The 52 strike aircraft of the three carriers launched simultaneously at 1330. Following takeoff from *Magnificent*, Cartwright's two flights shifted to *Bennington*'s control, being initially assigned to conduct a radar calibration run since there was a need to check out the carrier's radar system. Presumably, the Avengers would later detach and join in the overall strike as originally briefed with a low level torpedo attack on the fleet. Under *Bennington*'s control, the aircraft were established at an altitude of 10,000 feet and as Cartwright recalls, he could see an extensive band of low cloud which appeared to be moving in generally from a southerly direction. Although this weather pattern had been mentioned at the pre-flight meteorology briefing aboard *Magnificent*, it had not been given any particular emphasis. As the two flights climbed out to orbit over *Bennington*, they were given a course to fly toward the southeast, for about 30 minutes.

As Cartwright's formation was being vectored out, Paddy O'Connell in the Guppy, headed out on the same 'into wind' course as the fleet, climbing to altitude to commence his assigned long range radar surveillance. Very shortly after, he became aware that the band of cloud forming below, was much more extensive than as originally briefed. Noting a picket destroyer in the vicinity, he called the ship asking them to relay to *Magnificent* the deteriorating weather, being concerned that the cloud with its low ceiling and visibility would soon engulf the approaching fleet. His weather report message never reached *Magnificent*. O'Connell continued to climb out to his optimum altitude, but this was interrrupted shortly after by an immediate recall to return to *Magnificent*.

Cartwright had by now reversed course and noticed that the Task Force was also becoming obscured by what appeared to be low cloud. He was now a bit concerned about the abrupt weather change, so requested from *Bennington* the current weather and an altimeter setting. The only response from *Bennington* was a cryptic, "Wait."

In the meantime, the large USN air strike force heading outbound reported encountering low cloud which had rapidly thickened with cloud tops rising to 2000 feet. Weather reports from two AD Guppy aircraft had also been received. One 75 miles west of the force reported the weather still clear but visibility reduced in haze. The second, closer to the fleet, reported that surface fog was quickly forming.

Aboard *Bennington*, rapidly deteriorating visibility was evident, and at 1420 Admiral Goodwin ordered the recall of all aircraft. Fortunately, the aircraft closest to *Bennington* were the 14 Corsairs which were the last aircraft to launch. Ten actually managed to get aboard in rapidly forming fog. Ceilings were now down in variable fog conditions to less than 100 feet. The last Corsair to make an approach on *Bennington*, literally disappeared in the fog in front of the LSO's eyes and was forced to climb away. Visibility dropped so quickly, that in seconds the LSO could not even be seen from the Flying Control position. Cdr. Ben Preston, the Air Strike Coordinator had increased speed, leading his squadron of Skyraiders abruptly back to the fleet. They let down to 300 feet, but as the last four Corsairs had already found, they were also too late. The entire fleet was completely swallowed up in the thick fog. Aboard the carriers, the roar of the aircraft could be heard going over, nothing was sighted, neither by the pilots nor by those on the flight decks. The USN aircraft were directed to climb back up and hold at 3000 feet. A few selected pilots were then authorized to commence instrument approaches on a trial basis. It was ironic that the frantic efforts to get the aircraft back aboard were badly handicapped on that particular day, because the Carrier Controlled Approach (CCA) radar was unserviceable on all three carriers. The recovery attempts were of necessity rather basic, being restricted to radar vectors issued to the aircraft from the two USN carriers. Since *Magnificent* did not as yet have her aircraft returned to her own control, there was a mounting degree of frustration and helplessness felt by the Air Commander, (Cdr. Abrams). He had recognized the dangers of the fast moving fog bank initially reported by Page, which coupled with the narrowing gap between the temperature and dew point, made the formation of fog almost inevitable, particularly when moved by a brisk surface wind.

Magnificent having control of O'Connell in the Guppy, authorized him to make an approach using the high definition radar equipment aboard the aircraft. He recalls letting down on instruments, and still not breaking clear, asked one of the crew to report when the sea was visible. He continued on down, using the radar altimeter, passed through 100 feet and the water was then reported visible about an altitude of 60 feet, but there was no forward visibility from the cockpit. O'Connell flew on, closing in on the carrier on radar until the ship was lost in the sea return radar clutter. O'Connell then climbed away at the last minute, the drone of his aircraft was heard, but he was never seen, by those on the flight deck of *Magnificent.*

The "Wait" response from *Bennington* sounded ominous to Cartwright. Obviously during the general USN aircraft recall activity, the operator aboard *Bennington*, manning the air radio circuit controlling the Canadian flights, did not have the information, authority or perhaps even the priority, to respond quickly to Cartwright's query. After about ten minutes, Cartwright again requested the prevailing weather. He was deeply perturbed when the answer came, "Ceiling and visibility zero in heavy fog, wind 30-40 knots."

The overall aircraft control situation involving 42 aircraft was now turning into a real shambles, so Cartwright requested his flights revert to *Magnificent*'s control, which after a delay was granted. The two flights were detailed by *Magnificent* to commence orbiting about 10 miles to the northwest of the carrier, now completely obscured in heavy fog. It will always be a point of contention whether *Magnificent* could have managed to get some of her nearby orbiting Avengers aboard if they had been released from *Bennington* immediately the general aircraft recall order was given. The fact that 10 of the USN Corsair aircraft did get aboard *Bennington*, tends to support this view. In such a confused and fast moving situation however, it was inevitable that a delay in reaching and implementing a quick decision would occur, particularly observing the intricate chain of authority prevailing in a major Task Force of this complexity, with all its interlocking command and control communications procedures.

The cloud tops had now reached about 5000 feet, and the Avenger aircraft commenced holding on top of the cloud in a loose formation, the pilots choosing the most economical engine power settings for maximum endurance. This reduced the airspeed of the Avengers to about 100-110 knots, so they were literally wallowing through the air, which was how the rest of the afternoon was spent. Upon somebody's suggestion, all droppable items consisting of sonobuoys, smoke markers etc. were jettisoned, resulting in a saving of aircraft weight and drag, with a simultaneous loss of several thousand dollars worth of stores, (the least of anybody's worry). O'Connell, who had joined up astern and below the circling Avengers in his Guppy, will always recall the extraordinary sight of all the smoke floats and sonobuoys dropping away in front of his eyes and disappearing into the fog.

At this point Cartwright called *Magnificent*, requesting that the aircraft be allowed to commence individual approaches on their own radar, coupled with whatever additional radar monitoring that could be provided by the carrier. A further suggestion he made was to establish the feasibility of diverting the aircraft to the airstrip Bluie West One at Cape Farewell, on the southernmost tip of Greenland. He commented that although the airborne squadron aircraft did not have the necessary maps and airport landing details, an Avenger aboard *Magnificent* could conceivably be launched with the necessary information and then shepherd the two flights to safety. There was no immediate answer forthcoming to his proposals. Aboard the carriers, the possibility of reaching Bluie West One had already been considered by Admiral Goodwin (OTC) and his staff, but the 450 mile transit to an unmanned airstrip in Greenland was rejected as perilous, since it was calculated to be beyond the range that could be derived from the fuel remaining in most of the aircraft. Mike Page, on duty in *Magnificent*'s Operations Room, increasingly concerned about the now dangerous situation developing for his airborne squadron, remembers the prevailing weather at Bluie West One was also bad, with freezing rain and low visibility. An additional problem was that the unmanned strip had no night lighting or radio navigation aids. In the meantime, Paddy O'Connell flying the Guppy and having made his own independent calculations, estimated his actual position only 360 miles from the airstrip, insisting he could make it, if allowed to depart in the next twenty minutes. It was deemed prudent to deny his request. O'Connell did receive approval from *Magnificent* to separate from the formation and search for any possible break in the fog bank, which he proceeded to do without success.

Aboard *Bennington* and *Wasp*, frantic efforts continued to recover more aircraft. Pilots were told to not descend below 100 feet to provide a margin of safety, since the height of flight decks alone were at least 60 feet above the water. Some individuals went lower, in a desperate attempt to break clear as they followed radar vectors up to the carrier's wake. One pilot actually inched his aircraft down to an indicated 20 foot altitude on his radio altimeter, and sighted nothing.

After about an hour in the holding pattern, *Magnificent* contacted Cartwright and authorized him to attempt a single aircraft landing approach. He was vectored by the carrier and let down to an altitude of about 200 feet, where looking vertically, he could intermittently see the fog covered water, which was becoming increasingly choppy in the high wind. After being directed downwind to approach the carrier from astern, Cartwright was somewhat disconcerted to see the top of some ships' masts actually sticking up out of the fog, moving in the opposite direction at a speed relative to him in excess of 120 knots. In the high wind, the controlled approach pattern had taken him a long way astern, his attempt to break clear of the fog was unsuccessful, so he was then directed to return to the orbiting flights. No other approach attempts to get aboard *Magnificent* were made by the Avenger flights. Those aboard the carrier, shrouded in fog so thick you could not see the length of the flight deck, could hear the occasional aircraft droning by them in the futile attempts to reach the safety of the carriers. Aboard *Magnificent* it was going to be a long and arduous afternoon for the two LSOs, Lts. Bob "Willy" Williamson and Bob Falls. They would remain on their fog shrouded platform for the rest of the afternoon, anxiously waiting for an opportunity to bring an aircraft aboard.

As Cartwright was making his attempt to land, and while desperate recovery efforts were being carried out by the other two carriers, Admiral Goodwin ordered the battleship *Iowa* and her heavy cruiser screen changed from their normal formation. He dropped them astern of the carriers to reduce a collision risk with their high mast structures. These ships were no doubt part of the fast moving formation of masts Brian Cartwright had seen during his abortive approach.

For the rest of the afternoon, *Magnificent*'s aircraft remained orbiting in their two flights, the pilots flying their aircraft at maximum endurance speed, rendering their fuel state and reporting their aircraft radar serviceability at regular intervals. The massive size of the fog area was now becoming clearly evident, picket ships as far as 100 miles to the southeast of the Task Force were also reporting themselves blanketed in heavy fog. Spreading rapidly over a great ocean area, the fog was being formed by advection, as the relatively warm wind blew over the cold water, the overrunning air then cooling, condensing and creating a massive, rapidly moving, ever expanding fog bank. It was now readily apparent that a disaster of devastating proportions was in the making.

The Fleet Commanders frantically sought alternatives. Iceland and Newfoundland were examined as possible diversionary destinations for the longer range Skyraiders. Both locations were equally unacceptable. Not only was the transit distance greater, being some 660 and 780 mile respectively, but the weather there was also down with ceiling and visibility zero. The four remaining airborne Corsairs never did have an alternative. They were too short of fuel to go anywhere. Goodwin and his staff were forced to face an almost unthinkable alternative - mass bailout of all the aircrew ahead of the fleet! This would be a grim scenario with aircrew spread over a relatively large area in a cold and turbulent sea, obscured in fog. Another possibility discussed was a controlled ditching by a few aircraft at a time, with radar monitoring from the carriers. This had the definite advantage of a more easily controlled and localized ditching area. On the other hand the percentage of successful ditches that could be expected, coupled with the aircraft numbers involved, in a rough, fog blown sea, was certain to be low, and equally fraught with disaster.

By 1700, the aircraft had been airborne about three and a half hours, the Corsairs had about one hour's fuel remaining. Darkness would be closing in shortly after 1800.

While these torturous decisions were being made by the Task Force Commanders, the two Avenger flights from *Magnificent* continued to hold their solitary orbiting patterns. Brian Carwright felt the isolation becoming somewhat eerie and increasingly lonely. Surprisingly, he saw only two other aircraft in the distance, which considering that there were still thirty three of them from the other carriers in the air, it was almost unreal. He pondered on whether a peptalk to the others would be in order, but decided against it because the survival chances were obviously poor and it would be misleading to pretend otherwise. S/Lt. Weldy Paton, a member of Cartwright's flight, was equally pessimistic. He had been fortunate to walk away, only five months ago, from his crash in the fog shrouded hills around Greenwood, NS. This was building into a much worse situation, and it was becoming so drawn out. Paton had an added personal concern, since he had never even done a night carrier landing. There was also the continual waiting, with little to do but ponder one's own fate. With dusk closing in, he feared the fog would only get thicker.

Suddenly a little after 1700, an unexpected message was received by the fleet from a Blue Force submarine, USS *Redfin*, located 110 miles to the west of the carrier force. Although reporting heavy twelve foot seas running, the ceiling in the sub's immediate area was 100 feet, and the visibility had improved considerably to an estimated 2 miles. There was no time to be lost! This unexpected minor break in the fog blanket at the *Redfin*'s position was definitely enough to improve the chances of surviving a ditching, and there were no other options with darkness closing in and fuel rapidly being exhausted. The order was given to the USN aircraft, "Ditch alongside the *Redfin*!"

As Cartwright later recounted, "This would have been a horror show! The water was very cold and the submarine a small target to detect on radar. The aircraft would have to do an instrument ditching, and the difficulty the *Redfin* would have in trying to maneuver to find and retrieve the scattered crews of 42 ditched aircraft in heavy seas, was almost insurmountable." The captain of the *Redfin* was equally pessimistic, voicing his concern about the sea state. In actual fact, the aircrew survival percentages were estimated to be between 10% and 25% depending upon the optimism of the individual concerned. With regard to total numbers of aircrew, the Canadians with eight Avengers and the Guppy all with 3 man crews, totaled 27, while the American pilots flying primarily single seat aircraft, would probably number 36-38 aircrew, bringing the total to nearly 65 souls aloft.

Not discussed, but most assuredly given considerable thought by the pilots as they headed for the *Redfin*, was the knowledge that flying to the submarine over a distance of 100 miles, required not only an accurate departure point, but very accurate en-route navigation. During the abortive attempts to land aboard their carriers, the USN aircraft were naturally dispersed and their original formations had become scattered. Some pilots, after climbing back up through the fog, were unable to locate their original squadron flights, so they joined up with any formation they could find. For many pilots, it was now not only a question of accurate flying, but also the dire necessity of getting to the *Redfin* as soon as possible, while fuel and a semblance of light still remained. The sun was now slowly settling, then as it began to imperceptibly slide down through the fog shrouded horizon, the whole atmosphere became fraught with fear and deep foreboding.

Aboard *Magnificent*, the implications of the impending disaster were now felt throughout the ship. Probably the worst aspect of the situation for those aboard, was the utter hopelessness of the circumstances. All that could be done had been done! The few ship's boats and cutters were manned, blankets and equipment were assigned, and emergency sick bays (hospitals) were organized. On a religious plane, it is noteworthy to add that there was constant activity aboard, with a steady stream of personnel proceeding to the ship's chapel, to join with the naval padres in prayers for the salvation of the airborne crews.

At about 1705 the following unclassified plain language message was sent to Naval Air Station Argentia, Newfoundland, from Admiral Goodwin, Task Force Commander:

DISTRESS FORTY TWO AIRCRAFT THIS FORCE DITCHING LAT 5338N LONG 4120W AT 232040Z.

This naval aviation catastrophe with all its fatal implications was now released to the world.

There was an interesting discrepancy in the foregoing message, because as Brian Cartwright comments, "As far as I can recall, we never did receive any direct instructions to proceed to the *Redfin* position. All that was provided to us was an advisory from *Magnificent* that the USN aircraft had been given a course to the submarine and ordered to proceed." Consequently, *Magnificent*'s aircraft were still holding in their orbit near their carrier, while the USN aircraft raced to the ditching site. Yet from the wording of the Distress Message, it was clear that Admiral Goodwin had assumed that all airborne aircraft, including the Canadians, had departed for the *Redfin*.

Aboard *Magnificent*, fateful consultations between Commodore Rayner and Commander Abrams were continuing, to determine if there was any possible alternative to the desperate undertaking to ditch at the location of the *Redfin*. As Mike Page recalls, "They discussed a plan which conceivably might provide a better survival rate. Their option proposed the Canadian Avengers let down through the fog following a radar vector from the carrier, augmented by the individual aircraft radar sets, along a line of flares dropped astern from *Magnificent*. The aircraft would then ditch in a reasonably orderly manner, at the location of the last flare to be dropped. The carrier's boats and cutters (pitifully few in number) would be waiting, along with frogmen divers standing by to rescue any aircrew that successfully made it to the ditching location." Observing the prevailing weather of ceiling and visibility zero, darkness closing in, and heavy seas running, the chances of a successful rescue by small boats were obviously remote. Indeed, for the pilots to even know if they were at the correct smoke float to ditch, would be a problem in such reduced visibility. In the final analysis, the aircrew would have to survive a virtual ditching under instrument conditions, the inflation of their life rafts in twelve foot seas, and above all the 30 minute life expectancy in the cold water. Presumably, the authorities aboard *Magnificent* believed an attempted rescue of the nine Canadian crews at dusk in a nearby localized area, with the Canadian ships standing by, was a viable option. Certainly with the *Redfin* ditching scenario, there were enormous recovery problems involved with the fleet arriving four hours after the mass ditching, then attempting to locate and recover the scattered crews of 42 ditched aircraft in the black of night. Regardless of what action taken, the likelihood of success was depressingly low. In any event, the decision by *Magnificent* to implement any ditching instructions to the still orbiting Canadian aircraft were as yet not forthcoming, since Rayner and Abrams were still agonizing over their decision.

Meanwhile, the three carriers in a parallel line abreast formation, with the battleship and cruisers in the van, continued steaming into the wind toward the *Redfin*. Time however, was running out for the aircraft. The official estimates, calculated that some of the aircraft would be out of fuel by 1830, and for the mass ditching to have a marginal degree of success the operation would have to commence before darkness fell.

At about 1800, as the fleet raced through the gloom of the heavy fog, there was a gradual almost imperceptible change in the visibility, and then, in a few moments it was possible to vaguely see the previously mist shrouded outlines of adjacent ships.

Meanwhile, Commander Ben Preston had broadcast general briefing instructions to all pilots about the impending ditchings, "Ditch two at a time, one on each side of the submarine, use your landing lights, and don't land on top of someone in the water. The low state Corsairs are to ditch first." In order to obtain his own accurate departure point, Preston flew a course that would take him over the fleet and while doing so, he glanced down and saw the wake of a ship through a small hole in the fog below. He immediately queried *Bennington* on the weather in the vicinity. Simultaneously aboard the ships, it was now definitely apparent the ceiling and visibility had unexpectedly and dramatically improved.

Visibility continued to increase, and the ceiling definitely began to rise. An immediate decision was made! A general recall went out to the aircraft, some of which were now many miles ahead, proceeding to the position of the *Redfin*. Naval aircrew are by nature generally optimistic, but to intentionally fly toward a positive night ditching in the cold North Atlantic water was not a cheery prospect. Most of them realistically felt their arrival at the *Redfin* would be a rendezvous with disaster. The order for all aircraft to return to the carriers was therefore an unexpected and thankful reprieve. As the first returning aircraft reached the fleet, they were authorized to commence their approaches to the carriers, down through the fog which by now had even thinned somewhat. The base was now estimated to have risen to a ragged height varying between 100-200 feet. The three carriers continued steaming in line abreast into the wind, with *Magnificent* placed in the centre. It was now about 1800, and observing the critical shortage of fuel in the aircraft and the darkness of night closing in, the pilots were instructed to land on any carrier they could find. In order to facilitate the landings, all available ships' searchlights and the ceiling projectors of the carriers were trained skyward, while the continuous trail of flares dropped astern from the fleet provided a guiding surface reference line for the incoming aircraft to follow, as they let down through the murk.

Cartwright leading the two flights, was given clearance by *Magnificent* for the aircraft to commence their landing approaches. He sensibly proposed that the Avengers time their departures to let down and approach in pairs, rather than a mass letdown, fearing valuable time would be lost with unnecessary waveoffs, if there was not a degree of co-ordination by the pilots in their approach and landings.

Among the several USN AD Skyraiders airborne, there was one piloted by Ensign Jim Elster. He fortuitously took the landing instruction ,"Head for the nearest carrier" literally. He spied a well lit carrier and being desperately low on gas, made a straight in approach for "Maggie". Fortunately, LSO Bob Williamson seeing the AD heading his way and being familiar with the aircraft, promptly alerted the flight deck crews. Full arresting pressure was immediately set on the wires, and the big Skyraider came aboard with no trouble.

The visual perspective of the Canadian Avenger pilots varied to a considerable degree. The flight and two plane section leaders, scanning and watching ahead, were provided a relatively good appreciation of the fleet disposition and general visibility conditions as they let down. The wing men however, encountered a degree of disorientation. Flying formation in cloud they had seen little except the vague silhouette of their leading aircraft as they formated on down through the cloud to the landing pattern. On breaking clear however, the brightly lit fleet of ships all around was a revelation to all!

Lt. Bob "Doughie" Maclean with Lt. Bryan Hayter flying formation on his wing, suddenly broke through the darkening fog and recalls being utterly amazed at the multitude of lights illuminating the night. In his recollection it was so bright the fleet looked like a well-lit city. His observer, Lt. Jack Cairney, who had perversely refused to wear an immersion suit, (based on the assumption that a suit would only extend survival in the water a few more minutes) was probably one of the most thankful to see the reassuring outline of a carrier deck.

Hayter's recollection of the approach was as follows, "When my altimeter read 50 feet, the water below was still scarcely visible.

Suddenly, a row of flares appeared ahead of us, and as if a hand had swept the fog away, the shapes of ships took form. Surrounding the fleet was a dense bank of fog and the only clear spot was around the carriers. We found our ship, and though it was dark and her deck pitching, it was home and we were safe; I shall never forget the cheer that rose from Maggie's crew!" Hayter will also never forget the tot of neat rum handed to him by a thoughtful air maintenance man, as the crew stiffly climbed down from their Avenger, after almost five hours of the most dangerous and stressful flying they would ever experience.

Paddy O'Connell made his letdown through the fog, and the first thing he saw was a line of flares in the water. He followed these and suddenly saw a large carrier loom through the darkness. He called *Magnificent* to land aboard and was both frustrated and surprised by the reply to "Wait". He then ran through a patch of fog and was back on instruments. He broke out almost immediately and saw another carrier ahead, this time *Magnificent* with all lights blazing. Making a tight circuit, Paddy got aboard, although experiencing a degree of uncertainty as he momentarily lost sight of the LSO at the "cut" position.

When Lt. Bob Bovill was detached to approach with his wingman Lt. Ken Meikle, he suddenly noted that his aircraft artificial horizon instrument was inoperative, so he prudently passed the lead to his less experienced wingman to take them down through the fog. Meikle's observer, Diatchenko, picked up the fleet ahead on radar, homing them in. Then Meikle saw the flares as he lowered to 150 feet in altitude. Bovill recalls seeing the water for the first time from an altitude of only about 75 feet. Meikle reported he was visual with the flares and the response in a pronounced American accent was, "Follow them boy!" He next saw the silhouette of a large warship loom up. Being too close to go around, he flew over the stern. He subsequently learned this was the mighty battleship *Iowa*. On sighting the errant Avenger, the order had been piped throughout the *Iowa*, "Clear the fantail, prepare to receive aircraft." On sighting *Magnificent*, Meikle who had never done a night landing before, was not happy with his first approach, so elected to take his own waveoff, successfully coming aboard on his second attempt. This was to be Meikle's one and only night deck landing. He was the last Avenger to come aboard, parking alongside Elster's USN Skyraider. Remarkably, the other seven Avengers and the Guppy had all managed to get aboard successfully on their first pass.

Recovering the remaining 33 USN aircraft aboard their two carriers was a far more complicated and stressful ordeal. With the four Corsairs literally sucking their gas tanks dry, there was no time for them to spare. One Corsair pilot obviously conserving fuel, came downwind opposite *Bennington* with gear and flaps up, when he finally got them down, he was so low to the water that his hook was skimming the wavetops. He finally recognized his predicament, got his power back on and disappeared into the cloud as he frantically climbed away, taking his own waveoff.

Other pilots made their own priority approach from wherever they could. Some dropped through the ragged fog bank only to disappear from view as they climbed in and out of the fog.

Meanwhile, instead of joining the rat race to land, the two AD 4W Guppy Skyraiders did yeoman work, electing to remain aloft orbiting the fleet, augmenting the control efforts of the carriers with supplementary radar vectors. Their voice instructions provided a reassuring degree of stability to the other pilots making their desperate passes on any carrier they could detect in the now darkening night.

For individual pilots, there was a variety of reactions. One AD pilot described the area above the fog bank as being similar to the surface of a lake, with fish jumping; an apt description of aircraft plunging into the cloud, then popping back out again as they failed to break through the fog in their attempt to find a carrier.

Another pilot somewhat humorously described the feverish penetration attempts through the fog, whether singly or in formation as, "Lancer approaches, with each pilot making a stab at it!"

The pilots of one orbiting flight of 4 Skyraiders discussed their individual plans on their tactical frequency, noting the still heavy air congestion, the on-going landing attempts, darkness approaching, and the likelihood of still being forced to ditch. One of them, perhaps more resigned to his fate, had decided when down to his last 30 gallons of fuel, to ask for a Catholic Chaplain to accept his confession over the radio. No doubt to his immense relief, that ultimate decision was thankfully cancelled when his flight suddenly received their clearance to make their landing approach.

LCdr. Les Hofta senior LSO aboard *Bennington* was frantically giving directions with his illuminated night landing signals as soon as any aircraft came in sight, knowing full well there were pilots still airborne that had not yet qualified in night landings. He did not lack for traffic! At one point he counted nine aircraft approaching simultaneously; five of them making the normal curved approach after coming downwind, and another four making a straight in approach from well astern. He calculated his "wave-offs" were in the ratio of 5:1 to "cut signals", while determinedly taking control of each aircraft as fast as the landing area of the deck could be cleared.

Perhaps one of the last and most spectacular approach and landing aboard *Bennington* was made by Lt. (JG) Frank Guiterrez, a Corsair pilot. Having lost his leader he had already made two letdowns without seeing a carrier. On his third try he let down to about 50 feet to stay below the fog, saw the line of flares and followed them through the gloom almost to a collision point with the fantail of *Bennington*. Hofta signalled a frantic wave-off with accompanying red flares and yells over the radio. At the last second, Guiterrez saw the LSO, responded and "poured on the coal", pulling up for a wave-off. With his aircraft nose high he reached a near stall, agonizingly just missing the ramp of the ship. Instead of prudently leaping to the LSO safety net, Hofta stood his ground, then quickly gave the upward climbing Corsair a "roger" signal followed by an immediate "cut". Guiterrez instinctively reacted, closed the throttle, pushed forward, reaching an approximate landing attitude and thumped heavily down amongst the arrestor wires. The Corsair's engine stopped a few seconds later - out of fuel!

By 1828, the last of the 42 aircraft aircraft had successfully made it aboard, many with their fuel virtually expended. Considering all the stress factors on the pilots, including low fuel, pitching decks, poor weather and night at hand, their overall performance was extraordinary. One poor landing with a barrier engagement, might well have caused a critical delay, but thankfully this did not occur, due to the skill and determination of the pilots and their guiding LSO's. Fortunately, the high wind allowed the carriers to steam at a minimum speed, allowing precious extra time to traverse the small partially clear area. Minutes later, just after the last aircraft was safely aboard, the carriers ran out of that redeeming patch of the sea. The fog then closed in for the remainder of the night. The unlikely chance that a small, unpredictable body of warmer surface water would exist at that critical time and in that particular place, allowing the fog to temporarily thin out, was indeed miraculous.

Aboard *Magnificent* and the other two carriers there was great rejoicing at this almost unbelievable happy conclusion to what had been considered a hopeless situation, leading to a disaster of unprecedented magnitude. Bob Bovill recalls the stiff drink happily proffered to all 881 squadron aircrew by Cdr Abrams, and also the emotional vow that he would never let Maggie's aircraft out of his control again. Commodore Rayner, in spite of his reputation to be somewhat of a teetotaller, gracefully donated a case of scotch toward the wardroom officers' celebration, as he attended the festivities following the successful aircraft recovery. There were equally happy gatherings in the remainder of the ship's messes. Aboard the "dry" USN carriers, the pilots also had a boisterous celebration, which was greatly enlivened through the generous distribution of medicinal brandy to the thankful participants.

The following morning aboard *Magnificent*, there was a church service attended by virtually the entire ship's company. The lesson was read by the earnestly religious Commodore, in which he expressed thanks to the Almighty for the blessed deliverance. There were few disbelievers that day. It was 11 years later that Rayner, then a Vice Admiral and retiring as Chief of the Naval Staff, stated to an interviewing reporter that the fog incident, "Sticks out in my memory as vividly as my battle actions as a destroyer commander in the Second World War."

Perhaps one individual who will long recall the "fog incident" was Ensign Jim Elster, USN, the young AD pilot. He will be certain to remember *Magnificent* for not only the small flight deck, but also the three bars! He took off unexpectedly (to his dismay) the next morning in his aircraft, on the first launch with a vicious hangover. On each side of the fuselage of his AD, painted in the centre of the USN star emblem, was a small red maple leaf under which was printed

"Maggie". Unbeknownst to Elster, and while celebrating the safe recovery of all the aircraft, the air maintenance gang had enthusiastically covered almost the entire visiting Skyraider with typical flight deck graffiti. Commodore Rayner, always somewhat straitlaced, did not appreciate the humour involved and so ordered all the offending literature removed. Only the maple leaves and name survived. As Ken Meilkle relates, "Years later at Quonset Point, I came across Archie Benton, (USN exchange pilot aboard *Magnificent* in VF 871 during the fog incident.) He told me as of that date, the AD had been through two major overhauls including repainting, and the maple leaves were still there. The word had been clearly sent out that the loss of your pension was the least of your worries if the Canadian maple leaf memento was not preserved."

For the interest of the reader, the official verbatim summary of the entire fog incident as messaged from the Commander of the Strike Fleet is provided as follows:

To CICMARCHAN From COMSTRIKFLT

UNCLASSIFIED/PRIORITY

MARINER FOR CĪNB MARINER. NODUF. WITHOUT WARNING, FOG AN ANCIENT AND REALISTIC ENEMY OF SEAFARERS, CLOSED DOWN ON BLUES FAST CARRIER TASK FORCE WEDNESDAY AFTERNOON CATCHING 42 OF ITS PLANES IN THE AIR. WITH THE NEAREST LANDING FIELD 450 MILES NORTH ON THE SOUTHERNMOST TIP OF GREENLAND BEYOND THE FUEL CAPACITY OF THE AIRCRAFT. ONLY THE CO-ORDINATED EFFORTS OF THE SHIPS AND THEIR AVIATORS PLUS A LAST MINUTE MIRACLE OF NATURE, ENABLED EVERY PLANE TO LAND SAFELY ON CARRIER DECKS INSTEAD OF DITCHING AT SEA, FOR WHICH ORDERS HAD BEEN ISSUED. WHEN THE LAST PLANES LANDED ON THE CARRIERS AT 1830, THEY WERE TEN MINUTES BEYOND THE MOMENT WHEN THEIR FUEL TANKS WERE DUE TO BE EMPTY. THE CRITICAL SITUATION WAS CAUSED WHEN HEAVY LAYERS OF FOG BLEW IN FROM THE SOUTHWEST. NEAREST LANDING FIELD AND IT UNMANNED, WAS BLUIE WEST ONE IN GREENLAND. THE PLANES FROM THE US CARRIERS BENNINGTON AND WASP AND THE CANADIAN CARRIER MAGNIFICENT HAD

TAKEN OFF UNDER FAVOURABLE CONDITIONS SHORTLY
AFTER 1330. LIGHT AT FIRST, THEN RAPIDLY THICKENING THE
FOG ROLLED OVER THE OCEAN. RECALL FOR THE PLANES
WAS ISSUED AT 1420. TEN MANAGED TO LAND BEFORE THE
FOG SETTLED TO A CEILING OF 100 to 200 FEET. REPEATEDLY
ATTEMPTS WERE MADE TO COACH THE PLANES INTO THE
CARRIER DECKS BY RADAR. THE PILOTS COULD NOT GET
LOW ENOUGH TO SEE THE DECKS. REPEATEDLY THOUSANDS
OF ANXIOUS EARS ON THE SHIPS COULD HEAR THE UNSEEN
PILOTS RUN FROM SEA THROUGH THE SOLID WALL OF FOG.
REAR ADMIRAL HUGH GOODWIN TACTICAL COMMANDER
TCX OF THE CARRIER TASK FORCE ORDERED THE NORMAL
FORMATION BROKEN UP. THE BATTLESHIP IOWA AND
ACCOMPANYING CRUISERS ALL DROPPED WELL ASTERN OF
THE CARRIERS TO ELIMINATE THE HAZARD OF MASTS AND
HIGH STRUCTURES FOR THE AVIATORS. THE THREE CARRIERS
WERE POSITIONED PARALLEL TO ONE ANOTHER. AGAIN THE
PILOTS FOUGHT TO FIND THEIR DECKS. AGAIN IT WAS IM-
POSSIBLE. AT 1620 PLANES IN THE AIR HAD AN ESTIMATED
FUEL TIME OF EXACTLY TWO HOURS REMAINING. REPORTS
FROM PLANES ABOVE THE FORMATION AND FROM AVAIL-
ABLE OUTLYING SHIPS AND THE ESTIMATES OF FLEET AERO-
LOGISTS GAVE NO HOPE OF REACHING ANY OPEN AREA WITH
THE CARRIERS BEFORE EVERY PLANE WOULD BE OUT OF
FUEL. THEN CAME A MESSAGE FROM THE BLUE FORCE
SUBMARINE REDFIN 110 MILES TO THE WEST. CEILING IN ITS
IMMEDIATE VICINITY WAS 100 FEET WITH TWO MILE VISIBIL-
ITY. THOUGH THE CARRIERS COULD NOT REACH THE SPOT IN
TIME, THE PLANES COULD MAKE THE DISTANCE BEFORE
DARK. AFTER CONSULTATION BETWEEN VICE ADMIRAL
THOMAS S. COMBS AND REAR ADMIRAL GOODWIN, DECISION
WAS MADE TO HEAD FOR THE REDFIN'S POSITION, THAT THE
PILOTS MIGHT DITCH IN A GROUP IN THE IMMEDIATE VICIN-
ITY OF THE SUBMARINE IF NECESSARY. THEN JUST AS DARK-
NESS APPROACHED, THE FOG IN SHIPS COURSE BEGAN TO
THIN AND THE CEILING TO LIFT PERCEPTIBLY. SHIPS WHICH
HAD BEEN BLOTTED OUT FROM ONE ANOTHER TOOK SHAPE
THROUGH THE FOG. PLANES WERE TURNED BACK TOWARDS

THEIR CARRIERS, ONE BY ONE THEY SHOT DOWN THROUGH
THE WHITE BLANKET TO WHICHEVER CARRIER DECK WAS
CONVENIENT AND READY TO TAKE THEM. AT 1820 WITH
NIGHT AT HAND, TEN PLANES WERE STILL IN THE AIR,
THOUGH THEIR ESTIMATED FUEL TIME WAS GONE. LIGHTS
BLAZED ON ALL SHIPS THE FIRST TIME SINCE LEAVING PORT.
AT 1828 CAME THE WORD, LAST PLANE RECOVERED.
PERSONNEL ON EVERY SHIP WERE AS THANKFUL AS THE
AVIATORS THAT AN ISOLATED PATCH OF WARM WATER
ENCOUNTERED ENROUTE TO THE REDFINS VICINITY HAD
OPENED THE FOG AT EXACTLY THE CRITICAL MINUTE TO
PERMIT THE PLANES TO LAND ON FRIENDLY DECKS INSTEAD
OF IN THE COLD NORTH ATLANTIC. VICE ADMIRAL COMBS
SENT A WELL DONE TO ALL SHIPS AND PILOTS CONCERNED
AND THE RECOVERY OPERATION, WHICH PROBABLY CAN BE
CLASSED AS ONE OF THE MOST IMPORTANT EXPERIENCES IN
TRAINING THAT THE INVOLVED UNITS WILL OBTAIN IN THE
CURRENT EXERCISE.
   9 DIST-V-O N-LT WALLACE-A-A1-A2 ...//251259Z/T P/L
TOR 1320Z/9/53 SJD.
   Following the near catastrophe, there was a relatively quiet period
for the next four days. Severe south-westerly gales struck the fleet
with heavy seas requiring double lashings to the deck park of aircraft
on *Magnificent*'s heaving deck. During this period, there were extensive engine examinations carried out on the Avengers involved in the
flight during the fog incident. Several engines required changes or
major valve repair, their burnt condition caused by the very lean
mixtures and high cylinder temperatures resulting from flying the
aircraft at maximum endurance settings.
   In retrospect, it was indeed fortunate that the defending jet fighters
at ready status and the Sea Furies had not yet been launched for their
phase of the strike intercept sorties. With their limited fuel, relatively
poor ditching characteristics, and in the case of the Sea Furies, their
dangerous bale out record, the five fighter squadrons would most
certainly have undergone tragic losses in both aircraft and pilots.
Coupled with the 42 strike aircraft already airborne, there was indeed
the likelihood that the entire air group strength of the three carriers

Ensign Estler USN, being presented with souvenir of Magnificent by Cdr. Abrams following Mariner fog incident, September 1953. Credit PA1755003

USN AD. Skyraider aboard Magnificent preparing to launch on morning following dramatic fog incident. September 1953. Credit DND via Leo Pettipas

870 Squadron Sea Fury at Patricia Bay airport Victoria, BC.
September 25, 1953. Credit PA168879

871 Squadron Sea Fury at River Manitoba carrying out armament exercise, loaded with 2-1000 lb. bombs, January 1954. Credit PA153084

would have been in serious jeopardy.

The next phase of the exercise recommenced on 28 September, with the fleet augmented by the Royal Navy carrier *Eagle*, the battleship *Vanguard* (with her built in brewery) and an additional cruiser and escorts. These combined units now formed part of a heavy striking force, which headed for Denmark Strait. *Magnificent* and the rest of the carrier support group continued on to Reykjavic Iceland, *Magnificent* and her destroyers then forming a "Hunter Killer" group to counter opposing submarines. Sustained flying around the clock was carried out by the Avengers of 881 and the Guppy flight, while the Furies of 871 continued with intensive day fighter sorties.

The final phase of Mariner consisted of a series of Blue Fleet air strikes on 1 and 2 October against bases in the UK, while Orange Fleet aircraft attacked the "Blues" with bombing runs. The exercise wound up on 4 October with *Magnificent* continuing with anti-submarine sea and air exercises off Ireland. Before departing from the UK an additional nine new Sea Furies were picked up, these being the last to be purchased by the RCN. There was no further flying en route to Halifax for the CAG due to the large deck park of new Sea Furies. The long but highly productive cruise for *Magnificent* and the CAG ended on 2 November as the two squadrons flew ashore to *Shearwater*.

Flying intensity was not only at a high level during the cruise and exercise, but the professionalism displayed throughout the overall operations was particularly noteworthy, including sustained operations of an impressive standard. The tactical value of the Guppy flight was of marked significance, and the air and ground crews did yeoman service, virtually maintaining one aircraft on a surveilllance status at all times during the exercise. Maintenance was particularly good for both the Avenger and Fury squadrons. Considerable credit belonged not only to the engineering staff headed by LCdr. Dave Litle and Lt. Johnny Franks, but to the air maintenance personnel generally, who worked long and arduous hours for a large part of the time, often under less than desirable conditions. The success of the CAG's overall effort can be best confirmed by the flying hours achieved. During the actual cruise from August to October, which included periods of bad weather etc., and time alongside in foreign ports, 881 Avenger crews each averaged in excess of 110 hours, with 25% of these hours conducted at night. Over the 1953 year period, each pilot logged in excess of 350 hours and 65 day and night landings. In 871 Fury squadron, the hours were equally impressive with the pilots averaging over 300 hours during the year. During the cruise period, from August to October, the Fury pilots averaged about 70 hours and over 35 deck landings. The overall flying during Exercise Mariner was particularly productive at the operational level, as *Magnificent*'s aircraft flew 15 of the 19 days, totalling 357 sorties, with an additional 88 sorties flown by the plane guard helicopter.

Ashore, the transfer of the SAG to RCAF Station Summerside from Scoudouc in Sepember, was a necessary step for the winter months. The group was warmly received by the RCAF station personnel, with a well maintained hangar provided and all the attendant station facilities available for the comfort of the naval personnel. Additional naval support from *Shearwater* was sent to Summerside, consisting of an H04S helicopter and staff for Search and Rescue and utility duties.

The utility of the chopper was quickly put to use on one free afternoon (make and mend) when Pappy Macleod, myself and two others prevailed on Lt. Ted Fallen, the helo pilot, to drop us off on a likely looking but remote spit of land, to engage in some goose hunting. This he did, as part of a normal training flight and to activate the area, Ted commenced flying around a bit to stir up the birds, in a manner of speaking. This was of course not to be construed in any sense of the word as a "roundup" or a "goose herding" flight, which would obviously put the birds at somewhat of a disadvantage. We were greatly disconcerted a few minutes later to see a big puff of black smoke suddenly emit from the chopper, followed abruptly by the aircraft plunging from view. Our immediate thoughts were, but not necessarily in that order, "How do we get out of here?" "How are we going to explain this one?" "What do you suppose happened to Fallen and the chopper?" As it turned out, Ted had skillfully auto-rotated down to a nearby isolated spit of land, and the aircraft was undamaged, requiring only engine repairs. We spent some hours walking through the "boonies" until we found a house with a phone, in the meantime the interval gave us an opportunity to come up with a plausible summary of our afternoon's extra curricular activities. We never did see any geese.

With the intended Banshee jet fighter replacement for the Sea Furies scheduled for 1955, there was now a need to introduce jet training and conversion in the expanding Air Branch. This was initiated with approval for the Training Air Group (TAG), to send a fighter pilot to the RCAF jet instructor course at RCAF Station Trenton in late October 1953. Lt. Alex Fox, who had completed his tour on Sea Furies in 1951, and was now instructing in the TAG, was selected for the course. Due to a severe lack of jet instructors in the RCAF, the acceptance of Fox for the jet course by the RCAF was contingent on him being assigned to instruct on jets for a six month period at RCAF Station, Portage La Prairie. This arrangement was of mutual benefit, since Fox would be able to obtain valuable experience on the T33 jet trainers during that period, which would serve him in good stead on his return to *Shearwater,* as Officer in Charge of the jet flight in the summer of 1954.

The last flying for the year aboard *Magnificent* was carried out by the 31st. Support Air Group in December. Although only aboard for a five day period, both the Avenger and the Fury squadrons successfully re-qualified their pilots in day landings. As Pappy Macleod, Commanding Officer of 870 Fury squadron, noted at the time, "The RCN was now coming of age, the SAG deck period was successfully completed with no accidents, upholding the high standard of flying previously set by the operational squadrons of 30 CAG."

The award of the Safe Flying Trophy in 1953 to VF 871, an embarked fighter squadron, was encouraging, and positive proof that the Sea Fury had now come into its own as a superior naval strike day fighter. The excellent maintenance organization, dedicated ground crews and the high degree of professionalism demonstrated by the pilots, were all contributory factors, the sustained efforts finally paying off after experiencing several discouraging years of costly teething problems with the Sea Fury.

The 1954 year commenced with an unusually heavy period of snow and maritime winter storms, which effectively reduced flying in January and February. The new runway was now in service and taxed the station snow clearing to the limit. There was one fatal accident on

26 January 1954 when an Avenger of VU 32 crashed minutes after takeoff, killing the pilot, Lt. Leslie Terry, an RN officer on exchange. Very prompt action on the part of two pilots flying a helicopter resulted in the timely rescue of the Observer's Mate, once again demonstrating the value of the helicopter in the Search and Rescue role.

In January 1954, the first step was made by Canadian Naval Aviation to establish a West Coast presence, by the transfer of a detachment of two Avengers from VS 880, headed by Lt. D.J. Fisher, to the airport at Patricia Bay, B.C. to participate in torpedo running trials. This move precipitated further discussions by Naval Air Staff at Headquarters, which were to shortly lead to the establishment of a permanent Utility Squadron to be based at the Patricia Bay facility. The two Air Staff Officers involved in organizing the new squadron were LCdrs. Bill Atkinson and Hank Leidl. They paid their respects to the Flag Officer Pacific Coast on a visit to make initial plans for the squadron formation. The Admiral was supportive but balked initially because he had not received any documentation from the Naval Secretary informing him of the proposal. Atkinson neatly resolved that administrative hitch by using the services of a secretary in one of the staff offices to write such a letter. He signed it befittingly with a flourish on behalf of the Naval Secretary, from whom all such correspondence flows, the Admiral was satisfied, and the formation plans then proceeded.

The first change of command for the year took place in February with LCdr. Vince Murphy taking over VU 32 from LCdr. Jim Watson.

VS 881 Avenger squadron commenced a major transfer of aircraft and personnel in mid February by flying from Dartmouth to Quonset Point, remaining there overnight, then flying direct to Bermuda, where, at a distance of 180 miles out from the island, we were met by a US Coast Guard escort aircraft. This transit showed once again the long range capability and reliability of the Avengers, as they completed the leg from Quonset Point to Bermuda in a six hour flight. For the next five weeks the squadron participated in extensive anti-submarine exercises with both surface ships and submarines in the Bermuda area. The good weather and high aircraft serviceability resulted in excellent training, with each crew averaging in excess of

40 hours, virtually all of which was concentrated on exercises with the submarine.

Magnificent was alongside in Dockyard during January and February for self maintenance, then sailed to Portsmouth for a long electronic and general refit, lasting until June. The only aircraft aboard *Magnificent* on this non-flying trip were 14 surplus Fireflies of various types, which, having been sold to Ethiopia, were being ferried to the UK. This transaction had some humorous international entanglements, when the Ethiopian Government offered to purchase the old Fireflies. Gerry Daniel, who negotiated the deal, recalls the Ethiopians offered something in the region of $100,000 for the lot, and since at the time this seemed a reasonable sum, he accepted on behalf of the RCN. It was only after the Fireflies had been sold and paid for, that the Federal Crown Assets Corporation heard of the sale and were all upset because military aircraft were not to be disposed of by any authority, other than their own, and under no circumstances were such aircraft permitted to be sold to a foreign power. The story of the old RCN Fireflies was resurrected in 1989, when two of them were discovered to still be in existence in a military compound at Asmara in the province of Eritrea. Although somewhat the worse for wear by perforations from assorted bullet holes, and surrounded by rebels, the aircraft were still intact. Other than a recently rebuilt Firefly in the UK, these are believed to be the only other Mk I Fireflies still in existence. Attempts to purchase them, since their discovery, have been singularly unsuccessful due to the ongoing civil war.

The helicopter squadron became increasingly the subject of favourable publicity about this time, with participation in three separate rescue missions. One involved flying a doctor to Terrace Bay, NS., which was isolated with heavy snow, to provide emergency treatment for two children. Another rescue flight was made to a sealer, off the Magdelan Islands, to assist a sick crewman. The third mission was the airlift of three sick personnel from the American military transport, the USS *General Hodges*, for medical treatment ashore.

By the end of March 1954, VF 870 was now commencing to disband in preparation for re-equipping with the replacement Banshees. As often happens, the planned aircraft replacement schedule could not be adhered to. The delivery dates for the Banshees were

|complicated by the problems the USN were having with their Banshee replacement all-weather fighter, the F3H Demon. This delayed the scheduled transfer of used Banshees to the RCN, with the anticipated allocation of the aircraft now spread over a 30 month period commencing in late 1955, as compared to the original 12 month period.

As VF 870 was temporarily disbanded, the remaining SAG squadron VS 880 changed command, with LCdr. Fred Townsend taking over from LCdr. Ted Davis in March. This was followed by a period of ASW training by the Avenger squadron at Bermuda transiting there via Quonset Point. In the CAG there was also a change of command in March, with LCdr. Deke Logan assuming command of VF 871 Sea Fury squadron from Lt. Mike Wasteneys. Mike had the distinction of being the last officer to have command of an operational squadron while as a Lt. As can be seen, the wartime RCNVR FAA pilots and ex-RCAF pilots were now attaining the rank level of LCdr., and were no longer being appointed to squadron command in the lower rank.

With *Magnificent* away, an extensive program for VS 881 Avenger squadron commenced with their departure from *Shearwater* for a two week visit to the West Coast, where the squadron, working out of Patricia Bay, was to exercise with RCN ships of the Pacific fleet. On 7 April, the twelve aircraft left the air station and by 9 April were in Calgary. Things regrettably came to an abrupt halt there with suspected fuel contamination problems, which necessitated a four day delay while all the aircraft had to be checked and fuel changed. While in Calgary we were all in a quandry as to how to safeguard our personal issue of .45 calibre automatic pistols. This was resolved when we dumped them all on the desk clerk at the well established Palliser Hotel, with vague instructions to put them in the hotel safe. He quickly agreed and the two dozen guns were ceremoniously checked in the honoured tradition of the old west, before we entered the bar.

On 15 April, the Avengers arrived en masse at Pat Bay and settled in for a pleasant flying period in the balmy west coast weather. A good opportunity was presented to "show the flag" while on the West Coast, by conducting fly pasts at several B.C. cities. On 30 April, the squadron left the gentle climes of the Pacific, but ran into problems with one Avenger piloted by Lt. Bryan Hayter reporting a major fuel

Surplus Firefly aircraft after being sold to Ethiopia, aboard
Magnificent en route to UK, March 1954. Credit PA140260

Aerial view of Fairey Aviation Co. (Canada) at Eastern Passage, NS.
August 1954. Note Avengers in foreground awaiting conversion.
Credit PA136556

881 Squadron Avenger aboard USS Antietam angled deck carrier for first time after being diverted from Magnificent, September 3, 1954. Pilot S/Lt. Tony Cottingham. Credit PA140253

Formation of VU 32 Avengers over Nova Scotia, Summer of 1954. Credit DND via Leo Pettipas

leak. This ended up with all the squadron lobbing into the short airstrip at Cranbrook, which impressed the locals somewhat, particularly with all the "turkeys" doing a wing fold to give additional parking space at the end of the strip. The fuel problem was quickly repaired by our travelling maintenance team flying in the aircraft, and we all departed for Calgary the same day. All ended well in spite of the delays, the cross country barnstorming trip, ending as the squadron droned into *Shearwater* on 7 May.

Meanwhile on 6 May, an unusual fatal accident befell the young crew of an Avenger of VS 880 as the squadron was nearing the Nova Scotia coast about 75 miles south of Yarmouth, while returning from Bermuda. The aircraft crewed by SLt. James Holden, SLt. Robert Jones, SLt. John MacLeod and P.O. John White, inexplicably dropped unseen out of the formation, without any radio message, and disappeared. In spite of an intensive air and surface search, no survivors were found, the only telltale evidence located being an immersion suit and a wheel from the Avenger.

Also in May, a major re-organization took place with the disbanding of the Training Air Group. Recognizing the increased emphasis on the aircrew training requirements, 743 squadron was disbanded and VU 32 (Utility) was established as a completely separate unit and organized into its own hangar. The current Commanding Officer, LCdr. Vince Murphy, who had succeeded Jim Watson in the previous February, remained in command and the squadron with its Avenger aircraft played an increasingly important role in observer training, pilot proficiency flying and the varied utility commitments of the fleet.

In addition, an entirely new squadron was formed at the same time from the Training air Group (TAG) and re-designated VT 40 (Training). This new squadron was divided into two components; one being the Instrument Flying School, (IFS) and the other comprising the Operational Flying Training School (OFTS). The OFTS was divided into two distinct units, one being designated the Advanced Training Flight (ATF), the other consisting of the All Weather Flight (AWF). The responsibilities of VT 40 were now considerably expanded and included the training of pilots for the increasingly important Instrument Ratings, and the conversion and operational training of newly

graduated pipeline pilots. The organization of VT 40 was also designed to accommodate a jet flight, which was now in the process of being
organized to reflect the growing need for jet training in the RCN, for
the planned equipping with the Banshees. The Commanding Officer
of the newly formed VT 40 was LCdr. Pat Whitby who continued on
in command from the now defunct Training Air Group.

A further change took place with the abolition of the administrative organization of the Carrier Air Group (CAG) and the Support
Air Group (SAG). This resulted in each squadron assuming a greater
degree of autonomy allowing more individual squadron flexibility. The
need for an Air Group Commander was hardly justified, since in many
cases, squadrons were now being deployed separately according to
their role, aircraft type and their own particular program and operational status.

Magnificent arrived back at Halifax on 11 June 1954, and preparations were immediately begun to commence carrier qualifications
for the CAG in July. This period was also used to night qualify the
VS 881 Avenger crews and exercise both the Fury and Avenger
squadrons in joint armament training, culminating with strikes on a
smoke float target. This was a very intensive period which included
541 deck landings and was rounded out with day and night anti-
submarine exercises in the Gulf Stream area.

In VU 32, the command of the squadron changed in July with
LCdr. Vince Murphy turning over the squadron to LCdr. B.L. (Barry)
Hayter.

During the same period, Lt. (E) (A/E) T.S. "Dudley" Allan had
joined 871 Fury squadron, after undergoing the last Sea Fury Operational Training Course with the Royal Navy following his pilot
graduation. Dudley, one of the so called "Flying plumbers", only had
a couple of weeks to complete his deck landing qualifications before
Magnificent sailed, but he was in one respect already uniquely qualified. By virtue of having been recently temporarily attached to the
"Clockwork Mouse" squadron, he flew probably no less than 600
Field Carrier Landing Practice sorties (FCLP) before he ever even saw
a carrier deck. He no doubt obtained more Sea Fury flying time than
anybody else during his operational training course because he and
three other students were attached to an RN reserve squadron for the

second phase of their course. Since the squadron normally flew only on the weekends, and had 24 Sea Furies on strength, the four pilots under training not only had their own private instructor, but a virtually unlimited number of Sea Furies to play with during the week. Dudley happily settled into 871 squadron with great enthusiasm, filling a regular squadron pilot billet for the first year or so. This was followed later by shifting into the squadron Air Engineer Officer (AEO) assignment, while also continuing in a flying capacity.

During the summer, RCN pilots continued to add to the number of exchange appointments and serve with contemporary fighter squadrons of the USN. With the fighter emphasis on jet operations and the planned introduction of the Banshees in the RCN, the USN were extremely obliging in the acceptance of RCN pilots in their squadrons. At one point in the current period, there were three RCN pilots serving in a composite fighter group. Not only did the USN authorities recognize the seniority of the RCN officers, but they very generously gave them the prime assignments in the group. At one time Lt. Ron Heath was serving as Operations Officer of the Cougar jet squadron, Lt. Wally Walton holding the same position in the Panther squadron, while LCdr. Jim Hunter held the coveted Group Operations assignment. Within a year, both Walton and Heath would be flying with VC 3 aboard a USN carrier operating in the Strait of Formosa. Due to the subsequent confrontation between mainland China and Taiwan, and the United States monitoring the scene with USN forces, the two Canadians being foreigners were, much to their disappointment, denied any participation in the operational sorties being flown by the USN carriers.

For *Magnificent*, further exercises involving the CAG took place in August, operating off New York where anti-submarine exercises with two USN submarines were conducted. Change of command of VS 881 squadron also took place in August as LCdr. Bob Cocks relieved LCdr. Mike Page. A second squadron command change took place in September, with LCdr. Roy de Nevers, DFC assuming VX 10 from LCdr. Hal Fearon.

September was a heavy flying month for both embarked squadrons, with the Furies carrying out extensive armament and strike sorties. An RCN "first" also took place on 3 September 1954, when a VS 881 Avenger, piloted by S/Lt. Tony Cottingham, had to make an emergency landing aboard the USN angled-deck carrier *Antietem*, at a time when *Magnificent*'s arrester gear was temporarily unserviceable. This happened during a continuous flying period, in which day and night convoy support flying operations were being carried out in exercise New Broom II and was the first landing by an RCN aircraft aboard an angled deck carrier. Following the major exercise, *Magnificent* with *Quebec* in company headed south for the Panama Canal on the planned cruise to the West Coast. After transiting the Panama Canal on 28 September, there was a bit of a problem since our part time planeguard, the frigate HMCS *Stettler*, with a maximum speed of 18 knots, could not keep up with *Magnificent* in light wind conditions when 24 knots were required. This was partially solved by stationing the frigate ahead to port, so that as we flew the aircraft on and off, the frigate was more or less in position for a brief period of "passing by" time. During Avenger night operations when our planeguard chopper did not operate, it became a bit more complicated, but since the water was warm and it was not a common occurrence, we were not overly concerned with the frigates marginal capability. The weather changed somewhat as the carrier approached San Francisco and fog prevented further flying. A particularly enjoyable part of this cruise were the visits to both San Diego and San Francisco, where the natives were found to be particularly friendly.

One interesting sidelight during our stopover at San Francisco, was that of the newly arrived icebreaker HMCS *Labrador*, and aboard were Lts. John Laurie and "Duke" Muncaster, the pilots flying the ship's two Bell HTL helicopters. *Labrador* having just recently completed her east to west historic trip through the North-West Passage, was now en-route to Halifax via the Panama Canal, thus becoming the second ship in history to circumnavigate the North American continent. This was not only a particularly rewarding cruise for all aboard, but also provided a unique flying opportunity for the helicopter detachment to show its versatility in such an environment. John and Duke were extremely active during the trip, often each flew 4-5 trips per day, and between 23 July 1954 and 20 September, they averaged close to 70 hours apiece, particularly in August when the ship's scientific teams were very busy in surveying the coastal area. The value of the helicopters in this role was quickly recognized and was graphically evident, when 45 miles of surveying was completed in 4 days by the choppers, as compared to 10 miles being surveyed in 18 days using the previously laborious method, which utilized a land based Weasel (a tracked vehicle for use in rough terrain). There were many other specific duties carried out by the helicopters, which included inspecting the micro stations, mail pickup/delivery and medical missions. Probably the most important of all was the ice reconnaissance missions where the helo would scout ahead of the ship providing navigational guidance to circumvent the heavy ice floe buildup in the waters ahead.

Lt. A/E Bill Maxwell, who served aboard *Labrador* during the first two cruises, provides some comments on *Labrador*'s influence upon subsequent ship-based helicopter operations, as follows, "Shipboard aviation facilities aboard *Labrador* were basic, originally consisting of a skimpy flight deck canvas shelter and rudimentary fuel and support facilities. HMCS *Labrador* had a short commission in the RCN, but her design features had great influence on this aspect of the development of Naval Aviation. 1954-57 were the infant years of operating helicopters from small ships. Many naval authorities thought it impracticable to operate armed and equipped helicopters effectively from small ships in open ocean operational conditions. A fortuitous set of circumstances proved them wrong! A stabilized vessel, a helicopter with good deck handling equipment, and a capable crew would prove to be a winning combination. *Labrador* and her small teams of aviation maintenance personnel, supervised by highly qualified air technicians such as Chief Petty Officers Shorten and Turner, initially set the standards of maintenance and technical support for small ship helicopter operations. Subsequent cruises expanded and refined the concept over the next two years. This established a pool of experienced aviation personnel including both pilots and technicians, thereby forming a basis for future application and the eventual development of the RCN DDH, a new helicopter carrying anti-submarine class of ship."

Aboard *Magnificent* in the Pacific, dive bombing and other armament sorties were conducted by 871 Fury squadron after continuing on the northern leg to Esquimalt on 22 October, and by the end of the month both squadrons had progressed to a high level of combat readiness, as the hard working maintenance support teams provided excellent serviceability. This, coupled with the good flying weather as the carrier proceeded up the Pacific Coast, gave all the aircrew impressive flying totals with a corresponding low number of deck landing incidents. After a final day's transit where flying was disrupted by fog, *Magnificent* reached Esquimalt, B.C., on 25 October, where eight VS 881 Avengers and six Sea Furies of VF 871 flew ashore to the Pat Bay airport.

Meanwhile at *Shearwater*, there were two more squadron changes of command in October 1954. LCdr. V.M. "Mike" Langman, DSC. assumed command of VU 32 from LCdr. Barry Hayter, while LCdr. R.A. "Rod" Lyons took over VT 40 from LCdr. Pat Whitby.

Also at *Shearwater*, VH 21 helicopters were increasingly active with rescue missions. In October, the squadron received an emergency call for assistance to the lighthouse keeper on St. Paul's Island, located in Cabot Strait nearly 300 miles away. The man was suffering from a fractured skull and other injuries resulting from a dynamite explosion. Lt. W.E. "Sandy" James flew this mission with a crewman in a Piesecki HUP 3 one of three such recently arrived aircraft having been procured primarily for service aboard *Labrador*. This was a long and arduous flight in gale force winds and poor visibility. Sandy picked up a doctor at Sydney, N.S. then continued the difficult flight to his destination. The weather was so bad on landing, with blowing snow and high winds, that he was required to keep the aircraft rotors going for three-quarters of an hour while the doctor was giving emergency treatment to the patient. Sandy finally made it back to *Shearwater* after a gruelling trip of eight and a half hours of flying in most trying conditions. Sandy James was subsequently awarded with the Most Excellent Order of the British Empire for his courageous humanitarian action. As VH 21 increased its helicopter rescue services, many squadron pilots carried out similar missions of this type, some of whom were also subsequently honoured for their accomplishments. James, originally an RCAF pilot graduate, transferred to the RNVR in 1945, was demobilized then joined RCN Aviation in the air technical branch, serving as a Petty Officer in 19 CAG. He sub-

871 Squadron Sea Furies flying over Mount Baker, Washinton State USA, during Magnificent's cruise to the West Coast. Credit R.E. Quirt

Pair of 881 Squadron Avengers during Magnificent's return to Halifax, November 1954. Credit R.E. Quirt

881 Squadron Avengers flying over Rockies, April 1954, en route
to Patricia Bay BC. Credit R.E. Quirt via DNS 12488

sequently remustered to aircrew, regaining his pilot status.

Meanwhile, following a short stay at Esquimalt, the carrier then sailed to Vancouver for a welcome recreational and "show the flag" visit, which included a short day cruise on 5 November in local waters where both squadrons, after an air strike, were to put on a deck landing display for a large number of visiting members of the Vancouver Board of Trade. This was not exactly a howling success, since light winds in the Gulf of Georgia forced the Furies to divert to Vancouver airport, and it was only later when the wind picked up fractionally, with the carrier steaming flat out at 25 knots whipping in and around the heavy coastal shipping traffic, that the Furies finally made it aboard, albeight with more than a few dicey passes whining by, and late wave offs caused by the light wind conditions, and frequent but necessary alterations of course. All this frantic activity with it's attendant implications, was in a manner of speaking, really over the head of the mesmerized multitude of "goofers" aboard for the afternoon's entertainment, most of whom assumed that this rather untidy evolution was how carrier landings were normally carried out.

Lt. Ken Gibbs, one of the pilots crewing the H04S (Angel) helicopter on this cruise, was involved in an amusing incident concerning the Minister of National Defence, the Hon. Ralph Campney. Arrangements had been made for a ceremonial visit of the Minister to the carrier to view the Navy's pride and joy and to watch the air strike and landing display. Ken landed his trusty chopper on the parade square of HMCS *Discovery*, the Reserve Division to pick up the Minister for the flight to *Magnificent*. Campney, expressing interest in flying in the co-pilot's seat, was "assisted aboard", climbing into the window hatch. With the noisy rotors whizzing above his head, Campney could not hear Ken's boarding instructions all that well and ended up entering the cockpit head first, and grabbing at the aircraft controls (much to Gibbs' dismay) to pull himself in. In all the haste and confusion, he caught his pants on the access window latch and ended up with a large "L" shaped tear in the seat of his best Sunday trousers. As the chopper landed aboard Maggie, and the Minister made his ceremonial appearance, he was particularly conspicuous to all and sundry with "the arse torn out of his pants", and a prominent display of white underwear. Campney however, took all this in 'stride', and at the reception later in the wardroom, he was once again adequately covered. This was achieved by the not so expert repairs to his trousers by the Safety Equipment Petty Officer, who was much more versed in the mending of parachutes and dinghy packs.

Meanwhile, plans to re-equip the Canadian ASW squadrons with a Canadian version of the S2F, were in full swing and to gain experience on the operation and maintenance of the new aircraft, a group of officers and men from *Shearwater* were attached to VS 26, one of the USN squadrons operating S2Fs aboard the USS *Antietam*. One individual so involved was Petty Officer R. Spicer, whose quick thinking avoided a nasty accident on the flight deck. Spicer was in the cockpit of an S2F being towed forward on to the elevator by a tractor, when the elevator suddenly made an unplanned descent to the hangar deck below. Spicer immediately locked the brakes on the aircraft, stopping at the very edge of the elevator well. Although the towing arm was bent at right angles with the tractor dangling in mid air down the well, no damage was sustained to the aircraft or personnel. Spicer was subsequently officially commended by the Chief of Naval Staff for his prompt action, which most certainly saved a valuable aircraft and protected personnel from possible serious injury.

About the same time, Lt. Shel Rowell whilst undergoing LSO training was attached to another S2F squadron. This was one of the first S2F squadrons to go aboard, and as can be imagined, there was the usual number of deck landing accidents that took place in the process. One of the most incredible Shel ever witnessed, was one landing by an older ex navy transport pilot who wanted to have a late career attempt at carrier deck landings. His S2F bounced and went right down the deck, slammed into the barrier, and to everybody's astonishment, the tail end of the aircraft fractured at the centre section and folded like a huge hinge over the front cockpit, crushing the side windows absolutely flat. The pilot walked away from the pile of wreckage virtually unscathed. He also discontinued his attempt to have a career as a carrier pilot.

Flying from *Magnificent* recommenced on 10 November following departure from Esquimalt. The two frigates *New Glasgow* and *Stettler* were in company as were three minesweepers. At Long Beach, our remaining frigate *New Glasgow* (*Stettler* having returned to

Esquimalt) developed condenser difficulties and remained in harbour. This unfortunately restricted flying to daytime only for the Avengers, with only our trusty Pedro chopper available to carry out the plane guard rescue duty. Anti-submarine exercises however continued daily with the USN submarine *Carbonero* as we headed south for the eastern transit of the Panama Canal. After a quick passage of the Canal, *Magnificent* joined up with the cruiser *Quebec*, the two sailing on 27 November with heavy flying continuing by both squadrons. On reaching Bermudian waters the annual operational inspection of *Magnificent* by the Flag Officer Atlantic Coast (FOAC) took place, as the ships continued north on the last leg of their extended cruise. The two squadrons flew ashore to *Shearwater* in early December, and *Magnificent* then commenced her annual refit on 15 December, after a very busy year in which the carrier had steamed nearly 34,000 miles.

The air operations of the CAG in 1954 continued to be intensive. Over the recent embarked period from August to December, VS 881 crews were averaging in excess of 30 hours per month while at sea. The pilots, who were qualified for both day and night carrier landings, were averaging even more hours, carrying out half their flying at night. A high number of individual deck landings were also achieved with some pilots averaging in excess of 60 each, again with half of their landings carried out during night operations. VF 871 Fury pilots, also maintaining a high level of operational readiness, flew close to 25 hours per month each, while averaging 35 day deck landings per pilot during the same embarked period.

With the increased emphasis on night carrier flying, I had been aware, as an LSO for some time, of the limitations of our night equipment, which although of standard USN design was marginal in the distance the pilots could clearly detect signals from the LSO. Operating aboard the larger USN carriers with their greater speed, stability and deck space, the requirement for a high degree of accuracy and control in landing at night was certainly less than that required aboard a small carrier like *Magnificent* where the margin of error was greatly diminished.

The USN LSO night landing signal system consisted of a row of ultra-violet lights spaced on a bar at deck level a few feet from the

LSO platform. This light source shining on the fluorescent stripes of the LSO suit and paddles resulted in an illuminated "Day Glo" type of presentation, which provided the incoming pilot with the required signal display. There were two problems with this system. The first was the necessity for the controlling LSO to wear an aluminum shield around his neck to prevent the ultra-violet light from shining in his eyes, thereby destroying his night vision which was essential in order to detect the incoming aircraft. The shield was restrictive and difficult to keep in place so head movements had to be minimized. The second problem was that the light could not be suitably amplified to extend the range of the visual presentation for the landing pilot.

I believed that if a brighter light source could be provided from the LSO's suit and signal paddles, while still protecting his required night vision, the pilots would see the signals at a much greater distance. This would in turn provide the pilot a clearer focal point to concentrate upon, enabling him to respond earlier to the landing signals. I worked for a few months in the summer of 1954 developing such a system. This consisted of small lucite rods attached to the front of canvas overalls mounted in short sections, with a narrow strip of reflective red tape fastened on the rear of the rods. When illuminated by small bulbs enclosed at each end of the rods, the light was then projected outward and being directional would shine only ahead, thereby protecting the night vision of the LSO. Since the lucite rods could be curved and the light naturally followed the curvature, the paddles were shaped accordingly, again with the light being thrust forward. A rheostat control was provided to control brightness. The whole system operated on a 24 volt DC power source, and was constructed of material and electrical components available through naval stores. After conducting several night FCLP approaches, we were more than satisfied with the results and the electrical staff at both *Shearwater* and *Magnificent* responded enthusiastically to the concept, and in short order we had two suits and two sets of paddles in operation.

The pilots reported they were able to detect the signals at a considerably greater distance, and it was also noted that the haze or halo prevalent with the ultra-violet lighting was no longer evident. There was one problem I did not consider, which flared up later one

LSO night landing suit and paddles designed by Lt. Stu Soward
(left). On right, standard USN LSO suit worn by Lt. Shel Rowell.
Credit DND HS 44911

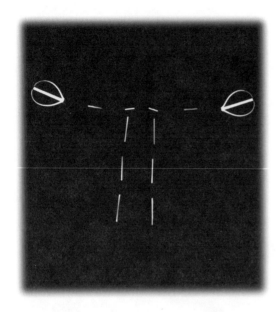

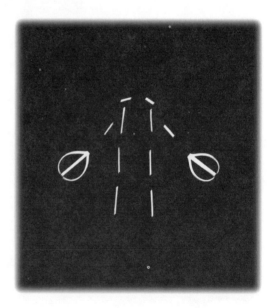

Views of illuminated LSO night suit by Soward while conducting night FCLP's at Shearwater, 1954. Credits DND MAG 7343, MAG 7358

night aboard the carrier when Ken "Big Nick" Nicolson was waving the aircraft aboard. The prototype electrical connections being made of modified soldered fixtures were not as robust as one might require, and Nick experienced a short circuit which presented him with a 24 volt shock every time he moved his arms. The outcome of this malfunction was some rather dubious and confusing signalling as Nick pranced about the platform, spasmodically jumping as each charge coursed through his body.

The equipment continued to be successfully used until *Magnificent* was returned to the Royal Navy. The paddles were actually retained, and continued to be in service as a backup to the mirror landing system subsequently installed in the replacement carrier *Powerful* (*Bonaventure*). There was considerable interest expressed by the USN in the design, but the rapid introduction of the mirror landing system in their carriers virtually eclipsed the requirement for an LSO and the equipment became redundant. However for my efforts, I was presented a year later with a cheque in the princely amount of $300 and a letter of commendation from the Chief of Naval Staff.

At *Shearwater*, major flying commitments were being met over the last two months of the year with VS 880 engaging in a month of advanced ASW training at Bermuda, where sea and flying conditions were eminently suitable for the support squadron to work up the newly arrived crews. As indicated previously, the increased flexibility, longer range and overall reliability of the Avengers was much in evidence, greatly expanding the ability of the air squadrons to deploy aircraft detachments in extended operations. VU 32 with its Avengers was also very busy with the on-going air training of observer's mates and the NATO observer classes, the Observer School having graduated their fourth course in the previous June.

There was one accident worthy of mention that occurred toward the end of the year involving an Avenger of VU 32. Lt. Paddy Moore, a WW2 FAA pilot, and a recipient of the Distinguished Service Cross (DSC), was one of a group of VU 32 pilots carrying out Field Carrier Landing Practice (FCLP). While he was flying the low pattern over the air station, a fuel line fractured and the Avenger caught fire. Paddy, in an incredible display of coolness and skill, was forced to partially vacate the smoke-filled cockpit, and managed to control the blazing aircraft from the side standing on the wing. With great difficulty he was able to keep the Avenger under control until he had flown over the built up area of the air station, including the large section of married quarters. Finally at a height of only about 800 feet, he leaped from the wing and parachuted to safety, landing in the station football field. His burning aircraft crashed nearby at the marine jetty, where the burning fuel exploded, fortunately with only slight damage to the jetty. This was a remarkably courageous act, for which Paddy deserved great credit. Being a very quiet and unassuming person, he modestly down-played his brave action, but there is no question he skilfully averted what probably would have otherwise been a major tragedy.

As the year ended, VS 880 was announced as the winner of the Safe Flying Trophy for 1954, ending a year of very successful flying both ashore and afloat.

After ten years of hard work, agonizing reflection and many instances of tragedy and heartache, Canadian Naval Aviation was now coming of age. New aircraft, better training, higher standards of leadership, improved flying practices and the establishment of adequate support facilities, had all been combined to provide a high level of confidence and professionalism. The consistently competent deployment of *Magnificent* on NATO exercises, and the high standards of operational flying being achieved, were particularly rewarding for all concerned, and a promising future and expanding role for the Branch now appeared to be at hand.

PRANGS - 1945-1954

The following photographs encompassing this ten year period of Canadian Naval Air history, portray accidents in which all the participants emerged virtually unscathed. As can be seen, in many instances it was indeed remarkable that the aircrew were able to escape without injury.

300

John Henderson's Firefly "flamer" landing aboard HMS Theseus
September 1946. Credit Stan Woods

Don Hockin's Firefly in port catwalk, Warrior 1946.
Credit S. Britton

Tom Wall's Firefly undercarriage collapsing on landing, Warrior, 1946.
Credit S. Britton

Art Liley and Firefly "floating" into barrier, Warrior, 1946.
Credit E.M. Davis

Clunk Watson and Seafire into barrier, Warrior, 1946.
Credit E.M. Davis

Hank Leidl's Seafire entangled in barrier, Warrior, 1946.
Credit E.M. Davis

Deke Logan's Seafire after veering into crane, Warrior, 1946.
Credit E.M. Davis

Howie Clark and Firefly hitting the dirt during ADDL at RCN Air
Section, 1946. Credit S. Britton

Al Woods pecking the deck with Firefly, Warrior, 1947.
Credit DND G1028

Stu Soward and Firefly coming to an abrupt halt at
barrier stanchion, Warrior, 1947. Credit DND G921

Dick Bartlett and Firefly torquing in....

....with a resounding splash! Magnificent, 1948. Credit R.E. Bartlett

John Roberts and Firefly parking in starboard catwalk, Magnificent, 1948. Credit PA138014 via Leo Pettipas

Untangling John Roberts' Firefly from #2 barrier, Magnificent, 1948. Credit PA138013 via Leo Pettipas

Charlie Bourque and Firefly ditching to port of
Magnificent, 1948. Credit DND MAG 1871

Doug Fisher's Firefly at rest in starboard gun sponson,
Magnificent, 1948. Credit DND MAG 1353

Anonymous pilot and Sea Fury slamming into barrier,
Magnificent, 1949. Credit PA168846

....and disentangling! Credit PA 168871

Joe MacBrien torquing with his Sea Fury into the sea, Magnificent, 1949.
Credit W. Maxwell

Anonymously piloted Firefly as undercarriage collapses on landing
Magnificent, 1949. Credit PA152288

Hal Welsh and his Firefly after stalling during FCLP at Kindley
Field Bermuda, 1950. Credit PA153019

Anonymous–Firefly flying into barriers of Magnificent after missing
all wires, 1950. Credit PA152270

Anonymous–Firefly draped over starboard side of carrier Magnificent,
May 1950. Credit Colbert, DND PA138018

Shel Rowell in Firefly sliding into forward deck park after "passing through barriers", Magnificent 1950. Credit MAG 2023

Bill Munro diving his Fury alongside port side, Magnificent, 1951. Credit MAG 2824

Roger Fink executing a "water landing" in Avenger alongside
Magnificent, 1951 MAG 2826

Anonymous–Sea Fury entangled in barrier, Magnificent, 1951.
Credit PA146261

Anonymous—Barrier-bound Fury charging up the deck to barriers after losing hook and tail wheel, Magnificent, 1951. Credit PA153042

Anonymous Fury crashing inverted on deck after slamming into
barriers, Magnificent, 1951-52. Credit MAG 2075

Al Shimmin's broken-backed Fury after engine failure near
Chezzetcook, NS. 1952. Credit PA153072

Monk Geary and his Fury "Trucking along" at Shearwater, 1952.
Credit PA153110

Bob Falls and Fury hurdling barriers of Magnificent, 1952.
Credit PA 180231

....and "parking" up forward. Credit PA163856

Bryan Hayter and Firefly wheeling up port side of HMS Triumph,
October 1952. Credit Bryan Hayter.

Paddy O'Connell with his
Avenger entangled in
barrier of Magnificent,
1952. Credit R. Duiven

Anonymous–Inverted Fury in snow, Shearwater, 1952.
Credit PA153107

Pat Ryan and Fury, embedded in barrier, Magnificent, 1952.
Credit R. Duiven

Brian Bell-Irving with his Fury undercarriage collapsing while
landing, Magnificent, 1952. Credit R. Duiven

Anonymous–Well wrinkled Fury after forced landing at Shearwater,
1952. Credit PA153111

Anonymous–Avenger hook about to engage barrier after floating over the wires, Magnificent, 1953. Credit MAG 4386

Jim Burns and his Avenger after dropping into golf course at Chester NS., 1953. Credit PA136525

Weldon Paton's burned out Avenger in trees near Greenwood,
NS., 1953. Credit W. Paton

Weldon Paton's Avenger suspended on port side of Magnificent during
night landing, 1954. Credit W. Paton

– Drifting away.

Anonymously piloted Avenger landing sequence:
– Lining up to port.

– Away we go.

– Port wing dropping.

– Splash one Avenger.

– Over the side.

– Chopper pickup. Credit P. Wiwcharuck

SYNOPSIS

The first ten years of Canadian Naval Aviation were plagued with all the problems and frustrations that could possibly be encountered when establishing a new and unique major Branch of the RCN.

The shift of the RCN in the closing year of the war from an escort force to a more traditional balanced fleet comprised of cruisers, destroyers and aircraft carrier(s), primarily came about because these were the type of ships required for the final stage of the Pacific war against Japan. With plentiful wartime manpower available for this task, the RCN could well fill the crying need to man the ships provided by the Royal Navy which had reached its limit of manpower resources. This balanced force concept could fulfill the primary role of the maritime defence of Canada and fitted well into the postwar fleet envisaged by Naval Board.

By 1945, the RCN was faced with the very difficult task of creating an entirely new Air Branch virtually from scratch, just as the war ended and the mass exodus of experienced personnel to demobilization commenced. This placed an undue strain upon the dwindling available resources required to establish the peacetime infrastructure and training facilities to provide support to the already in place, first line air squadrons operating both ashore and afloat.

The foregoing lack of experienced personnel at all levels, the operational wartime attitudes still in effect, and the introduction of new and more advanced aircraft without adequate support, all had a detrimental impact on the overall development of the new branch. The most obvious outcome of these factors was the initially high accident rate which unfortunately included many fatalities.

From September 1945, when RCN Aviation came into being, to December 1954, 58 young Canadians of all ranks and trades perished whilst serving in Canadian Naval Aviation. Pilot error, in many instances was certainly responsible for several accidents in the first four years, but often it was the consequence of operating under conditions for which the pilots had not been adequately trained. In the early years, this was particularly applicable to the Seafire XV accidents which occurred in both bad weather and under unexpected instrument conditions. For various such reasons, including the period of engine supercharger problems, the Seafire was not successfully operated to any extent aboard the carrier. Additionally it could not be effectively applied in the operational training role due to inadequate spare parts and an insufficient number of trained maintenance personnel.

Although the naval airmen on staff at Naval Headquarters made determined efforts to obtain Hellcats from the USN, these attempts were doomed to failure by the strong pro British RCN Naval Board, their undue procrastination and the perceived lack of Hellcat support from the RN advisors. It was generally recognized that a purchase of Hellcats for use in an operational training capacity would have provided an excellent interim naval fighter replacement for the Seafire. This would have allowed the Air Branch to develop a nucleus of well trained fighter pilots operating a proven day and night carrier fighter. In turn, the RCN would have gained some valuable time, allowing a delay in the introduction of the Sea Fury until some of the initial major problems associated with the aircraft's engine were resolved by the Royal Navy. No doubt there would have been a considerable saving in both lives and money if this course of action had been allowed to take place.

The early introduction of the Sea Fury to replace the Seafire XV however, was a bold step and when the aircraft was finally clear of the major engine problems and the deck landing difficulties were to a great extent overcome, it became for all intents and purposes the best carrier-based fighter bomber of its time. Indeed, the Canadian Sea Fury fighter squadrons not only performed on a par with those in the Royal Navy but provided for several years the only operational fighters available in the Canadian military.

Some critics have stated that the Sea Fury was just too "Hot" for the RCN, but upon examination, the facts do not support this contention. True, most accidents that occurred during the first ten years were with the Sea Fury. Of the 8 fatal accidents involving this fighter from its introduction in 1948 to the end of 1954, six could be blamed on pilot error or inexperience. Other non-fatal accidents could be similarly attributed. On the other hand, there were estimated to be over 30 accidents both ashore and afloat, two of which were fatal and directly attributable to engine associated malfunctions. Many of these were caused by the subsequently rectified design flaws in the Centaurus engine oil circulation system. It is probably more accurate to say that the Sea Fury was put in RCN service before either the aircraft and the Air Branch were ready. Further, lack of sufficient operating experience at all levels was compounded by an initial shortage of trained maintenance personnel, spare parts and a decided lack of suitable maintenance publications.

There were only two fatal Sea Fury accidents from 1951 to 1954 and accidents of all types were greatly reduced. During this period the aircraft was flying extensively and fully operationally both ashore and afloat. The overall accident rate had dropped dramatically and the deck landing accident rate was comparable to the RN. The original RAF, non-naval design of the aircraft certainly resulted in a higher rate of deck landing accidents than those experienced by comparable USN aircraft, which were specifically designed from the outset for carrier operations. By 1952 however, the Fury was emerging as a first rate interceptor-fighter and fighter-bomber, with an unmatched performance. For the next two years the combat readiness of the fighter squadrons was maintained at their highest level and the quality of maintenance support was first class.

The shift to the USN Avenger from the RN Fireflies was probably the most progressive step taken by Canadian Naval Aviation during this ten year period. The resulting dramatic increase in the hours flown, the greatly improved equipment configuration, the ease of maintenance and reduced accident rate all considerably enhanced both the operational readiness of the squadrons and the training standards of the support squadrons.

From the perspective of policy and planning, the Air Branch was now being staffed at adequate levels by qualified naval airmen at Naval Headquarters. The influence of the Royal Navy had waned and the USN, now our closest ally, had become the major source of replacement aircraft, safety equipment, air stores, pilot training facilities and specialized technical training for the maintenance air trades.

The purchase and modernization of the aircraft carrier *Powerful* to Canadian standards was however, viewed in some quarters with a degree of justifiable concern. This was due to the considerable operational limitations imposed by the ship's slow speed, limited deck space and lack of potential to accept any future generation of naval aircraft. Calculations established that the operation of Banshees and S2F aircraft aboard the ship could be accomplished, but in some cases only marginally since the flight deck equipment was operating at near maximum limits. The planned introduction of the Banshees to meet the prescribed role for an all weather fighter defence capability for the fleet was a necessary development. The question of how well the Banshee would be able to carry out this role from the modified *Powerful* was yet to be established. The selection of the S2F twin-engined aircraft to replace the Avenger was viewed with considerable acclaim, ensuring the RCN of an aircraft with impressive performance over a long term.

By the end of the ten year period covered in this Volume I, the formation, organization, consolidation and expansion of the Canadian Naval Aviation Branch had been achieved. The Branch appeared to be on a firm footing, plans to establish and develop realistic goals were underway, and there was every expectation that Naval Aviation would be flying high in the years ahead.

Perhaps however, one area of concern among the Naval Aviation Staff and particularly those involved in long term planning, was the implications of the comment made in 1953 by Commodore Keighly-Peach, RN. His statement that the operational strength of the air squadrons had remained virtually unchanged over the first decade while the surface fleet of the RCN had doubled, was disturbing. This, coupled with the recent trend to reduce the percentage of aviation expenditures in comparison with the total RCN budget, was an indication that Naval Aviation may well be facing a degree of uncertainty in the years ahead due to the shifting financial priorities of the RCN.

ABBREVIATIONS

ADDL	Aerodrome Dummy Deck Landing
AEW	Airborne Early Warning
A/S	Anti-submarine
ASWTNS	Anti-submarine Warfare Tactical Navigation System
CAP	Combat Air Patrol
CARQUAL	Carrier Qualification
CBE	Commander of the Order of the British Empire
CJAT	Canadian Joint Air Training
CNMO	Canadian Naval Mission Overseas
CAG	Carrier Air Group
CAS	Chief of the Air Staff
CNS	Chief of the Naval Staff
COAC	Commanding Officer Atlantic Coast
COMAIRCANLANT	Air Commander Canadian Atlantic Sub-Area
COMCANLANT	Commander Canadian Atlantic Sub-Area
CVE	Carrier Vessel Escort Class
CVL	Carrier Vessel Light Class
DFC	Distinguished Flying Cross
DLCO	Deck Landing Control Officer
DLT	Deck Landing Training
DNAD	Director Naval Air Division
DSC	Distinguished Service Cross
DSO	Distinguished Service Order
ECM	Electronic Counter Measures
EER	Explosive Echo Ranging
EFTS	Elementary Flying Training School
FAA	Fleet Air Arm
FCLP	Field Carrier Landing Practice
FOAC	Flag Officer Atlantic Coast
FOPC	Flag Officer Pacific Coast
FRU	Fleet Requirements Unit
GM	George Medal
HMAS	His/Her Majesty's Australian Ship
HMCS	His/Her Majesty's Canadian Ship

HMS	His/Her Majesty's Ship
LSO	Landing Signals Officer
MAD	Magnetic Anomoly Detection
MCA	Maritime Central Airways
NAAFI	Navy Army and Air Force Institutes
NAF	Naval Air Facility
NAMS	Naval Air Maintenance School
NATO	North Atlantic Treaty Organization
NAVEX	Navigation Exercise
NSHQ	Naval Service Headquarters
NHQ	Naval Headquarters
OBE	Officer of the Order of the British Empire
OFS	Operational Flying School
OTC	Officer in Tactical Command
OTU	Operational Training Unit
RAF	Royal Air Force
RAAF	Royal Australian Air Force
RCAF	Royal Canadian Air Force
RCN	Royal Canadian Navy
RCNAS	Royal Canadian Naval Air Service
RCNAS	Royal Canadian Naval Air Section
RCNAS	Royal Canadian Naval Air Station
RCN(R)	Royal Canadian Naval (Reserve)
RCNVR	Royal Canadian Naval Volunteer Reserve
RFC	Royal Flying Corps
RN	Royal Navy
RNAS	Royal Naval Air Service
RNAS	Royal Naval Air Station
RNVR	Royal Naval Volunteer Reserve
RNVR(A)	Royal Naval Volunteer Reserve (Air)
SACLANT	Supreme Allied Commander Atlantic
SAG	Support Air Group
SNAM	School of Naval Air Maintenane
SFTS	Service Flying Training School
TAG	Training Air Group
TCA	Trans Canada Airlines
TF	Task Force
TG	Task Group
TBR	Torpedo Bomber Reconnaissance

UK	United Kingdom
UN	United Nations
UNEF	United Nations Emergency Force
USA	United States of America
USNAS	United States Naval Air Station
USS	United States Ship
VC	Victoria Cross
VC	Heavier-than-air Composite Air Squadron
VDS	Variable Depth Sonar
VF	Heavier-than-air Fighter Air Squadron
VH	Heavier-than-air Helicopter Air Squadron
VS	Heavier-than-air Search Air Squadron
VT	Heavier-than-air Training Air Squadron
VTOL	Vertical Take-off and Landing
VU	Heavier-than-air Utility Air Squadron
VX	Heavier-than-air Experimental Air Squadron
WEE	Winter Experimental Establishment
WRNS	Womens Royal Naval Service
W/T	Wireless Telegraphy

BIBLIOGRAPHY

Airpower and the Royal Navy	Geoffrey Till.
A History of Canadian Naval Aviation	J.D.F. Kealy and E.C. Russell.
Banshees in the RCN	Carl Mills.
Carrier Glorious	John Winton.
Carrier Operations in World War Two, Vol. I Royal Navy	J.D.Brown.
Damn The Torpedoes	Paul Hellyer.
Death of the Battleship	Richard Hough.
Fleet Air Arm Aircrew Canadian Register	B.K.West.
History of the Royal Canadian Air Force	Christopher Shores.
"It's Really Quite Safe"	G.A. Rotherham.
Memoirs of a Mariner	Admiral H.N. Lay.
Midway! Incredible Victory	Walter Lord.
North Atlantic Run	Marc Milner.
Operation Skua	Maj. R.T. Partridge.
RCN in Retrospect	J.A. Boutilier, Ed.
Reflection on the RAN	J.A. Boutilier.
The Bonnie HMCS Bonaventure	J. Allan Snowie.
The Fairey Firefly in the RCN	Leo Pettipas.
The Fleet Air Arm History	LCdr. J.Waterman.
The Grumman Avenger in the RCN	Leo Pettipas.
The Hawker Sea Fury in the RCN	Leo Pettipas.
The Longest Battle, The War at Sea 1939-45	Richard Hough.
The Mainguy Report - Report of Incident on board HMC Ships ATHABASKAN, CRESCENT and MAGNIFICENT, Board of Enquiry Minutes of Witness - LCdr. C.G. Watson	Rear Admiral E.R. Mainguy, RCN., L.C. Audette, Leonard W. Brockington.
The Mariner Miracle	Capt. Wynn F. Foster USN (Rtd).
The Price of Admiralty	John Keegan.
The Squadrons of the Fleet Air Arm	Ray Sturtivant.
The Supermarine Seafire in the RCN	Leo Pettipas.
They Gave Me A Seafire	Cdr. R.M. Crosley.
Wings Across the Sea, The History of Australian Naval Aviation	Ross Gillett.
Wings of the Morning	Ian Cameron.

The following Appendices extracted from A History of Canadian Naval Aviation by J.D.F. Kealy and E.C Russell, have been modified where applicable to conform to the context of this recollective history.

APPENDIX A

SENIOR OFFICERS FOR NAVAL AVIATION

Officers	From	To
ASSISTANT CHIEF OF NAVAL STAFF (Plans) (Air)		
Commodore H.N. Lay, OBE, RCN, (Act.)	Apr '48	Dec '48
Commodore H.N. Lay, OBE, RCN	Jan '49	Apr '49
ASSISTANT CHIEF OF NAVAL STAFF (Air)		
Commodore 2nd Class C.N. Lentaigne, DSO, RN	Apr '49	Mar '51
Commodore 2nd Class C.L. Keighly-Peach, DSO, OBE, RN	Mar '51	Jun '53
Commodore 2nd Class W.L.M. Brown, DSO, OBE, DSC, RN	Jun '53	-

APPENDIX B

DIRECTORS OF NAVAL AIR DIVISION
& DIRECTORS OF NAVAL AVIATION

Officers	From	To
DIRECTORS OF NAVAL AIR DIVISION		
Commander (P) J.S. Stead, RCN, (Temp) (Act.)	Apr '44	Apr '45
Commander (A) J.H. Arbick, OBE, RCNVR, (Temp)	May '45	Feb '46
Captain R.E.S. Bidwell, CBE, RCN	Feb '46	Dec '46
Captain G.A. Rotherham, DSO, OBE, RN, (Act.)	Jan '47	May '48
DIRECTORS OF NAVAL AVIATION		
Captain G.A. Rotherham, DSO, OBE, RN, (Act.)	May '48	Jan '49
Captain C.N. Lentaigne, DSO, RN	Jan '49	Apr '49
Captain H.C. Rolfe, RN	Sep '49	Oct '51

APPENDIX C

COMMANDING OFFICERS OF AIRCRAFT CARRIERS
AND AIR STATION

Officers	From	To
HMS *NABOB*		
Captain H.N. Lay, OBE, RCN, (Act.)	Oct '43	Sep '44
HMS *PUNCHER*		
Captain R.E.S. Bidwell, CBE, RCN	Apr '44	Jan '46
HMCS *WARRIOR*		
Captain F.L. Houghton, CBE, RCN	Jan '46	Jan '47
Commodore H.G. DeWolf, CBE, DSO, DSC, RCN	Jan '47	Mar '48
HMCS *MAGNIFICENT*		
Commodore H.G. DeWolf, CBE, DSO, DSC, RCN	Apr '48	Aug '48
Commodore G.R. Miles, OBE, RCN	Aug '48	Jun '49
Commander A.G. Boulton, DSC, RCN	Jun '49	Sep '49
Commodore K.F. Adams, RCN	Sep '49	Oct '51
Captain K.L. Dyer, DSC, CD, RCN	Oct '51	Mar '53
Commodore H.S. Rayner, DSC and Bar, CD, RCN	Mar '53	-
ROYAL CANADIAN NAVAL AIR SECTION DARTMOUTH		
Commander (P) H.J. Gibbs, RCNVR, (Temp.)	Nov '45	Dec '45
Commander (P) H.J. Gibbs, RCN(R), (Temp.)	Jan '46	Sep '46
Commander A.E. Johnson, RCN(R), (Temp.)	Sep '46	Jun '47
Captain H.S. Rayner, DSC and Bar, RCN, (Act.)	Jun '47	Jun '48
Commander (P) A.B.F. Fraser-Harris, DSC and Bar, RCN	Jul '48	Nov '48
HMCS *SHEARWATER*		
Captain A.B.F.Fraser-Harris, DSC and Bar, RCN, (Act.)	Dec '48	Aug '49
Captain E.W. Finch-Noyes, CD, RCN	Aug '49	Jun '51
Captain D.L. Raymond, CD, RCN	Jun '51	Feb '53
Captain A.H.G. Storrs, DSC and Bar, CD, RCN	Feb '53	-

APPENDIX D

COMMANDING OFFICERS OF AIR GROUPS

Officers	From	To
18th CARRIER AIR GROUP		
Lieutenant-Commander (P) W.H. Bradley, RCN, (Act.)	Jul '47	Nov '48
Lieutenant-Commander, (O) R.I.W. Goddard, DSC, RCN, (Act.)	Dec '48	Apr '50
Lieutenant-Commander (P) R.E. Bartlett, RCN	Apr '50	May '51
30th CARRIER AIR GROUP		
Lieutenant-Commander (P) R.E. Bartlett, RCN	May '51	Mar '52
Lieutenant-Commander (P) R.A.B. Creery, RCN	Mar '52	Mar '53
Lieutenant-Commander (P) J.W. Roberts, CD, RCN	May '53	Apr '54
Lieutenant-Commander (O) M.H.E. Page, RCN	Apr '54	Jun '54
19th CARRIER AIR GROUP		
Lieutenant-Commander (P) H.J. Hunter, RCN, (Act.)	Jul '47	Sep '49
Lieutenant-Commander (P) V.J. Wilgress, RCN, (Act.)	Sep '49	Jan '51
Lieutenant-Commander (P) N. Cogdon, RCN, (Act.)	Jan '51	May '51
31st SUPPORT AIR GROUP		
Lieutenant-Commander (P) N. Cogdon, RCN	May '51	Mar '52
Lieutenant-Commander (P) J.B. Fotheringham, RCN	Mar '52	Apr '53
Lieutenant-Commander (P) D.W. Knox, CD, RCN	Apr '53	Jun '54
No. 1 TRAINING AIR GROUP		
Lieutenant-Commander A.B.F. Fraser-Harris, DSC and Bar, RCN	May '47	Jul '48
Lieutenant-Commander (P) R.A. Monks, RCN	Jul '48	Nov '48
Lieutenant-Commander (P) L.R. Tivy, RN	Apr '49	Jun '51
Lieutenant-Commander (P) J.G. Wright, DFC, RCN	Jun '51	Aug '53
Lieutenant-Commander (P) J.P. Whitby, RCN	Aug '53	May '54

APPENDIX E

COMMANDING OFFICERS OF AIR SQUADRONS

Officers	From	To
803 SQUADRON		
Lieutenant-Commander (P) A.J. Tanner, RCN, (Act.)	Jan '46	May '46
Lieutenant-Commander (P) C.G. Watson, RCN, (Act.)	May '46	May '47
Lieutenant-Commander (P) H.J.G. Bird, RCN, (Act.)	May '47	Aug '48
Lieutenant (P) J.P. Whitby, RCN	Aug '48	Sep '48
Lieutenant-Commander (P) V.J. Wilgress, RCN, (Act.)	Sep '48	May '49
Lieutenant-Commander (P) N. Cogdon, RCN,(Act.)	May '49	Dec '50
Lieutenant (P) D.D. Peacocke, RCN	Dec '50	May '51
870 SQUADRON		
Lieutenant (P) D.D. Peacocke, RCN	May '51	Nov '52
VF 870		
Lieutenant (P) D.D. Peacocke, RCN	Nov '52	Feb '53
Lieutenant-Commander (P) D.M. Macleod, RCN	Feb '53	Apr '54
883 SQUADRON		
Lieutenant-Commander (P) R.A. Monks, RCN, (Act.)	May '47	Jan '48
Lieutenant-Commander (P) J.B. Fotheringham, RCN, (Act.)	Jan '48	Nov '48
Lieutenant-Commander (P) R.A.B. Creery, RCN, (Act.)	Dec '48	Apr '50
Lieutenant (P) W.D. Munro, RCN	Apr '50	Apr '51
871 SQUADRON		
Lieutenant (P) W.D. Munro, RCN	May '51	Nov '51
Lieutenant-Commander (P) D.H.P. Ryan, RCN	Nov '51	Jul '52
Lieutenant (P) R. Heath, RCN	Jul '52	Nov '52
VF 871		
Lieutenant (P) R. Heath, RCN	Nov '52	Mar '53
Lieutenant (P) M. Wasteneys, RCN	Mar '53	Mar '54
Lieutenant-Commander (P) J.W. Logan, RCN	Mar '54	-

Officers	From	To

825 SQUADRON

Lieutenant-Commander (P) O.W. Tattersall, DSC, RN, (Act.)	Jan '46	Jan '47
Lieutenant-Commander (P) R.E. Bartlett, RCN, (Act.)	Feb '47	Aug '48
Lieutenant (P) D.D. Peacocke, RCN	Aug '48	Sep '48
Lieutenant-Commander (O) J.A. Stokes. RCN, (Act.)	Dec '48	Apr '50
Lieutenant-Commander (P) D.W.Knox, RCN,(Act.)	Apr '50	May '51

880 SQUADRON

Lieutenant-Commander (P) D.W.Knox, RCN,(Act.)	May '51	Nov '51
Lieutenant (P) E.M. Davis, RCN	Nov '51	Nov '52

VS 880

Lieutenant-Commander (P) E.M. Davis, RCN	Nov '52	Mar '54
Lieutenant-Commander (P) F.G. Townsend, RCN	Mar '54	-

826 SQUADRON

Lieutenant-Commander (P) J.B. Fotheringham, RCN, (Act.)	May '47	Jan '48
Lieutenant-Commander (O) R.I.W. Godddard, DSC, RCN, (Act.)	Jan '48	Nov '48
Lieutenant-Commander (P) J.W. Roberts, RCN, (Act.)	Dec '48	Apr '50
Lieutenant-Commander (P) J.N. Donaldson, RCN, (Act.)	Apr '50	May '51

881 SQUADRON

Lieutenant-Commander (P) J.N. Donaldson, RCN	May '51	Oct '51
Lieutenant-Commander (P) W.H.I. Atkinson, DSC, RCN	Oct '51	Nov '52

VS 881

Lieutenant-Commander (P) W.H.I. Atkinson, DSC, RCN	Nov '52	Aug '53
Lieutenant-Commander (O) M.H.E. Page, RCN	Aug '53	Aug '54
Lieutenant-Commander (P) R.W.J. Cocks, RCN	Aug '54	-

Officers	From	To

743 FLEET REQUIREMENTS UNIT

Lieutenant (P) J.N. Donaldson, RCN	Sep '46	Aug '47
Lieutenant-Commander (P) W.E. Widdows, RCN, (Act.)	Aug '47	May '48
Lieutenant-Commander (P) C.G. Smith, RCN, (Act.)	Nov '48	Jun '49
Lieutenant (P) R.J. Watson, RCN	May '52	Jan '53
Lieutenant-Commander (P) R.J. Watson, RCN	Jan '53	Feb '54

VU 32

Lieutenant-Commander (P) V.J. Murphy, RCN	Feb '54	Jun '54
Lieutenant-Commander (P) B.L. Hayter, CD, RCN	Jul '54	Oct '54
Lieutenant-Commander (P) V.M. Langman, DSC, RCN	Oct '54	-

VT 40

Lieutenant-Commander (P) J.P. Whitby, RCN	May '54	Oct '54
Lieutenant-Commander (P) R.A. Lyons, RCN	Oct '54	-

VX 10

Lieutenant-Commander (P) W.H. Fearon, RCN	Mar '53	Sep '54
Lieutenant-Commander(P) (O) R.O. de Nevers, DFC, CD, RCN	Sep '54	-

NUMBER 1 HELICOPTER FLIGHT

Lieutenant-Commander (P) J.D. Lowe, CD, RCN	Sep '51	May '53

VH 21

Lieutenant-Commander (P) J.D. Lowe, CD, RCN	May '53	Aug '53
Lieutenant-Commander (P)(O) J.H. Beeman, RCN	Aug '53	-

VU 33

Lieutenant-Commander (P) D.J. Fisher, CD, RCN	Nov '54	-

APPENDIX F

SPECIFICATIONS OF AIRCRAFT CARRIERS

HM SHIPS *Nabob* and *Puncher*

Smiter Class Escort Carriers

	Nabob D.77	*Puncher* D.79
Displacement	15,390 tons	14,170 tons
Overall Length	495' 8"	492' 0"
Breadth at flight deck	107' 2"	102' 0"
Breadth at waterline	69' 6"	69' 6"
Draught	25' 5"	24' 8"

Armament: Two 5" thirty-eight calibre dual purpose guns with Bofors and Oerlikons for anti-aircraft defence.

Aircraft: 20

Propulsion: Geared turbines; single screw; full speed 18 knots.

HMCS *Warrior*

Improved Colossus Class Light Fleet Carrier

Displacement	18,000 tons full load
Length on waterline	682'
Length on flight deck	700'
Beam (waterline)	80'
Draught	23'
Breadth of flight deck	112' 2"

Armament: Six quadruple two-pounder pompoms and 19 Bofors guns for anti-aircraft defence.

Aircraft: 34

Propulsion: Parsons geared turbines; twin-screw; full speed 25 knots.

HMCS *Magnificent* RML 21

Majestic Class Light Fleet Carrier

Displacement	18,000 tons full load
Length overall	694' 3"
Beam on waterline	80'
Draught	23'
Breadth of flight deck	112' 5"

Armament: Thirty Bofors guns for anti-aircraft defence.

Aircraft: 34

Propulsion: Parsons geared turbines; twin-screw; full speed 25 knots.

APPENDIX G

DETAILS OF RCN AIRCRAFT 1946-1954

Fairey Swordfish

Description	Carrier-based torpedo-spotter-reconnaissance aircraft. Crew of 3 for reconnaissance or 2 for torpedo strikes. Metal structure, fabric covered. The Swordfish IV, as used in Canada, had an enclosed cockpit.
Engine	One 690-HP Bristol Pegasus III M3 or 750-HP Pegasus XXX.
Performance	Maximum speed 139 m.p.h. Cruising 104-129 m.p.h. Range 546 miles with normal fuel and one 1,610-lb. torpedo. Maximum range for reconnaissance with no bomb-load and extra fuel, 1,030 miles. Service ceiling 10,700 feet.
Armament	One Vickers gun forward and one Vickers "K" gun or one Lewis aft. One 18-inch torpedo or one 1,500-lb. mine or 1,500-lb. weight of bombs.

Supermarine Walrus

Description	Spotter-reconnaissance amphibian for carrier-borne or catapult duties. Crew of three. Metal hull and composite wood and metal wings, fabric covered.
Engine	One 775-h.p. Bristol Pegasus II.
Performance	Maximum speed, 135 m.p.h. Cruising 95 m.p.h. Range 600 miles. Service ceiling 18,500 ft.
Armament	One Vickers gun in bows, two amidships. Light bombs below wings.

Supermarine Seafire XV

Description	Single-seat carrier-borne fighter, fighter-bomber or tactical reconnaissance aircraft. All-metal stressed-skin construction.
Engine	One 1,850 h.p. Rolls-Royce Griffon.
Performance	Maximum speed, 383 m.p.h. at 13,500 ft. Cruising 255 m.p.h. Range 430 miles (normal) or 640 miles (with auxiliary tank). Service ceiling 35,500 feet.
Armament	Two 20 mm guns and four .303 guns.

Fairey Firefly F.R. I

Description	Two-seat carrier-borne fighter reconnaissance aircraft. All-metal stressed-skin construction.
Engine	One 1,990 h.p. Griffon.
Performance	Maximum speed, 316 m.p.h. Range 1,300 miles. Service ceiling 28,000 feet.
Armament	Four fixed 20 mm guns in wings. Provision for eight-60lb. rocket-projectiles or two 1,000-lb. bombs below the wings.

Fairey Firefly IV

Description	As for Fairey Firefly F.R.I. with following changes: - wings clipped; beard radiator replaced by coolant radiators extending from leading edges of centre section; four-bladed airscrew in place of earlier three-bladed type.
Engine	One 2,250 h.p. Rolls-Royce Griffon 74.
Performance	Maximum speed, 386 m.p.h. Range 1,300 miles. Service ceiling 28,400 feet.
Armament	As for Fairey Firefly F.R.I.

Fairey Firefly V. (A/S)

Description	Two-seat carrier-borne anti-submarine reconnaissance and strike aircraft. All-metal stressed-skin construction.
Engine	As for Fairey Firefly IV.
Performance	As for Fairey Firefly IV.
Armament	Four fixed 20 mm guns in wings. Provision for sixteen 60 lb. rocket projectiles or two 1,000-lb. bombs below the wings or sonobuoys.

Hawker Sea Fury F.B. XI

Description	Single-seat carrier-borne fighter-bomber. All-metal stressed-skin construction.
Engine	One 2,550 h.p. Bristol Centaurus 18.
Performance	Maximum speed, 460 m.p.h. Range 700 miles at 30,000 feet or 1,040 miles with two 90-gallon drop-tanks.
Armament	Four fixed 20 mm guns in wings and provision for twelve-60lb. rocket-projectiles or two 1,000-lb. bombs below the wings. Alternatively sonobuoys can be carried on the rocket stations.

Avro Anson V

Description	Twin-engined monoplane.
Engine	Two 450-h.p. Pratt & Whitney Wasp Junior.
Performance	Maximum speed, 188 m.p.h. Range 790 miles. Service ceiling, 19,000 feet.

Grumman Avenger A.S.3

Description	Three-seat carrier-borne or shore-based anti-submarine strike aircraft. All-metal stressed-skin construction.
Engine	One 1,750 h.p. Wright Cyclone.
Performance	Maximum speed, 261 m.p.h. Range 1,130 miles. Service ceiling, 22,600 feet.
Armament	Four depth-charges and one homing weapon. Sixteen sono-buoys for submarine detection.

North American Harvard ("T-6")

Description	Two-seat Primary and Advanced Trainer. Low-wing cantilever monoplane. All-metal structure with aluminum-alloy spars.
Engine	One 550 h.p. Pratt & Whitney radial air-cooled.
Performance	Maximum speed 205 m.p.h. Range 750 miles. Service ceiling 21,500 feet.

Bell HTL

Description	Two-seat General Utility Helicopter.
Engine	One vertically-mounted 178 h.p. Franklin six-cylinder fan cooled.
Performance	Maximum speed, 92 m.p.h. Range 212 miles. Service ceiling 11,500 feet.
Accommodation	Side-by-side seating in convertible open or covered compartment.

Sikorsky S-55 (HO4S-3)

Description	Twelve-seat Utility or Anti-submarine Helicopter.
Engine	One 700 h.p. Wright R 1300.
Performance	Maximum speed, 112 m.p.h. Range, 360 miles. Service ceiling, 10,600 feet.
Accommodation	Pilot's compartment seats two side-by-side. Cabin located below main lifting rotor, seats from seven to ten passengers. Can carry up to six stretchers, which can be loaded by hydraulic power-operated hoist while aircraft is hovering.
Armament	Homing torpedo or depth-bombs.

Piasecki/Vertol HUP-3

Description	Medical evacuation and light cargo helicoptor.
Engine	One 550 h.p. Continental R-975-46.
Performance	Maximim speed, 105 m.p.h. Range 340 miles. Service ceiling 10,000 feet.
Accommodation	Crew of two and four passengers or three stretcher cases.

Beechcraft Expeditor (C45)

Description	Twin-engined light transport. Low wing cantilever monoplane. All-metal structure. (Used as navigation and multi-engine pilot trainer.)
Engine	Two 450 h.p. Pratt and Whitney Wasp Junior radial air cooled.
Performance	Maximum speed 230 m.p.h. Range (with nose tank), 1500 miles. Service ceiling, 20,500 feet.
Accommodation	Pilot's compartment in nose, seating two side-by-side, with dual controls. Passenger cabin seating five to seven people.

INDEX

Abrams 246, 247, 264, 271, 277
Accident Investigation and Prevention Section, AIPS 155
Acheron, HM Submarine, 244
Adams 158, 185, 198, 207
Admiralty 1-3, 5, 8, 11-15, 17-19, 21-25, 27-29, 31, 33, 45, 64-66, 71, 82, 91, 206, 219, 220, 222, 223, 235, 236, 250
Advanced Training Flight 287
Aerial Patrols 4, 5
Aerodrome Dummy Deck Landings, ADDL 38, 55, 56, 64, 85, 112, 144, 166
Agnew 92, 93
Air Board 9, 10
Air Mechanics 58, 74
Air Ministry 3, 13, 14, 3
Air Supply Directorate 163
Airborne Early Warning, AEW 111, 112, 196, 210, 231, 258, 262
Airspeed Oxford, aircraft 65
Albacore, aircraft 30
Alcide, H.M. Submarine 134, 216
Alexandria 15
Alford 90
Algonquin, HMCS 257
Allan 115, 288
Anderson, AVM 25
Anderson, Jim 36
Anderson, AB John 37, 53, 54, 61, 63, 72
Anderson, Lt. John 221
Andrew, HM Submarine 184
Angled Deck 64, 219, 223, 235, 253, 290
Annual Senior Officers Conference 189
Anson, aircraft 61, 62, 70-72, 156-158
Anti-Submarine Warfare 133, 189, 213, 252
Antietam, USS 235, 253, 294
Antigonish, HMCS 135
Arbick 32, 33, 57
Arbroath 29, 30, 36, 37
Ark Royal, HMS 18, 19, 29, 30
Arnoldi 168
Arpin 69
Asmara 285
Athabaskan, HMCS 135

Atkinson 86, 179, 207, 255, 257, 284
Atlee 45, 46
Attacker, aircraft 243
Audette 136, 137
Auster, aircraft 148
Avenger, aircraft 31, 173, 174, 184, 191, 192, 195, 197, 202, 203, 211, 216, 219, 221, 222, 225, 226, 230-233, 236, 241, 242, 253-257, 259-262, 265-268, 273-275, 281, 283, 284, 286-288, 290, 297, 298, 303, 304
B17, aircraft 125, 126, 159
B29, aircraft 158, 159
Babbitt 44, 134, 142, 158, 159
Baker Point 7-9, 57, 61, 127
Baker-Falkner 16
Ballantyne 7, 10
Banshee, aircraft 194, 202, 222-224, 228, 229, 235, 240, 244, 254, 255, 262, 283, 286, 304
Barracuda, aircraft 16, 30, 47, 50, 51, 93
Barter 91
Bartlett 15-17, 29, 48, 51, 69, 70, 75, 83, 96, 102, 104, 119, 120, 173, 178, 218
Batista 169
Bays 123, 270
Beach 36
Bearcat, aircraft 169, 171, 217, 247
Beatty 2, 3
Bedell 6
Beeman 65, 158, 159, 256
Belfast 37, 38, 48, 99, 110, 111, 227, 228
Bell, aircraft 201, 290
Bell-Irving 228
Bennington, USS 260, 262-265, 267, 272, 275, 276, 278
Benton 246, 247, 278
Berge 109, 123, 132
Bermuda 75, 84-88, 99, 135, 143, 164, 166, 183, 184, 191, 192, 221, 232, 284, 286, 287, 297
Bice 53, 86, 115, 121
Bidwell 26, 63, 64, 243
Bird 65, 90, 97, 194, 221, 222, 244
Birks 207, 248, 259
Birtwhistle 69
Blinkhorn 85
Blue Force 257, 269, 279

Bluie West One 266, 278
Boak 78, 130
Bonaventure, HMCS 297
Bourque 44, 51
Bosquet 261
Bovill 262, 274, 277
Bowman 41
Boyle 53
Bradley 52, 91
Bray 98, 143, 144
Bristol Brabazon, aircraft 149
British Cabinet 14, 28, 45, 46
Britton 50, 78
Brown, Al 96
Brown, W.L.M. 250
Bullock 262
Burchell 187
Bureau of Aeronautics 11, 254
Burns, Jim 97, 117, 141, 248, 250
Burns, John 256
Burscough 51, 55, 56
Byrd 4, 8
Byrne 72
Cabinet 24, 26, 28, 33, 60, 65, 74, 119,
    164, 172, 206, 219, 222, 244, 255
Cairney 262, 273
Caldwell 134
Cambray 141
Campbell, "Rocky" 127
Campbell, Roger 160
Campney 293
Canadian Air Force 5, 10
Canadian Commercial Corporation 173
Canadian Joint Air Training Centre,
    Rivers 91, 92, 108, 116, 117, 123,
    147-149, 160, 162, 236, 237, 239
Canadian National Exhibition 73, 153
Canadian Naval Air Service 2
Canadian Naval Member 92
Canadian Naval Mission 27
Cape Farewell 266
Capri 201
Carlson 262
Carmichael 237
Carrier Air Group, CAG 29, 30, 85,
    89-91, 95, 96, 99-106, 108, 109, 111,
    112, 115,116,120-124, 126, 132, 134,
    135, 142, 144, 147, 148, 154,
    158-160, 163-166, 168, 172, 178,
    179, 180, 190-196, 207, 211, 218,
    221, 224, 225, 228, 231, 235-237,
    243-245, 257, 281, 283, 286, 288,
    289, 292, 295
Carter 65
Cartwright 49, 51, 56, 262, 263, 265-
    267, 269, 270, 273
Carver 30
Catapult 64, 131, 219, 222, 223, 241,
    253
Charleston 168
Chatham 105
Chezzetcook 190, 209
Chief of the Air Staff 54, 58, 119, 248
Churchill 19, 28
Clark 51, 67
Clarke 143
Claxton 91, 206
Coastal Command 20, 30, 215
Cocks, Harvey 115
Cocks, Bob 165, 166, 203, 289
Cogdon 154
Combs 260, 279, 280
Conner 113
Constellation, aircraft 149
Copeland 262
Coral Sea, USS 26, 142
Coronation Squadron 243, 245, 247
Corsair, aircraft 47, 48, 86, 140, 264,
    265, 275, 276
Corsican, RMS 8
Cottingham 207, 290
Coultry 71, 72, 132
Courageous, HMS 16, 238, 292, 298
Cranbrook 287
Crawshaw 262
Creery 126, 134, 162, 178, 185, 218, 243
Crescent, HMCS 60, 76, 83, 135
Crosley 153, 154
Crown Assets Corporation 285
Cuba 84, 142, 169
Cull 4, 5, 7, 8
Cummings 204
Cunningham, Sir John 18
Cunningham, Vern 248, 249, 259
Cupples 65
Curtis 119, 120
Cushman 245
Cyr 36, 38, 39
Dakota, DC3, aircraft 62, 108
Daniel 59, 113, 130, 131, 150, 151, 209,
    241, 285
Dardanelles 225

Darling 42
Darlington 253, 254
Dartmouth 32, 57, 58, 60-62, 66, 72, 73, 79, 86, 88, 94, 96, 97, 100, 111, 118, 119, 121, 122, 124, 129, 149, 284
Davis, "Dai" 51, 55, 67, 69
Davis, Ted 55, 155, 156, 185, 207, 286
Dawson 226, 236
Deck Landing 46, 47, 59, 64, 66, 83, 89, 99, 106, 107, 109, 115, 135, 144, 146, 147, 158, 163, 166, 172, 192, 195, 221, 235, 244, 253, 275, 288, 292-294, 302, 303
Deck Landing Control Officer, DLCO 55, 72, 83, 87, 92, 112, 145, 146, 158
De Havilland 255
Demon, aircraft 244, 286
de Nevers 65, 66, 167, 174, 289
Department of Public Works 4, 8
Desbarats 10
DeWolf 21, 82, 87, 99, 110, 115
Diatchenko 262, 274
Diogo Gomes 228
Director Naval Air Division, DNAD 57
Director of Air Engineering 94, 134, 241
Director of Naval Aviation 63, 64, 91, 112, 143, 163
Discovery, HMCS 104, 285, 293
Doherty 94, 150, 196, 219, 220, 254, 255
Donaldson, J.N. 70, 174, 178, 207
Donaldson (Observer) 262
Doucette 262
Douglas, Mel 36
D'Oyly-Hughes 19
Dunn 103
Dyer 57, 77, 78, 207, 243
Eagle, HMS 4, 30, 48, 77, 281
East Haven 30
Edwards 18, 42, 132, 139, 237, 238
Eglinton 95, 96, 100, 104, 105
El Centro 174
Ellison 63
Elster 273, 275, 277, 278
Elton 115, 153
Esmonde 30
Esquimalt 74, 75, 78, 79, 81, 292-295
Esquimalt, HMCS 97
Etchells 192, 198
Ethiopia 285
Eversfield 73

Ewasiuk 69
Exercises: Caribex 50, 169; Castinets 224, 225; Homecoming 185; Mainbrace 229, 230; Maple Leaf 6, 183, 202, 277, 278; Mariner 23, 257, 260, 261, 278, 281, 282; New Broom II 290; Scuppered 97; Symphonie Deux 202
Fairey Aviation 86, 133
Fairey Aviation of Canada 95
Fairey Battle, aircraft 20
Fairey Gannet, aircraft 250
Falls 36, 86, 216, 267
Farouk 225
Farrell 69, 239
Favreau 68, 77, 111
Feagan 68
Fearn 30, 50
Fearon 36, 38, 49, 71, 111, 160, 241, 289
Field Carrier Landing Practice, FCLP 146, 182, 184, 191, 195, 216, 217, 288, 296, 297
Finch-Noyes 154, 157, 165
Fink 36, 191, 192
Firebrand, aircraft 198
Firefly, aircraft 30, 31, 51, 55, 56, 59, 60, 63, 67, 69, 71, 79, 81, 83, 84, 88, 89, 93, 95, 97, 99, 102, 107, 111, 115, 116, 117, 120, 122, 124-126, 133-135, 140, 142, 144, 145, 146, 158, 159, 163, 166, 167, 169, 171, 172, 173, 180, 181, 190, 196, 285
Fisher, Ralph 68
Fisher, Nigel 112
Fisher, D.J. 284
Flag Officer Atlantic Coast, FOAC 295
Flag Officer Pacific Coast 284
Fleet Air Arm, FAA 12-16, 18, 20-24, 28, 29, 32, 36, 39, 47, 48, 51, 58, 99, 109, 126, 138, 154, 176-178, 198, 223, 286, 297
Fleet Requirement Unit, FRU 61, 65, 70, 71, 75, 98
Flying boats 4, 5, 9-12, 62
Foley 32, 59, 96, 100, 102, 106, 120, 201, 221
Forbes, Admiral 18, 20
Forbes, Andy 36, 37
Formidable, HMS 16, 30, 86
Fort Worth 201

Fotheringham 69, 90, 99, 117, 177, 218, 220, 228, 232, 243
Fox 283
Franks 281
Fraser-Harris 112, 114, 127, 133, 144, 154
Frost 236
Furious, HMS 20
Gallery 230
Gavel 51, 77, 82, 83
Geale 242
Geary 53, 154
General Hodges, USS 285
Geraghty 96, 111, 241
Gibbs, Cdr. 57
Gibbs, Ken 45, 46, 109, 112, 124, 140, 141, 144, 146, 293
Gibraltar 182, 227
Gill 51
Glasgow 59, 207
Glasgow, HMS 142
Glorious, HMS 16, 19
Gneisenau 19
Goddard 99, 127, 165, 178
Goodwin 260, 263, 264, 266-268, 270, 279
Grady 69, 180
Grant 139, 140
Gratton-Cooper 185, 192, 211
Gray, Don 36
Gray, T.E. 15, 17
Gray, Hampton 15, 21, 29
Green 262
Greene 115
Greenwich 43, 45, 46
Greenwood, George 65
Guantanamo 142, 143, 172
Guiterrez 276
Guppy, aircraft 231, 261-266, 269, 275, 281
Haida, HMCS 97, 135, 159
Hal Far 197, 198, 227
Halifax 1, 3-5, 7-9, 57, 59, 60, 62, 66, 67, 81, 83, 85, 97, 99, 111, 115, 118, 121, 126, 134, 135, 151, 158, 162, 166, 172, 183, 184, 188, 190, 192, 203, 207, 209, 216, 221, 230, 232, 247, 281, 288, 290
Hand 67
Harley 15, 16, 20, 258
Harris 44, 140

Hart, Capt. 74
Hart, Johnny 227
Hartle 36, 191
Harvard, aircraft 36, 48, 61, 71, 109, 188, 216, 245
Harvie 95, 259
Havana 84, 169
Hawthorne 262
Hayes 77
Hayter, Barry 53, 288, 292
Hayter, Bryan 262, 273, 274, 287
Heath 19, 42, 48, 53, 101, 152, 153, 193, 225-227, 243, 289
Helicopter 32, 201, 202, 215, 221, 237, 238, 256, 258, 282, 284, 285, 291, 292
Hellcat, aircraft 38, 64, 65, 86, 90, 169, 302
Hennessy 67
Hermes, HMS 16
Hilliard 262
Hinstock 49, 50
Hoare 104
Hockin 51
Hoffus 36
Hofta 276
Holden 287
Hopkins, S.V. 6-8
Hopkins, George 65, 122
Houghton 57, 77, 82
Howe 141, 255
HU 21 237, 249
Hughes 241, 253
Hullah 190
Hunt 65
Hunter 42, 55, 87, 91, 100-103, 123, 132, 148, 154, 160, 161, 162, 172, 221, 228, 230, 251, 252, 281, 289
Huron, HMCS 180
Hutchison 36, 220, 221
Hutton 140, 141
Iceland 257, 260, 268, 281
Idlewild 111
Illustrious, HMS 29, 115
Indefatigable, HMS 30
Indomitable, HMS 224
Inskip 14
Instructional Centre 91
Iowa, USS 260, 267, 274, 279
Irish Free State 49
Iroquois, HMCS 239

Istanbul 225, 226
It's Really Quite Safe 2
Jackson 8
Jamaica 75, 135
Jamaica, HMS 135
James 60, 102, 287, 292
Jantzen 36
Janusas 114, 130
Jeffries 36
Jellicoe 9
Jet Flight 283, 288
Johnson, A.E. 59, 69, 70, 91
Johnson, Major 165
Johnson, Observer 262
Johnstone, M. 157, 165
Jones, G.C. 54
Jones, Robert 287
Keighly-Peach 194, 202, 210, 213, 221,
    222, 224, 229, 240, 249, 250-253
Keindel 262
Kenora 260
Kenya, HMS 88
Kindley Field 85, 86, 166, 192
King-Joyce 30, 53
Kingston, Ontario 18, 72, 245
Kingston, Jamaica 75, 135
Kinross 124, 243
Kniffen 130, 210
Knox 69, 92, 146, 165, 166, 177, 178,
    181, 182, 207, 243, 256
Kohl 46
Königsberg 17
Korea 219, 223, 236-240
La Hulloise, HMCS 257
Labrador, HMCS 201, 290-292
Labrador 261
Laidler 53
Lakehurst 22, 201
Laming 262
Lamon 95
Lancaster, aircraft 62, 152
Landing Signals Officer, LSO 145, 146,
    158, 159, 171, 182, 202, 203, 211,
    216, 217, 232, 264, 273, 274, 276,
    294-297
Langman 292
Laramee 104
Laurie 41, 290
Lavack 71
Law 111
Lay 21, 23-26, 110, 143, 173, 189, 190,

212-215, 222
Learmouth 65
Leckie 9, 54, 58
Lee-on-Solent 38, 57, 199, 244, 246
Leeming 97
LeFaivre 69
Legare 242
Leidl 36, 61, 199, 247, 248, 284
Lend Lease 32
Lentaigne 143, 163, 186, 194
Lewry 68, 77, 180
L'Heureux, 256
Liaison Section 91
Light Fleet Carriers 26-28, 33, 60, 74,
    93, 206
Liley 51
Lindberg 48
Lisbon 182
Litle 281
Lockheed Neptune, aircraft 215
Logan 36, 37, 39, 61, 70, 90, 92, 93, 95,
    96, 101, 143, 225, 286
Lowe 51, 55, 75, 201, 221, 237, 238,
    256
Lucas 90
Lynch 51
Lyons 95, 292
Macauley 262
Macaw, HMS 36, 39-42
MacBrien 124, 135, 231, 238, 239
MacDermid 36
Macdonald Lake 126
Macdonald, CPO 143
Mackay 207
MacKenzie, Cam 36
Mackenzie, Andy 232
MacLaurin 8, 9
MacLean 262, 273
Macleod, D.M. 192, 193, 197, 208, 236,
    248, 256, 259, 282, 283
Macleod, John 287
MacNab's Island 140
Mae West 168, 197
Magdalen Islands 120
Magnetic Anomoly Detection, MAD
    212
Magnificent, HMCS 28, 57, 65, 82, 95,
    99, 110, 111, 115, 121, 133, 134,
    135-137, 139, 142-144, 147, 158,
    159, 166, 169, 170, 171, 178,
    180-182, 184-187, 190-193, 195-198,

202, 203, 206, 207, 211, 219, 220, 221, 224-233, 236, 237, 239, 240, 243, 244, 246, 254, 257, 258, 260-268, 270-272, 274, 277, 278, 280-283, 285, 286, 288-295, 298
Mainguy 135-138, 140, 176, 214
Mainguy Report 135-138
Malahat, HMCS 245
Malta 16, 197, 199-201, 204, 225-227
Marine Section 57, 61, 140, 151, 209
Marlow 53, 70
Martin 242
Mason, PO 50
Mason, John 221
Maxwell, Bill 74, 148, 291
Maxwell, "Kam" 97
McCuaig 36
McCubbin 100
McEwan 137, 138
McKay 95, 96
McKerran 262
McMillen 207
McNab 52
McNicol 73, 140
McPhee 198
Mead 53, 145, 146, 158, 159
Medicine Hat 259
Meikle 262, 274
Messerschmitt, aircraft 192
Micmac, HMCS 67, 135, 180, 197
Miles, GR 115, 137, 158
Miles Magister, aircraft 20
Mindora, USS 219, 229, 230, 253
Miramar 218
Mirror Landing Aid 64, 211
Missouri, USS 169
Mitchell, Chris 129
Mitchell bomber, aircraft 167
Monks 52-54, 90, 99, 140, 141, 143
Montcalm, HMCS 245
Monteith 94
Montreal 67, 73, 94, 95
Moore 297
Morehouse 193
Morris 100, 188
Mortimer 57, 78, 79, 87, 88
Moss 190, 192
Munro 36, 92, 154, 156, 157, 178, 180, 191, 193, 194, 200, 201, 207, 208
Murphy, John 65, 220 221
Murphy, Vince 102, 215, 222, 284,

287, 288
Murphy, Tom 123
Murphy, Frank 149
Mustang, aircraft 92
Myers 53, 162
NAAFI 103
Nabob, HMS 26, 27
Naples 200-202, 226
Nash 36, 38
National Air Show 259
Naval Air Division 22, 27, 57
Naval Air Facility 248
Naval Air Maintenance School, NAMS 209, 210
Naval Air Staff 139, 173, 224, 235, 248, 250, 284
Naval Air Stores 119
Naval Aviation 3, 5, 7, 8, 11-13, 19, 21, 22, 24, 26-28, 33, 54, 57-59, 63-65, 90, 91, 93, 94, 98, 99, 110, 112, 119, 127, 138, 141, 143, 144, 155, 163, 164, 174, 175, 177, 178, 186, 189, 208, 209, 211, 212, 213-215, 220, 222, 233, 235, 237, 238, 248, 250, 255, 261, 270, 284, 291, 303-305
Naval Aviation Conference 185
Naval Board 22, 27, 28, 33, 59, 62-65, 85, 90, 91, 93, 110, 111, 118, 139, 141, 155, 163, 174, 228, 249, 301, 302
Naval Member 92
Naval Staff 13, 21, 24-28, 54, 64, 65, 85, 93, 94, 98, 110, 138, 139, 141, 143, 163, 194, 213, 214, 233, 240, 244, 247, 248, 277, 294, 297
Neptune, aircraft 215
New Glasgow, HMCS 294
New Liskeard, HMCS 97
Newfoundland 22, 268, 270
Nicolson 44, 53, 297
Noble 259, 260
Nonsuch, HMCS 72, 98
Nootka, HMCS 75, 97
Norseman, aircraft 108
North Atlantic Treaty, NATO 63, 111, 133, 180, 183, 189, 202, 203, 207, 213, 216, 228, 229-231, 237, 249, 252, 257, 297, 298
North Sydney 4
Nova Scotia 1
Nova Scotia Government 238

Nutts Corner 30, 37, 38, 50, 52-54
O'Connell 262, 263, 265, 266, 274
O'Neil 241, 242
O'Rourke 179
Observer School 249, 297
Observer's Mate 262, 284
Ocean, HMS 27, 202
Ocean, Indian 28, 29
Olson 47
Ontario, HMCS 135, 142
Operational Flying Course 249
Operational Flying Training School 287
Operational Training Unit, OTU 52, 60, 75, 86, 90
Orange Force 257, 261
Oriskany, USS 219
Oslo 230
Page 142, 257, 261, 262, 264, 266, 271, 289
Panama Canal 75, 290, 295
Panshangar 65
Panther, aircraft 262, 289
Paton 242, 262, 269
Patricia Bay 79, 81, 284, 286
Patuxent River 111, 216, 218, 253
Peacocke 49, 51, 78, 82, 92, 120, 145, 146, 182, 193, 228, 236
Pearl Harbour 26, 76, 99
Peever 44, 167, 168
Pensacola 24, 171
Phantom, aircraft 244
Philippine Sea, USS 170, 171
Pickering 134
Piers 110, 135-139, 158
Pintail, HMS 30
Pitt 114
Plomer 127
Pompeii 201
Port Mouton 144
Portage La Prairie 283
Portsmouth 59, 110, 225, 243, 285
Powerful, HMS 2, 38, 142, 169, 196, 199, 219, 220, 222-224, 236, 240, 241, 255, 258, 297, 304
Premier, HMS 47, 48
Prescott 36
Preston 264, 272
Prince of Wales, HMS 18
Privy Council 1
Pulfer 46, 96, 140, 141
Pullen 97

Pulsifer 62
Puncher, HMS 26, 27
Quarton 36, 110
Quebec 67, 245
Quebec Conference 24
Quebec, HMCS 220, 230, 243, 257, 260, 290, 295
Quirt 51, 231
Quonset Point 145, 184, 190, 278, 284, 286
Ratcliffe 37, 74, 113
Rattray 30, 50, 68
Ravager, HMS 46, 47
Raymond 210, 236
Rayner 91, 97, 112, 243, 246, 257, 271, 277, 278
RCAF Station Dartmouth 58, 60
RCAF Station Greenwood 118, 156, 162, 163, 166, 188, 242, 269
RCAF Station Portage La Prairie 283
RCAF Station Summerside 282
RCAF Station Trenton 283
Redfin, USS 269-272, 279
Reed 110
Reid 98, 99
Repulse, HMS 18
Reserve 9, 28, 59, 60, 65, 71, 72, 82, 219, 245, 289, 293
Reykjavic 281
Rice 97, 124, 241, 242
Rikely 36, 54, 86, 195, 201
Ritchie 157, 158
Roberts, Al 36
Roberts, J.W. 127, 134, 165, 178, 216, 243
Rolfe 164
Ross 97, 180, 181, 219, 229, 253
Rotherham 2, 18, 90, 91, 112, 143
Rounds 36
Rowell 109, 142, 158, 159, 165, 169, 180, 181, 294
Royal Air Force, RAF 2, 3-15, 10, 19, 20, 24, 30, 48-50, 58, 65, 92, 94, 198, 213, 215, 223
Royal Australian Air Force, RAAF 93, 94
Royal Australian Navy, RAN 47, 67, 77, 78, 87, 93, 94, 112, 117, 118, 123, 144, 149, 152, 157, 176, 184, 185, 191, 193, 225, 228, 274, 277, 286
Royal Canadian Air Force, RCAF 9, 11,

23-26, 29, 32, 34-36, 39, 44, 48, 51-54, 57, 58, 60, 62, 66, 71, 74, 79, 86, 91, 92, 94, 105, 108, 113, 117-121, 125, 127, 130, 131, 152, 154, 155, 156, 162, 165, 167, 178, 188, 189, 192, 196, 204, 207, 209, 212-215, 227, 228, 232, 235, 237, 247, 248, 249, 251, 252, 282, 283, 286, 292

Royal Canadian Naval Air Service, RCNAS 5-11, 24, 26, 34

Royal Canadian Naval Volunteer Reserve, RCNVR 21-23, 29, 31, 32, 35, 36, 42, 47, 50, 52, 53, 57, 59, 178, 286

Royal Canadian Navy, RCN 6, 9, 11, 13, 15, 21-28, 30, 31, 33, 35, 38, 42, 52, 54, 57-66, 71, 74, 81, 83, 85-88, 91, 92, 94, 95, 99, 105, 107, 110, 111, 115, 117-119, 121, 127, 133, 135, 136, 138, 139, 147, 149, 152-155, 164, 167, 172-174, 177-181, 186, 189, 190, 194-196, 198, 201, 202, 206-216, 219, 221-224, 227-229, 231, 233, 234, 237-240, 244, 245, 250-255, 258, 283, 285, 286, 289-292, 301-304

Royal Canadian Navy (Reserve), RCN(R) 38, 48, 52, 53, 57, 60, 81

Royal Flying Corps 2

Royal Naval Air Service 2, 3

Royal Naval Volunteer Reserve, RNVR 21, 23, 29, 31, 32, 35, 36, 39, 42, 45, 50-52, 67, 69, 154, 178, 249, 292

Royal Navy, RN 3, 8, 10-19, 21-26, 31, 35-37, 39, 40, 44-47, 51-53, 57, 60, 66, 79, 84, 88, 89, 91, 92, 94, 99-101, 103, 106, 108, 109, 111-113, 133, 134, 135, 139, 153, 175, 176, 180, 190, 194, 195, 206, 209, 211, 219, 222, 223, 231, 235, 236, 243, 250, 281, 288, 297, 301, 302

Runciman 44, 45, 148

Russell 36

Ryan 207, 208, 225

Sabre, aircraft 189, 207, 228

Safety Equipment 143, 144, 294

Saint John 121, 144, 156, 162

Saipan, USS 146, 163

Salkus 192

San Diego 79, 173, 174, 218, 290

Sandes 171

Scapa Flow 20

Scharnhorst 19, 29

Schellinck 109, 135, 162, 167

Scoudouc 248, 256, 259, 282

Sea Fury, aircraft 64, 65, 90, 95, 96, 100-102, 105, 106, 110, 113, 115, 121, 122, 132, 135, 139-141, 148, 152, 153, 162, 166, 171, 179, 182, 186, 190, 193, 194, 198, 199, 221, 223, 225- 229, 232, 233, 236, 237, 242, 247, 258, 283, 286, 288, 302, 303

Sea Gladiator, aircraft 15

Sea Hornet, aircraft 112, 113, 115

Sea Vampire, aircraft 111, 245

Sea Venom, aircraft 222-224

Seaborn, HMS 57

Seafire, aircraft 29-31, 36-39, 50, 59, 62, 85, 88-90, 97, 99, 105, 108, 109, 117, 119, 121, 123, 127, 130, 141, 149, 153, 154, 302

Second Fleet 260

Secretary of the Navy 11

Seddon 1

Shaw 127

Shearwater, HMCS 108, 115, 126, 127, 129, 131, 133, 140, 142-144, 147, 54, 156, 157, 160-162, 166, 175, 177, 179, 183, 184, 186-188, 190, 193-196, 201, 209, 210, 215, 220, 221, 224, 228, 231, 236, 237, 239, 241-243, 245, 247-249, 253, 282, 283, 286, 287, 292, 294-297

Sheffield, HMS 88, 233

Sheppard 69, 86, 123

Shorten 291

Shortt 60

Sidewinder 244

Sikorsky 32, 210, 221, 237, 256, 258

Skua, aircraft 16, 17

Skyraider (AD), aircraft 111, 169, 170, 171, 217, 273, 275, 278

Sloan 36, 115, 216, 218

Smith, Derek 53

Smith, LAM 72

Smith, Neil 94

Smith, Observer 262

Smuts 2, 3

Sonar 212, 215

Sonobuoy 200

Sorrento 201

Spicer 294
Spithead 57, 243-245
Squadrons, Air, RCAF: 410 Squadron 207
Squadrons, Air, RCN: 803 29-31, 36-39, 49, 52, 53, 57, 59,62-66, 73, 75, 85, 86, 90, 95, 96, 99, 101, 103, 108, 110, 120, 126, 132, 134, 142, 147, 154, 185, 190, 193, 195
  825 29-31, 50-52, 55, 57, 59, 62-64, 66-69, 74, 75, 81, 82, 83, 85-87, 89, 90, 96, 101, 106-108, 111, 120, 126, 134, 135, 142, 144, 146, 160, 162, 164, 165, 169, 178, 180, 182, 183, 185, 190, 195
  826 30, 31, 57, 59, 63, 90, 95, 97, 99, 117, 124, 126, 127, 134, 135, 144, 164, 165, 167, 170, 172, 174, 178, 184, 185, 190-193, 195
  870 195, 229, 232
  871 195-199, 203, 207, 216, 221, 224, 228
  880 195, 207, 216, 232
  881 195-197, 199, 203, 207, 215, 216, 221, 224-227, 229, 230
  883 30, 31, 38, 50, 53, 57, 59, 62, 65, 85, 90, 97, 99, 123, 126, 134, 142, 147, 178, 180, 185, 190-193, 195
  VC 921 245
  VC 922 245
  VC 923 245
  VC 924 245
  VF 870 233, 236, 242, 285, 286
  VF 871 233, 236, 243, 245, 246, 262, 283, 286, 292, 295
  VH 21 256, 292
  VS 880 233, 284, 286, 287, 297, 298
  VS 881 233, 236, 237, 258, 284, 286, 288-290, 292, 295
  VT 40 287, 288, 292
  VU 32 284, 287, 288, 292, 297
  VX 10 241, 289
Squadrons, Air, RN: 806 111-113, 115
  825 20, 30
  826 30
  803 29
  883 30
Squadrons, Air, USN: VC 3 289
  VS 22 219, 229
  VS 25 174

VS 26 174, 294
St. Merryn 48
St. Vincent, HMS 68
Stadacona 69, 74, 114, 115
Station Flying Orders 157, 175, 177
Stead 27
Steel, Jack 69, 88
Steele 187
Stephens 50
Stettler, HMCS 290, 294
Stewart 127, 141, 255
Stock 52, 154
Stokes 126, 169, 178, 201, 231
Storrs 236, 238, 242
Stovin-Bradford 30, 50-52
Submarines 5, 134, 180, 200, 216, 224, 230, 251, 252, 257, 281, 284, 289
Summerside 282
Support Air Group, 19th 85, 109
Support Air Group, 31st 235, 283
Support Air Group 190, 228, 233, 235, 283, 288
Supreme Allied Commander Atlantic, SACLANT 230
Supreme Court 158
Surprise, HMS 245, 246
Sutcliffe 142
Swainson 68
Swansea, HMCS 257
Sweeting 50, 51, 69
Swiggum 50, 53, 121, 123, 152, 156, 174
Swordfish, aircraft 30, 32, 57-59, 61, 62, 71-73, 75, 133, 150
Sydenham 48, 110, 228
Sydney, N.S. 1-5, 7-9, 292
Sydney, HMAS 182
T33, aircraft 283
Takali 198
Tanner 36, 52, 64
Taranto 26, 99
Tarawa, USS 240
Task Group Alpha 252
Tate 36, 258
Tattersall 51, 52, 81, 83, 154
Taylor 74
Tecumseh, HMCS 72, 245
Tennant 88, 135
Tern Hill 48, 49
Terrace Bay 285
Terry, Leslie 284

Thatch 252
Theseus, HMS 229, 230
Thomas 45
Tiger Moth, aircraft 65, 66, 113, 131
Tivy 143, 196
Torrie 170
Tovey 18
Townsend 81, 286
Tracker, aircraft 255
Training Air Group 130, 143, 196, 283, 287, 288
Trans-Canada Airlines 62
Treasury Board 173
Trenchard 2, 12
Trinidad 192
Tuck 133, 134, 175
Turkey 47, 225
Turner, Les 53
Turner, John 100, 101
Turner, Mike 193, 197, 221
Turner, CPO 291
Uganda, HMCS 76, 83, 85
United States Navy, USN 3-5, 8, 10, 11, 15, 22-25, 27, 32, 33, 64, 65, 76, 90, 91, 105, 107, 110-112, 139, 140, 142, 144-147, 149, 155, 156, 158, 164, 167, 169-174, 179, 186, 189, 190, 194-196, 201, 202, 206, 215, 216, 218, 221-224, 226, 227, 229- 233, 235, 239, 240, 244-249, 252- 255, 257, 260, 261, 264, 265, 269, 270, 273, 275, 277, 278, 286, 289, 290, 294, 295, 297, 302-304
Utting 167, 174
Vampire, aircraft 105, 111, 152, 198, 226, 245
Vanguard, HMS 281
Victoria Cross 21, 32
Victorious, HMS 30, 53, 86, 140
Voodoo, aircraft 244
Wade 36, 38
Wakeham Bay 121
Wall 51, 55, 56
Walrus, aircraft 57, 61, 62
Walton 53, 289
Wardrop 53, 115, 116, 182, 197, 198, 208, 239, 240
Warnock 102
Warren 109
Warrior, HMCS 27, 28, 31, 38, 55, 57, 59-61, 67-69, 73-77, 81-86, 88, 89, 94, 95, 99, 106, 108, 115, 138, 172, 207, 236, 249
Washington 3
Wasp, USS 204, 230, 260, 262, 267, 278
Wasteneys 72, 199, 243, 245, 257, 258, 286
Watson, Jim 50, 51, 55, 69, 242, 284, 287
Watson, C.G. 57,64, 90, 137, 138, 153, 154, 176, 177
Webster 258
Welsh 116-118, 166, 190
Westwood 47, 53, 72, 109, 163
Whitby 36, 95, 101, 103, 253, 288, 292
White 287
Wilgress 53, 120, 154, 162, 190
Wilkinson 29, 36, 52
Will 240
Williamson 216, 267, 273
Willoughby 19
Windover 72, 114
Winter Experimental Establishment 71, 110, 152
Wisconsin, USS 230
Wood, Stan 108, 109, 117, 118, 124
Woods 81, 84, 243
Worcester, USS 258
Wraith 260
Wright, J.G. 196, 253
Wright, USS 230
Wright's Lake 193
WRNS 39, 40
Yankee Lake 237
Yeovilton 31, 42
York, HMCS 245
Zeals 42